THE OROMO OF ETHIOPIA

A history 1570–1860

MOHAMMED HASSEN

THE RED SEA PRESS
Publishers & Distributors of Third World Books
15 Industry Court
Trenton, NJ 08638

THE RED SEA PRESS, INC.

15 Industry Court
Trenton NJ 08638

Cover Design and Illustration by Carles J. Juzang

Library of Congress Cataloging - in - Publication Data

Hassen, Mohammed.
    The Oromo of Ethiopia : a history, 1570 - 1860 / Mohammed Hassen.
        p. cm
    Originally published: Cambridge : Cambridge University Press,
    1990. With new introd.
    Includes bibliographical references and index.
      ISBN 0-932415-94-6 (HB) –   0-932415-95-4 (PB)
    1. Oromo (African people) --History. 2. Gibbe River Valley
(Ethiopia) --History. I. Title
DT390.G2H38 1994
963'.3--dc20

93-44124
CIP

To Pat, Paul, Aziza, and Birmaji

Contents

Oromo glossary

Abba	father or title of respect
Abba Bokku	father of *bokku* (keeper of *bokku*) i.e. a leader of gada in power
Abba Dula	father of war
Abba Gada	father of gada in power
Abba Lafa	father of land (possessor of land)
Abba Mizan	father of balance (an official responsible for trade and foreign affairs)
Abba Muda	the spiritual head of traditional Oromo religion
Abba Qorro	a provincial governor
Afkala	Oromo traders from the Gibe region
bokku	wooden scepter kept by an Abba Gada in power
butta	one of the most important Oromo festivals, which each member of a gada-group in power celebrated by slaughtering a bull
butta war	a war which followed *butta* festival
chafe assembly	meadow assembly (the Oromo parliament)
dadhi	mead made of honey
dhalatta	"he who is born" i.e. he who is adopted into a clan
donachaw	crown prince
gabbaro	men of low social status because they were not of "pure" Oromo descent (i.e. conquered men who were required to serve)
genne	lady of royal blood
gindo	state prison
gossa	clan or tribe
ilma gossa	a son of a clan (i.e. he who is adopted into a clan)
jarra	a ceremony that was observed every eight years at the beginning of a new Oromo year
lemmi	messenger(s) of a clan or ambassador(s) of a king
massera	a residence of a king (palace)
moti	king or conqueror

viii

oda	the "holy" sycamore (tree)
ogessa	the skilled ones
Qallu	a ritual expert or a priest of traditional Oromo religion
qubsisa	late settlers or late-comers
sorressa	wealthy dignitary
Waqa	traditional Oromo god (i.e. sky-god)
yahabata	*gabbaro* cavalry which were despised because of their low social origin but feared because of their skill in warfare

Maps

Preface

Starting in the fourteenth and fifteenth centuries and increasingly during and since the sixteenth century, the Christian literature of Abyssinia, the Muslim literature from Harar, and European travelers' accounts make considerable reference to the Galla. This was a name, applied by outsiders, by which the Oromo were known until recently. The term is loaded with negative connotations. The Oromo do not call themselves Galla and they resist being so called. In this study I employ Oromo, the name which they have always used.

The Oromo constitute a good half of the population of Ethiopia. They are also the largest national group in the Horn of Africa and have been so at least since the nineteenth century. However, careful examination of the sources on Ethiopia reveals that much has been written on the Oromo by anthropologists, while Oromo history has been totally neglected. Take, for instance, the important work of Dr. Taddesse Tamrat covering the period from 1270 to 1527, which was published in 1972.[1] Nothing is said about the Oromo in this book. It does provide an excellent background to the Christian and Muslim conflict in the region, and yet Dr. Taddesse failed to see that some elements of the Oromo nation were indeed the victims of the fourteenth-century conflict, while other Oromo groups participated on both sides in the conflict in the sixteenth century.

Detailed research into the history of the peoples of southern Ethiopia has only just begun, and the need to go deeper in time and to undertake field work has become steadily clearer to scholars in the field.[2] However, the identity of the peoples who inhabit the present administrative region of Shawa and the area south of it has not yet been established apart from the general attempts to categorize them under a few headings such as "Sidama"[3] or "Sidama Afar and the Semitic military colonies,"[4] or Hadiya, both Cushitic and Semitic.[5] Scholars have so far not considered seriously the question of whether some Oromo groups could have been within the region either before or during the fourteenth century. Much that has been written about the early history of the peoples of southern Ethiopia seems to be conjecture. Until careful and detailed research into it is undertaken, the early history of several Ethiopian peoples will remain obscure. Until then a student in the field will have to pick his way

1 Modern administrative regions of Ethiopia

"warily among the debris of half-erected and half-demolished hypotheses" which the historian without the effective use of various oral traditions, linguistic evidence, and social practices can neither complete nor raze to the ground.

I feel compelled to state clearly at the outset that there is conclusive evidence which demonstrates beyond the shadow of a doubt that some settled sedentary agricultural Oromo groups lived in and to the south of what is today the administrative region of Shawa before the fourteenth century.[6] This is a fascinating subject. The thesis is new and its implications could have far-reaching consequences for the history of the Oromo and other peoples of southern Ethiopia. The evidence is not new material. It is a new interpretation of the rich written Amhara oral tradition and religious literature, even though that interpretation does not have the support of scholarly works hitherto undertaken. I believe that in the main this story is correct, despite the fact that earlier scholars support me only in part and in some cases appear violently to contradict me when I dealt with this subject elsewhere.[7] To discuss it as part of this study would have encumbered the main theme with many digressions. Here it should suffice to say that the historical wisdom that was accepted for a long time and which claims that the Oromo arrived in the Christian kingdom only in the sixteenth century is incorrect for the following three reasons among others. First, it is incorrect because it is based on an inaccurate historical premise which seeks to establish the origin of the Oromo as outside the present boundaries of Ethiopia thus making them "newcomers" to the country. The Oromo belong to the eastern Cushitic language-speaking group of peoples who are known to have lived in the Ethiopian region for thousands of years. In fact, the Oromo are the largest group of Cushitic-speaking people. We do not know when the Oromo evolved their separate national identity and language, but we do know that they had lived in the highlands of southern Ethiopia for the greatest part of their history. They are one of the indigenous peoples of Ethiopia.[8] To consider them as newcomers is a claim which has no historical foundation whatsoever. Secondly, it is incorrect because it is based on the assertion that all Oromo were nomads before and during the sixteenth century. We know that originally the Oromo were not nomads. They were engaged in mixed farming.[9] Some of them began to become pure pastoralists only after they moved from the highlands to the lowland areas,[10] where an environment conducive to grazing induced them to abandon farming and depend on pastoralism.[11] Thirdly, it is incorrect because it is based on the assertion that all Oromo lived in one place before their sixteenth-century migration. In reality, a group of pastoral Oromo lived in what is today the administrative region of Sidamo, while others lived in what is now the administrative region of Bale. Furthermore, a number of sedentary agricultural Oromo communities lived in historical Dawaro,[12] Ifat,[13] Waj,[14] and other Muslim principalities of southern Ethiopia,[15] which were conquered by Emperor Amda-Siyon (1314–1344). These settled agricultural Oromo communities which existed before the fourteenth century were not part of the sixteenth-century pastoral Oromo migration. It is the latter group which is the main focus of this study.

With the exception of three studies, even the history of the sixteenth-century pastoral Oromo migration has not received the attention it deserves. Of the three studies, Dr. M. Abir's book published in 1980 devotes a chapter to the Oromo history,[16] although it contains very little new information about the migration. Dr. Braukamper's work, published in the same year, contains useful data on the migration.[17] However, the author has been unable to free himself from the often-repeated but incorrect view of history which claims that the Oromo entered documented history and the territory of the Christian kingdom only in 1522. The only study which deals at some length with the history of Oromo migration is Dr. Merid's excellent thesis, which is not yet published.[18] The central theme in his work is not the history of the migration, but the effect it had on the Christian kingdom and the Muslim state of Harar. While Merid gives an impressive account of the migration, the work is nevertheless not free from limitations. First, Merid failed to see that some of the people he calls "Galla invaders" were actually returning to the land which earlier had been taken from them by the Christian authority, at least in and south of what is today Shawa. Secondly, in his attempt to explain the Oromo success, Dr. Merid overemphasizes the civil war that afflicted the Christian society after 1559. But by then, the success of the Oromo was inevitable and the civil war itself was generated mainly by the inability of the Christian leadership to stop the Oromo advance.[19] Thirdly, one major reason for the Oromo success was the endless slaving-raids which the Christians conducted against their pagan subjects and neighbors.[20] These raids were carried out with thoroughness, purportedly to finance the war against the Oromo. They not only failed to stop the Oromo advance, but instead contributed to their rapid spread. Merid does not seem to have grasped fully that the slaving-raids in the southwestern provinces actually depopulated the region, creating a vacuum into which the Oromo moved rapidly without meeting much resistance.

Oromo pastoralists arrived in the southwestern region of what is today Ethiopia in the 1570s; and several decades after the disintegration of Ennarya (the most important state in the Gibe region) in 1710, a new order was created in the area. In the course of the Oromo settlement in the Gibe region, the ground was prepared and the stage set for the transformation of the Oromo mode of production from pastoralism to sedentary agriculture, combined with cattle-keeping. This in turn set in motion a new, dynamic political process that culminated in the formation of the five Oromo Gibe states shortly after 1800. Although the existence of these states spanned no more than a few decades before their annexation by Menelik, the Amhara king of Shawa, this brief period was packed with events of crucial importance. It witnessed a rapid agricultural, social, cultural, political, religious, and commercial progress unsurpassed in any of the other Oromo areas of Ethiopia. Although the works of Drs. M. Abir and H. S. Lewis have shown the importance of the history of the Gibe states, so far there is no coherent work which deals with Oromo migration to and settlement in the Gibe region, the process of the Gibe state formations, their political organization, economic foundation, and ideological orientation.

The present study has been undertaken with a view to filling this gap. In attempting to shed fresh light on the history of the Oromo, it analyzes the profound cultural, social, economic, and religious changes the Oromo in the Gibe region had undergone. As a result of this study, I believe we have a coherent work which will provide a basis for further work on the Oromo in Ethiopia. However, I must admit to one lacuna in the present study, namely the period from 1710 to the second half of the eighteenth century. This is because of the lack of written information about this period.

This book is based mainly on the last section of my Ph.D. dissertation presented to the School of Oriental and African Studies, London University, in June 1983. The sources which I have used for this study can be grouped into three categories. One source is the traditional Christian materials, mainly the royal chronicles[21] of more than two centuries, together with a number of Christian[22] and Muslim[23] historical documents produced during the tumultuous sixteenth century. The first two chapters are based on these sources. The second source is accounts by European travelers and missionaries of the last century who either visited or lived in the Ethiopian region and have left us some information on the Oromo society of the time. Their accounts, when supplemented by the works of modern anthropologists, provide a wealth of information about the Oromo people in general and the gada system in particular. Although I was unable to go back to Ethiopia to do field work, I was extremely fortunate in that some inaccessible manuscripts and a number of other very useful documents became available to me. The manuscripts were written by Oromo authors on Oromo history, while the documents dealt with the Oromo history, economics, and politics. These materials constituted my third source. I will comment on these manuscripts and documents at the appropriate places in the book; here it suffices to say that these Oromo sources give the Oromo view of their own history. The last four chapters of the book are based on the second and third sources mentioned here.

I conducted research at the Public Record Office and the India Office Library in London, at the Ministère des Affaires Etrangères and the Archives Nationales in Paris, and also at the Propaganda Fide, Archivo Storico della Societa Geografica Italiano and Ministro degli Affari Esteri in Rome. All these archives contain useful and very interesting information on northern Ethiopia, Shawa, and Harar generally, but these were not of much direct help to me. The archival material which I found most useful for my purpose is mostly in the Bibliothèque Nationale, Paris.

I am very grateful to the British Council, my sponsors for three years. They also facilitated my visits to some important archives in Paris. A grant from the Central Research Fund of the University of London enabled me to visit some of the Italian archives in Rome. For this, I am grateful. I am also grateful to the African Educational Trust for its financial support.

It is impossible to acknowledge fully the range of my indebtedness. Many persons have contributed to this study in various ways. Among them the following deserve particular mention. I am deeply indebted to Professor Roland Oliver, who supervised my research at the School of Oriental and African Studies. He was truly a patient guide, and it was his encouragement which led me to develop the last section of my dissertation into this book. I owe a debt of gratitude to the late Dr. Richard Caulk for providing me with photocopies of the Jimma Interview Programme and a number of invaluable documents; to my friend Mahdi Hamid Mude for providing me with a copy of the manuscript of Abba Jobir Abba Dula, the last king of Jimma; to Dr. Gunnar Hasselblatt for providing me with the 330-page unpublished manuscript of Tasaw Merga, which covers Oromo history from the beginning of the sixteenth century to the end of the nineteenth century; to Dr. A. Trulzi for allowing me to photocopy some of his documents and manuscripts which deal with the history of Oromo in Wallaga; to Shaykh Mohammed Rashad, who generously provided me with copies of a number of Shaykh Bakr Sapalo's manuscripts, which are otherwise inaccessible; to Ms. Bonnie Holcomb, Professor Lucy C. Grigsby, Professor Asmaron Legesse, and Dr. Paul Baxter for reading the manuscript and for their comments and suggestions; to Professor Earle D. Clowney for his help with the French materials, Haile Larebo for translating Geez materials and helping with the Italian materials, and Kulan Gudina for translating German materials. Similarly, I greatly appreciate the kindness and assistance of the following people while I was in London – Demissie Tulu, Dinkensh Beyene, Mohammed Kitesa, Drs. R. J. Hayward, Donald Crummey, Solomon Inquai and too many others to list. I am greatly indebted to Dean Ruby Thomson and Atlanta University for their assistance with this project. I am deeply indebted to my wife, Aziza Usso, who tirelessly and patiently encouraged me to finish this book. Finally, I thank Karen Nails, Carolyn Clark, Andrea B. Williams and Pauline Moore for typing the manuscript.

Standardization of the spelling of Ethiopian names used in this study

Ethiopian linguists have not agreed on correct spelling in English of Ethiopian names, not to mention words in the Amharic and Oromo languages. As a result, there are variant spellings of the same name which confuse a reader. The following list shows the spellings which have been used in the text.

Variant spellings	*Versions used*
Aba (father or title of respect in Oromo)	Abba
Abay, Abai (river)	Abbay
Abba Boko (king of Jimma)	Abba Boka
Abessinia	Abyssinia
Amaras	Amharas
Amoleh (salt bar)	Amole
Bagemder, Begemder, Bagemdir (province)	Bagamder
Bareytuma, Barettuma	Barentu
Bideru	Bidru
Boku	Bokku
Boran	Borana
Caffe	Chafe
Dedjazmatch, Dejazmach	Dajazmach
Dembya (province)	Dambiya
Enarya, Inarya, Innarya, Narea, Hinnario (province)	Ennarya
Gabaro	Gabbaro
Gooderoo, Goodro	Gudru
Hadya	Hadiya
Kabie, Kabiyye	Qabie
Kafa	Kaffa
Lemi	Lemmi
Limu	Limmu
Macha	Matcha
Nono, Nunnu	Nonno
Nur Husain	Nur Hussein
Saka, Sakka, Saqa	Saqqa

Sapa	Sappa
Sapara, Suppera, Supira	Sapera
Sheikh	Shaykh
Sheikh Husain	Shaykh Hussein
Shewa, Shoa, Showa (province)	Shawa
Soresa	Sorressa
Sudecha	Sadacha
Tigre, Tigrai (province)	Tigray
Tuloma	Tulama
Tunique	Tinnqe
Waka	Waqa
Wallagga, Wollaga, Wellaga (province)	Wallaga
Wallo, Wello (province)	Wollo
Warra Himano	Warra Himanu

Introduction

This study deals mainly with the history of the Oromo of one area – the Gibe region. It covers a period of three centuries. The story begins at a time when the medieval Christian kingdom of Abyssinia was rapidly disintegrating and ends shortly before the creation of the modern Ethiopian empire. During this long period, the Oromo led an independent existence as masters of their destiny and makers of their own history. The Oromo of the Gibe region lived as neighbors with, but beyond military control and political influence of, the medieval Christian kingdom of Abyssinia. The latter came to constitute only a small part of what today is Ethiopia. The Oromo developed their own cultural, religious, and political institutions which shaped their history and expressed their world view.

The independent existence of the Oromo was brought to an end abruptly and rudely by the creation of the modern Ethiopian empire during and after the 1880s. The conquest and annexation of their territory not only deprived the Oromo of their sovereignty but also of their history, because the creation of the empire consolidated myths and untruths long held and circulated in the Christian kingdom about the Oromo, who were generally portrayed as people without a history. To set the record straight this introduction considers two themes that are unrelated but each necessary to the understanding of the history of the Oromo. First, the introductory chapter briefly depicts how the Oromo problem is either presented falsely or even ignored in the Ethiopian historiography. The second and larger part of the chapter deals with the Oromo social organization on the eve of their sixteenth-century migration.

During the sixteenth and subsequent centuries much was written on the military conflict between the Oromo and the medieval Christian kingdom of Abyssinia. The Oromo were generally described simply as "the enemies of the Amhara" and what was written about them by the Christian chroniclers mainly expressed the intense prejudice which was deeply rooted in Abyssinian society.[1] Even the enlightened historian and great intellectual of his time, Abba Bahrey, who wrote "History of the Galla" in 1593 opens his invaluable work with these words: "I have begun to write the history of the Galla in order to make known the number of their tribes, their readiness to kill people, and

1

the brutality of their manners."[2] Since the time of Abba Bahrey the purported brutality of Oromo manners has been magnified and embroidered with grotesque distortions of history, which depicts the Oromo as "barbarian hordes who brought darkness and ignorance in their train."[3] In such writings the Oromo were never credited as creators of an original culture, or as having religious and democratic political institutions which flowered in patterns of their own making and nourished their spiritual and material well-being. On the contrary, unsubstantiated myths and untruths were created and the Oromo were arbitrarily degraded to a lower stage of material culture, as people who needed the "civilizing mission" of their Abyssinian neighbors. Although the Abyssinian society has had a fascinating history, to maintain that its elite members had an historic mission "to civilize the barbarians" is nonsense historically. The Abyssinian elite, especially the Shawan Amhara rulers, who laid the foundation of and created the modern Ethiopian empire, had everything to gain in attributing a "civilizing mission" to themselves – it has been the common cry of colonizers. In fact, the new Ethiopian ruling class, typified by Emperor Menelik, the creator of the modern Ethiopian empire, found it necessary and profitable to denigrate the Oromo people, their culture, and their history in all ways great and small. This ruling class especially perceived the danger of the larger Oromo population to its empire. Consequently, the ruling class systematically depicted the Oromo as people without history, and belittled their way of life, and their religious and political institutions. It is not an exaggeration to say that no people have had their history so distorted or ignored and their achievements and human qualities undervalued as the Oromo have in the Ethiopian historiography. Bogumil Jewsiewicki's observation in his Introduction to the *African Historiographies* seems apposite.

> Because of its alliance with the state structures, separate from the true needs and concerns of the people, the historiography of the savants is, in Africa as elsewhere, the dominant form by which the past is described. But such an alliance also requires the creation of myths which pretend to be exclusive truths and portray themselves as capable of overcoming all other means of understanding the past.[4]

Until very recently, Oromo history has been either neglected, as M. Abir admits,[5] or it has been totally ignored,[6] or it has been distorted by prejudice. The Ethiopian ruling class even succeeded in elevating its anti-Oromo prejudice to the plane of state ideology, which was uncritically repeated in the name of scholarship.

> The Galla had nothing to contribute to the civilization of Ethiopia, they possessed no material or intellectual culture, and their social organization was at a far lower stage of development than of the population among whom they settled.[7]

These words written in 1960, by a well-known scholar of Semitic languages, are a good illustration of such long-held common historical prejudice. A number of other scholars have expressed similar historical prejudice less eloquently.[8a]

These biases derive from several sources. The very presence of a vast and readily available corpus of chronicles and texts in the Semitic languages of the northern kingdoms and chiefdoms has fitted in with the biases of European historians and classical linguists towards written sources; however dubious their contents, texts have been rated as more scholarly than oral sources, "proper" history only existing in writing and records. The northern Abyssinian texts, moreover, were written in Semitic languages of the same family as those used by the founders of the great Middle Eastern religions, Judaism, Christianity, and Islam and enshrined in the holy books of those religions. That, in itself, gave them prestige in the eyes of Orientalists. Further, Oromo, by not being a "written language" was not available to European scholars in libraries; not being available meant that it did not exist (Tutschek 1844 is an honorable exception). Amharinya, Tigrinya, and Geez pointed towards the Middle East and Abyssinians stressed myths such as the Solomonic legend (which was taught in schools as historical fact) and they played down their Africanness. Christian and Negro were often cited as opposites, as good and evil. Oromo, or Galla as it was called, derived from Black Africa. Further, the study of the north flourished when European colonial empires were flourishing: Britain, France, Germany, Italy, Belgium, and Portugal also saw themselves as having "civilising missions." In a way Menelik and his nobles became honorary, if second-class, bearers of the "white man's burden."[8b] Similarly, Christianity, even of the Ethiopian variety, just had to be an indicator of a higher level of civilization than a traditional African religion which did not have a "book": just as in a society stratified by class, the predatory state was at a higher level of cultural evolution than the "primitive democracies" or "simple states" of the Oromo.

Addis Ababa, the capital of the empire, was at the end of the railway line and was the stopping-point for most diplomats and scholars; beyond that was wild bush country populated by wild people and wild game. Certainly foreign travelers, diplomats, and the rare traveling scholar had to set out from the seat of the empire if they wished to penetrate its peripheries. So their own experiences, directed as they were from the center, took on the perceptions of the center, and those perceptions were arrogantly colonialist and Amhara-centered. Such observers could hardly have known that the Ethiopian ruling class sought not only to destroy the Oromo people's pride in their achievements, but also needed to keep them chained, with no faith in themselves, their history, and national identity.

I believe that a true knowledge of the history of the various Ethiopian peoples will create confidence and trust among the peoples of that country. Therefore, it is with this goal in mind that I have endeavored to write an objective history of the Oromo of the Gibe region, but from an Oromo point of view, though I do not neglect the history of the other people with whom the Oromo interacted. Above all, it is a history whose unexpressed message stresses the importance of and the need for building bridges of understanding and tolerance between the various peoples of Ethiopia.

Oromo social organization

At the time of the sixteenth-century migration, the pastoral Oromo consisted of two powerful confederacies named Borana and Barentu. In the national myth, Oromo was the "father" of both. But in the separate Borana genealogy, Borana had a "father" called Sapera. Bahrey[9] was the first historian to record that Sapera was the father of the Borana.[10] Antoine d'Abbadie,[11] on the basis of numerous genealogies gathered in the Gibe region, concluded that the "father" of the Borana lived around A.D. 1400 in Walal (see map 3, p. 19). D'Abbadie's information is important not for what it purports to tell us, but for what it implies. According to d'Abbadie it would appear that the Borana had already migrated to Walal before the fifteenth century, from their original home in the highlands of historical Bali,[12] where they must have lived for a long time together with the Barentu group. This interpretation is supported by a recent study which claims that some portion of the Oromo were living in the region of Walabu in the twelfth century.[13] The question of the original home of the Oromo has been discussed at length by E. Cerulli, I. M. Lewis, E. Haberland, H. S. Lewis, U. Braukamper, and other scholars;[14] I therefore dispense with the details. I follow the main conclusion of Haberland, which is supported by Oromo oral tradition.[15] Professor Haberland believes, and rightly, that the ancestral home of the Oromo was in the cool highlands in the region of Bale.[16] In one Oromo tradition, there is a reference to a faraway land, the land which is consistently claimed as the first home of the Oromo people, the birthplace of the nation. This land is known as Fugug[17] (see map 2, p. 5). Today the land of Fugug[18] and Mount Fugug are located in the administrative region of Arsi, the heartland of historical Bali. The Oromo people who lived in the highlands of Bali engaged in mixed farming, while the lowlands in the valley of river Ganale became the grazing ground for the pastoralists, who drifted away from the main group due to the transhumant nature of their economy. As Professor Haberland has observed:

> The main section of the tribe lives in the highlands and practices agriculture while the young manhood looks after the herds in the lowlands. Each group follows its distinct way of life and thus the cultural elements associated with cattle-rearing come more strongly to the fore in the lowlands. There are plenty of cases where whole groups settled down for long periods in the lowlands and later became separate tribes. Favourable grazing conditions had led them to settle in the lowlands in order to live exclusively by cattle-rearing . . . The vegetable foodstuffs needed for nourishment are procured by barter with the highland tribes.[19]

At this point it must be stated clearly that there was no such thing as a "pure" Oromo tribe derived from a single founding father. This aspect will be discussed fully in the next chapter and here it suffices to say that the history of the Oromo people is not a collection of histories of individual tribes or group of tribes, but a story of fusion and interaction by which all tribes and groups had altered and been transformed constantly. This was made possible by a dynamic Oromo institution (the gada system), the process of adoption, continual

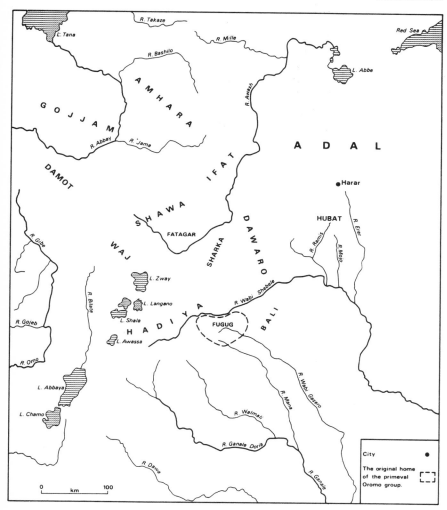

2 The probable location of Fugug around 1330

migration, conquest, assimilation, and interaction with other groups. All of these aspects will be discussed in more detail later.

Owing to the transhumant nature of their economy, the different Oromo groups moved in different directions; however, since the fourteenth century their movement to the north, to the east, and to the west, seems to have been checked by the southward-expanding Christian state.[20] In fact, it is clear that some Oromo groups were affected by Amda-Siyon's (1314–1344) wars of conquest.[21] Without going into details of Amda-Siyon's wars, it should suffice to say that the Christian and Muslim struggle during the first half of the

5

fourteenth century seems to have encouraged the movement from the highlands of historical Bali to the huge lowlands south of the same province, that is to say, from the region where there was conflict and control to the region where there was no conflict or control. It was in the lowlands south of historical Bali, that is in the valley of the Ganale river, that the Borana and Barentu developed into two separate fully fledged confederacies.

The problem of reconstructing the separation of Borana and Barentu becomes all the more difficult when one attempts to define the time-depth involved. The only safe way of putting it is that it probably happened before or during the fourteenth century.[22] It seems that at the initial stage of the separation the group that moved to the region west of the Ganale river acquired the appellation Borana,[23] while the other group, which remained in the region east of the Ganale river, retained the old Cushitic name of Barentu. Because of the "masculine" attribute associated with Borana, this group acquired the status of the "eldest son," which accorded its descendants seniority in the national myth.[24] After the sixteenth-century migration of the pastoral Oromo, the term Borana became a mark of distinction to express feelings of cultural and social superiority, or it was used to emphasize the "purity," fictitious or real, of one's genealogy. To this day, Borana signifies to Oromo speakers a "cultural and linguistic purity" which is more apparent than real. By the beginning of the nineteenth century in the Gibe region of western Oromoland the term Borana had already acquired the meaning of noblemen, rich in cattle and slaves. In fact, in this part of Oromoland, the Borana became the wealthy ruling class, who distinguished themselves from the plebeians by the marks they made on their left arms and by following certain food restrictions.[25]

In the highlands of Bale and the valley of river Ganale, the various Oromo tribes seem to have shared a common language, a culture, an oral literature, customs and manners, law, a "government," and institutions such as the office of Abba Gada, Qallu[26] and the *bokku*.[27] In short, they shared a common Qallu institution and gada system, which encompassed the totality of their existence. The Qallu institution and the gada system are discussed briefly so as to show their importance in the history of the Oromo nation and, indeed, their continuing influence.

The Qallu institution

A Qallu was a high priest who was the spiritual leader of Oromo traditional religion. The national myths which surround the origin of the first high priest, though varied in form, are similar in content.[28] The first Qallu was of divine origin. Some say he "fell from the sky itself," and others say he was found with the first black cow. And still others say he was the "eldest son of Ilma Orma."[29] Because of his origin and his role in the traditional ceremonies, the Qallu was the center of Oromo religion. As the "eldest son" of all Oromo, the national myth confers upon him the title of the father, the source of customs and traditions, "the prophet of the nation" who guarded the laws of Waqa (the sky god) and their interpretation.[30] Waqa was both the sky god and the sky itself, manifesting the dual nature of the two moieties within the nation, controlled fertility, peace, and lifegiving rains which were the *sine qua non* for farming and pastoral society. Prayers for peace, fertility, and rain are at the center of Oromo religion.[31]

The Qallu institution and its relation with Waqa were the core of traditional religion. Adult men visited the Qallu for blessing. This brings us to the story of Abba Muda. "The term Muda, when used by itself is the name of the ceremony that is celebrated once every eight years in honor of the Qallu." The Muda ceremony was important because it was the point at which the Qallu institution and the gada system intersected. "It is one of the critical foci of the Oromo polity."[32]

Bahrey, who first wrote about the military aspect of the gada system, did not mention the pilgrimage to Abba Muda. This is one of the many indications that Bahrey's knowledge of the Oromo society of the time was limited. What is more, Bahrey does not appear to have gathered information about Oromo history from the Oromo themselves, who were in the army of the Emperor Sarsa Dengel (1563–1597). But a few years later, around the beginning of the seventeenth century, Azaj Tino, one of the authors of the chronicle of Susenyos, described the pilgrimage to Abba Muda in glowing terms. He says besides their belief in one Waqa, the Oromo believe in one single person whom they call Abba Muda. As the Jews believe in Moses and the Muslims in Muhammad, the Oromo believe in their Abba Muda. They all go to him from far and near to receive his blessings.[33]

Four important points emerged from Tino's vital piece of information. First, Abba Muda was the spiritual leader whom the Oromo regarded as their prophet. Secondly, the land of Abba Muda which the pastoral Oromo regarded as sacred and the cradle of their birth, was located in the highlands of the middle south. Thirdly, the pilgrims to Abba Muda were delegates, who were the representatives of their clans. And finally these pilgrims could be either Borana or Barentu.

European travelers and missionaries of the nineteenth and early twentieth centuries have reported a strikingly similar picture of the pilgrimage to Abba Muda. Perhaps what Cecchi says about the journey to the land of Abba Muda may sum up the important points, though not all of what others have to say:

> The journey to Abba Muda is made partly to honour him and partly to receive his blessings and anointment, which qualify the pilgrims for ritual functions in their own home region. Only those who have committed no serious crimes may make the journey ... They must be married and circumcised. This means that they must have undergone the butta ceremony and thereby completed their forty-year participation in the gada system. During the journey they are said to be dressed as women and to receive food from women. They wear their hair cut short and bear no weapons. As an offering to Abba Muda they bring a bull, and as a sign of their peaceful intentions they drive a sheep. When they reach Abba Muda, the pilgrims' leader offers food to the snake that guards Abba Muda's grotto. After

communal prayers Abba Muda anoints the jila and gives them myrrh. He commands them not to cut their hair and to be righteous, not to recognize any leader who tries to get absolute power, and not to fight among themselves.[34]

Those who went to Abba Muda and received his blessing and anointment were called *jila*.[35] *Jila* were considered the link between the spiritual father and the nation.[36] As the *jila* were inviolable, no one touched their cattle either in war or in raids between villages. People who herded their cattle were unarmed as a sign of their peaceful intentions. A common story runs that *jila* was "brother" of Borana and Barentu. Each had his own law and, the descendants of *jila* having become extinct, men can acquire "his law" by the pilgrimage to the spiritual father of the nation.

On the arrival of the *jila* at the spiritual center of Abba Muda, the latter asked them about the law of Waqa and the customs of the Oromo people (Ilma Orma). We are told that the Abba Muda denounced the danger of abandoning the way of life of the fathers, and urged them to stick to the simple pastoral life that guaranteed the continuity of the ancient traditions. The prayers and blessings which Abba Muda showered on each pilgrim underline the ideal type of prosperity he wished for the Oromo.

> Prosper, O son of Orma, return home to your family and Abba Boku. May the milk of your herds flow in abundance. May the whole village drink of your superfluity [of milk]. May you be loaded with goods. May your favourite cow's udder be full of milk, from which none drinks but the father of the family, from which none drinks but the mother of the family, from which none drinks but he who has received Unction [Muda]. It is the wish of my heart that you should prosper. May Waqa be with you.[37]

According to a number of sources the pilgrimage to Abba Muda was abolished around 1900, by Emperor Menelik, who saw the danger of Oromo unity in this practice;[38] before that happened pilgrims from Harar used to go to Mormor in Bale. Those from Shawa, Wallaga, and the Gibe region went to either Walal or Harro Walabuu. The Arsi went to Dallo Baruk or Debanu.[39] As can be seen, before the sixteenth-century pastoral migration, the different groups sent their representatives (*jila*) to their spiritual father in the country of their origin. This in turn abundantly demonstrates that even in the sixteenth century the nation did not have a single spiritual father. It seems that after the separation into the highland and the lowland groups, each group had its own high priest. Despite the multiplicity of the high priests, they seem to have performed almost identical duties and shared a common heritage.

Today among the Borana, who live in southern Ethiopia and northern Kenya, the Qallu stands for the moral quality, the peace and the unity of the people. "His path is that of peace and truth." He represents the Borana ideal of generosity and unreserved concern for fellow brothers. "Qallu is the life spirit of Boran."

> Neither Boran society nor culture can be understood without consideration of the part played by the qallu. All Boran acknowledge the sanctity of the qallu; it is by the qallu that all their essential customs were ordained and by them endowed

with a moral force and divine order. Further, it is their possession of the qallu which, above all else, distinguishes the Boran tribe from the "junior" tribes and makes them all superior to their neighbours.[40]

Whatever their role within gada politics, the Qallu's spiritual center seems to have represented the continuity of peace within the nation even in early times. After the separation of the Borana and Barentu, and more particularly during the great migration, it seems every fully fledged tribe went with its own Qallu. The religious leaders who accompanied the migrating tribes were not Qallu in the real sense of the term. They were called *irressa*, "the right hand" of the Qallu, his emissaries, who received the "right to exercise their functions from the high priest in the south."[41] This explains the continuous link maintained through the *jila* pilgrimage every eight years to the "birth place" of Abba Muda in the south. What all these had in common was that, despite the separation of the tribes from each other over a long period, they all recognized that the cradleland, the nation's spiritual center, was in the highlands of the middle south. For them this area was, as Mecca is for the Muslims, a place of pilgrimage. So the Qallu institution developed among the Matcha only after 1900, when the contact with the spiritual center was stopped.[42] Before the separation and migration, the possession of Qallu and the common gada government seem to have been the "special mark" of the Oromo nation. After migration and the adoption of a large number of people into the Oromo nation, the office of Abba Muda and the institution of Qallu remained in the hands of the descendants of the Borana or Barentu, who are termed in the national myth as "pure" Oromo.[43]

The gada system

The term gada is very difficult to define precisely. It is a term loosely used for so many varied concepts that it has lost any single meaning. The dividing-line between the various definitions is very shadowy and indistinct unless one takes into account strictly the context in which the term is used. This is because the interpretations of Oromo terms, idiomatic expressions, and proverbs related to the gada have meanings other than their surface meanings.

> The meaning of the word only becomes intelligible when the total context in which it has been uttered is taken into account. The words which express cultural values – the "key-words" of a culture – cannot be understood unless one is thoroughly acquainted with the society in question. They are untranslatable except by lengthy descriptive explanations.[44]

My purpose in calling serious attention to the definition of gada is not because I have an alternative handy definition, but because the realization of the weakness of the definition of gada itself is an essential point to be kept in mind when dealing with this complex system. Below, an attempt is made to define gada from various perspectives.

In his *Oromo Grammar* published in 1867, Massaja derived the etymology of gada from *gaddisa* (shelter, shade, that protects from the heat of the sun). It is used in three contexts. The first use is in the sense of taking advantage of the shelter. The second is in the sense of protecting oneself with the shelter, taking refuge in it, or in him, or using its or his good name for protection. The third is in the sense of giving somebody a shelter, protecting him, or them, taking them under one's umbrella. In common speech in the language people say, "gada balaa" (wide gada), meaning a haven for refugees, a large shelter for all. When reduced to the essentials, the above concepts of gada refer to the practice of "adoption" by the national assembly and the indisputable protection which the assembly accorded to those it adopted. This is an incomplete definition. According to Professor Asmarom:

> The term gada cannot be given a univocal interpretation. It stands for several related ideas. It is first of all the concept standing for the whole way of life that is the subject of study. More specifically, however, it refers to any period of eight years during which a class stays in power.[45]

To a speaker of the language, the term gada has very strong resonances of time: *Gafa gada kami?* (during which gada?). It has the meaning of an official: *Inni gada* (he is gada, i.e., an official). The term can also be used in the following context: *Gada nagaya* (gada of peace), *gada qufa* (gada of plenty), *gada lola* (gada of war), *gada keyna* (our gada), etc. Gada is a measurement of time, but according to Angelo Mizzi it also has a religious sense. *Gadoma* (sacredness) is associated with circumcision and thereby maturity for political power.[46]

The different definitions reflect different attributes of the system. One definition cannot be complete because it leaves out the other attributes. However, for our purposes in this introduction, we adopt the following definition of Professor Asmarom, which stresses the military and political aspects of the gada system.

> The gada system is a system of classes (luba) that succeed each other every eight years in assuming military, economic, political and ritual responsibilities. Each gada class remains in power during a specific term (gada) which begins and ends with a formal power transfer ceremony. Before assuming a position of leadership, the gada class is required to wage war against a community that none of their ancestors had raided. This particular war is known as butta and is waged on schedule every eight years.[47]

The male members of the Oromo society were classified into generation-sets and gada grades. The set is the group of people "who share the same status and who perform their rites of passage together, whereas the grades are the stages of development through which the groups pass."[48] Our main concern here is with the gada grades. It is impossible to reconstruct fully the names of the original gada grades, because after the migration the various groups adopted slightly different names. This has led to confusion at two levels, the first on the names of gada grades[49] and the second on the names of the gada in power.[50] The gada grades will be discussed first. According to many authors, the full cycle of the gada system was ten grades. An individual entered the first grade at birth and left the last grade at the gada age of eighty. After that, he retired. The first five grades according to one source were the "practical schools" during

10

which young men were trained militarily, politically, and ritually to take over the leadership of the nation.[51] These were: *Daballe* grade (1–8 years), *Folle* grade (8–16 years), *Qondalla* grade (16–24 years), *Raba* grade (24–32 years), and *Dori* grade (32–40 years).

The full cycle of the gada system was ten grades. This full cycle was divided into two periods of forty years each. Among the Borana in southern Ethiopia and northern Kenya, where the gada system is still a living institution, the period of forty years is known as *gogessa*. However, among northern Oromo the period of forty years was known as *mesensa* (a thread that links two points). In this case, it means a blood tie that links members of one full cycle of forty years. This is because children of a single father, regardless of their ages, all belong to one branch *mesensa*.[52] The gada of the father, the first forty years, had particular names, and that of the son, the second forty years, also had their names. The system worked on the pattern in which the forty years of the father were followed by another forty years of the son. This seems to have been the core of the system. "The basic rule of the gada system is that the newly born infant boy always enters the system of grades exactly forty years behind the father regardless of the age of the father; father and son are five grades apart at all times."[53]

The movement of the forty years was cyclical, repeating itself after every eighty years. The following gada names were recorded by Bahrey in 1593. Other names are listed in the footnote.[54]

Fathers	Sons
(1) Melbah	Harmufa
(2) Mudana	Robale
(3) Kilole	Birmaji
(4) Bifole	Mulata
(5) Michelle	Dulo[55]

A number of writers on the Oromo in Ethiopia strongly emphasize the political significance of the system,[56] while others find less political significance in it.[57] Those who claim that the gada system had less political significance than the Qallu institution tend to ascribe higher authority to the latter than to the former. This is incorrect to say the least. The gada system existed because of its political importance and the rituals stressed in it were part of the politics. However, what is not in dispute is the fact that it seems impossible to draw a clear demarcation between the ritual and the political functions within the gada system. Both were part of the same body politic. Since both dealt with the good of society, it was unnecessary to distinguish between them. Furthermore, within the gada system, the political "power" was held by the gada class, and not by one person or a few individuals. The officers selected were simply the representatives of the "reigning set," and they did not have powers separate from the one given to them by the *chafe* (meadow) assembly.[58] There was no permanent power invested in the officers. The ultimate source of power was the assembly, which exercised this power in specific circumstances.

Hence, the system seems to have worked ideally for small groups whose members knew each other and met face to face when the situation demanded. With a large group spread over a wide territory the system did not work effectively. Instead of having one supreme assembly, several competing assemblies sprang up in different areas. That is why, although the Oromo nation was under a single gada system, they did not have a common government; instead they had what became the confederacy governments.

As already indicated, there were five gada grades that led to the Gada – the stage of political and ritual leadership. This forty-year period of the five gada grades was concluded with the *dannisa* ("fatherhood") ceremony (which brought to a conclusion forty years of development of the gada class).[59]

An important institution in the gada system, the *butta* war, was the kernel of the complex military preparation. Bahrey does not mention *butta* by name. But he describes the practice known as *dulaguto*.[60] This is a composite term consisting of *dula*, war, and *gutu*, full or complete, which means full or complete war. And *butta* was indeed a complete national war conducted every eight years. According to Cerulli, *butta* was a great Oromo festival which each tribe celebrated every eight years. These celebrations were followed by a *butta* war.[61] From this it follows that two concepts are embodied in the term *butta*: the grand feast that preceded the ritual war and the war that followed the feast. The war was part of the ritual requirement of the system. As such it was directed against either big game or enemies, depending on the gains involved.[62] At least by the sixteenth century there is evidence that the *butta* war was the major source of booty for Oromo warriors. (This aspect becomes clear from Bahrey's description.) What made the *butta* war economic in character was the fact that it was preceded by the grand feast, for which all the gada class without exception sacrificed animals, depleting their herds. The booty that followed the feast was undertaken to replace the depleted stock.

The grand feast of meat and butter eating and milk drinking was one of the most joyous times in the life of the nation every eight years.[63] The feasts were accompanied by dances, love songs, and above all boastful war songs that intoxicated the participants. The boasting war songs were of two kinds. *Farsa* were long poems with short verses, in which were celebrated the most famous warriors of the tribe, particularly by recalling their ancestors on the fathers' and mothers' sides. They were "poetical expressions of the bonds which united the members of the tribe. They were the boasting songs of the tribe as a whole."[64] *Gerarsa* were the boasting songs about a single warrior's "bravery." Its accompanying characteristics were "virtues of the highest order" depicted through *gerarsa*. The following short and moving song describes a joyous welcome which was given to a valiant warrior after his return from a successful raid. During the emotional days of the grand feast, the successful hero recited his achievements and moved both young and old with tears of joy.

> The gucci[65] [ostrich] loves the sun. I have descended to the narrow valley and I have pulled down the horsemen . . . the beautiful girls will adorn my comb. My friends will kiss my mouth. The children will say to me, "You have killed well."[66]

Through *farsa* songs, eloquent heroes found their poetical expression, which set members of their tribes aflame with pride. Through these powerful songs the dead heroes of the nation were reincarnated and the living heroes were elevated to a higher plane; bravery was almost worshiped as a religion. Through *gerarsa*, individual warriors won the hearts of their mistresses and the respect and admiration of the participants. The meat feast and the emotionally charged war songs seem to have prepared the ground for immediate offensive. The war was ritual in form and economic in content. The immediate economic and psychological advantages were buried under a religious cover. Then "they attack a country which none of their predecessors have attacked."[67] It thus appears that the direction of *butta* was decided by economic prospects of a new country that had not previously been raided. All the warrior classes seem to have participated in *butta* war because of its far-reaching economic and psychological implications.

Gada: (the stage of political and ritual leadership Borana)[68] 40–48 years

The Gada stage was the heart of the system, the kernel of the whole complex institution. In the true sense of the term the Gada stage was a landmark in the history of the grade that was coming to power. It was at this stage that every "reigning set" left its mark on the nation through its political and ritual leadership. "The strongest indication that the class was in power is the fact that it imparted its name and its ritual attributes to the period of history when it was Gada (VI)."[69]

Gada government

Before I embark on discussion of the gada form of government, a few points must be made clear. Among the Oromo of the sixteenth century different confederacies seem to have had a similar form of government. However, the variations from confederacy to confederacy were pronounced enough to warn against generalization. Two points of caution are mentioned below. The form of government which each confederacy adopted was based on a number of factors peculiar to itself, factors such as the size of its population, the geographical features of its region, and the predominant mode of production at the time. This means that although before the separation of the nation there was probably a common form of government, after the separation, and eventually after the migration, the different confederacies developed along slightly different lines, modifying their modes of life and government to suit their new environment and requirements.[70] Secondly, government among the Oromo, at both the confederacy and the clan level, was essentially by assembly. The confederacy assembly had the power to legislate for the whole confederacy. This assembly concerned itself with matters of supreme importance – war and peace, legislation, the settlement of inter-confederacy or inter-clan disputes, hearing cases that were brought from the lower assemblies.

13

Ordinary day-to-day problems were left to the clan assemblies, which were based on the model of the bigger and broader government.

The composition of gada government, while varying from region to region, conformed to a certain general pattern which justifies us in speaking of a gada government. We are told that there was an extensive election campaign, ranging from weeks to months, extending over long distances among different clans.[71] The oratorical talent expected of the candidates, the traditional fund of knowledge which they were supposed to have acquired, the wisdom for settling disputes and taking quick action in difficult situations, tangible past military achievements that they could boast of during the election campaign, all these constituted criteria for leadership which seem to have precluded many from the offices. Three qualities – oratory, knowledge of the history and traditions of the society, and past military achievements with recognizable potential for future leadership – constituted these three major criteria.[72] In all there was an Abba Gada (the father of the gada in power). During the eight-year period, the Abba Gada was a central authority, a single political head and the spokesman for the confederacy. His residence was the seat of the government and the capital of the confederacy. The assembly was held in the *chafe* (the meadow) under the life-giving shade of the *oda* ("the holy sycamore tree"), which traditionally was believed to be the most "respected" and the most "sacred" of trees, the shade of which was the source of peace and the center of religion. The shade of the *oda* was not only the "office of the government," the meeting-ground for the elders of the confederacy, but also the sacred place for the religious duties. Hence, all the sacrifices undertaken by the gada class were performed at this spot. When the government met under the *oda*, the Abba Gada sat on the right and the other dignitaries on the left, by seniority of the tribe or clan and the age of the participants. The debate followed this hierarchical order.[73] When the assembly met, all those present participated in the debate and decision-making. Once a policy was adopted by the "reigning set" its implementation became the task of all. This was both the strength and the weakness of the gada government: strength because unity symbolized in a common political head was strengthened through a common action, which in turn ensured that no one group became entrenched and assumed despotic powers; weakness because the gada government lacked political integration at a national level. The Oromo nation broke down into autonomous confederacies and the nation was not able to hold the confederacies together under a unitary national government.[74]

In each, there was the Abba Dula ("the father of war"), who was an orator and tactician versed in the military exploits of the past generations. The history of the past military success was the material upon which the leaders drew in the psychological preparation for war. The Abba Dula marched at the head of the warriors and recited exciting war poems that put the brave aflame and hardened the coward. In each, there was the Abba Sera ("the father of the law"), an expert on traditional law, whose duty it was to memorize the results of the assemblies' deliberations and furnish them when needed. In each, there was the *saylan* (Sagalan, Borana or Barentu), the nine judges who were elected from the retiring officers. In each, there were the *lemmi* (the messengers), sent to each clan to resolve differences and settle disputes to preserve the peace and stability of the region. It was an inviolable Oromo law, next to that of the *jila*, that the ambassadors were not hurt. To hurt them was an insult to the whole clan or confederacy and a cause for war.[75] In each, the gada government was the government of "the reigning set." The election and the "transfer of power" took place at the time of the *jarra* ceremony. *Jarra* was the event that ended the gada of the previous eight years and started the new one. It was the beginning of the new period, the building of the new future, which the European travelers and missionaries of the last century compared with the Greek Olympiad.[76]

Jarra was the end of one era and the beginning of another. It was the time of feasting and extensive ritual activities, during which the hopes for the next eight years were expressed and the strength and weaknesses of the past eight years were told. It was the time when the "soul" of the nation met under the *oda*. *Jarra* was the pivot of the Oromo calendar, the dividing-line betwen gada periods.

After the "transfer of power" the preceding Abba Gada handed over the *bokku* to the new Abba Gada, and that signaled the end of one gada period and the beginning of a new one.[77] *Bokku* was a very popular term in oral literature. It has two meanings. The first and more important was the one attached to the wooden scepter kept by the Abba Gada in his belt during all the assembly meetings. As the emblem of authority, the *bokku* represented the independence of a tribe, and it served as a symbol of unity,[78] common law, and common government. Secondly, it referred to the keeper of the *bokku* – Abba Bokku.[79] With the transfer of the *bokku*, the change of the government was completed. Then the new government and the leaders together with the assembly made a "new law" that lasted for the next eight years.

Before the debate on the substance of the new law commenced, the new Abba Gada (Abba Bokku) slaughtered his *butta* bull,[80] and dipped a branch of green tree into the blood of the sacrificed victim and planted it in the assembly.[81] The sacrificial blood symbolized the unity of the confederacy as brothers descending from a common founder, real or fictitious. The branch of a green tree represented peace, plenty, and fertility of Ilma Orma (the Oromo people).

Once the debate started, the members of the assembly spoke according to their seniority. Every important point raised by the speakers was scored by the sounding of *wachafa* (sling) by the person who was assigned to do this specific duty. The sounding of the sling was used for applauding the speaker and for counting his impressive points. It was the official registration of the valid scores (points to be taken into the "new law" and regulations). The public debate on the law served as a "practical school" for the young to learn proverbs, genealogy, and local history. It was a forum for ambitious men to establish their reputation and the platform for the old to articulate their wisdom.[82] Each speaker was allowed a few minutes to recapitulate and enumerate the points he forgot earlier. Once his speech was over, the Abba Gada asked the assembly if there was a proposition for the law.[83]

In Oromo there are two terms that express the concept of law. The first is *ada*, "custom, habit, tradition, way of life, etc." and the second is *sera* (or *hera*), the law in the formal sense of the term. It is difficult to demarcate the boundary between the two. Both were kept in the "living constitution" of the nation, the hearts of the elders.[84] The law seems to have embodied the spirit of unity, common identity, and common internal peace. Baxter has shown that the Borana identity, unity, and sense of oneness are strongly stressed in the *ada*. He says, "The Boran 'people' consists of all those persons who speak the Boran language, call themselves Boran and acknowledge the 'peace of Boran'."[85] The symbol of the law was kept in the *bokku*, the Abba Gada's sign of authority. In this context, the law, the national authority, and the Abba Gada were interconnected by the *bokku*. The essence of Oromo law is expressed in the following quotation:

> Sera is, though not the whole of the law, the core and in a sense the symbol of it. Ada, custom, or a way of life, is, however important and constantly present in people's awareness, too diffuse a thing for the value which is attached to it to lie ritually expressed in a direct way. Sera – a more or less short list of important maxims in a memorable form, can be the object of such expression and thus act as a permanent symbol of law in the wider sense. Among these communities which lack kings, the law, like his insignia, is handed on from one Gada chief to the next, it reigns permanently, while its representatives come and go.[86]

After the assembly finished "making law," the Abba Gada led his Gada set and the nation in prayer. He prayed on behalf of the nation. Here the politics and the rituals intersect and overlap, one influencing and the other determining the duty of his office.[87] After the prayer, the Abba Gada, and he alone, declared the law from the stage of piled stone which was known as *dhaga koru sera labsu* (the proclamation of the law from the stage of the piled stone). From the stage, the Abba Gada announced orally each article, and the assembly repeated after him in chorus, which symbolized signature. Now the law was "signed" and "passed" by the assembly. The stage of piled stones represented the supremacy of the new law. Most of the "new" laws were reiteration of "old" traditional laws. Once proclaimed, they were not changed for the next eight years. From then on, the main duty of the Abba Gada (Abba Bokku) and his government was to guard and administer them.[88] In the interpretation of the law, the new Abba Gada was supported by legal experts who were old, retired judges. Because "old age in general was a sign of wisdom and associated with peace the retired judges contributed" to the maintenance of peace among the part of the whole. As they were recruited from the retired officers, they knew the law by heart. This underlined the importance and the continuity of the law. In the implementation of the law, the major force behind the Abba Gada was strong public opinion.[89]

Finally, in the above necessarily incomplete discussion, I have tried to show the importance of the Qallu institution and the gada system in the history of the

16

Oromo people. In the later chapters, we shall see how the Qallu institution continued to be important despite the Islamization of part of the Oromo people while the political importance of the gada system decreased as the result of profound transformation within the Oromo in the Gibe region. However, before we embark on the fascinating discussion of the changes that the Oromo underwent in the Gibe region, it is indispensable that the process that took pastoral Oromo to the Gibe region itself be considered. The following chapters will discuss this process, which spread the pastoral Oromo to the Gibe region and beyond, altering the political landscape of what is today southwestern Ethiopia.

1

The migration of pastoral Oromo to the southwestern parts of Ethiopia and their settlement in the Gibe region from 1570 to 1600

The first part of this chapter deals with the Borana Oromo migration to what is today the administrative region of Shawa. The second and larger part of the chapter concentrates on their migration to the Gibe region and beyond. The Borana section of the Oromo was divided into three confederacies, namely Tulama-Matcha, the southern Borana[1] and Gujjii. The Tulama-Matcha lived together under one *chafe* assembly at Harroo Walabuu located some 48 to 64 kilometers east of Lake Abbaayaa.[2] The southern Borana lived in Tullu Walal, while the Gujjii lived around Harroo Gerjjaa on both sides of the Ganale river (see map 3, p. 19) The migration of the southern Borana and Gujjii is not discussed here, only that of the Tulama-Matcha (the northern Borana). These migrated in two stages. During the first stage, they migrated in small numbers, while during the second stage they migrated in very large numbers. The linking thread through both stages was that their custom was to set out together to war, although after a period they eventually separated.[3] This separation occurred only in the last quarter of the sixteenth century. The sources are unanimous in claiming that after their migration from Harroo Walabuu, the two groups had a common *chafe* in Fatagar at a place called Oda Nabi, in Dukam, about 30 kilometers southeast of Addis Ababa. Bahrey makes a clear distinction between the first and the second stages. As for the first, he states that "the Galla came from the west and crossed the river of their country, which is called Galan, to the frontier of Bali in the time of the Hase Wang Sagad." On the basis of internal evidence this had been proved to be in 1522. And for the second stage, he states that "those of the Borana who stayed, came out of their country by way of Kuera, that was the time when Fasil attacked them and was killed by them."[4] This took place between 1578 and 1586, when the powerful Birmaji gada was in power.

During the first phase of their migration, the Tulama-Matcha, like their brethren, the Barentu,[5] took considerable advantage of the situation created by the jihad of Imam Ahmad (1529–1543). This was because the jihad was accompanied by warfare on a scale hitherto unwitnessed in the area. What is more, it sent different groups fleeing from the "storm center," abandoning their ancestral homes. This process triggered a chain reaction which affected

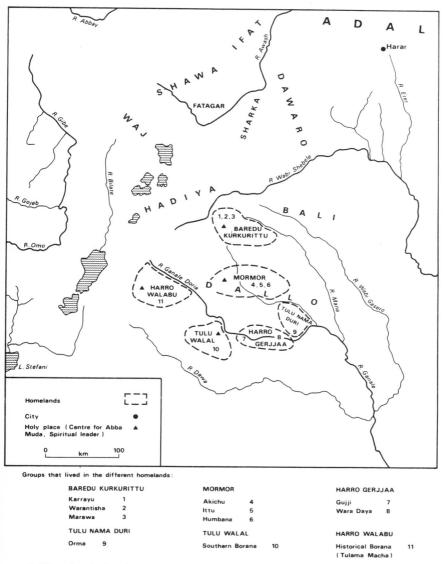

Groups that lived in the different homelands:

BAREDU KURKURITTU		MORMOR		HARRO GERJJAA	
Karrayu	1	Akichu	4	Gujji	7
Warantisha	2	Ittu	5	Wara Daya	8
Marawa	3	Humbana	6		
TULU NAMA DURI		TULU WALAL		HARRO WALABU	
Orma	9	Southern Borana	10	Historical Borana	11
				(Tulama Macha)	

3 Homelands for the Barentu and Borana groups on the eve of their sixteenth-century migration

wide areas. The dispersal of the displaced people was accompanied by carnage and destruction on an appalling scale. Many probably died from famine during the jihad and the anarchy that followed its failure. This was particularly true of some regions which were devastated by jihadic war, following which a great number of people seem to have abandoned their ancestral lands to seek

19

refuge in difficult mountainous regions or other areas which held out hope of asylum.

> While some inhabitants fled to escape the sword, others fled famine and misery which had ruined much of the country . . . In addition, aside from the war itself, mass movements and famine, epidemics played havoc in sections of the country as well. Whole villages were abandoned, the land left uncultivated and the survivors migrated to other areas in the hope of finding some means of subsistence.[6]

A major consequence of the jihad was that the Christians and the Muslims devastated each other. With appalling massacre and destruction on both sides went the fall and destruction of the defense systems of both. The Christian military colonies in the southern region were broken up, most of the men were killed, sold into slavery, or fled from the region. All semblance of defense and authority disappeared. The previously occupied area between the Christian kingdom and the Muslim state of Harar was emptied of its inhabitants, who sought refuge in an inaccessible mountainous area. The area became a "no-man's land" as the result of the conflict. It is not so much that, as many scholars have presumed, "the so-called Galla invasion" destroyed both kingdoms, as that the kingdoms so battered each other that the way was made clear for surges of advance by the Oromo pastoralists. In other words, scholars seem to forget that the sedentary communities on both sides destroyed each other and by so doing destroyed the very dam that had checked the migration of the pastoral Oromo for many centuries. The sedentary agricultural Oromo who lived in the Christian and the Muslim areas appear to have lost their identity in the jihadic struggle. Hence, according to the general view of historians, no group of this people played an integral part in the mutually destructive struggle in the Horn. But the monumental book of Arab Faqih makes it abundantly clear that some groups of Oromo people who lived in the hotly contested areas suffered severely from the jihadic war.[7] I have discussed this aspect elsewhere.[8] Here it should suffice to mention three crucial points. First and foremost, during the jihad of Imam Ahmad (1529–1543) when the Muslims and Christians in the Horn of Africa were engaged in wars of mutual destruction, the sedentary agricultural Oromo who were in the zone of conflict were equally devastated. Secondly, Oromo pastoralists who were on the periphery of the zone of conflict were not affected by it. Thirdly, before the Christian kingdom fully recuperated and re-established its military colonies in the southern provinces, the migrating Oromo dislodged what was left after the jihadic wars and thwarted new attempts at settlement. The regions which had been sparsely populated before the jihad were left empty by the shifting of population during the jihad. This explains why the Oromo easily entered huge areas in a short time. At this early stage in their migration, the pastoral Oromo seem to have manifested unique characteristics of adaptability. They easily adapted to another environment and coalesced with indigenous people, and at the same time they imparted their language and the complex gada system, which eventually replaced the Islam of the conquered people. The desire to participate in the spoils of the Christian and Muslim states may have attracted various non-Oromo groups to join the Oromo groups that entered in the course of the battles. An unusual aspect of Oromization was that many of the absorbed groups were nomads. The Oromo genius for assimilation quickly claimed any non-Oromo, defeated or otherwise.

An important Oromo institution which seems to have facilitated the process of the migration was the process called *moggaasa* (adoption). One form of *moggaasa* is known as *guddifacha* (a foster parent adopting a child). This still exists. Traditionally, the adopted son was looked upon as a real son,[9] and he enjoyed all rights of a true son. Even if foster parents had a son of their own after they had adopted a son, the first remained *angafa* (the oldest son) with all the rights and privileges.[10] The second form of adoption, which has special relevance to our subject, is known as *moggaasa*, adoption into a clan or tribe. The adopted individual or group could be either Oromo[11] or non-Oromo. The adoption was undertaken by the Abba Gada on behalf of his *gossa* ("clan").[12] Before adoption, animal(s) were slaughtered and a knife was dipped in the blood of the victim and planted in the assembly, composed of the elders of the *gossa* and the representatives of other *gossas*. Then the Abba Gada said a prayer blessing the new members and the adopted individual, or groups touched the knife planted in the assembly, repeating in chorus what the Abba Gada had to say. "I hate what you hate, I like what you like, I fight whom you fight, I go where you go, I chase whom you chase, etc. . . ."[13] This oath was binding and "unbreakable" on both sides. The adopted groups now became collectively the "sons" of the *gossa*. The blood symbolized the brotherly unity of the *gossa* and its new "sons" and the knife symbolized the readiness of the *gossa* to fight for the right of its new members, while the new members pledged themselves to fight for the rights and the cause of their new *gossa*. By this oath of mutual responsibility and obligation, clans or tribes quickly enlarged their members, while the weak Oromo or non-Oromo groups gained both protection and material benefit – material benefit, because at the time of adoption the clan contributed whatever was available for the support of new members. Any property or cattle given to the adopted members were considered as *andhura*[14] and therefore untouchable by others. *Andhura* means umbilical cord, and in this sense it is a special gift which a father gives to his son at his birth. This is the only property over which the son has full authority before the death of his father. However, in the case of adoption, *andhura* symbolized a father–son relationship between the clan and its new members. Thus *moggaasa* was inspired by political, military, and economic considerations on both sides. This may explain why the Oromo assimilated more than they were assimilated by others. After adoption, the concept of belonging was extended to include not only the clan that adopted, but also the tribe or confederacy to which the clan belonged. Through the new genealogy, the new members now became part of the Oromo people, counting their ancestors several generations back to the hypothetical founder of the confederacy.

What all this amounts to is that Oromo tribes were fluid groupings: some members were lost and others incorporated through the continual process of migration, conquest, assimilation, and interaction with their neighbors. This was made possible by the fact that the migrant Oromo speakers seem to have been especially well equipped with qualities that made the adjustment of their own culture to new conditions easy. If any feature seems to have been widespread among the Oromo-speaking groups at this time, "it was their flexibility among new peoples, their ability to adopt and to absorb." [15]

This explains why adoption was accompanied by Oromization. The wide dispersal of the pastoral Oromo from the southern region was mainly responsible for the Oromization which embraced many non-Oromo groups. Oromo pastoralists absorbed into their socio-political structure Cushitic- and Semitic-speaking tribes as clients or serfs *gabbaro* (see below for full discussion of this category). The importance of adoption is that for new members it brought gada from the periphery into the center of communal life.[16] The Oromo pastoralists penetrated easily and assimilated quickly where there were already pockets of Oromo-speaking communities. This was particularly true of old Bali, Dawaro, Hadiya, Waj, and other provinces (see map 3, p. 19).

According to the chronology of the Oromo migration recorded by Bahrey, it was during the period of the Melbah gada (1522–1530) that the Borana invaded Bali. Since the last part of the Melbah's years in office coincided with the period of major confrontation between the Christians and the Muslims, the Oromo seem consciously to have avoided the zone of conflict. They do not appear to have harassed either Muslims or Christians. What they did was probably no more than to dislodge a few isolated communities. Since Bali was the theater of jihadic operations between 1529 and 1532, the pressure from pastoral Oromo probably was limited.

During the time when the Mudana gada was in power (1530–1538), the Oromo crossed the Wabi. The reference is certainly to the Shabelle, which means the northern "frontier of Bali proper." [17] The inference from this is that by this time the pastoral Oromo already had established their presence in the province of Bali. Two factors could have made that possible. First, after the fall of Dawaro to the Muslims in August 1532, the Christian force was wiped out by Wazir Adole, the Muslim general who became the first governor of Bali.[18] Secondly, once the people accepted Islam, the Muslim leader, leaving behind only a skeletal force, moved on to the central and northern parts of the Christian kingdom. The Muslim leaders, who were accustomed to pastoral raids in their own country, did not develop any coherent policy towards the troublesome Oromo in Bali, whether by involving them in large numbers in their jihadic wars, or by containing them in that province. On the contrary, they hastily deported some Hadiya nomads from the zone of conflict. This not only thinned the already sparse population of the region, but also contributed to the further weakening of the defenses. Thus, it is safe to assume that between 1530 and 1538 the path for Oromo migration to both the north and northeast was wide open.

Even at this early stage, a three-stage process of migration can be discerned

22

from what Bahrey tells us. These stages were scouting, surprise attack, and settlement. Scouts seem to have been sent a long distance, sometimes taking many days, from the Oromo base area. Scouting was a preparatory stage during which information was gathered about the neighboring territory, concerning its strong and weak points, the presence or absence of organized resistance forces, and its economic resources. Scouting seems to have played an extremely important role in the early phase of Oromo migration, when pastoral Oromo seem to have been bent on avoiding direct contact with both the Christian and Muslim forces because of the latter's possession of firearms, while the Oromo had none.

The second stage was characterized by surprise attacks carried out mainly during the night. The purpose of these attacks was to collect booty and trophies as quickly as possible, while at the same time unnerving the enemy. The attacks were carried out during the night so as to avoid detection while the attackers were coming and pursuit while they were retreating. Since these attacks were carried out at a long distance and under cover of darkness, the enemies were not able to repay in kind by following the attackers to their base areas. Safe base areas, where women, children, and animals were kept, formed a cornerstone in Oromo strategy, and it seems this effective policy was adopted after a long period of trial and error. This strategy itself is a strong indication that pastoral Oromo had long experience of border warfare with the Christian kingdom. Bahrey makes clear that up to 1554 after every campaign the Oromo returned to their safe base area near the Wabi Shabelle river.[19] This highly useful piece of information demonstrates beyond any doubt that, once the Oromo crossed the Wabi between 1530 and 1538, the Muslim force in Bali was unable to repulse them, and that the Wabi Shabelle area, the boundary between Bali and Dawaro, became a safe base area during the time when Imam Ahmad was at the height of his power.

The second stage in the process of migration was very important in a double sense. First and foremost, the evening surprise attacks were repeated on selected weak targets at intervals until the resistance of the opponents was broken. The opponents either evacuated their own territory, fleeing to safer areas, or they submitted to the pastoral Oromo, accepting their supremacy, which was more apparent than real. The defeated and subjected groups were turned into fighting units through adoption. Thus the conquered people joined the Oromo in the next attack on other groups. The conquered people increased the fighting capacity of the Oromo and widened their knowledge of the terrain. Adoption marked the loyalty of the vanquished and their eventual assimilation with the conquerors, while it assured safety, protection, and equal sharing of booty in the next raids. Secondly, the evening surprise attack made the Oromo an invincible enemy. Neither peasants nor traders in settlements and towns were prepared for the Oromo war of attrition. It was only after the Oromo discovered their muscle that they started changing their tactics into those of conventional warfare, in which they suffered repeatedly from the enemy's firepower.

The third stage in the process of migration involved the culmination of the first two. Now the former frontier and enemy territory which had been won during the second stage was turned into the base from which the next war for new territory would be launched. The process would repeat itself until the Oromo had vastly increased both the size of their territory and their people. It was these processes that seem to have taken the pastoral Oromo through the length and breadth of their huge territory.[20]

The period of the Kilole gada (1538–1546) coincided with the drastic change in the fortunes of the jihad. Imam Ahmad, who was undefeated between 1529 and 1542, was routed utterly in March 1543. The imam was slain, and a large proportion of his force put to the sword. So ended abruptly, as it started, the reign of the most powerful Muslim leader of the time in the Horn of Africa. His death ended his empire. The victorious Christian emperor, Galawdewos (1540–1559), ordered his famous regiment, Adal Mabraq, to stop the Oromo advance. Unfortunately for Galawdewos, it was already too late. The Kilole gada defeated and drove Adal Mabraq out of lowland Dawaro in 1545.[21]

During Bifole gada (1546–1554), the Christian emperor Galawdewos fought against both the Barentu and the Borana, but he was not able to slow down their spirited attack on Waj, Fatagar, and other provinces. It was the Bifole gada which devastated the whole of Dawaro and began to make war on Fatagar.[22] Compared with his campaigns against pastoral Oromo, Galawdewos achieved spectacular results against the Muslims.[23] The reason for the success, as compared with the struggle against the Oromo, is quite simple; it was due to the nature of the war he conducted against each. The Muslims fought in a conventional style, in which Galawdewos seems to have had considerable advantages in both men and firepower. Furthermore, the Muslims were settled communities who could be pursued and punished in their own homes for their attack upon and incursion into Christian territory. With the Oromo, the situation was entirely different. The emperor had trained manpower and considerable firepower which the Oromo lacked. However, the elusive character of Oromo warriors made this apparent advantage insignificant. Whenever possible the Oromo avoided engagement with his highly destructive striking force. But the repeated Oromo attack on the settled Christian military colonists proved impossible to stop. Their night attacks caused considerable damage to men and property, and also eroded the morale of the Christian forces. By the time the local Christian troops recovered from the shock and wanted to hit back, the Oromo warriors would have disappeared from the area, taking away its spoils, usually consisting of many head of cattle and trophies. It was the elusive character of the Oromo warriors that was their strength and prevented the Christians from taking advantage of their superiority in numbers and weapons.

The period of Michelle gada (1554–1562) was a real landmark in the whole history of the Oromo migration, a landmark because the power of both the Christians and the Muslims dramatically decreased during this period, while the power of the pastoral Oromo increased in the same proportion. The sudden and radical transformation in the balance of power quickly brought to an end two centuries of struggle between the Muslims and Christians, replacing it by the struggle of both against the Oromo for the next three centuries. In short, the period of this gada opened the chapter of rapid spread for the pastoral Oromo which changed the course of history in the region. In the words of Bahrey:

> It was he who killed the Jan Amora corps and fought against Hamalmal at Dago; he devastated all the towns and ruled them, remaining there with his troops, whereas previously the Galla invaded from the Wabi had returned there at the end of each campaign.[24]

It was the Borana Michelle gada which destroyed the famous Jan Amora corps in Fatagar. This province, which had been the headquarters of Amhara emperors for almost a century,[25] now became the headquarters of the Borana (Tulama-Matcha) with their famous *chafe* at Oda Nabi. The Oromo success during Michelle gada was brought about by the fact that the Christians and the Muslims once again battered each other in 1559, clearing the way for the Oromo surge forward. In fact, 1559 was a watershed in the history of the struggle between the Christians and Muslims in the Horn of Africa. In March 1559, the Muslims from Harar, under their leader, Amir Nur, routed the Christian force in Fatagar and destroyed its leadership, including Galawdewos the Amhara emperor. The death of Galawdewos marked a turning-point in every sense of the term. Not only did his death produce terrible grief throughout the Christian land, it left the political scene uncertain and fluid as well. Furthermore, and for our discussion more relevant, it left the Christian defense system in utter ruin and marked the end of the era of Amhara dominance. After this battle, the Amhara force was never able to regain its full strength and failed to stop the migration of the pastoral Oromo.

Galawdewos, having no son, was succeeded by his younger brother Minas (1559–1563). Minas drew a wrong conclusion from the Muslim victory on March 22, 1559. Whereas he had expected them to follow up their success by moving deep into the heart of the kingdom, they withdrew from Fatagar and Waj and quickly returned to Harar.[26] Thus, as the victorious Muslims abandoned Fatagar and Waj, so did Minas, who moved the seat of his government from Waj to Mengesta Semayat in eastern Gojjam. By the rash transfer of the capital across the Abbay (the Blue Nile) he tacitly abandoned the provinces east of the Abbay to the Borana, who now made Fatagar their safe-base area, from where they radiated their attack on Waj, Shawa, Damot, and beyond (see map 4, p. 26).

After a short while, the top Christian leaders, who escaped from the massacre on March 22, 1559, held a great council at the residence of Minas in eastern Gojjam. This highest state council decided upon making Dambiya the rainy-season residence of Minas.[27] The choice of Dambiya may have been influenced by the wealth and safety it provided. This decision also proved another landmark in the history of the kingdom. Since 1270, when the Shawan Amhara dynasty was formed, especially after Amda Siyon (1314–1344)

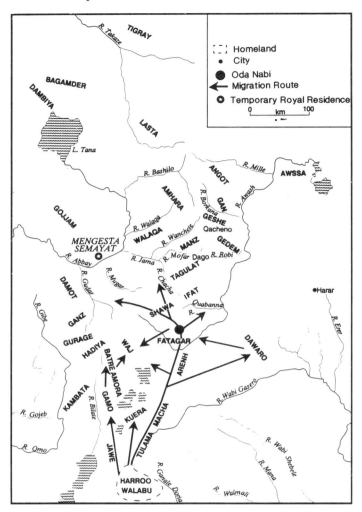

4 The Matcha–Tulama migration to Fatagar and other provinces

established a strong Christian empire, the provinces east of the Abbay were the center from which Amhara colonization was directed to the south. By the transfer of the residence of the king, the Amhara nobility was unconsciously transferring the center of political and military gravity of the kingdom across the great river. The queen mother and other high dignitaries followed Minas to Dambiya,[28] where he soon founded his capital at Gubay in Emfraz, "a mountainous area overlooking the northeastern shore of Lake Tana."[29]

It was at this juncture, when a weak Amhara leadership[30] tacitly abandoned the eastern provinces and moved its headquarters to Dambiya in northwestern

Ethiopia (see map 4, p. 26) that the period of Michelle gada (1554–1562) came to an end. It was succeeded by the period of Harmufa gada (1562–1570). It was during this gada period that the pastoral Oromo began migrating to the southwestern region of what is today Ethiopia.

The migration of the Matcha to the southwestern region and their settlement in the Gibe region

The previous section followed the course of the Borana migration to Fatagar. The rest of the chapter will examine the further migration of the Borana, mainly to the southwestern regions of Ethiopia. The Matcha section, which spearheaded and dominated the whole course of the migration, is the subject of this section. At the same time, since the history of the Matcha cannot be analyzed apart from the peoples of the area through which the Matcha passed, considerable attention will be given to the history of the people of Ennarya,[31] thereby showing the dynamism of conflict, interaction, and change which occurred over two centuries. Before going on to describe the course of the migration, we should briefly look at some of the factors that made Damot, Shat, Konch, Bizamo, Bosha (see map 5, p. 28), and other districts too weak to resist the migrating Matcha, while Ennarya alone proved to be too strong for the Matcha arms to overcome. It is only by looking at the underlying forces of disintegration in the area that we will be able to explain the dynamism of the Oromo migration.

After 1560 the southwestern regions were in much the same predicament as Harar and the Christian kingdom. As for the former, the battle of Hazalo in 1559 dealt a *coup de grâce* to the Muslim military power of Harar.[32] Harar, the center of Islamic learning and civilization, the political capital of the mighty Muslim empire for fifteen years, and the long-time entrepôt for the lucrative long-distance trade, now suddenly found itself reduced to a town exerting little influence beyond its walls, deprived of its historic functions, and thrown back on its own resources.[33] Likewise, the Christian kingdom, although it quickly recovered from the devastating jihadic wars, rapidly lost ground to the migrating pastoral Oromo.[34] In the discussion on the dynamism of the sixteenth century, I have referred to the jihadic period because I believe it critically conditioned the period which followed. The jihad, which was really the beginning of a radical transformation of the political landscape of the Horn, facilitated the process of pastoral Oromo migration. A brief glance at the Gibe region during the jihadic war of Imam Ahmad over the general course of history of two neighboring provinces which shared many common characteristics would clarify the point under discussion. I mention two examples of different responses to the jihadic situation, those of Damot and Ennarya, which shaped their subsequent histories. Both provinces were part of the Christian kingdom. However, while Damot fought on the side of the Christians, Ennarya did not involve itself in the conflict. Under the hail of blows from the Muslim army, the Christian kingdom disintegrated. The king

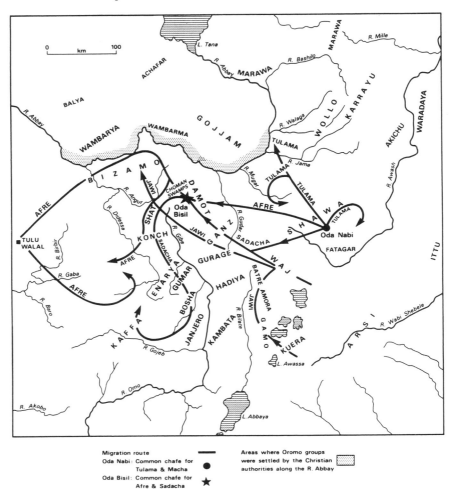

5 The Matcha migration to the southwestern provinces

saved himself by flight. The disaster which had overtaken the Christian leadership had also engulfed Damot. The rulers of the provinces suffered a series of defeats from the invading Muslim army. Thus, the Christian forces of Damot were left in complete disarray; some fled, and others surrendered. There was nothing the Amhara Christians could do to assist Damot, and the Muslims moved in to exact their revenge for the stiff resistance put up against them.

The tragedy which had affected Damot did not extend, however, to Ennarya. At the beginning of the jihad, Ennarya tried to remain neutral. Once the direction of the tide became clearer, the ruler of Ennarya made a firm decision which delighted the Muslims and saved Ennarya from their swords.

When the Muslims went into the country of Damot, Balaw Sagad . . . ran away with thirty horsemen and crossed the Gibe. He stayed . . . in Ennarya, in the hope that the ruler of Ennarya might save him from the Muslims. However, the ruler of Ennarya chained all of them and brought them to Wazir Adole. The ruler of Ennarya brought 1000 ounces of gold tribute and rich presents to Adole. The latter was delighted and gave the former beautiful clothes, and sent him back to his country with honour.[35]

By these practical measures, the Ennarya ruler not only maintained himself in power but also saved his country from the Muslim swords. As we shall see below, time and again the leaders of Ennarya showed a touch of realism in dynamic circumstances. The cry around which the leaders rallied support was to keep enemies out of their land, which was balanced by playing tribute to and trading with any powerful leader who was in control of the region of the Christian kingdom. In other words, they were jealous of their internal autonomy and they paid regular tribute and gave rich gifts so as not to provide any pretext for interference in their internal affairs. What is remarkable about the leaders of Ennarya is the consistency with which they maintained this policy. They were ready to fight any enemy who crossed the frontier of their land, but they were particularly reluctant to fight beyond their own frontiers. In this they were greatly helped by the topography of their land, as well as by the unity and self-confidence of their people, which made them ever ready to punish any enemy unwise enough to cross into their territory.[36]

Once the jihad ran its course and the weakened Christian authority was restored in the region, Ennarya was the first to adjust to the changed situation, without resorting to war. In 1548, Galawdewos conducted a devastating six months' campaign on the frontiers of Damot.[37] The expedition had at least three purposes. First, it was directed against the governor of Konch, who had refused to pay the tribute.[38] Secondly, it was meant to punish the inhabitants of Bosha, who were reported to have killed Christians during the jihad. Thirdly, it was meant to replace the depleted resources of the Christian treasury by a veiled act of brigandage. Once again, the sword of the conqueror fell on the defenseless inhabitants of the neighbors of Ennarya. It was with the riches, slaves, cattle, and gold taken at this time that Galawdewos financed his last and expensive expedition to Harar in 1550.[39]

Ennarya gave no opportunities for Galawdewos to invade her territory. On the contrary, as he approached the border, the ruler surprised him with pleasant and conspicuous generosity, lavish gifts, and tribute, with humility and words of loyalty on his lips. His choice of time for paying tribute was excellent, his understanding of the financial difficulties of Galawdewos was profound, the choice of place appropriate, and his delivery impressive. He gave form and expression to Galawdewos's desire to reconstruct the devastated kingdom. In short, he won the respect and admiration of Galawdewos. In the congenial atmosphere generated by Ennarya's gold, the past was forgotten and forgiven. Ennarya was left undisturbed. She enjoyed peace and prosperity.

The fate of the pagan neighbors of Ennarya was the exact opposite. Many of the pagan communities of this area had begged Galawdewos to convert them to Christianity. Their sudden clamor for Christianity probably was not out of love for it, but because they thought this a sure way of escaping from the devastating slave-raids conducted upon them by the Christian leaders. In the words of a Jesuit father who was in the kingdom in 1555, the pleas for baptism went unheeded.

> And that you may know what sort of people these are: persons who should well know about it affirmed to me several times that many of those pagans who border upon them and who pay them tribute begged them many times that they make them Christians and that, thus, they would happily continue to pay them their taxes. And they did not want to do so that they may continuously make raids on them, which they do and they take from them their children and wives and possessions. And they send them to the sea to be sold to the Turks and Moors, to whom those of this kingdom sell every year more than ten or twelve thousand slaves, of whom there would not have been one person who would not have willingly become Christian.[40]

It was ironic that Galawdewos, who has been reported to have been the most humane king ever to sit on the Christian throne,[41] and who was regarded as a torch for the spread of Christianity, did so much to reduce not only the chance of spreading the faith, but also undermined the future resistance of these non-Christian communities as well.

Minas came to power in 1559 and died in 1563, a year which saw a series of developments that contributed to the rapid spread of the migrating Oromo to western Shawa, Damot, Bizamo, Shat, Konch, and several other districts (see map 5, p. 28). When Sarsa Dengel succeeded to the throne in 1563, Hamalmal, the old general, rebelled against the young king. During the interval between his quarrel with and reconciliation to Sarsa Dengel, Hamalmal settled in western Shawa with his large army. The pagan Gafat tribes of this area became an easy prey and the victims of plunder by his soldiers. "Hamalmal had overlooked the problems of feeding the continuously increasing regiments. Gafat villages of Endagebatan and the neighbouring district of Gendabarat were wantonly pillaged."[42]

Many Gafat chiefs, who were outraged by the pillage, saw the salvation of their people in submission to Sarsa Dengel. Hamalmal thereupon reconciled himself to the young king, but the plight of the people of Gafat continued. For example, when the soldiers of Rom Sagad, the governor of Shawa, were ordered back to their eastern garrisons (which they had abandoned since 1559),[43] they refused to go. Instead they plundered Gendabarat, Endagebatan, and Mugar.[44] To add to their misery, Sarsa Dengel pacified the notorious Giyorgis Haile regiment by settling them in Mugar, where they continued with their wanton destruction and plunder.[45] In their shortsighted policies, the Christian political and military leaders were not only causing the slow death of the Gafat people,[46] but were creating as well a vacuum into which the pastoral Oromo would move. Thus a few years later, when the first group of Borana cavalry passed through the region, Gafat had no strength left to resist. The Gafat pastoralists who were impoverished,[47] and the farmers who were uprooted against their will, had either to submit to the Oromo and become part of them, or to run *en masse* across the Abbay, to seek refuge in the province of Gojjam. Some did the one, some the other.

The history of the Gafat people of western Shawa runs parallel with that of the Damot. During the rebellion of Hamalmal, Damot was governed by Taklo, a man who is described (with some justification) as "intelligent, and famous for his sagacity and wisdom."[48] He was instrumental in aborting Hamalmal's rebellion, but though he secured the throne for Sarsa Dengel, he did so at a great cost. His large force was continuously increased by the addition of rebellious soldiers who refused to return to the eastern districts. In order to pacify them, Taklo had to be lavishly generous to them. This pillaging, sacking, and extortion became the rule, and seeking fair tribute the exception. As we shall see below, these undisciplined and disloyal soldiers were brave among the defenseless peasants, but cowardly before the Oromo. They rebelled against Taklo for no other reason than his excessive liberality, which failed to appease them. Taklo found it impossible to keep them in the province, for which reason Damot was taken from him and given to an adventurer by the name of Fasilo, who soon became the gravest menace to the man who appointed him. In 1566, Sarsa Dengel wanted to pass the rainy season in Damot, but his soldiers refused on the pretext that it had an unhealthy climate.[49] Sarsa Dengel had no alternative but to abandon his plan. The real reason for the soldiers' refusal, however, is hinted at in the chronicle. Damot, which only a few years earlier had been described as one of the richest provinces[50] in the kingdom, was by 1566 largely denuded of its wealth by the continuous pillaging and plundering by the rebellious soldiers, who had come and gone through the strategically located province. The young king, who knew the root cause of the rebellion, moved to Endagebatan in western Shawa, where his soldiers found fresh pasture for their rapacity. Fasilo, who was supposed to keep the provincial soldiers of Damot at their post, marched against Sarsa Dengel at the head of mutinous soldiers with the proclaimed intention of chopping off his head. In the battle of August 1566, Sarsa Dengel would have perished had he not received timely warning and saved himself by flight. The victorious Fasilo looted Sarsa Dengel's camp and put his soldiers to the sword. Frustrated by the escape, Fasilo marched through and plundered from Gendabarat to Gojjam. Despite the failure of its main objective the consequences of Fasilo's rebellion were drastic. The misery it inflicted on the people of Damot and western Shawa was beyond calculation. Sarsa Dengel became captive to the demands of his soldiers in the time to come. Thus, the flame of endless slave raids which burned the non-Christian minorities between the second half of the sixteenth century and the first half of the seventeenth was already alight at this early date in the reign of Sarsa Dengel. As with the Gafat in western Shawa, the people of Damot received a heavy blow from which there is good reason to assume that they did not recover before the Borana assault a few years later.[51]

But all was not gloomy for Sarsa Dengel. In 1566, the governor of Konch gave him shelter and treated him kindly. By the beginning of 1567, the soldiers of the adventurer Fasilo surrendered to him. This was followed by the submission (albeit temporary) of Yishaq of Tigray. At the beginning of 1568, Sepenhi, the clever politician and famous ruler of Ennarya, delighted Sarsa Dengel with rich tribute.

> Sepenhi came towards him with an army as numerous as locusts covering the earth. Then he went into the royal reception, according to his law, among the men, some had arranged, in a sign of deference, their clothes of blue silk, others . . . their velvet(s) each one in its own colour. After that Sepenhi gave to the king his tribute, composed of a sizable quantity of gold, such that those who had preceded him in the office of governor of Ennarya had never given an equal mount of it to the kings who had existed earlier.[52]

There could never have been a more difficult time than this, as Sarsa Dengel needed gold to replenish his looted camp and empty treasury. Once again the ruler of Ennarya surprised Christian leadership with his farsightedness, his understanding of the spirit of the time, and his demonstration of total loyalty, backed by a show of strength, in warning the king that it was not possible to let loose his slaving raids on Ennarya with impunity. This mixture of humility and strength had the desired effect. Sarsa Dengel never conducted slaving raids in Ennarya. For Ennarya there was nothing new in this policy. It was part of her established tradition to pay in full what was due to her masters, but at the same time to keep them at bay. For Sarsa Dengel this was a historic compromise dictated by economic and political considerations. Thus, of all the non-Christian provinces of his kingdom, Ennarya alone escaped from the devastation of his slave raids, a significant achievement. More was to come in the decades to follow.

The governor of the province of Bosha neither learned anything new from the practical and pragmatic policy of his neighbor, Sepenhi, nor forgot and forgave the terrible misery Galawdewos had inflicted on his country. He refused to pay tribute to Sarsa Dengel, and so invited punishment on his people. Under the combined pressure of the forces of Sarsa Dengel and Sepenhi, the unwise governor surrendered and submitted tribute and rich gifts to calm the king's wrath. What is interesting to observe here is not Sarsa Dengel's easy victory, but Sepenhi's co-operation in the attack on Bosha. It may be that he was simply obeying an order from the king; but one suspects that Sepenhi also had other motives for involving Ennarya in her first attack on her pagan neighbor. It seems that Sepenhi was well aware of the rapid spread of the Oromo in the eastern provinces. By 1568, Sarsa Dengel already had lost many provinces east of the Abbay to the Oromo.[53] One suspects that Sepenhi may have realized that the Oromo would reach the Gibe region shortly. It may have occurred to him that Ennarya by herself was in no position to stem the tide.

Like the governor of Bosha, Aze the Muslim governor of Hadiya refused to pay tribute to Sarsa Dengel. But unlike the governor of Bosha, Aze had a formidable force of 1,700 cavalry and 500 armed *malasay*,[54] and a large contingent of infantry. The Muslims of Hadiya who earlier had suffered at the hands of the Oromo, no longer had any desire for war with the Christians. The attitude was expressed by the action of Aze's soldiers, who refused to fight with Sarsa Dengel. Only the *malasay*, the Muslim force from Harar,[55] fought. Deserted by their fellow Muslims and outnumbered by Sarsa Dengel's men, they were easily crushed. Aze reconciled himself to the king, who was magnanimous in return. The king left Aze in his office, but stripped him of real power. Takla Giyorgis was made the commander of the provincial soldiers.[56] With this success in Hadiya, Sarsa Dengel proceeded to Waj, where he left the Muslim force under Asma-ad-Din undisturbed.[57]

In 1571, during his stay in Waj, the king again appointed Takla Giyorgis as the "governor of Damot and *dajazmach* of the Gibe/Awash region."[58] The appointment was strikingly similar to those of 1559 and 1548. In 1571, Takla Giyorgis was made the *dajazmach* of a vast region. In 1559, Hamalmal had been made the *dajazmach* of all the provinces east of the Abbay, while in 1548 Fanuel was appointed[59] with authority over Dawaro and its dependencies. In all three cases, the appointment was made at the eleventh hour to stop the advance of the Oromo forces. All three appointments were followed by the departure of the monarchs from the storm centers. In all three cases the withdrawal of these officials was accompanied by the massive exodus of Christian refugees. The appointment of 1548 and that of 1571 were made at the time when both Galawdewos and Sarsa Dengel were powerful. But that of 1559 was made at the time when the Christian power had reached its nadir.[60]

The beginning of the Matcha migration to the Gibe region

Having appointed Takla Giyorgis, Sarsa Dengel left Waj for Dambiya in 1571 at the very time when the Borana Robale gada (1570–1578) was moving toward Shawa and Waj. The simultaneous Borana attack on both provinces was devastating and swift. Alarmed at the success of the Borana, the king returned to Shawa in 1572, where he ordered quick mobilization and administered a quick sharp shock to the Borana, which forced the latter to withdraw from Waj.[61] After this success, he campaigned for two years at the head of his large army, first towards western Shawa, and then to Damot and Bizamo, everywhere inflicting heavy damages on the pagan communities. As we shall see below, the king had been engaged in extensive depopulation for two years. Just as he was completing the debilitating round of slave raids among the non-Christian communities, the Robale gada attacked Gojjam. Shortly after, Zara Yohannes, the experienced governor of Gojjam, was killed by the Oromo.[62] His death led to the rebellion of the garrisons in the province. The pacification of the garrisons in Gojjam took the king's time and energy, and it meant that the Borana were left undisturbed in the provinces east of the Abbay.

When the Muslim forces from Harar invaded Bali and Waj in 1576 (see map 3, p. 19), the Borana deliberately withdrew from the storm centers, avoiding conflict with both the Muslims and the Christians. This is one of the many examples which show how the Oromo maintained neutrality in the conflict between these two groups. There are two earlier examples. First, in the 1520s when Imam Ahamad invaded the Christian kingdom, the pastoral Oromo remained beyond the range of the Muslim sword; and again in 1559, when Amir Nur entered the Christian kingdom, the Oromo withdrew from the storm center, keeping themselves in reserve at the time when the Muslim army plunged its feeble sword into the disintegrating body of the Christian kingdom. Once again, in 1576, the pastoralists kept themselves out of the conflict between the two enemies. The outcome of this last war proved to be the end of the political importance of Harar and at the same time weakened the Christian kingdom. The invading Muslim force was liquidated. "The whole Moorish army perished this day, except the horse, either by the sword or in the river, nor had the Moors received so severe a blow since the defeat of Gragne by Claudius [Galawdewos]."[63] But the Christian force was also left too feeble to stop its new enemy. Thus once again, as in 1559, the real victors were the Oromo. In other words, the Christian force succeeded in dealing the death blow to their enemy at the cost of sustaining deep injuries themselves. Unlike the two previous times, when the Muslim conquests prepared the soil for the Oromo success, in 1576 the Oromo reaped where the Christians had sown. This is shown by the fact that the Borana were apparently well established in Waj before Sarsa Dengel had left Shawa in 1577. The Borana impact on Waj sent a wave of terror throughout western Shawa, where the Christian community rightly guessed that the next blow was to fall on them. Their fear was succinctly expressed by the mother of the king.

> Then, while he was there, his mother learned that her son wanted to go to the Tigre: she left Genda-Barat immediately (for she was living there at that time) and rushed to go find him at Sabarad. That day she began by telling him: "O my son, why have you decided to do this thing against me and your brothers? Do you then want to deliver us to the Galla? Does not our loss cause you any sadness?" With these words and other similar ones, she touched his heart and persuaded him, for he was obedient to his mother and . . . when he renounced going to the Tigre, he resolved to go to the country of Waj to fight the Galla who were there.[64]

Sarsa Dengel's change of heart was only temporary and intended to mitigate mounting criticism against him and to allay the fears of the Christians in western Shawa. His campaign against the Borana was short-lived and it inflicted no lasting damage on them, since they dispersed before him. With an insignificant success to his name, Sarsa Dengel withdrew all the Christian regiments east of the Abbay and marched to Dambiya, from where he led a more successful expedition against Yishaq in 1579.

One of the most singular documents written by an unknown compiler in the first half of the eighteenth century sums up the history of this period in a striking sentence. "When . . . the country was wasted by the hands of the Galla Malak Sagad was exiled and came to Dambiya."[65] The use of the term exile has profound meaning. Sarsa Dengel's withdrawal to Dambiya shattered the

Christian authority east of the Abbay. Even though he tried time and again to restore his authority in the region, all attempts failed ignominiously and therefore his withdrawal to Dambiya remained an exile in the true sense of the word.

Sarsa Dengel's decision to take all the eastern regiments to Tigray in 1578 fortuitously coincided with the period of a new Borana gada, which was undoubtedly the most successful militarily of all the Borana gada that had fought so far. This was the Birmaji gada (1578–1586), which continued the war with vigor and revolutionary innovation. This was the adoption of ox-hide shields of body length, which made the poisoned arrows of the Maya warriors irrelevant in war. It probably was the Maya poisoned arrows which kept the Borana out of Waj for a long time. The effect of the new shield was dramatic and the consequences shattering.

> This Birmaje of the Borana made ox-hide shields of body length and attacked the Maya, who were skilled archers, but were beaten because there was no place for their arrows to strike, since the shields were made of stiff ox-hide.[66]

The Maya were respected and dreaded by all for their deadly weapons. The Borana adopted the body-long ox-hide shields only after they had suffered repeatedly at the hands of the Maya warriors. Once adopted, the new shields revolutionized the course of the Borana warfare. As the large-scale use of cavalry by the Michelle gada (1554–1562) quickened the pace of Barentu spread,[67] so did the adoption of the protective shield for the Borana Birmaji. In every sense this was a real turning-point in the course of the Borana migration.

> Birmaje pressed hard on Azmach Daharagot, commander in chief of the king's army, and killed Zena and his guards. At first Daharagot defeated the Galla many times; but by the will of God, because the sins of the Christians were not expiated, the Galla devastated Arena, the country of which Daharagot was governor and killed Gato Batro, Badlo, Amdo, and other personages.[68]

As a result Daharagot withdrew, abandoning all the provinces over which he had been appointed governor. The Borana Birmaji, insured for future success by the protective shields, attacked and devastated Damot. The Christians in Damot fled to Gojjam. Some of the indigenous people too fled across the Abbay to Gojjam, and across the Gibe to Ennarya. But the majority of them seem to have accepted the new masters, by whom they were adopted *en masse*. "Among the countless people who had fled to Gojjam were Selus Haila (the mother of the king) and other members of the royal family."[69]

The Borana Birmaji quickly overran "the whole low country between the mountains of Narea and the Nile."[70] In this vast area they attacked Gojjam, Konch, Shat, Ennarya, Bizamo, the Choman Swamp, Gumar, and Bosha (see map 5, p. 28). The widespread and scattered formation thinned their numbers and mitigated the effects of their sudden attack. Even then, many provinces suffered a great deal. Only Gojjam, because of its size, its topography, the density of its population, and its military establishment, and Ennarya, because of the quality of its leadership, and the impregnability of its defense system, were unscathed. As for the other provinces, it was their first shock, which hastened the short journey of their disappearance into historical oblivion.[71] The period of the Birmaji gada came to an end at the time when Damot became the headquarters from where the Matcha attack was to be deployed in all directions.

The Mulata gada (1586–1594) continued to wage war in all directions. Most of the Borana Mulata held their *jarra* ceremony[72] in the safe-base areas in Damot, but one part of them held it in Gojjam.[73] This is the first time we hear of the *jarra* ceremony taking place west of the Abbay. Before 1586 it seems to have been held east of the Abbay. We do not know why the vanguard of the Borana held its ceremony in Gojjam this time, but assume that it may have been due to the degree of self-confidence which they had gained after their spectacular victories in Waj, Shawa, and Damot. Unprepared for the thunderbolt that was to strike them, the Borana bands continued to feast themselves on the cattle they had acquired from the peasants of the area. Sarsa Dengel, who was on his way to Damot, realized the threat the Borana posed to his refugee mother in Gojjam and rushed to her rescue, administering a very severe blow to the Borana. He attacked them suddenly with his crack force, consisting of musketeers and cavalry armed with iron helmets. The Borana shields proved useless and irrelevant in front of firepower and swords handled by drilled soldiers. Those Borana who bravely faced the firing were mown down. The rest sought safety in flight. As all of Sarsa Dengel's troops were fresh, they were able to pursue the scattered Borana with great vigor; many were slain, and the rest perished at the hands of the local peasants. In the words of a contemporary historian:

> He did not act according to the custom of the kings of his ancestors who when making war were in the habit of sending their troops ahead, remaining themselves in the rear with the pick of their cavalry and infantry, praising those who went forward bravely and punishing those who lagged behind. This time, on the contrary, our king put himself at the head of his brave troops and fought stoutly; seeing which the army threw itself like a pack of wild beasts on the Galla, who were all killed without survivors. Most of them fell over a precipice, so that the inhabitants of the country and the labourers killed them where they found them.[74]

That day Sarsa Dengel, who was determined to restore his lost prestige, raised the morale of his Christian subjects and humiliated his opponents, the pastoral Oromo. He distinguished himself in the midst of the Borana by fighting like a common soldier.

The conversion of the ruling house of Ennarya to Christianity

Sarsa Dengel's resounding victory in Gojjam had its intended effect on the Borana in Damot, who were at the time invading Ennarya. It not only relieved the pressure, but boosted the morale of the governor of Ennarya as well. Subsequently Sarsa Dengel decided to go to Ennarya, a move that proved to be advantageous for him. From a military viewpoint, it was a timely and necessary decision. From a religious point of view, it turned out to be a landmark in the history of Ennarya. From the political point of view, the decision was important; economically it was overwhelming.

> The king desirous to open a communication with a country where there was a great trade, especially for gold, crossed the Nile on his way to that province, the Galla flying everywhere before him. He was received with a very great joy by the prince of that country, who looked upon him as his deliverer from those cruel enemies. Here he received many rich presents, more particularly a large quantity of gold. And he wintered at Cutheny, in that province, where Abba Hedar his brother died, having been blown up with gun powder with his wife and children.[75]

During Sarsa Dengel's stay in and around Ennarya in 1588, the governor of Ennarya came to meet him and brought tribute of gold. The meeting turned out to be the most important event of the decade.

Before the arrival of the Borana in the Gibe region, no record indicates whether the leadership in Ennarya had the desire or pressing need for conversion to Christianity.[76] But times had changed, and there was now an urgent desire among the leaders of Ennarya to convert themselves and their people to the ideology which Christianity provided. We have seen above that the Christian leadership time and again refused to baptize the pagan communities. As Galawdewos ignored the pagan request, so did Sarsa Dengel. For example, "in 1564, the Shanesha of Bizamo had repeatedly begged a relative of the emperor to stop raiding them and give them priests to convert them."[77] But their request fell on deaf ears. Now times had changed, and the Christian leadership had to change its attitude. This was first seen in 1581, when Sarsa Dengel gave permission for the conversion of the Gafat in Shat.[78] Interestingly, this was at the time when the Borana were establishing themselves in Shat. At about the same time, the governor of Ennarya, and the successor of Sepenhi, named La'asonhi, approached the Christian court for baptism. The chronicler, who wanted to whitewash the king in this affair, squarely put the blame on his chief treasurer.

> He [Sarsa Dengel] learned that the father of Badancho, chief of Ennarya, named La'asonhi, wanted to become a Christian, but that the azaj, in charge of the finances of the kingdom, had not given him their permission, because they had been restrained by material concerns, by love of money.[79]

In 1581, perhaps the Christian leadership may not have realized the ideological importance of converting both the leaders and the people of Ennarya to Christianity. However, by 1588

> the growing power of pagan Oromo forces throughout the territories surrounding Hinnario [Ennarya] at this period clearly demonstrated to all Christian overlords the dire need to fortify these lucrative markets. A non-Christian ruling class in Hinnario would have succumbed to the Oromo advance much earlier than a staunchly Christian one. Sarsa Dengel's move was a calculated one intended to prolong control of the Northern Ethiopian empire in a wealthy area rapidly falling out of this control.[80]

In the variant of the long chronicle of Sarsa Dengel it is even suggested that the king not only negotiated with Badancho – "We will diminish your tribute, if you become Christian and renounce idolatry, which God forbids"[81] – but showered him as well with gifts of clothing and jewelry after he had accepted Christianity. From this it would appear that the initiative of 1588 for baptizing the leaders and the people of Ennarya came from Sarsa Dengel himself.

> The king reminded Badancho that his father loved the Christian religion, and that he had not received the grace of a Christian baptism because the time had not yet come. Now show through action what your father had meditated in his heart; make a reality of that which he had begun as a wish [desire] . . . In order to have him accept this advice, he sent to him some doctors [of theology] to preach to him.[82]

It was Sarsa Dengel's good luck that he arrived in Ennarya after gaining a formidable victory against the Borana in Gojjam. It was Badancho's good luck that the king arrived after Ennarya had weathered the storm and forced the Borana into retreat. The king was delighted with the governor's performance, and the governor was relieved at the arrival of the king. Rarely did the mood of both men alter so dramatically in a single year from despair to jubilation. The old practices and doctrines gave way to new realities. Ideological unity between the Christian leadership and that of Ennarya opened a new chapter in their relationship.

From the description of the chronicler, Badancho appears to have been a very intelligent man, a statesman *par excellence*, wholly determined to resist the Borana assault. For his non-Christian background he compensated by his sincere desire to embrace Christianity.[83] He was considered as the center, the life and soul of his people's desire to embrace Christianity. According to the chronicler, he appreciated and delighted in every manifestation of spreading Christianity. The marvelous thing about the way the chronicler describes Badancho is that it conveys the impression that he was a particularly impressive, brilliant man, even at his most profound never far removed from Christian ideals. Such a description is amusing, of course; but above everything else, it is unique, and perhaps of all his attributes described and celebrated in this chronicle, it is his "uniqueness" which is the consistent thread, the ideal most manifestly embraced. We are made to feel that limitless advantage flowed from his baptism, both for the Christian church and for Ennarya. This may or may not have been the case, but one thing remains certain: Badancho was a wealthy ruler who was very generous and liberal towards political as well as religious leaders at the camp of Sarsa Dengel. Beneath his generosity and spiritual craving, Badancho was a calculating and meticulous leader who knew what he was doing. He was not born into organized religion, but he did have that precise grasp of the ideological advantage an organized religion offers at a time of crisis.

> The next day, at dawn, the baptism began. King Sarsa Dengel at Badancho's baptism . . . was his godfather, according to the law of the unique Orthodox church, and he said to him: "You are my son, and I am your father from this day

forward." He was given the name Za-Maryam which is a Christian name, since all the believers take a new name on the baptismal day. This name then was the baptismal name of one of the sons of the king, who loved him very much. The king spoke in the presence of all the inhabitants of the country of Badancho saying: "This is my son, whom I love! Obey him!" ... After he had been baptized, he was dressed, by order of the king, in magnificent robes.[84]

The baptism of Badancho and his people was the spectacular bloodless revolution of 1588. It was an overwhelming achievement. Without doubt the star of the day was Sarsa Dengel, paying his first visit to Ennarya for spiritual reasons. It was Christianity which lured him to Ennarya, and now the occasion was being converted into a festival of ideological unity.

> The same day, the king gave a great dinner to the chief of Ennarya and to the chiefs of the tribes which carried out his orders; he had ordered tables prepared, each one in its own way and with its particular dishes; he had ordered slain selected fattened calves and bulls. The day was spent in great joy – eating and drinking.[85]

The flood of feeling which wells up through the chronicle transforms the ceremony from an ordinary baptism to an elaborate and emotional time when the depths of Christian patriotism overflowed. Under these circumstances the triumph of Christianity might have been expected to be more sure, swift, and lasting. But it came too late, and, like other measures of Sarsa Dengel which were taken at the eleventh hour, it was bound to fail.

The last campaigns of Sarsa Dengel against the Borana (east of the Abbay)

Within two months, Sarsa Dengel had achieved three victories. He had opened the route to Ennarya. He had received no less than three thousand ounces of gold tribute from that country. He had gained a momentous victory for the church by the baptism of Badancho and his people. After guaranteeing the establishment of the church in Ennarya, Sarsa Dengel set out for Waj with a firm resolution to punish the Borana who had earlier inflicted considerable damage on the Christians of the province. After a long march, he arrived at Sef Bar, the old court of Galawdewos, but found no enemy to face him.

> But as soon as the Galla learned the news of his arrival, ... they were seized with fear and trembling, and they fled with their wives, their children and their flocks; they scattered along all roads, just as smoke dissipates under the force of the wind.[86]

As usual, the Borana avoided confronting Sarsa Dengel in the field. In this they were helped by the nature of his large, slow-moving army, which included more camp followers than combatants. The useless baggage train and camp followers hampered rather than helped the movement.

> The number of men at arms ... even if it should be less, makes an excessively big camp because the camp followers and the baggage train amount to many more than the soldiery. The reason is that usually there are more women than men in the camp. Besides the king's being accompanied by the queen, and all or nearly all

39

the ladies who are usually at court, widows, married ladies and even many unmarried ones, and the wives of the chief lords and captains, so that they go to war with their households and families, besides this, every soldier has one or many women with him.[87]

The Borana did not have this type of problem. Their women, children, and cattle were kept out of the zone of conflict as far as possible. Any Borana band included only warriors, who carried dried meat prepared with butter, which was nourishing and easy to carry. As a result the Borana retreated when the king advanced, and advanced when he withdrew. Rapid movement was the source of their strength. The policy of choosing a soft target and a right time was one of their greatest tactics. In the sparsely populated eastern provinces the tactic was most effective, and the Christians found no alternative but withdrawal to provinces which were more densely populated and therefore easily defendable.

Having failed to punish the Borana in Waj, Sarsa Dengel decided to try his luck against the Jawe, who were the terror of the Christians. The Jawe were a branch of the Borana, who devastated several provinces east of the Abbay. The Christians in Waj and Damot, who complained that they were harassed a great deal by the Jawe, compared them with an incurable skin disease called *dawe*, and accordingly they gave them that name. "The Abyssinians call them Dawe because of the trouble they have brought to them."[88]

> The king decided to go fight the Galla who were in Bater-Amora, and who are called Jawe. They were the ones who had devastated Fasilo and his army. But when they learned the news of the arrival of this terrible king . . . they fled in the distance, so that the traces of their shelters were not even discernible. Then the great men of the kingdom held counsel saying, "Where shall we seek [them] now? The trail of the Galla has disappeared; we do not know where they went; there is no more corn [grain] to pillage or to buy. Now famine will truly torture our camp. Let us return to our campsite [Gubay][89] which is a meeting of the apostles!"[90]

Several important points emerge from the above. First, the slow movement of Sarsa Dengel's army enabled the Borana warriors to disappear into their dense forests with all their cattle, children, and womenfolk before his arrival. While on the road, Sarsa Dengel's army often resorted to looting to replenish its supply, and this acted as an alarm bell to the Borana bands, who were seldom caught off guard. Whenever they were surprised, they were slaughtered, as we have seen earlier.[91] Secondly, it appears that the damage the Jawe caused in Bater-Amora[92] was considerable. The governor, who also seems to have been the military commander of this province, was one Fasilo. He decided to meet the Jawe before they ravaged his land. This was a bold and dangerous strategy, by which he hoped to avert the series of defeats of the kind that put Darahagot into flight. It was bold also because he took the initiative to meet them before they had entered the strategically important district of Kuera. By so doing he had hoped to defend Kuera and assure the safety of Gamo, the buffer district between Kuera and Bater-Amora. It was dangerous because he committed the classic mistake of meeting the Jawe in a field of their own choice and at a time before they were exhausted by fighting, or burdened with booty. Fasilo's much hoped-for victory failed to come. Instead, it backfired with catastrophic consequences. Fasilo and his entire army perished somewhere between Gamo and Kuera in late 1586 or early 1587.

> Then the Dawe began to make war on the Christians ... and they devastated the two districts of Bater-Amora and Waj ... The Dawe chased this prophet,[93] laid waste his country, which was called Gamo, and looted all that he possessed.[94]

Sarsa Dengel's spirited expedition against the Jawe in 1588 seems to have been inspired by his desire to avenge not only the death of Fasilo, but also the ravages the Jawe had caused in the three districts. As we saw above, the Jawe disappeared before the thunderbolt intended for them was launched. To follow them into their dense forests was not feasible, nor was it possible to wait for their return to Bater-Amora. The unsettled conditions in Gamo, Waj, and Bater-Amora had already turned the arable land into pasture. The Borana depended for their livelihood on their cattle, which they supplemented with agricultural produce, through exchange with their neighbors. The Christian soldiers depended on corn (grain), which they supplemented with animal produce. With the Borana dispersal before Sarsa Dengel there was neither grain nor cattle to buy or loot.[95] The reaction of the soldiers to this desperate economic situation was an explosion of the fear of hunger, which surpassed in degree the Borana fear of them. We catch a uniform note of panic: "It is better to die fighting than to die starving."[96] The hunger issue dominated all others. The soldiers' decision to recross the Abbay was irrevocable. "The king heard them, saying, 'Yes, let it be done as you have just said!' Having spoken thus, he turned around and headed towards the Guraghe; he walked very swiftly."[97] On his homeward journey in 1588, Sarsa Dengel baptized the governors of Bosha and Gumar, along with their people. Here too, Christianity was not destined to succeed because it came too late. Finally, Sarsa Dengel crossed the Abbay without inflicting any injury on the Borana. Whatever hope he might have had of creating a semblance of authority east of the Abbay could not be sustained once he had crossed the river because the dispersed Borana regrouped and decided to show him that to come back was well-nigh impossible. According to a contemporary historian, they devastated both Shawa and Damot,[98] and kept up the pressure on Ennarya and Gojjam. Sarsa Dengel spent the rest of his life west of the Abbay, mainly conducting slave raids.

The separation of the Matcha from the Tulama

Before their separation, the Matcha and the Tulama had a common *chafe* assembly, at Oda Nabi in Fatagar.[99] Since the Matcha and the Tulama shared a *chafe*, they were under a common government and common law. As brothers who obey common law, they fought in support of one another. Every eight years each group sent its delegation to Oda Nabi for the gada election. The gada leaders who were elected at Oda Nabi executed the duties of central *chafe*, settled disputes between the Matcha and the Tulama, marshaled their resources for the common cause, declared war and concluded peace. The separation of the Matcha from the *chafe* assembly at Oda Nabi was first precipitated by the formation of the Afre confederacy (i.e., the confederacy of the four), composed of the Hoko, Tchalliya, Gudru, and Liban. According to Bahrey, the Afre confederacy was formed during the period of the Robale gada (1570–1578). During the period of the Birmaji gada (1578–1586), the second Matcha confederacy, the Sadacha (i.e., the confederacy of the three), was formed. This was composed of Obbo, Suba, and Hakako.[100] The Afre spearheaded the Matcha migration to the southwestern region. They crossed the Gudar river into Damot during the period of the Robale gada. During the Birmaji gada, the Sadacha also crossed the Gudar river and joined with the Afre in Damot. By trekking in the footsteps of the Afre, the Sadacha were completing the separation of the Matcha from the Tulama. Once the two groups arrived in Damot, the distance between them and the central *chafe* at Oda Nabi (in the heart of the Tulama land) became too extended owing to difficult terrain and unsettled conditions. Travel to Oda Nabi became less common, and the Matcha broke from it and founded their own central *chafe* in the region of the upper Gibe river, some 250 kilometers west of Oda Nabi.[101]

The new center, called Oda Bisil (or Tute Bisil), was located between the Gedo, Billo, and Gibe rivers. This location was in an ideal environment, endowed with abundant pasturage and adequate water from numerous rivers. In addition to its fertility, good weather, and abundant rainfall, Oda Bisil was located in a strategic position; it was surrounded by a number of hills and enveloped in a deep forest, both of which served as buffers against sudden enemy attack. It was from here that the Matcha directed raids against Ennarya, Bosha, Gumar, and Janjero in the southwest and south, against Hadiya and Gurage in the east, against Bizamo, Shat, and Konch in the west, and against Gojjam in the north.

Oral tradition gives two versions of the separation of the Matcha from the Oda Nabi. The Matcha tradition views it as a peaceful act undertaken with the consent of the Tulama. The tradition was recorded at the beginning of this century and remains current in the area. It claims "that before they began their march, the Matcha and Tulama gathered at the Awash river [i.e., in the region of Oda Nabi] and said farewell to each other weeping."[102] On the other hand, the Tulama tradition places all the blame on the Matcha.

> . . . before they left the iron bokku was with the Matcha. The Gombichu and others sent ambassadors to Matcha to request them to return the bokku. The Matcha refused. Then Gombichu and others made raids against the Matcha; but before the Gombichu retrieved the bokku, the Matcha escaped and went further from the attack of the Gombichu. The Gombichu, Ada and other Tulama groups already settled in Shawa held a meeting to decide about the new bokku. The old men said "cut an olive tree and make of its wood a bokku and honour it." So it was settled in that way, and from then onward, the Matcha became hereditary enemies of the Tulama.[103]

In its main aspect, this tradition deals with three points. First, it dimly refers to the time when the two groups had a common "iron" *bokku* and lived together in peace. Secondly, it deals with the importance of the *bokku* in Oromo society. The third aspect is part of the second. It deals with the consequences of the proliferation of the *bokku*. When the Tulama and the Matcha had a common *bokku*, the constant friction between them was settled through dialogue in the gada assembly at Oda Nabi. The gada leaders constantly toured by themselves, or sent their delegates to settle disputes.[104] This seems to have provided an outlet for friction before it exploded into bloodshed. In addition, the central gada leaders directed the military wing of the Oromo society against their enemies.[105] This was made possible because of the common *chafe* and the common *bokku*, which embodied the spirit of unity and served as a living constitution. *Bokku* was a wooden scepter which was used as an emblem of authority by the gada leader.

At this point, it is pertinent to state briefly the importance of this ceremonial emblem in the Oromo society of the time. The following analysis depends heavily on the precious materials of Shaykh Bakri Sapalo,[106] an outstanding Muslim Oromo intellectual from Harar, and the invaluable manuscript of Abba Jobir Abba Dula, the last king of Jimma. What follows is a summary of the important points contained in the works of both authors. In the above tradition, the common *bokku* is referred to as being made of "iron." According to these authorities,[107] this was not the case. The term "iron" should not be taken literally. They imply that it is the quality of iron rather than iron itself which is referred to in this connection. In fact, the *bokku* always had been made of wood. It was a multi-purpose emblem which had ritual, political, and perhaps also military significance. Ritually, every public prayer was concluded with a display of the *bokku*. The gada leader kept it in his belt during the assembly meeting and whenever there was disorder he took it out and showed it to the assembly, upon which calm was immediately restored. This shows the awe and reverence in which the *bokku* was held. It was seen not only as the symbol of political power, but also as a "sacred" object as well. This may be the reason why the Tulama tradition also stresses the point of honoring[108] it, and why Abba Jobir Abba Dula compared it with Orthodox Christian *tabot*.[109] As an honored emblem, the *bokku* was kept only with the leader. "Nobody except the Abba Gada carried it. At the end of his tenure of office, the incoming leader took it directly from the hand of the outgoing leader."[110] Abba Jobir even claimed that the *bokku* was capable of changing the fortunes of a war.

> It was used in a war. When a war became bad for the Oromo, the gada leader took the bokku out of its container and he went with it in his hand from one part of the field of battle to the other striking the ground with it. This raised the fighting capacity of the Oromo and weakened that of the enemy, resulting in the defeat of the latter.[111]

The practical usefulness of the *bokku* in war is open to question. What is not in doubt is that neither the Oromo political organization of the time, nor their unity, could be understood without recognizing the special role of this object.

Both sources acknowledge that the *bokku* was not only the symbol of supreme authority, but was also enshrouded in an aura which inspired awe and fear. It was by the *bokku* that all essential celebrations, blessings, and legislation received the final touch, and by it were endowed with moral force and divine sanction. Further, it was the possession of a common *bokku* which above everything else distinguished the earlier unity of the Matcha and the Tulama from their later disunity. Thus, the common *bokku* engraved in the core of their unity represented the highest expression of peace that bound them together. In their introduction to the *African Political Systems*, Fortes and Evans-Pritchard made an interesting observation which may have some relevance to the point under discussion.

> Members of an African society feel their unity and perceive their common interests in symbols, and it is their attachment to these symbols which more than anything else gives their society cohesion and persistence. In the forms of myths, fictions, dogmas, ritual, sacred places and persons, these symbols represent the unity and exclusiveness of the groups which respect them. They are regarded, however, not as mere symbols, but as final values in themselves.[112]

As is common among other confederacies, Tulama tradition cited above refers to an iron *bokku* for reasons which are not difficult to explain. The quality of iron symbolized confederacy. Like iron, a confederacy was hard to break or destroy so long as it had a common *bokku*. As iron made the best of all known weapons of war, so the *bokku* made for the best unity. When the Matcha escaped with the "iron" *bokku*, the Tulama tried to retrieve it instead of making another one. In other words, they tried and failed to impose unity on the Matcha. Once the hope of unity was damaged beyond repair, the Tulama elders said, "Cut an olive tree and make of its wood a bokku and honour it."[113] The olive tree according to Oromo tradition is the best of all trees because of its strength, the good smell of its leaves, the medicinal value of its trunk, and the several uses made of its stem.[114] Internal peace was maintained only among those groups who shared a common *bokku*. Once the symbol of their unity no longer kept them together, conflicts over scarce resources found expression not through dialogue in the assembly, but through war.

With their central *chafe* at Oda Bisil, the Matcha people lived together under a common *bokku* for three decades before the common *chafe* was divided and replaced by independent Afre and Sadacha *chafes* in what are today Wallaga and Kaffa provinces respectively. According to a very popular Matcha tradition, a certain historical figure called Makko Billi played a decisive role at an early stage in the life of the Matcha *chafe* at Oda Bisil. His contribution is well preserved in the tradition, and his name still is recalled fondly among the Matcha. The French traveler Antoine d'Abbadie, who was in the kingdom of Limmu-Ennarya[115] in 1843, interviewed many elders, some of whom were reported to be a hundred years old.[116] On the basis of the information he gathered from these men, d'Abbadie stated that Makko Billi was a great Matcha leader who had invented the gada system. From the number of generations given to him by his informants, d'Abbadie placed the time of the

44

invention of the system in 1589. He arrived at the date on the basis of the number of the gada periods which had taken office between 1843 and 1589. The estimate is plausible, not because the gada system was invented in this year, but rather because of the mentioning of this date in connection with the time of Makko Billi. The system was clearly much older[117] than that suggested by d'Abbadie, but the date is nonetheless extremely important for the period under discussion. The date of 1589 corresponded with the time of the break of the Matcha from the Tulama central *chafe*. From this we may assume that Makko Billi probably existed at this formative stage in the history of the Matcha.

The Matcha tradition claims that Makko Billi was "an able leader, a great law-giver and *raajii* ('prophet') at the same time."[118] As an able leader, he succeeded in establishing the famous Matcha *chafe* at Oda Bisil. As a law-giver, he instructed the Matcha in the "gada laws." Some of these laws dealt with the "art" of settling disputes over land,[119] the importance of performing *butta* (the slaughtering of bulls by the members of the new gada set) every eight years and the observance of new-year ritual annually.[120] As *raajii* Makko Billi spoke to the Matcha in the name of Waqa (the Oromo god) and instructed them to follow "the way of Waqa."[121]

Among other Oromo (even among the Tulama, their Borana brethren) both the name and the law of Makko Billi are unknown. However, among the Matcha, Makko Billi is still remembered not only for his "qualities" mentioned above, but as well for an important Matcha concept which is connected inextricably with his name. This is the concept of *saffu*, which is very difficult to translate into English. It embodies a concept somewhat closer to the Marxist dialectical law of unity of the opposites. But it differs from this law in that the opposites do not struggle in unity. They live without struggling against each other because the moment they do, the basis of their peaceful coexistence will be destroyed. Lambert Bartels, who has lived among and studied the Matcha Oromo for over two decades, defines *saffu* as "the Matcha's view of the cosmic and social order as it was given to them by Waqa from the beginning."[122] He adds that, "being *saffu* to one another means having to respect one another's place in the cosmic order and in society." From this perspective, *saffu* expresses the Matcha view of the universe.

> Matcha see the world and particularly their own society, as Waqa's creation in which all things have been given a place of their own ... All are unique, different from one another ... They must keep distance from each other, each of them has to follow his own way; they must not overstep the boundaries put between them by Waqa; they must not get mixed up.[123]

It appears that the main ideas embodied in the concept of *saffu* are harmony, respect, avoidance, and distance. *Saffu* is mutual. In this sense, it is said that "thorns and the soles of the feet are saffu to one another ... Ashes and flour are saffu ... Old and young are saffu ... Slave and master are saffu to one another."[124] This *saffu* came from Waqa and it was Makko Billi, who in the name of the Oromo god, "applied" this cosmic law of the Matcha. Makko Billi was Matcha. This explains why both his name and his laws are unknown among other Oromo.

Makko Billi must have played a dramatic role at the time when the Matcha formed their independent *chafe*. This may explain why his name has been so deeply involved in the Matcha oral tradition. In fact, one Matcha traditional historian categorically asserts that Makko Billi was the great Matcha leader who played a dynamic role at the time when the Matcha first formed their own independent central *chafe* at Oda Bisil.[125] The same source makes Makko Billi even a martyr. It is claimed that when a huge *gabbaro*[126] force suddenly and unexpectedly encircled Oda Bisil, thus exposing the Matcha to destruction, he quickly devised an ingenious stratagem that enabled his followers to break out of the encirclement. According to this tradition, Makko Billi himself was killed while trying to escape, but his strategy saved the Matcha from extermination.[127] Much remains to be understood about Makko Billi "the law-giver," "the prophet," and war strategist, but enough is already clear to frame a picture of an extraordinary leader who was active in the early stages of the formation of the Matcha central *chafe* at Oda Bisil.[128]

We now continue with our discussion on the progress of the Matcha in the Gibe region, which we left in 1588 when we followed Sarsa Dengel's march to Waj. It appears that shortly after 1589, the pressure on the Matcha eased owing largely to the suspension of the Matcha campaigns by the king. By 1590 under constant pressure from the Barentu, Sarsa Dengel's court at Gubay was itself unsafe. As a result, he was forced to change his court to Ayba.[129] By then he had abandoned his attempts to baptize the pagans and commenced a new policy of slave raids against them. The outcome was as usual, the same as all the previous slave raids: extermination, slavery, and depopulation, all of which contributed to the dissipation of resistance against the Oromo. In 1590, Sarsa Dengel's slaving raids were directed against the Gambo people, who lived in the fertile lands east of the Choman Swamps. The ideological justification for the raids was as a punitive measure "to avenge the Christian blood which had been shed there."[130] The justification was in reality an excuse, as the Gambo were an easy prey to his soldiers. Since 1564, the king had made a number of slaving raids among the pagans in the regions of the Choman Swamp and Bizamo. The disorganized Gambo proved a soft target. Their men, women and children were taken captive, their cattle looted, and those who resisted put to the sword. The raids were at the time when the territory of Bizamo, which bordered on the land of the Gambo people, was overrun by the Afre branch of the Matcha people.

Some writers on the Ethiopian history of the period observe little but ruin in the Oromo migration.[131] However, these writers failed to consider the continuous enslavement and pillaging to which the Christian leadership subjected their pagan minorities and neighbors. As indicated earlier,[132] the Christian leadership spared only those who accepted their faith. The pagans were fair game and easy victims for plunder and enslavement by the Christians. Without a doubt, it was this process which facilitated the Matcha migration to the southwestern region. Moreover, as we shall see further in the discussion,[133] the Christian soldiery in some cases brought more ruin to their own peasantry than the migrating pastoral Oromo. What is more,

> Judging from the evidence of the chronicles, the brutality of the professional soldiers, be it to decapitate or emasculate men or to enslave women and children, does not seem to have been matched by the reputed savagery of the Galla.[134]

The people of the southwestern region were caught between the attack of the migrating pastoral Oromo and the Christian leadership's heavy-handed collection of tribute, slave raids, and sometimes wanton pillaging.[135] At all events after their recovery from the initial shock and attack of the migrating Oromo, the people of the region seem to have come to terms with their new masters. Adoption may have facilitated the process of integration. What cannot be doubted is that the people in the region were left to manage their own affairs. This aspect will be dealt with later.[136] Here it should suffice to say that by the end of the sixteenth century the Matcha had already become the masters of vast territory in the southwestern region of what is today Ethiopia. It was only Ennarya that was able to resist the Matcha assault up to the beginning of the eighteenth century. The celebrated resistance of that state is the subject of the next chapter.

2

Ennarya and the Sadacha 1600–1710

In the previous chapter the course of the Matcha migration to the southwestern regions of what is today Ethiopia has been followed. Here their migration will be charted into the rest of the region, mainly to Ennarya, the only state which proved to be too hard a nut for the Matcha arms to crack. Before doing this, however, it may be useful to make two points very clear at the start. First, we have seen above that the Matcha section of the Borana was divided into two major confederacies. These were the Afre confederacy (i.e., the confederacy of the four) composed of the Hoko, Tchalliya, Gudru, and Liban. This confederacy was formed during the Robale gada (1570–1578). The other Matcha confederacy was the Sadacha (i.e., the confederacy of the three) composed of Obbo, Suba, and Hakako and this was formed during the period of the Birmaji gada (1578–1586). The two Matcha confederacies broke away from the Borana (i.e., Matcha-Tulama) *chafe* assembly at Oda Nabi in Fatagar. They crossed the Gudar and Mugar rivers in the 1570s and formed their own independent *chafe* in the 1580s at Oda Bisil in Damot, some 250 kilometers west of Oda Nabi. Secondly, by the beginning of the seventeenth century, two directions of Matcha movements were visible. Whether it was by agreement or accident, the Sadacha branch of the Matcha directed their entire efforts towards the south and southeast, namely the Gibe region, of which Ennarya formed the dominant part, while the Afre branch directed their movements towards the west and southwest, the vast land which today constitutes the administrative regions of Wallaga and Illubabor.

The Sadacha, which spearheaded and dominated the struggle against and eventually became the masters of Ennarya, is the subject of discussion in this chapter. At the same time, since the struggle of the Sadacha cannot be presented, much less analyzed, apart from the history of the people of Ennarya, I have given (as in the previous chapter) considerable attention to the fascinating history of Ennarya, thereby showing the dynamism of conflict, interaction, and change which occurred between 1600 and 1710. For over a century, Ennarya resisted the Sadacha attack with more than usual vigor. It was this resistance which expressed the heroism of her people, demonstrated the strength of her institutions, and constituted the glorious chapter of her history.

48

We have already seen in the previous chapter that during the Mulata gada (1586–1594), the Matcha invaded Ennarya. They not only threatened Ennarya militarily, but also seem to have impressed upon the Christian leadership the pressing need to convert both leaders and the people of Ennarya to the ideology which Christianity provided. The 1588 Matcha attack on Ennarya seems to indicate that the Christian defense establishment in western Shaw and Damot was slowly but surely disintegrating. The disintegration of the provinces east of the Abbay led to the exodus of refugees, some of whom fled to Ennarya. Apparently with the intention of raising the morale of his people and increasing the number of fighters in his country, Badancho, the wise politician and the first Christian leader of Ennarya, started using the refugees for the cause and in the interest of Ennarya. For the time being the fleeing refugees provided Ennarya with an inexhaustible fighting force. Consequently, between 1588 and 1594, Ennarya repulsed a number of Matcha attacks with shame and loss.

However, during the period of Dulo gada (1594–1602), the balance of force (for a while) changed in favor of the Matcha (the Sadacha). In 1594, the first blow of the Sadacha fell on Ennarya. Though they failed to knock Ennarya out of political existence, they succeeded in deflecting the course of her history. The Sadacha attack on Ennarya was so terrible that it forced the latter to abandon all the fertile land between the main Gibe and Gibe Ennarya, the last of which became the strategic center from which Ennarya resisted the Sadacha assault to the uttermost. In the 1580s, it was from the main Gibe that Ennarya resisted the Sadacha. By 1594, the arable land between the two rivers had turned into pasture. The Sadacha attack on Gumar and Bosha left these districts enfeebled. Ennarya, which had lost a piece of fertile territory in the north, took advantage of the feebleness of her two neighbors and occupied some parts from the two districts. By so doing, Ennarya gained back what she had lost to the Sadacha. The ruling houses of Bosha and Gumar desperately resisted both the Sadacha attack on their lands, and Ennarya's enrichment at their expense. Harassed between the irresistible Sadacha and expanding Ennarya, the ruling families of Gumar and Bosha were forced to seek refuge across the Gojeb river in Kaffa. The last rulers of Ennarya were to follow suit almost a century later.

Guamcho, the new governor of Ennarya, while resisting the Sadacha attack on the one hand, and expanding at the expense of his disintegrating neighbors on the other, appealed to Sarsa Dengel for military aid. We have seen above the special relation between Badancho, the father of Guamcho, and Sarsa Dengel. Badancho came to power as a pagan but died a Christian in the early 1590s. During his governorship, there had been moments of glory and times of tragedy, war and peace, euphoria, and near despair. Sarsa Dengel, who virtually depended on Ennarya for his gold tribute, was very anxious to support the son and successor of Badancho. Accordingly, he led a swift expedition to Ennarya in 1595. By the time he reached Ennarya, the latter had already weathered the heavy storm, and the Sadacha dispersed before the well-armed force of Sarsa Dengel. As a result, the king was unable to cause any damage to the Sadacha. His long march was not without a result, however. He baptized Guamcho, as he had Badancho before him. It is probably for this reason that one source claims that Sarsa Dengel introduced Christianity into Ennarya at this time.[1]

> He left an additional number of priests and monks to instruct them in the Christian religion, though there are some historians of this reign who pretend that it was not till this second visit that Ennarya was converted.[2]

With the pressure on Ennarya removed, the safety of the route assured, and the baptism of Guamcho accomplished, Sarsa Dengel collected whatever gold tribute the new governor was able to give and commenced his homeward journey without fighting a single battle with the Matcha in general. At this time, the Afre were overrunning Konch, Shat, the Choman Swamps, and Bizamo. The pagans of these areas, long subjected to intermittent slave raids, were very far from possessing any strength for resistance, whether organizational or numerical, which enabled Ennarya to withstand and repulse the attacks. While the art of war, that is dependence on cavalry for offensive attacks and fortifications for defense, had made considerable progress in Ennarya, it was at a rudimentary stage in the areas mentioned above. A central leadership that marshaled all the common resources, harmonized skills and animated the mass into action did not develop here. They were equally unskilled in the arts of constructing elaborate fortifications and defending them resolutely in the way that Ennarya did. The non-Christian communities seem to have trusted their defense more to their forests than to their fortifications, and more to their power of flight than to that of combat. Above all, they were disorganized, lacked unifying leadership, and were linguistically divided and thus easily defeated. Consequently, the Afre became masters of much of these districts. Between them, the Afre and the Sadacha were now in possession of extensive lands of exceptional fertility, excellent pasturage intersected by many streams and rivers which drained either to the Abbay or the Omo, and enveloped in dense forests interspersed with the sacred *oda* (sycamore trees), under the life-giving shades of which the Afre and Sadacha assemblies met. Game, which was a source of food for adults, and a means of practical training for the young in the wielding of arms, was plentiful. These opportunities seem to have increased the spirit of adventure among the Matcha pastoralists. The abundant wild fruits supplemented their animal diet. The numerous beehives set either in the hollow of big trees or in cavities of rocks provided additional food. The abundance of rainfall and the luxuriance of the vegetation also contributed to the increase in the size of the human and animal population.[3]

A number of Cushitic-speaking pagan communities of Bizamo and the adjacent districts fled across the Abbay into Wambarma, Achafar, and Wambarya. The Afre followed them. Probably the majority remained on their land and submitted to their conquerors, by whom they were absorbed *en masse*.

The Sadacha who fled before Sarsa Dengel in 1595 regrouped the following year, thereby cutting the caravan route to Ennarya. This directly affected Sarsa

Dengel, who in 1597 made an ambitious attempt to take the vast land between Ennarya and Gojjam from the Matcha who had occupied it. The whole purpose of the expedition seems to have been to attack the Matcha in their sanctuaries in Damot. With that intention, he crossed the Abbay and went to Damot, with the Matcha fleeing everywhere before him. From Damot he went to Shat, where he was suddenly taken ill and died on October 4, 1597. Since his return from the long expedition to Waj in 1588, all the provinces east of the Abbay, except some parts of Shawa, had been lost. By 1597, all the provinces south of the Abbay, except Ennarya, were in the hands of the Matcha. A great kingdom which had become what it was by virtue of having been for centuries the strongest in the Horn of Africa now suddenly found itself cut off from its former provinces, deprived of its historic role, and thrown back to the areas north of the Abbay. Between 1597 and 1603, the leadership in the Christian kingdom turned a blind eye to what Sarsa Dengel had done in the thirty-four previous years. It became clear to the weak and indecisive Christian leadership that, while the king's soldiers were strong enough to rout the Oromo warriors time and again, they were not strong enough to pacify them in all the provinces they had progressively occupied. Thus, all the campaigns to the south or east of the Abbay were abandoned. However, some elements within the Christian society had been able to produce suitable ideological clothing in which to dress the necessities of coming to the rescue of the lost provinces.[4] It was at this juncture, when the Christian kingdom was very weak, that the period of the Dulo gada (1594–1602) came to an end and was succeeded by the Melbah gada (1602–1610).

After eighty years (1522–1602), during which ten successive gadas had carried out with varying degrees of success the migration into the central, north, and southwestern parts of what is today Ethiopia, a new cycle of gada names began repeating the same series in the same order. To recapitulate, the earlier discussion on the migration opened with the Melbah gada in 1522.[5] In 1602, another Melbah gada began. However, the distance between the place from which the first gada started, and the place where the cycle began again, is probably more than 800 kilometers. The Melbah of the Borana continued with raids in all directions. The major assault of this gada, and of several subsequent ones, was concentrated on the Gibe region and Gojjam. Although the Christian kingdom was at its weakest at this time, the Oromo did not derive much benefit from their enemy's weakness.

In 1603, the Tulama from Walaqa and the Afre from Bizamo mounted a simultaneous heavy raid on Gojjam. This had serious consequences for the internal politics of the Christian kingdom. It must have been this and other pressures which forced Ya'eqob to go against the triumvirate at a tender age.[6] Once in power, the young king had the luck to defeat Ras Athantius and Za-Sellassie but he reinstated the former and exiled the latter to Ennarya. The adventurer Za-Sellassie was described by one historian as "a man esteemed for bravery and conduct, beloved by the soldiers, but turbulent and seditious, without honour, gratitude, or regard either to his word, to his sovereign or to the interest of his country."[7] By exiling Za-Sellassie to Ennarya, Ya'eqob probably hoped both to deprive the triumvirate of the use of this able general and consummate conspirator, and more importantly to tap the energy and organizational skill of this restless adventurer in helping Ennarya to strengthen her defenses, which were under threat at the time. We do not know what contribution, if any, Za-Sellassie had made to the defenses of this province, but one thing remains certain. Very soon, Ya'eqob himself was overthrown and exiled to Ennarya, while Za-Sellassie was freed and called back to a prestigious and lucrative position under Za-Dengel who, in the hope of using the military talents of this notorious general, even gave him his own sister in marriage.

While Ya'eqob was in exile in Ennarya, the province was subjected to the most devastating Sadacha attack yet seen. The people of Ennarya put up a very spirited resistance against the Sadacha behind the main Gibe. However, under a heavy assault from the Sadacha, Guamcho, Ennarya's able and brave governor, withdrew his force and moved behind the impregnable fortress of Gibe Ennarya. The Sadacha misinterpreted Guamcho's tactical withdrawal for general flight, and not for the first or last time they followed vigorously, thus becoming easy victims for his traps. Guamcho's elaborate network of trenches and fortifications, which were defended with an inexhaustible and irresistible supply of stone missiles, all contributed to the Sadacha defeat. On that day more Sadacha probably were killed by the flying stone missiles than by all the arrows, spears, and swords of Guamcho's men put together. The humiliated Sadacha were repulsed with shame and great loss.

By choice or accident, the adventurer prince, Susenyos,[8] presented himself to the Sadacha at the very moment when they needed his services most. Shortly before, he had been defeated by Sidi, the governor of Hadiya, and deserted by his own followers. Both found what they wanted in each other, Susenyos safety and booty, and the Sadacha his leadership. In his desire to share in the loot of Ennarya, Susenyos readily lent his services to the Sadacha.[9] Susenyos was an excellent horseman and able leader, who could endure want of food, and his mind and body were alike suited for the hard life of a warrior.[10] He possessed undisputed courage, which animated the pastoralists. He quickly raised the morale and restored the courage of the Sadacha by reorganizing them to face Guamcho. Susenyos's fame and popularity, his oratory, and his knowledge of their language,[11] all made him an ideal leader for the task in hand. He promised them victory, in return for which they promised him rich reward in booty, neither of which ever materialized. The Sadacha, who neither forgot nor forgave Guamcho for what he had done to them, rallied behind Susenyos with one mind. For three consecutive days, Susenyos stormed the stronghold of Guamcho with heavy losses on both sides.[12] On the fourth day, Susenyos introduced a new element in his strategy, which was at first effective, but later proved his undoing. Susenyos, who realized the difficulties of using cavalry in the maze of Ennarya's trenches and fortifications, left behind the Sadacha horses in the forest and attacked Guamcho's strongholds with infantry. The people of Ennarya, who were expecting a cavalry attack, were taken by surprise. Susenyos's strategy at first succeeded so well that his men were able to penetrate Ennarya's stout defenses. Credit for the success must without a doubt go to Susenyos, who after three days of indecisive engagements changed the course of the war. His battle plan was excellent, though the initial successes were not exploited with sufficient energy and imagination. Guamcho and his men were reeling under the shock of surprise when Susenyos's storming party began decapitating his soldiers deep inside his fortifications. This spectacle had just the opposite effect from that which had been intended. Inflamed by the rate at which his men were being decapitated, Guamcho resolved to die like a brave warrior by exciting his men into action. Intoxicated with anger, Guamcho threw himself upon his enemy with great courage. He, and a number of his comrades, fell under the blows of their enemies. Susenyos drew the wrong conclusion from the death of the leader. He thought that this would be the end of the battle. He and his men indeed became so jubilant that they neglected the fighting and began looting Guamcho's camp. The huge booty taken added to the bitterness felt by the people of Ennarya. To add insult to injury, Susenyos decorated with Guamcho's golden sword the man who had killed him.[13]

In their moment of trial, the people of Ennarya behaved with admirable discipline and a sense of self-preservation, and chose a new leader. The mantle fell on the nephew of the fallen hero. The search for booty which diverted the attention of Susenyos's men enabled the new leader to restore control and surprise the enemy. The cruelty of the enemy inflamed them rather than causing them panic. The warriors of Ennarya, who seem to have realized the catastrophe that would strike them if they were defeated, did not spare themselves. The new leader channeled this popular fury and poured their anger on the enemy. Being numerous and very familiar with the topography of the area, they rained their arrows, spears, and stone missiles on their enemies. Susenyos's men were stunned by the fury of the counter-attack. Rarely had the fortunes of a war altered so quickly, and the mood changed dramatically from jubilation to panic. Oppressed by numbers and shocked by the showers of arrows, their ruin would have been inevitable had not Susenyos's ability to escape from grave situations prevailed. The adventurous prince soon found that he was overcome by the superior morale of his enemy. To fly was the only sure way of survival. The Sadacha men, startled by the flight of the prince, took to their heels. Susenyos's followers were nearly all destroyed either in the field or in the flight, and as result about 700 horses fell into the hands of the victorious Ennaryans.[14]

This disaster, which Susenyos brought upon his Sadacha followers by walking into the Ennarya fortifications, decisive enough as it was by the rout of his men and the loss of their horses, became still more so from two consequences that followed. First, it brought to an end the alliance between the Sadacha and Susenyos for the loot of Ennarya. As he came with a hope of rich booty, he disappeared in a wave of disaster. He neither gained booty nor rescued his reputation. But a lot of life and pride had been lost. Susenyos[15] escaped to Gurage, where he made peace with Sidi, the governor of Hadiya. The Sadacha abandoned in panic the land between Gibe Ennarya and the main Gibe, and retreated behind the latter.

Secondly, and more importantly, this victory assured Ennarya's existence for one more century as a political entity. It was an overwhelming victory, and the defeated Sadacha were not able to pull themselves together and attack Ennarya for the next six years (the rest of the Melbah gada, 1602–1610).

At about the same time (1604), when the Sadacha launched their massive offensive on Ennarya, their brethren the Afre, from Bizamo, crossed the Abbay and invaded the district of Wambarma. The Agaw inhabitants of this district, who had been victims of slave raids earlier, offered very little resistance. Encouraged by the happy turn of events in this district, the Afre entered Gojjam with apparent determination to take it over. Their vanguard party alone routed Ras Athnatius, the governor. King Za-Dengel arrived on the scene and after a hard-fought battle changed the fortunes of the Christian force. They

> Bore down the Abyssinians with so much violence that the captains finding their battalions recoil, persuaded the king to betake himself to an early flight. He disdained the motion, as arguing effeminacy, leapt from his horse and advanced with his sword and buckler, cry'ed out, here will I die; you if you please escape the fury of the Gallas but never the infamy of deserting your king. The Abyssinians moved with such speech and countenance of their prince, cast themselves into a globe, and with a prodigious fury, like men prepared to die, broke in among the Gallas and constrained them to give back. Which the fugitives perceiving presently returned and renewing the fight gained a glorious victory, such a slaughter of the enemy that a greater had not been made among them at any other time.[16]

This was destined to be Za-Dengel's first and also major victory against the Oromo, who left behind no less than 1,700 dead.[17] However, at the very time when Za-Dengel was defeating the Afre in Gojjam, a plot was afoot to dethrone him in Dambiya. Some months later he was killed as a result of a rebellion among the Christian soldiers.[18]

The disaster of the Afre in Gojjam and that of the Sadacha in Ennarya halted the high-spirited Matcha offensive under the Melbah gada. With apparent intentions to recover their strength and replace losses, both the Afre and the Sadacha retreated to the region of their central *chafe*. Thus for the next six years of the remaining Melbah gada, we do not find much report in the Christian literature on the activities of the Matcha. Between 1608 and 1610, Susenyos fought a number of major battles, against either the Barentu or the Tulama.[19] The Afre's half-hearted attempt to raid Gojjam was easily repulsed. During the same period neither Susenyos, nor his governor of Gojjam, was able to cross the Abbay.[20]

The Mudana gada (1610–1618) came to office at the time when the Matcha were still nursing their wounds and replacing their losses. In 1610, the Afre from Bizamo crossed over into Wambarma and Wambarya. However, when they heard the news of Susenyos's arrival in Gojjam, they retreated to Bizamo in fear before they completed their looting and were fully satisfied. The Sadacha were much more successful in their raids on Ennarya. We have seen above that in 1604 the new leader of Ennarya succeeded in routing and chasing Susenyos and the Sadacha beyond the main Gibe river.

Perhaps it is necessary to say a few words about the complex Gibe river system at this point.

> The main or great Gibe rises near Haratu on the west of the [Choman] swamp. About 55 miles south of Haratu near Sogido it is joined by another river called the Gibe Ennarya and some 30 miles south-east from this junction it is reinforced by the Gibe Jimma, the two taking their attributes from the states through which they flow, and both of them flow northwards to the main river. The three united rivers, the great Gibe, join the Omo about 7 miles north of Abalti where the Omo is joined by yet another river called Wabi on the maps, coming from Hadya.[21]

During the assault of 1604, the men of Ennarya fought behind the Gibe of Ennarya. However, they managed to push the Sadacha beyond the main Gibe. The Sadacha, hovering along the banks of the main Gibe, made it the base from which they attacked Ennarya in 1610. The people of Ennarya were astonished by the Sadacha's repeated incursions into their country. Perhaps they were ignorant of the cause, the attraction of the wealth of their land for the Sadacha. Through repeated attacks, the Sadacha secured entrance into the area between the main Gibe and Gibe Ennarya. However, the people of Ennarya seem to have lived in full security as long as the Sadacha were kept beyond the Gibe Ennarya and their defense was still impregnable. The continuous Sadacha assault, however, showed how that defense was vulnerable; the Sadacha had acquired a detailed knowledge of the topography of the area. Soon they devastated the land from the Gibe Ennarya to the Gibe Jimma, and the highland Ennarya was now opened for constant Sadacha inroads. Here the Sadacha were unable to gain new grounds. They diverted their energy towards what may have appeared to be a softer target, the plain and the wealthy district of Bosha, which possessed all that would attract and very little that could resist, once Ennarya was weakened. This change in the fortunes of Ennarya and Bosha was graphically described by a report of an eyewitness in 1613:

> Father Antonio Fernandez and the ambassador left the court of Narea and thence forward always travelled eastwards. On the first day they arrived at a place where the officer was, who had to provide a guard for them . . . He made them wait here eight days and finally gave them only 80 soldiers to accompany them to the borders of Narea. With this company, they advanced for four days, by long stages, through country that was uninhabited because of the Gallas who often used to raid it, being a level plain, where they have a great advantage, as they may have many horses . . . On the fourth day the Nareas withdrew. The father and his companions were rather frightened but journeyed on in haste . . . After midday, they began the descent of a high mountain from which open country was to be seen. It is called Baterat and belongs to the province of Boxa. Here the Galla commonly graze their cows.[22]

From the above, three important points clearly emerge. First, on the eastern front it was safe from the Sadacha attack for only a short distance from the court of the ruler. Secondly, a large part of Ennarya already had been wasted and abandoned because they were unable to stop the Sadacha cavalry in the plains. In other words, Ennarya's defense on the eastern front was slowly but surely disintegrating. Thirdly, and more importantly, the flat district of Bosha was under the firm control of the Sadacha. It already had become a safe area, where they grazed their immense herds and kept their women and children. It seems that some members of the ruling families of Bosha fled across the Gojeb river to Kaffa.[23] "Those of its inhabitants who were not taken captive had withdrawn into the southern and western parts of Ennarya."[24]

The Sadacha attacks on Ennarya seem to have had far-reaching consequences for the internal politics of Ennarya. We do not have written evidence for what had taken place in Ennarya between 1610 and 1611, but from the subsequent activities of the leader elected in 1611, two things can be said with certainty. First, the struggle for power created instability in Ennarya.[25] Secondly, the struggle for power was generated by Ennarya's inability to stop the Sadacha advance.

We have seen above that Ennarya was forced constantly to use her military resources to keep the Sadacha out of her territory. In her three earlier resistances (1580, 1595, and 1604), Ennarya had managed successfully to repulse the Sadacha with shame and loss. Between 1585 and 1588, Ennarya was supplied with a large source of manpower in the form of the fleeing refugees from the fallen provinces east of the Abbay. Probably it was the alluring prospect of using this stream of manpower which pushed Ennarya to occupy some parts of Gumar and Bosha in the 1590s. By the beginning of the seventeenth century, Ennarya was surrounded by the Sadacha on all sides except the south. The Sadacha continued making deep raids into the heart of highland Ennarya. The people defended themselves with more than usual firmness and success in their highland areas, but in the process Ennarya lost the flower of her manhood. The Sadacha success of 1610 precipitated an internal power struggle which culminated in the rise of Banaro. Thus by 1611, this energetic man was at the helm of Ennarya's leadership. We do not know anything about the fate of the man who saved Ennarya in 1604. But we do know that the transfer of power was not peaceful.[26]

Banaro (1611–1620) was perhaps Ennarya's best-equipped leader both physically and mentally. As we shall see soon, he had the talent, self-confidence, imagination, and courage to cope with the situation. But Banaro was ruthless with all his internal enemies.[27] Beneath his cruelty and ruthlessness, he was an intelligent man who gave the highest priority to the defense of Ennarya. He was not only an able leader, but had the superior skill and knowledge to assign the right officer to the right task in the right place. For example, in 1613, his defense minister, Abecan, was placed at the key stronghold of Gonqa, on the border with the district of Konch, which was then under control of the Sadacha. "They entered Narea and climbed a steep mountain called Ganca, fully inhabited, where the chief military commander of that kingdom usually lives, since it is their frontier against many enemies with whom they are at war."[28]

The reasons why the military commander of Ennarya lived at such a long distance from Banaro's court are clear. First, Banaro had a precise grasp of Ennarya's strength and importance within the Christian kingdom. The stronghold at Gonqa was the key strategic trading center through which all the merchants to and from the Christian kingdom had to pass when coming to and going out of Ennarya. The safety of the Gonqa area was indispensable to the commercial prosperity of Ennarya. Banaro knew very well that Ennarya's importance and survival depended on the continuity of the trade that passed through Gonqa. Secondly, the most fertile, and therefore most densely populated, part of Ennarya was located in southwestern Ennarya, which had to be defended by an able military officer. Abecan proved equal to the task.[29] By strengthening the fortifications, assigning the right men to the right task, and by moving quickly from one point to the other,[30] Banaro raised the morale of his fighters and assured the safety of his country. By 1613, Ennarya was still the seat of wealth and commerce. The sources of her prosperity and her industrious inhabitants are described below in glowing terms by a contemporary historian.

> It is because of the trade there is with Cafraria [Kaffa?] that Narea has so much gold; it is acquired from the Cafres in exchange for clothing, cows, salt and other goods... A considerable quantity of gold is found in it, but the greater part comes from outside. The natives of Narea are the best in the whole of Ethiopia, as all the Abyssinians admit... They are men of their word and deal truthfully without the duplicity and dissimulation usual among the Amaras. The country is rich in foodstuffs and all kinds of cattle, mules and horses. They pay gold by weight, ... but small pieces of iron also circulate as money . . . Since he succeeds by inheritance from a father to son the ruler of Narea is strictly speaking a king... Nevertheless, since he had been subject to the emperor he has no longer been called king, but . . . governor. They habitually pay him their native loyalty, the situation being such that if they wanted to free themselves from it, he could hardly go and wage war upon them in the midst of the Gallas.[31]

The rapid recovery and military revival of Ennarya under Banaro was evident by the beginning of 1613. In March of the same year the Sadacha raided, displaying a fierce bravery, eluding Abecan and overrunning the fertile part of western Ennarya, but it seems to have been less costly in human lives. Banaro's court, which was located at six days' journey from the stronghold of Gonqa, was undisturbed by the news of the Sadacha attack. Banaro was calmly entertaining the ambassador from Janjero at his court, while the people in the areas under attack withdrew to safety, without the confusion and panic which usually followed such withdrawals both in the Christian kingdom and in Harar. For example, when in March 1613 Father Antonio Fernandez went to Banaro's court, he saw no sign of panic and disorder.[32] The father and the ambassador found amazing calm and peace, which probably reflects the degree of self-confidence prevailing at the court. Banaro's kind treatment of his guests demonstrates his political shrewdness and the importance he attached to his relationship with Susenyos, though the latter was in no position either to help or to harm him. "He gave the father 50 gold crusados to help on his way and made many excuses for giving so little, because it was the time when he had to send his customary annual tribute to the emperor, which is a thousand ounces."[33]

Interestingly, the said tribute was collected by the messengers of Susenyos in early 1614.[34] By this time Banaro, through good luck and decisive leadership, had managed to put Ennarya back where she had been in the 1580s. This rapid recovery probably surpassed his own expectations and that of his people, but it did not last long.[35]

The conflict among the Oromo and the rebellion of their subjects

The previous sections have indicated some aspects of the strength of Oromo society in the sixteenth century which allowed them to expand over wider territory. Hiob Ludolf has summarized the factors within Oromo society which enabled the pastoralists to migrate to new areas.

> An encouragement of boldness and hardiness to adventure that by such a conspicuous mark, the sluggish and cow-hearted should be distinguished from the bold and daring. In their banquets and feasts the best bit is always set in the middle and he that takes it must be the first in any perilous undertaking; nor is there any long consideration; every one person prepares to win honour to himself, ambition stimulating their fortitude . . . But their most prevailing encouragement in battle is that because no man should be thought to fight for base hire, or out of servile obedience for another man's honour, but only for his own reputation, the plunder is equally divided among them all. They go to war, as if they had devoted themselves for victory, with a certain resolution, either to overcome or to die. From whence proceeds great obstinacy in combat.[36]

The factors which made for the strength of the Oromo society in the previous century were becoming a source of weakness for a society which had spread over such a large area. When the Oromo were on the move, fighting for individual honor unleashed a dynamic spirit to push forward; but once they began settling down, fighting for individual honor became the source of conflict among themselves. When common interest united them, they were a terror to their enemies. With their spread over wider territory, it became very difficult to reconcile the interests of various groups. Clan interest replaced the wider interest of the confederacy. Disharmony undermined their unity and their fighting capacity. With the break-up of confederacies, different groups fought against each other as much as they fought their enemies. By turning against each other, they gave some breathing-space to their enemies, and encouraged the rebellion of their subject people. By the beginning of the seventeenth century, Oromo social organization was starting to break down; a contemporary historian has explained it in terms of the will of God. "If God had not blinded them and willed that certain families and tribes among them should be at war with one another constantly, there would not have been an inch of land in the empire, of which they are not masters."[37] While the Oromo strength was consumed in their own quarrels, their enemies rejoiced in the important discovery of the weakness. It was Susenyos who, through his long contact with the Oromo, made the discovery and tried to turn it to his own advantage.[38] In less than ten years, Susenyos managed to widen the division among the Oromo. This was a considerable political achievement, unmatched in the history of the Christian kingdom during the previous half-century. For example, in his report of July 22, 1607, the Jesuit Azevedo spoke of the "great concern the Galla had on matters of interest to them."[39] By 1614 some sections of the Oromo groups had already broken away from the nation and became loyal subjects of Susenyos. This was the result of his calculated policy aimed at weakening the unity and widening the division among the Oromo. On the one hand, he followed a policy of administering a "quick, sharp shock" to a weak Oromo group, thus forcing it into submission; while on the other hand, in any conflict between two or more Oromo groups, he extended protection to the weak one, thus encouraging the latter to break away from the body of the Oromo nation. We have many examples of this in this chronicle. Perhaps the best one is the following. In 1612, Susenyos decided to punish the restless small Oromo group called Warantisha. He ordered full mobilization and attacked the Warantisha at the time when they least expected it. The unsuspecting men were massacred, their women and children and cattle were taken captive by the victorious king, and the survivors fled in disarray.[40] The dispossessed and weakened Warantisha had to replace their lost stock for their survival. They were too weak to attack the Borana, and too enfeebled to cross the Abbay to loot Gojjam. They had no alternative but to turn against their brethren the Ittu, who came all the way from Charachar to help them. The Ittu were suddenly caught off balance and looted. It took some time before they had gathered strength to repay the Warantisha in kind. The Warantisha appealed to the Christian leadership for help. In 1612, Susenyos had devastated the Warantisha, and two years later, although they had neither the love for him nor the desire to ask him for help, they were forced to appeal to him owing to the pressure on them from other Oromo groups. Susenyos, who appears to have understood the cause of their restlessness, was quick to grasp the opportunity and supported the Warantisha in the struggle against other Oromo. He made a bold and brilliant attempt to drive the Warantisha's enemies out of Walaqa; the attempt failed and he therefore moved the entire Warantisha with their cattle across the Abbay in 1614 and settled them in key strategic positions, where they became a secure bulwark against other Oromo attacks on Gojjam. Although Oromo unity was still strong from time to time, the clash of interest produced conflicts too wide and too deep to be closed by the political discussion at the traditional *chafe* assembly. The conflicts spread, owing to the breakdown of the confederacies and the insensitivity of individual groups to the interest of the others.

After settling the Warantisha in Gojjam, Susenyos had other opportunities to settle a considerable number of Oromo in the region west of the Abbay. It was this group who settled among the Christian Amharas and furnished the state with an inexhaustible number of soldiers against other Oromo. In short, internal conflicts were the cause for the breakdown of Oromo unity which had been maintained earlier by the remarkable gada system. External as well as internal factors worked against the proper functioning of the gada, including the topography of the land, the differentiation in wealth, and the rapid increase in population. The three factors were more pronounced among the Matcha by the beginning of the seventeenth century than in any other Oromo group. First, the Matcha lived in "much more mountainous and inaccessible [land],"[41] which hindered contact between groups. The *chafe* assembly functioned on the basis of contact among people, during which differences were resolved and disputes settled in open discussion. The differentiation in wealth, other than cattle, was brought about among the Matcha through the enterprising activities of merchants and landowners. On occupying the fertile land between Ennarya and the Abbay, the Matcha realized that it would be advantageous to maintain caravan routes to and from Ennarya. They depended on the routes that passed through their land for salt, cloth, and other essential commodities. The whirlwind of activity let loose by the Matcha arrival in the region temporarily diminished the volume of trade. Nevertheless, the small but aggressive merchant community in the kingdom had a vested interest in the lucrative trade in gold, ivory, slaves, and other items with Ennarya and beyond. Both Susenyos and Banaro had a vested interest in continuing the trade, and with their encouragement and support merchants organized large caravans. Since the trade which passed through the Matcha territory primarily benefited the elite within Matcha society, they actively supported and protected it. The benefits from trade, in the form of both liberal gifts – for protection and for prominent persons – and taxes at key posts went to a limited number of individuals. The key posts and passes at which important Matcha men taxed the caravans in 1613 were probably already hereditary; in 1845, Plowden wrote that "Some rights of duty in different markets have descended in certain families from father to son . . . perhaps to seven or eight generations."[42] If we take a generation as thirty years, and count back eight generations, the practice goes back to the beginning of the century under discussion.[43] Some wealthy Matcha individuals who championed the cause of commerce and provided extensive protection to many merchants were themselves owners of extensive land. Perhaps the richest of them all was a certain Amuma. His power and prestige rested on his wealth and not his position within the *chafe* assembly. He was part of an emerging class that effectively eclipsed the prestige and usurped the traditional authority of the *chafe* assembly. Amuma was the *de facto* leader for the Oromo groups which lived between Bali and Hadiya.[44] His favor and protection were sought by merchants as well as by the Muslim ruler of Hadiya, the Christian governor of Gojjam, and by Susenyos himself. Information on the prestige and power of Amuma was related to Almeida by Father Fernandez, whose life Amuma saved in 1614.

The emperor's messenger Baharo asked him if he knew another Galla called Amuma, a great man and a close friend of his. The Galla replied that he was his servant and that his master was near at hand. They promised him a valuable reward if he would go and call him quickly, and they promised Amuma that they would give him a horse if he would come, Amuma came within the hour and with his coming their fears and all danger were at an end. He was a great and powerful man; he assumed responsibility for the father and ambassador and all their men and took them under his protection. So none of the Moors of the country dared to take up arms against them.[45]

The emergence of wealthy men like Amuma undercut the effectiveness of the *chafe* assembly from within. It was they, more than the voice of the majority, who had effect at the assembly. Decisions were made in their favor, sometimes going against the interest of the larger group, by the assembly which was supposed to defend that interest. War was fought in the name of the assembly but for the benefit of the new class. A good example is again what Amuma did in 1615. Alico, the Muslim ruler of Alaba, had given a number of his daughters in marriage to some important Oromo leaders,[46] perhaps including Amuma himself. Alico was an ambitious man who wanted to expand his territory. Amuma, too, was an ambitious man, who wanted to assert his authority over a large territory. Perhaps at the instigation and on behalf of Amuma, and certainly with the support of Amuma's kinsmen, Alico was deposed by his own cousin in 1615.[47] The new leader of Alaba was a meek and docile person who was amenable to the manipulation of Amuma.

In short, during the seventeenth century among the Matcha, wealthy individuals were not only making names for themselves, but were becoming hereditary leaders as well, a practice contrary to the established tradition of the gada system. While the gada leaders marched at the head of the Matcha warriors and fought against their enemy, the wealthy individuals were making peace with the same enemy. The best example is Abeko, the wealthiest man among the Liban, who belonged to the Afre confederacy. When Iyasu invaded the land of the Liban, their Abba Gada Dilamo fought against Iyasu, and died like a brave leader.[48] At the very time when Dilamo was fighting against Iyasu, Abeko was sending Iyasu a large gift consisting of numerous cattle, many slaves, and a lot of honey. In return, Iyasu gave a golden saddle to Abeko and decorated his sons with beautiful ornaments.[49]

While the gada leaders marched with men and cattle from pasture to pasture as soon as the forage of a place was consumed, the wealthy individuals settled permanently on the land. Their cattle were looked after by Oromo servants and non-Oromo slaves. The regular movements of the gada leaders seem to have encouraged the transfer of power and authority from one group to another from time to time, while permanent settlement on the land seems to have encouraged the concentration and control of authority in the hands of a few individuals permanently. While the movement in search of forage seems to have diffused the spirit of adventure and the desire to advance into new lands in search of riches, permanent settlement seems to have instilled fear of unknown lands, thus weakening the adventurous spirit of conquest that carried the pastoral Oromo over wide territory. While the authority of gada leaders had been based on the voluntary and democratic will of the people, that of the wealthy men was based on their own resources, and it was imposed on others. The gada leaders had been desirous of maintaining the support of the people; the wealthy were eager to dominate them. While the pastoral gada leaders adopted many of the vanquished people as members of their own clan or tribe, with all the rights to share equally in the advantage of any victory, the wealthy men substituted for the noble institution of adoption into the gada system an entirely new element of slavery and servitude of the vanquished people. Most of the conquered people who earlier had submitted with little or no resistance to the Matcha found that they were no longer equal members of a clan within which they were incorporated, but slaves of the wealthy, and were used as gifts and commodities for sale. The conquered people, whose pride was humbled in the dust of slavery, and whose number was reduced through sale, realized that the only hope of safety was open rebellion against their arrogant masters. One result was a celebrated uprising of conquered people against the Matcha, in the region between Ennarya and the Abbay. However, before this interesting episode is described, it is necessary to mention two points; first, the effect of the rapid population increase on the gada system, and second, the background to the uprising of the conquered people.

As we have seen, the Matcha spread over a wide area within three to four decades. Their campaign was stopped in the south by the people of Ennarya, to the east by the people of Hadiya, Gurage, Kambata, and Janjero; to the north the Abbay provided a natural barrier which mitigated the effect of their sudden attack on Gojjam, while at the same time saving them from the rapid pursuit of Christian forces. To the west they found extensive land with a thinly scattered population. Without enemies to impede their progress, they spread over the fertile land, reaching the western part of present Wallaga Province, which "they sanctified by making Walal their sacred mountain." [50] The beautiful mountain of the region, which resembles mount Walal in Walabu, the region of Borana dispersal in the early sixteenth century, aroused nostalgia for the Borana's original homeland.

> When the [Matcha] who did not forget the mountains of Walabu in their oral tradition looked at this wonderful mountain which stood silhouetted pointing up to the sky like a pole from the surrounding region, it aroused their longing for their ancient region . . . They named this mountain as Walal . . . made it the holy region . . . [for butta ceremony as well as for the chafe assembly]. [51]

Throughout this vast area the Matcha lived among the conquered people, who probably outnumbered them nine to one, [52] a ratio which seems to have quickened the pace of the internal changes of the gada system. [53] Finally, these three factors, the mountainous nature and the inaccessibility of the Matcha country, the emergence of a new class, and the sudden conquest of a huge non-Oromo population, presented the Matcha gada with serious problems. Whether it was owing to these factors or others, the Afre and the Sadacha were at war with each other between 1616 and 1618. The intensity and bitterness of the conflict, which led to the break-up of the common *chafe* at Oda Bisil, is well preserved in the tradition of the Afre as well as the Sadacha. Understandably, the tradition of each group tends to blame the other for the break-up of the common *chafe*, but both traditions agree that the originators of the conflict were "bad" individuals who, against the advice and wisdom of the assembly, destroyed Matcha unity. The sources give several names of the "bad" individuals, all of them wealthy and newly emerging leaders who turned Matcha against each other. Perhaps the most notorious person whom the Afre tradition condemns is a certain Na'aa Doro, who is reported to have burned Oda Bisil.

> When Na'a burned Oda Bisil out of madness . . . the Tulama come to attack the Matcha. Na'a fought and drove back the Tulama to where they came from. Na'a then advised the Afre to spread in different directions. So the Guduru took one direction, Horro took another. Sibu took one direction and Limmu took another . . . So every tribe took different directions and moved out of Oda Bisil.[54]

From the content of the tradition, it seems that Na'aa Doro wielded more power than an ordinary Abba Gada would have possessed. He led the Afre in their fight against the Sadacha and the Tulama. It was during one of his engagements with the Sadacha that he burned Oda Bisil. He burned the sacred land, where all gada rituals were performed and where the assembly was held. Perhaps Na'aa Doro was a defeated Afre leader. In the tradition, he is referred to as a "madman," which probably should not be taken literally as it only implies that he acted in an extraordinary way not acceptable to the assembly. The tradition claims that Na'aa defeated the Tulama. But this does not seem to have been the case. On the contrary, there is evidence that the Afre, oppressed by the combined force of the Sadacha and the Tulama, were forced to withdraw from the region of Oda Bisil.[55] The main reason which led to the break-up of the Matcha central *chafe* (according to one authority) was the shortage of land around the *chafe*. "The fertile land around Oda Bisil was not wide enough for both the animal and human population."[56] Be that as it may, while the Matcha were fighting among themselves, they were suddenly engulfed by the rebellion of their own subjects.

Even as early as the time of the Bifole gada (1546–1554), Bahrey reported that the Oromo had made the conquered people *gabare*.[57] But neither Bahrey nor any other Christian source mentions anything about the rebellion of the conquered people before 1618. Hence, we take the latter date as the start of the rebellion. The term *gabare* describes the obligatory relation between the conquerors and the conquered. The vanquished, still owners of their plot of land, became serfs or clients of the pastoral Oromo, who now demanded service and tribute from them. The Oromo term for the conquered people was *gabbaro* ("those who serve"). The Oromo adopted the *gabbaro en masse*, giving them clan genealogy, marrying their women, and taking their young into service for herding. Simultaneously, adult men were recruited for military service in times of war, and worked on the land in time of peace. While *gabbaro* was the common term used for describing conquered people, other terms were also used in a different place. For example, both the Barentu and the Tulama used the term *dhalatta* ("he who is born") to describe the status of the conquered people. The phrase "he who is born" does not have anything to do with real birth. It only describes the ideal type of relationship that should exist between the conquered and the conquerors after the latter adopted the former. The special role of adoption within the gada system, as well as its effect on the success of Oromo migration, has been shown in the previous chapter.[58] What we need to add here is that the "adoption ceremony was performed before the whole people and sacrifices were offered."[59] The central figure, the Abba Gada, slaughtered the sacrificial animal, led the prayers, and concluded the binding oath on both sides. The adopted individuals or groups now became collectively the "sons" of the *gossa* (clan or tribe) by whom they were adopted. In other words, they were now "born" into a new *gossa*. The Oromo term *dhalatta* describes this type of unusual birth. Instead of *dhalatta*, the Matcha used the direct and simpler term *ilma gossa* ("the sons of the *gossa*"). However, the Christian historians of the seventeenth century wrote *ilma guozit*, instead of *ilma gossa*, causing some confusion for later historians.[60] The Matcha also used another more popular and prestigious term, *yahabata* ("those who are mounted"). The Matcha used *yahabata* to distinguish the *gabbaro* cavalry from other ordinary *gabbaro*. The term describes the brave *gabbaro* who swelled the ranks of the Matcha cavalry. Probably earlier it was with the support of the *yahabata* that the Matcha won victories against numerous enemies. It was not without reason that the rebellions of the *gabbaro* were led by the *yahabata*.

When the rights of the *gabbaro* were trampled upon, their women and children sold into slavery by their Oromo masters (who tasted the material benefit of the trade), the *yahabata* rebelled all over the Matcha land. The conflict among the Matcha added fuel to the fire of their rebellion. The incitement from the governor of Gojjam and that of Ennarya gave self-confidence to the *gabbaro*. Tradition claims that the *gabbaro* rebellion was preceded by a peaceful protest.[61] The Matcha failed to react to the demands. As the patience of the *gabbaro* was exhausted, swords were drawn and the first Matcha head that rolled down became the signal for the declaration of war. From that day, the *gabbaro* renounced their servitude to the Matcha and decided to liberate themselves. The news of the *gabbaro* rebellion was received with jubilation at the courts of both Sela Christos, Governor of Gojjam, and of Banaro. "During the rainy season (1618) a great conflict broke between the Galla and the yahabata of the Borana. They fought bitterly because God sent them Satan who caused them to err and destroyed the wall of love between them."[62] Sela Christos had his own plan to build a new wall of love between the *yahabata* and the Christians. As a result of the conflict, the Matcha found themselves spread over a vast area among enemies more numerous than themselves. Tradition claims that the Matcha panicked and made considerable political concessions to the *gabbaro*.[63] The same tradition claims that the *gabbaro* rebellion was led by a certain Kuti Bose, a brave *gabbaro* who is reported to have killed five elephants.[64] It claimed that Kuti struggled to gain the right of forming a separate gada assembly for the *gabbaro*. Kuti was killed while fighting.[65] The same tradition claims that the cause for which Kuti died was immediately realized. The Matcha granted the *gabbaro* the political right to form their own assembly. If true, this was a major victory for the *gabbaro* and a great concession on the part of the Matcha. We cannot verify this claim from other written sources of the time. However, two things can be said with certainty. First, whether it was as a result of this rebellion or not, we find two assemblies in all the Matcha country after this time. One assembly was called Borana *chafe* (for the "true" Matcha) and the other the *gabbaro chafe* (for the conquered people).[66] Secondly, the name of Kuti Bose is immortalized in the tradition of all the *gabbaro* as "a hero of the oppressed." From this, it would appear that he was probably an important leader at the initial stage of the rebellion. Be that as it may, the policy of concession failed to conciliate the *gabbaro*, either because it came too late or because it merely encouraged them to fight. The hope of military support from both Gojjam and Ennarya may have hardened the attitude of the *gabbaro*, whose military challenge brought a sense of realism to the Matcha. Since the *gabbaro* rebelled against both the Afre and the Sadacha, the two groups made peace with each other. They forgot their recent quarrels and became fused together with a new spirit of self-preservation which never left them until the danger was over. Convinced by experience that it was an opportune moment to make peace with the Tulama,[67] the Matcha appealed to the latter for help. The Tulama's response was quick and positive. Both the Tulama and the Matcha acknowledged their past errors and assessed the present danger. They agreed to settle (albeit temporarily) their dispute peacefully and declared that they were at peace with each other.[68] The *gabbaro* seem not to have expected such a turn of events. The capacity of the Matcha to compromise was found to be greater than the determination of the *gabbaro* to fight alone. The news of the arrival of the Tulama to assist the Matcha seems to have spread terror among the *gabbaro*. With one voice they acknowledged that their only hope of safety was to call upon Sela Christos to come and move them across the Abbay. "Behold we have quarrelled with our masters the Galla. We have fought them until we have both shed blood. Come quickly and receive us for from old our origins and descent is from you and not from the Galla."[69]

Sela Christos was animated by the prospect of easy victory, while the hope of rich booty excited the valor of his soldiers. Only a few years before his soldiers had refused to follow him across the Abbay into Bizamo. But now they were too impatient to wait until the end of the rainy season. Sela Christos was not carried away by his soldiers' passion for immediate marching on Bizamo. He respected his men's desire to march, but decided to follow them with cautious step.

> Ras Sela Christos sent Asgadir, his general, with a large number of soldiers in order to receive the yahabata and fight the Galla. Dajazmach Buko also crossed

65

> the Abbay with a large number of his soldiers. The two commanders met in Damot from where they went to Bizamo. Here the yahabata and ilma guozit [ilma gossa] were delighted by their arrival and they all fought against Chalya and Obo. They massacred many and captured their children, women and cattle.[70]

The Chalya and the Obo were taken by surprise. It seems they only saw the enemy in their settlement and were warned of their danger by the sound of enemy cavalry. In a moment, this changed the fortune of the Matcha groups. Panic produced disorder; disorder was followed by flight and utter confusion. In their flight, the Matcha lost the greatest part of the booty which they had taken from the *gabbaro* earlier. As they flushed their soldiers with confidence, Asgadir and Buko won the day with little or no loss to their men. The easily gained victory and booty transformed the day into an occasion of great jubilation. This victory was won without cost "because the yahabata who knew the topography of the land, as well as the secret dwelling place of Chalya and Obo led the Christian force to the spot."[71] With the assistance of expert *yahabata* guides, nothing could remain inaccessible; resistance was suicidal and submission was equally fatal to the Matcha. Only flight held any hope for survival.

Asgadir and Buko sent messages of congratulation to Sela Christos. The latter was delighted with the news. But still he moved cautiously. His experience of the past seven years as the governor of Gojjam had taught him not to leave his province on the spur of the moment. His experience seemed to inspire him to ensure first the safety of his province. Thus, before crossing the Abbay, he wrote to Susenyos, asking him to come to Gojjam.

> The Galla and Yahabata have quarrelled and fought, and . . . there is no peace between them and they no longer live together. As a result, I am going to receive the Yahabata and ilma quozit, and also to fight with the Galla . . . come soon to Gojjam, before the Tulama comes to assist the Matcha, as we assist the Yahabata. Please, come to help us and reach us soon.[72]

Two points can be made from the above. First, before their quarrel, the Matcha and the *gabbaro* seem to have lived in peace, to the discomfiture of the Christian kingdom. Secondly, Sela Christos knew that the Tulama would come to assist the Matcha. The governor knew that the Tulama would attack Gojjam so as to relieve the pressure on the Matcha in Bizamo. That must have been the reason he urged Susenyos to come to Gojjam. Armed with Susenyos's assurance, Sela Christos crossed the Abbay around November 20, 1618, at the head of a large army.[73] After a rapid march, he arrived in Bota land where he was warmly welcomed by the two victorious commanders and the multitudes of the *gabbaro*. After indulging the *gabbaro* with splendid feasts,[74] he turned his attention to the Matcha, whose strength was increased by a stream of Tulama volunteers. The news of Sela Christos's arrival soon spread terror among the Matcha, who fled in fear. By their flight, the Matcha had time and again saved themselves from destruction, but this time their flight increased their calamities. Hot pursuit and devastation was the only measure which could restore the confidence of the *gabbaro* and vindicate the honor of the Christian leadership. The *gabbaro*, who forgot their earlier peaceful relations with the Matcha and remembered only their late quarrel with them, put at the disposal of Sela Christos their knowledge of the topography of the land and their large cavalry. Sela Christos took the Matcha by surprise, but killed only a few and captured little booty, because the majority had fled before the attack. The next day he left Bota land at dawn and surprised the Matcha in their forest hideout at a place called Gogatta.

> There he attacked and massacred the brave men of Chalya and Obo, and captured their women, children and cattle . . . He ordered the yahabata cavalry to pursue the flying Chalya and Obo, who escaped from destruction. They followed and met them in the land of Jiran, where a lot of the Matcha were killed and a large number of their women, children and cattle were taken captives . . . Few days later, he sent another commando unit against the Obo, who fled on the first sight of the Christian force, abandoning everything. The victorious soldiers captured Galla women, children and cattle, more than the eye could see.[75]

On this occasion the abilities of Sela Christos were found to be even greater than he had demonstrated in the past seven years as the governor of Gojjam. He did not waste time on unnecessary caution. Unlike his previous engagements, he was not disposed to sacrifice any solid advantages to avoid risk. Sensible of the benefits which would result from quick action, he ably directed the valor of his soldiers and the *yahabata* desire for revenge against the flying Matcha. By their flight, the Matcha only encouraged the hardy and fast *yahabata* cavalry to terrorize and disconcert them, everywhere inflicting wounds on the back of the flying enemy.[76]

The Matcha found themselves under attack from two directions. As Sela Christos marched south through Bizamo, everywhere destroying and looting the Matcha, Banaro, the ruler of Ennarya, marched north through Konch, everywhere slaughtering them.[77] Banaro accomplished feats too hard for any Christian force a few years earlier. "Banaro fought against the Galla called Hakako, whom he destroyed. He captured their children, women and cattle. He completely wiped out their adult men."[78] The victorious Banaro probably caused more havoc among the Sadacha than Sela Christos had among the Afre. This may be one of the reasons why the Sadacha avoided meeting Banaro in the field, while the Afre continued to put up resistance from time to time. In short, the Matcha were now attacked and pursued on both sides by the allied forces of Gojjam and Ennarya. The flower of their youth perished and the bulk of their cattle was looted. The Afre had neither safety nor much property left in Bizamo. Under the shock of repeated massacre, the Afre abandoned Bizamo for Sela Christos and fled *en masse* to the vast land west of Bizamo, where Sela Christos was unable to follow them. In this flight alone the Afre had a solid advantage over Sela Christos. With whatever cattle they had, the Afre marched several days' journey through the deep forests of the west, where they seem to have supplemented their meagre supply of flesh and milk with abundant wild fruit and game.

> The fact that they do not sow is of great use to them in that the Abyssinians cannot penetrate far into their country; when the Gallas know that they are invading with a strong army they retire with their cattle many days journey into the interior. The Abyssinians therefore never seize, or can seize supplies, and are thus compelled to withdraw to their own territories, often with heavy losses of men from sheer hunger.[79]

The sudden dispersal of the Afre had the intended effect upon Sela Christos. Since farming was abandoned in Bizamo during the unsettled years of conflict, Sela Christos could not find provisions either to buy or to loot. For fear of effecting reconciliation between the Afre and the *gabbaro*, the latter were not looted. The shortage of provisions seems to have diffused a spirit of restlessness among his soldiers. The connection between hunger and rebellion was so strong that the slightest exposure to this deadly enemy would have exposed Sela Christos to danger.[80] Thus after six days' stay in Bizamo the governor abandoned the land he had won from the Afre and "returned to the land of Bota, where he previously left his provisions."[81] The *gabbaro* for whose cause he had imposed so much devastation upon the Afre thought of only one thing – the Matcha revenge if they were to remain in Bizamo. They asked Sela Christos to take them across the Abbay. He gladly accepted them, since it was part of his strategy to strengthen the defenses of his provinces by settling them in key places on the other side of the Abbay. He was generous in moving them with all their cattle, women, children, and arms in hand, but his liberality was accompanied by one vigorous condition. They were to be settled where he wanted it and not where they chose. They were conducted without delay, and when their strength was collected on the other side of the Abbay, their new settlement assumed the atmosphere of a solid and dependable fortification for the defense of the region. Their swift horses and unquestionable hatred for the Matcha excited the pride of Susenyos and elated the hopes of the Christians for the safety of their land. In the words of the chronicler:

> The emperor was delighted with his achievements and received him with honour, for his victory against the Galla, and for bringing the yahabata . . . The emperor went from Baguna and chose from Wambarma a large and beautiful land convenient for horse racing and for military parade. There he ordered that each of his soldiers should carry shield and spear and all should organize themselves in chifra according to their origin as if they were going to battle. The cavalry appeared in full battle dress. The yahabata were stunned with the number of his soldiers and impressed with the quantity and quality of their weapons. Then the yahabata greeted him with humility and signs of submission and subjugation. The emperor said to them, "Thanks to God who saved you from death and liberated you from the servitude of your Galla masters. In the land of Christianity you are now free. Accept Christ so that we all will be equal in his kingdom." From among the yahabata some said, "Let it be according to your words." Others said, "Leave us until we complete the period of gueta [butta ceremony] so that our laws would not be transgressed untimely" . . . He organized them in Machakal, Emfesya, Badene, Arbuke and Yemakal.[82]

The purpose of this grand show was to impress upon the *yahabata* that

Susenyos was mighty – much more powerful than their earlier Matcha masters. In that respect, it was particularly successful. The *yahabata* were baptized and they increased the size of the Catholic population in the country. But there are two points worth considering in some detail from the above quotation. The first is about *gueta* (*butta*) and the second about Wambarma and Wambarya, the two districts where the entire *gabbaro* people were settled.

We have already seen that the *butta* ceremony (which is generally referred to as *gueta* in the Christian literature) was performed after every forty years by the gada class going out of power.[83] This was done at the time of the *jarra* ceremony, which concluded the end of the previous eight-year gada period, and signaled the start of the next eight-year period, with the coming to power of new gada leaders. Thus, the *jarra* ceremony was the time at which the two pivotal ceremonies within the Oromo society intersected in time and space. In the above quotation, we have seen how some *yahabata* requested Susenyos not to baptize them before they performed their *butta* ceremony, that is, their fortieth year in the gada cycle.[84] We do not know from our source whether or not Susenyos had granted the *yahabata* the short delay they requested before they were baptized but we do know that a new Matcha gada came to office shortly after. This was the Kilole gada (1618–1626). What is important to note here is that those *yahabata* who wanted to perform their *butta* were already part of the complex gada system. Culturally, and probably linguistically, too, the *yahabata* may have had much more in common with their Matcha enemies than with their new masters. Shortly after, whether it was owing to this or other factors, some *yahabata* reconciled themselves with the Matcha and returned to Bizamo. This alarmed Susenyos so much that he quickly moved all the *yahabata* from the two districts and settled them in Bagamder and central Gojjam in the midst of a predominantly Christian Amhara population. However, in 1618, Susenyos settled all the *yahabata* in Wambarya and Wambarma and other districts bordering along the Abbay. The obvious reason for doing so was that he wanted them to act as a shield against the Matcha incursion from across Bizamo. The *yahabata* were excellent horsemen and brave fighters and above all they had a unique advantage: because of their long association with the Matcha they knew their war tactics as well as the likely time they would make raids. Thus, it was easy for the *yahabata* to intercept the Matcha raiding party before it caused any damage. However, the deeper reason for settling the *yahabata* in the districts mentioned above is given indirectly by his own chronicler.[85] The Agaw inhabitants of these districts were either sold into slavery or exterminated in the continuous slaving raids which Susenyos and his governor of Gojjam had conducted between 1607 and 1616. This does not mean that there were no slaving raids in the region before the time of Susenyos. Indeed Sarsa Dengel, Za-Dengel, and Ya'eqob had all conducted slaving raids in the same area, but Susenyos intensified it out of all proportion. As with the Gafat people in western Shawa during the reign of Sarsa Dengel, so the Agaw inhabitants of the two districts were the victims of devastating slaving raids. Susenyos came to the throne officially for the second time in 1607.[86] He had no sooner done so than he took a decision which was bound to depopulate these districts. The Agaw inhabitants of the area lacked military organization as well as political unity. Owing to this they were unable to marshal their resources and to defend themselves. For reasons unclear from our sources, they were unskilled in the arts of constructing or defending established fortifications. They had few cavalry. Their small and badly organized war bands were easily dispersed, even by the Matcha, who were not as well armed as Susenyos.[87] Thus, when Susenyos's men suffered any loss among the Agaw, it was probably occasioned more by the quarrels of his men over booty than from the enemy missiles. It was probably owing to this weakness of the Agaw that Susenyos time and again led his restless soldiers to their favorite amusement of plundering the Agaw. The first act of Susenyos's reign in 1607 was to raid the Agaws of the area. The purpose of this raid was to replenish the exhausted imperial treasury and to buy the loyalty of his growing army by liberal gifts of cattle and slaves. He was conscious of the economic difficulties which his court had faced at Qoga. The provinces under his control were exhausted and the gold from Ennarya was inaccessible at the time. He probably knew both the weakness and the wealth of the Agaw and forgot about the effect of his action on them, remembering the immediate necessity of supplying his soldiers. Accordingly, he devastated the Agaw districts of Wambarya and Wambarma with insatiable thirst for slaves and merciless determination against those who resisted him. Such sad spectacles were repeated a number of times between 1607 and 1616.

> The raids of 1610, like those of 1607 and 1608, extended from Alafa to the west of Dambiya. All the way south to the camps of the Gonga refugees along the Blue Nile. The long procession of captives, consisting mainly of women and children as they were driven into Qoga, is movingly described by Paez. His intercession gained freedom for almost 12,000 of them, but his warning that these raids were opening the way to the Galla, who were massed on the other side of the Blue Nile went unheeded. The 1614 expedition against all the Agaw of Gojjam, allegedly brought by their lawlessness and insubordination, was particularly destructive. The Agaw of Achafar considerably debilitated and reduced by earlier raids abandoned their homes and sought refuge among other Agaw of Chara and the Shanqela of Matakal, to which district the emperor followed. Not contented with the cattle and slaves he and his soldiers acquired in the province . . . So many cattle were taken in this . . . that they offended the eye. Many men and women slaves . . . were captured. There was much rejoicing in the camp because of the large quantity of takings. There is not a man in the army of the king, who did not from the spoils then taken come into possession of cattle and slaves . . . And the king made gifts of all the cattle which were taken to those who had caught them. As for the slaves, he reserved for himself and did (with them) as he wanted.[88]

It was this type of slaving raid which was the immediate cause of the depopulation of the Agaw districts opposite Bizamo. Susenyos made war against the Oromo almost a regular job of his soldiers. To finance the war, he introduced systematic and methodical plundering of the pagan minorities and raised cruelty to the "art" of government. In the process, he left behind him in the districts of Wambarya and Wambarma carnage unprecedented in the history of the Agaw people. The cattle and slaves which Susenyos captured were employed in buying the loyalty of his formidable army. In other words, the conquest of the pastoral Oromo was the object of his hopes and preparation; but he ruined the Agaw without achieving anything. It is no exaggeration to state that the wars which the Matcha conducted from Bizamo into Wambarya and Wambarma and other districts along the Abbay for almost three decades before Susenyos came to power were much less destructive than the slaving raids which were conducted between 1607 and 1616 by the Christian emperor.

The fall of Ennarya

In 1618 Banaro was marching to the north through the district of Konch (see map 5, p. 28) to continue with his devastating war against the Sadacha. He was marching towards Bizamo with the hope of meeting with Sela Christos. While *en route* Banaro received a letter from Sela Christos which contained an urgent message. "I have crossed the Abbay from Gojjam and I am in Bizamo to fight against the Galla. Come and join us so that we destroy them together."[89] Apparently, the letter was written before Sela Christos fought with the Afre. Banaro, whose preparation for the war against the Matcha impressed everyone, including Sela Christos, was on his way to Bizamo when he received the news that the latter had left Bizamo because of the shortage of provisions.[90] Banaro changed his direction and continued with his fight against the Sadacha. The Sadacha were either unwilling to meet with him in the field or unable to stop him, and abandoned the districts of Konch and Shat and fled across the Gibe into Damot. By arms, diplomacy, and gifts, Banaro attracted a number of *yahabata* warriors to his standard. Satisfied with the discovery of his own strength and the weakness of his enemy, animated with the prospect of winning even more *yahabata* warriors to his cause, Banaro returned to Ennarya at the head of an army enlarged by the *yahabata* warriors and encumbered with the Sadacha captives and booty.

Banaro, who seems to have been intoxicated with his victory beyond the boundary of Ennarya, soon led his second expedition against the Sadacha. He passed through Konch, Shat, and to Choman Swamp without meeting any resistance from the Sadacha. He then crossed into Damot, where he met with stiffer resistance than he had reason to expect from the fleeing Sadacha. The stream of Tulama volunteers who came to help the Sadacha joined hands with the latter and answered Banaro's challenge. They put up a resistance worthy of their name. After a number of engagements, Banaro was forced to withdraw from Damot. He was satisfied neither with his men's performance nor with the outcome of the expedition. Perhaps at the suggestion of his captains, or else by his own decision, Banaro did not return to Ennarya. Instead, he marched towards the edge of the Abbay valley, where he surprised and massacred a number of small Sadacha groups. In his own words, "I went up to Warab and fought the Borana and killed a great number of them, captured their women, children and cattle. As a result, many yahabata cavalry and infantry surrendered to me."[91] This was contained in a message Banaro sent to Susenyos in early 1619. Shortly after, Banaro met Susenyos and delighted him with his gold tribute. "Banaro ... brought tribute of gold, together with his son whose name was Yaman Christos. He said to the king, 'Oh, my Lord! Here is your tribute of gold as well as my son, your servant!'"[92]

It was at the moment of his triumphal return to Ennarya, at the height of his power, that Banaro took a step which had all the appearance of success, but because of the circumstances failed to materialize, culminating in his tragic end. To the people of Ennarya it was the defense of their own country which was important.[93] To Banaro, it seems the defense of Ennarya could not be guaranteed without the conquest of the Sadacha in the surrounding districts. His main objective was to conquer the Matcha in the surrounding districts. This difference in outlook on matters of defense had unexpected consequences. It alienated Banaro from his people. To them, it seems it was the price which Banaro's policy involved that counted most. To Banaro, no price was too high to strengthen the defense of Ennarya. For a man who probably came to power by force, and certainly had strong political enemies,[94] this was an unnecessary gamble, but he did not stop here. Banaro proposed to Sela Christos a joint offensive against the Borana.[95] He did this not only for policy considerations but because he also wanted to strengthen his ties with the governor of Gojjam. Although he was at the height of his power, Banaro was conscious of the activities of his internal enemies. His exceptionally good relations with both Susenyos and Sela Christos were thus intended to frighten and disarm his enemies. In 1619, Banaro sent messages and gifts to the court of Sela Christos in Gojjam. The gifts, for which the people of Ennarya must have been taxed,[96] were intended to win favor and the friendship of the governor. In the same year, Banaro himself took the annual tribute of Ennarya directly to Susenyos. Double taxation may have angered the people, since they accused him of exploiting them. This was his undoing, and yet at the cost of incurring even deeper public hatred, Banaro continued to flatter Sela Christos with his liberality. The governor of Gojjam was impressed not only with Banaro's gold, but also with his bold proposal for the conquest of the Borana.[97] This animated Sela Christos, who soon entertained a grand project aimed at "the recovery of Damot and the Gafat districts beyond the Blue Nile,"[98] an idea which was buried with Sarsa Dengel in 1597. However, before the project was carried out, it was to be superseded by events which changed the course of history.[99]

It was probably Banaro's bad luck that the usual weakness of the Christian leadership and the ability of the Oromo to recover after defeat converged at a critical moment when he expected swift action. The Afre, who in 1618 dispersed and disappeared from Bizamo, regrouped and appeared with strength at the beginning of 1620. Sela Christos soon received an intelligence report which claimed that "the Matcha wanted to attack Gojjam and Ennarya."[100]

Alarmed, Sela Christos appealed to Susenyos for immediate assistance. The latter quickly mobilized his force and arrived in Gojjam. Their two forces met at the confluence of the Bir and Qachamo rivers, where they discovered that the news about the Matcha attack on Gojjam was false.

> Both have agreed not to cross the Abbay by raft towards Bizamo, because of the number of their soldiers. They said, "It will take us more than seven days to cross the river, and if the Galla hear we are coming to attack them they will have seven days' start in removing their cattle and property. We will not be able to find them as they can go wherever they like."[101]

These few lines sum up the hidden strength of the Matcha. Whenever the Matcha got wind of an enemy's movement they dispersed and disappeared into their forests covering several days' journey, where their enemy could not follow them. Dispersal and disappearance were part of the strategy by which they minimized casualties, even when they were vigorously pursued by a strong enemy. This was one of the reasons they were able to regroup and come back with strength. The Matcha bands usually consisted of six to eight thousand men.[102] Even if an entire band was massacred (which had happened many times), the loss to the strength of the whole group was not so great. Any misfortune to one band was the signal for a general dispersal of the whole group over many days' journey. The mobility of the Matcha bands, the unpredictability of their attack and retreat, their flight in the face of danger all added to reduce the damage to them. Christian forces usually moved in large numbers and their movement was slow and predictable. Any Christian victory usually lulled their own people into a sense of false security. It was at such a moment, when their enemies least expected it, that the Matcha attacked and caused considerable damage. There are many good examples of this in the chronicle of Susenyos. Perhaps the best one is the following. Within eight days from when Susenyos and Sela Christos separated, thinking that the Matcha were not crossing the Abbay at that time of the year, the Matcha poured on the Gojjam with flood-like speed. They attacked Gojjam on two fronts simultaneously, causing considerable havoc and terror in the province.

> Half of the Matcha have crossed via Guman to attack Gonga and Jigat, Agaw as far as Zigan, Min, Matakal . . . and Dagar. The other half had crossed via Machakal and had camped in the highland. Now I have decided to fight either for life or death. This is the time and hour to come and reach us soon.[103]

Crossing the Abbay at places where they were not expected, coming at a time when they were not expected, and attacking an area which was unguarded, was a complex Matcha strategy which the Christian leadership found it difficult to cope with. It was to overcome this difficulty that the Christian leaders adopted the policy of settling numerous Oromo who "from wars among themselves, have gone over to the king . . . and obtained lands on the banks of the river opposite to the nation they have revolted from, against which they have ever been the securest bulwark."[104]

The governor of Gojjam appealed to Susenyos, and he arrived at Addis

Alem, the headquarters of Sela Christos, at the time when the latter was under heavy Matcha attack. When Susenyos descended on the Matcha like a whirlwind from the hill above Addis Alem

> The Galla fled like animals chased by a lion and they were killed wherever they were found. When the Galla fly, they do not say this is a precipice, this is thorn, but jump upon everything as if it is a plain where there is no obstacle. If it was not for the darkness of the night that covered them, no one would have escaped to tell the tale.[105]

Shortly after this battle, the Tulama came to the support of the Matcha, overrunning and looting almost half of Gojjam, and devastating all the lands inhabited by Shime, Chome, Gafat, and other Agaw tribes.[106] The attack on Gojjam by the Matcha and the Tulama at a few days' interval in separate places was a deliberate common strategy which had three main purposes: first, they wanted to divide and weaken the Christian forces arrayed against the Matcha. Secondly, it seems they wanted to loot the riches of Gojjam to replace the losses they suffered since 1618, and thirdly and most importantly, it seems they wanted to put an end to the alliance between Ennarya and Gojjam, thus isolating the former while harassing the latter. The first two purposes met with varying degrees of success. The third was particularly successful, with tragic consequences for the ruler of Ennarya.

We have seen above that Banaro came to power at a time when Ennarya was under heavy Sadacha attack. By providing dynamic and creative leadership, he was able to save his land from anarchy and disintegration. He restored Ennarya's prosperity and strengthened the defense of the highland area. In both fields he succeeded all too well. Animated by his successes and deceived by the difficulties of the Sadacha, he started attacking them in the neighboring districts. He won repeated victories. These victories had been his personal achievements. He had fought beyond the Gibe until he had reached the edge of the Abbay valley, where no previous governor of Ennarya had ever fought. Between 1618 and 1619, he returned from a number of expeditions with military strength and prestige greater than any previous ruler of Ennarya had ever enjoyed. It was at this moment of triumph that Banaro wanted to extend his conquest to all the Borana. On this issue, he staked the wealth of Ennarya and his prestige. The great stimulus for his project came from the weakness of the Matcha, but the Matcha managed to overcome their weakness. Their alliance with the Tulama dismayed their enemies. The Borana eruption on the Gojjam changed the course of events.

Towards the end of 1619, Banaro sent his son, Yaman Christos, to the governor of Gojjam with a rich gift and a proposal to launch a joint offensive against the Borana. In early 1620, instead of coming back with much-hoped-for good news, Yaman Christos came with two alarming pieces of information from his short visit to the court of Sela Christos. First, the hope of joint action against the Borana was distant and doubtful, as the Borana had put heavy pressure on Gojjam itself. Secondly, and even more alarming, Yaman Christos seems to have told his father that the Sadacha, who had lately fled before his sword, had returned to the surrounding districts of Konch and Shat and that they were agitated with the prospect of revenge and hopes of booty from Ennarya. Either to repeat his earlier victory, or to intimidate the Sadacha, Banaro led his last expedition against them. It is not clear how far he might have gone this time, but he does not appear to have gone beyond the Gibe Ennarya. It seems Banaro had been disappointed by the refusal of his men to go beyond this river. Probably they were persuaded by their experience that the Gibe Ennarya was the only line of defense that could save them against the sudden attack of the Sadacha. Perhaps to show moderation, or suspecting some secret plan against him, Banaro decided not to proceed further, and returned to his court without any engagement with the Sadacha. His political enemies, who condemned him for everything, took this as a sign of weakness and decided to act. The opposition to Banaro was led by a man called Sisgayo, who seems to have been related to the old ruling house which Banaro overthrew in 1611. It is said that Sisgayo's party "had killed [Banaro] by treachery."[107] What this treachery involved is not clear from our sources, but two things can be said with certainty. First, it seems Sisgayo attacked Banaro at an unguarded moment, when the latter probably was accompanied by few of his supporters. Banaro was killed while fighting. We do not know how many of his supporters were killed with him, but we know that some of them hid and saved the life of his son, Yaman Christos. Secondly, the opposition to Banaro seems to have been supported by a large segment of the population. It was probably his heavy taxation which angered the people, on top of his wars beyond the Gibe, which had exhausted their resources.

The sad end of Banaro changed in a moment the dynamic policy that characterized Ennarya between 1611 and 1620. The new leader was not a military man like Banaro, but possessed abilities which enabled him to assess realistically what Ennarya could and could not do. Instead of aspiring to continue with the aggressive policy of his predecessor, Sisgayo limited his attention to the vital defense of highland Ennarya. It seems a number of fortifications built by Banaro in surrounding districts were abandoned. When the party of the dead leader smuggled Yaman Christos to Gojjam, Sisgayo knew that neither Sela Christos nor Susenyos was in any position to restore Yaman Christos to power in Ennarya. Nevertheless, the kind treatment Yaman Christos received at the court of Sela Christos angered Sisgayo, who used it as a pretext for making a veiled attack and warning to Susenyos not to meddle in the affairs of Ennarya.

> They sent a written message saying that "we have killed Banaro because he massacred the people without justice, and amputated the hands and legs of some and pulled out the eyes of others." He showed no mercy even towards the young and old . . . He kept for himself the tribute of the king which he extracted from our houses . . . He enriched himself through rapine and fraud . . . He practised adultery and took wives of others . . . As a woman conceives for nine months and gives birth to a baby in the tenth month . . . we kept in our stomach all his iniquities for nine years and gave birth to his death in the tenth. We killed him because he vigorously continued with the destruction of all the people of

> Ennarya. Instead of the cruel and unjust man, we have appointed a nice and pious man whose name is Sisgayo.[108]

From the content of this bold and insulting letter four things can be said with certainty. First, it seems Banaro was killed by a large number of people. Secondly, it appears that the opposition to Banaro simmered underground for nine years before it exploded in the tenth. Thirdly, it appears that Banaro oppressed the people by heavy taxation, all of which he seems to have used either for financing his aggressive policy against the Sadacha, or for winning favor at the court of the Christian leaders. Fourthly, and most importantly, it also appears that Banaro's wars against the Matcha in the surrounding districts were not popular with the people. It seems the people were persuaded by their past experience and fear to distrust the aggressive policy of Banaro, which sacrificed the lives of the people in the areas far from the frontiers of Ennarya. The choice of a "nice and pious" man to replace a "cruel and oppressive" one was regulated by the difference of their policies. Banaro was a man of war while Sisgayo was a man of peace. Two of the actions which Sisgayo took leave no doubt that he wanted to break with the policy of his predecessors. First, he suspended sending tribute to Susenyos. Secondly, he abandoned fighting with the Sadacha beyond the Gibe Ennarya. Susenyos's reaction to the above letter and the suspension of tribute by Sisgayo was a mixture of an explosion of anger (which he poured out in the following letter) and a pragmatic approach and friendly gesture to Sisgayo.

> He dictated a letter and message of anger to the people saying, "If Banaro was bad to you and if he had offended you with all his iniquities, and bad things, you should not have killed him. You should have sent us your grievance and notified us to demote him and appoint another instead of him. Why did you kill our governor who was appointed nine years ago? You have not done a good thing. You have committed greater arrogance by your own will by killing him without our order. As for Sisgayo, since he had not joined in the killing of Banaro, let his appointment be confirmed. However, send us our tribute and compensation as well as gift for confirmation." Having dictated this, he sent Mustaf Basha [a Turk captain in his army] with all the Turks towards Ennarya.[109]

From the above, it appears that Sisgayo had the support of the people. Susenyos did not want to go against the man who had this support, and instead, he decided to derive the best possible material benefit from the situation. Thus, he requested the people of Ennarya to send him tribute, compensation for the blood of Banaro and a gift for confirming Sisgayo's appointment. He backed his request with a show of strength by sending his message by Turkish musketeers from his army. Sisgayo, who did not want to incur the anger of the Turkish musketeers at close range, or offend the pride of Susenyos at a distance, seems to have sent rich gifts, but was "unable to meet the repeated demands made upon [him for tribute]."[110]

While Susenyos was absorbed by the consideration of material benefit from the changed situation in Ennarya, Sela Christos remained loyal to Banaro and treated his son with affection. Sela Christos, who was an ardent Catholic converted Yaman Christos to Catholicism, and gave him his own daughter for marriage. His kindness towards the young man was not without effect, nor Yaman Christos's prospect for return to power without success. The young man gave an account of himself as a loving husband and "a good Catholic."[111] He was highly thought of as the torch for the spread of Catholicism in Ennarya. It was the irony of history that Yaman Christos came to power in Ennarya in 1632 at the very time when the spread of Catholicism was irreparably destroyed in the Christian kingdom.[112]

Sisgayo ruled Ennarya between 1620 and 1632, for which period we lack sufficient information on which to base an in-depth analysis. However, the following remarks can be made with certainty. During the twelve years Sisgayo ruled, the strength of Ennarya was wasted in useless inactivity. Relieved from the pressures of Ennarya, the Sadacha spread themselves over the fertile land as far as the edges of highland Ennarya. The Sadacha attacks on Ennarya could not be stopped by the leadership, whose spirit of resistance appears to have been exhausted. The failure to stop the Sadacha created instability in Ennarya. It seems that even the ardent supporters of Sisgayo in 1620 had by 1632 questioned his abilities and started deserting his sinking cause. In contrast to this, the supporters of Banaro maintained their loyalty to his exiled son. The attempt to end the rule of Sisgayo in the manner by which he came to power culminated in 1632 when "Those of Benero party killed him [Sisgayo] and all his minions and then sent for his son Emana Christos to put him in control of the kingdom."[113]

Satisfied with the actions of his supporters, delighted with the revenge of his father, and excited at the prospect before him, Yaman Christos returned to Ennarya after an exile of twelve years. His supporters were elated by the memorable return of a Catholic prince, who was destined to be the first king of independent Ennarya. Yaman Christos (1632–1642) seems to have possessed a considerable share of the vigor and ability of his father. His triumphal return restored the courage, raised the morale, and animated the spirit of his people for resistance. However, it is very difficult, if not impossible, to know whether or not Yaman Christos was able to stop the Sadacha advance. This is not because he was inactive, but because we lack information on his period. In fact, our sources of information on Ennarya stop in 1632, with his return to his land.[114] Following the civil war of June 1632 in the Christian kingdom, the death of Susenyos in September of the same year, the removal of Sela Christos from office and his subsequent execution, the political link between Ennarya and the Christian kingdom was damaged beyond repair. Ennarya became a little kingdom under Yaman Christos. Our information on Ennarya sadly ends with the end of political contact between the two.

Fortunately, however, we have some information about the situation from the oral history of Ennarya. According to this, during the second half of the seventeenth century, Ennarya was characterized by intense internal conflict and external war with the Oromo.[115] There is reason to believe that the debilitating factional conflict was generated mainly by the inability of the leadership to stop the Oromo advance. It is essential to note here that in their earlier struggle against the Oromo, the heterogeneous[116] population of Ennarya were united. In fact, unity was the source of their strength. Their basic goal was simple, their vision clear: to keep their enemies out of Ennarya. During the second half of the seventeenth century, the people hoped that their leaders would strengthen their unity and inspire them to resist the Oromo within highland Ennarya, if not lead them to victory in the plains. To their disappointment, their leaders forgot their responsibility to the survival of their land and remembered only factional interests, thus inflicting real wounds on Ennarya. The leaders not only alienated themselves from their people, but also caused doubt to creep into the hearts of the different groups of people. It seems that each group began to depart to its own ethnic camp, drifting ineffectively with no plan for unity and no joint action against the Oromo.[117] The great irony of the history of the people of Ennarya was that they lost unity when they needed it most. In short, during the second half of the seventeenth century Ennarya not only lacked a single leadership, but also her feuding leaders probably fought more with each other than with their common enemy.

It was only in 1704 that some information about Ennarya was reported in the Christian literature. This was in connection with Iyasu I's war against the Matcha. At that time, Ennarya was a divided land on the verge of political disintegration. Without doubt, it was the developments which took place between 1632 and 1704 which led to its disappearance as a political entity in 1710. It seems Ennarya survived so long because of the strength of her political institutions, her economy, and topography. We do not know whether the debilitating factional conflicts flared up while Yaman Christos was on the throne, but we do know that while Ennarya's public strength was consumed in internal quarrels it was surrounded on the north, west, and east, and was continuously harassed by the Sadacha. Highland Ennarya itself seems to have become the theater of Sadacha attack. In the process the flower of Ennarya' men perished in the struggle without end and hope. In the face of ever increasing Sadacha attack, the people of Ennarya were unable to close ranks and stand together. The factional conflict was bitter and it was the fight of despair against sorrow and anger. Usurpation of power by factions involving either the Sadacha or the rulers of Kaffa became common practice in the politics of decaying Ennarya.

> Internal struggles for power marked the closing years of the Hinnaro [Ennarya kingdom ... A considerable part of the competition involved factions of the Kat Minigo ruling dynasty expanding their power base throughout the Kafa high lands in the late seventeenth century and the Hinnaro–Busaso dynasty rapidly losing their positions of power during the same period. Both were to lose area north of the Gojeb river to the third competitor: the Oromo.[118]

As the political institutions of Ennarya were disintegrating, so was her economy. Both agriculture and commerce rapidly declined. In other words, the Sadacha raids and internal power struggle damaged agriculture and diminished trade. The exhausted land could no longer afford to provide luxury for the quarreling aristocracy of Ennarya. Everyone seems to have been ignorant of the causes for the economic decay of their land. Each faction put forward its own leader to salvage the situation and save Ennarya. Thus, they neglected the unity of the people and inadvertently contributed to and hastened the destruction of Ennarya. The following interesting song was supposed to have been produced by a certain Sini, the wife of Tumi Taki[119] (who was on the throne of Ennarya in the early eighteenth century).[120] She supported a certain Sisti, a would-be usurper-lover, against her usurper-husband on the throne. Her song expresses the intensity of factional conflicts and the degree of economic decay in Ennarya.

> After the death of Gamma Kegocci,
> Tumi Taki has left me empty-handed.
> There are cows full of milk,
> but he never orders the people to milk them!
> There are beehives full of honey,
> but he never orders the people to empty them!
> There are oxen ready for plowing,
> but he never orders the people to harness them!
> He has become just like a commoner!
> He has become just like a medium!
> Since he has become king:
> sorghum does not grow.
> . . . Since he has become king:
> the royal trumpet is hardly blown.
> I am surrounded by weeds!
> Let Sisti become king!
> . . . And make the country great!
> The kingship would be in good hands with him.[121]

It seems that, owing to the bitter factional conflicts, highland Ennarya itself was divided into two parts and ruled by rival leaders, who probably fought more with each other than with the Sadacha. When in 1704 Iyasu arrived at Gonqa, the earlier stronghold fortification of Ennarya on the Gibe river, two rival rulers applied to him for investiture.

> The emperor confirmed the governorship upon one of the rivals, he took no steps to prevent the renewal of fighting between the supporters of the two rulers. If Iyasu's assaults on Konch and particularly on the markets near the Gibe river, were intended to help the ruler of his choice, his intervention was more harmful than useful. His licentious soldiers looted all the defenders whom they were unable to kill.[122]

Unable either to come to terms with each other, or to stop the advancing Sadacha, the rival rulers of Ennarya, urged by fear and despair, fled one after the other to take refuge across the Gojeb river in Kaffa. So ended the existence of Ennarya as a political entity in the Gibe region. It existed first as a kingdom on its own; it became part of the Christian kingdom in the fifteenth century, while retaining considerable internal autonomy. At the beginning of the seventeenth century it seemed capable of expanding. By 1632, it became a small independent kingdom which was to disappear at the start of the next century. Its political extinction, so complete and irretrievable, was owing chiefly to its own internal weakness.

The Sadacha were now in possession of Ennarya a land of uncommon fertility, blessed with all that they needed. There was nothing to resist the Sadacha advance up to the Gojeb river, and considerable wealth to attract them. At this time, the little state of Seka, located between Ennarya and the Gojeb river, had a king by the name of Bedi Gaecci. This man tried to come to terms with the situation by absorbing into his administration the energy of ambitious Sadacha individuals. This proved to be the cause of his destruction. By favoring the Oromo at his court, Bedi Gaecci alienated his own people. The ambitious Oromo individuals at his court harnessed the popular fury to their own advantage. The following song expresses the anger of this king.

> Are you angry with me?
> You are just like a pot covered with mud.
> I washed you and made you clean.
> I wish I had never washed you.
> You were bent just like a crooked tree.
> I made you straight.
> I wish I had never straightened you.
> O, Galla, you are not thinking correctly,
> . . . Yesterday Wadagi came;
> I wanted him as a son-in-law;
> I gave him my daughter.
> Today Dali came,
> I gave him a bride for his bed alone.
> He had no ring of copper;
> I gave him fat golden ring!
> You are just like a small animal,
> which has seen some food.
> You are just like a fox,
> which runs into its hole.
> O, Galla, you are lying.
> I am the creator of wars!
> . . . Bring your allies.
> Bring forty local leaders,
> . . . If I come to you,
> you would defecate!
> . . . O you foolish men;
> let us fight.[123]

They fought, and the outcome was a foregone conclusion. The Sadacha won decisively. The aristocracy of this little state also fled to Kaffa across the

Gojeb. The triumphal advance of the Sadacha was stopped at the valley of the Gojeb river. Here they found formidable natural barriers that opposed their advance towards Kaffa. The hot valley of the Gojeb, infested with both terrible mosquitoes[124] and tsetse flies, covered with tall grass and dense forest, made rapid cavalry attack and retreat virtually impossible. This natural protection which the Gojeb valley afforded to Kaffa was further strengthened by elaborate and highly complex man-made fortifications which protected all the entrances to that country. To all intents and purposes the defense system of Kaffa was impregnable. Thus, Gojeb remained the boundary between the Oromo and Kaffa.[125] With their further progress stopped at the Gojeb, the Sadacha were obliged to settle in the Gibe region and henceforward devoted their energies to developing a system of agriculture combined with cattle-keeping.

To summarize what has transpired thus far: as we saw earlier in the chapter, the Matcha crossed the Gudar and Mugar rivers in the 1570s. By the first decade of the eighteenth century, they were the masters of the vast land which extended from the Gojeb in the south to the Abbay in the north, from the western and southwestern parts of what is today Shawa province in the east, to the provinces of Wallaga in the west and Illubabor in the southwest. The Afre section of the Matcha spread mainly to the region of the latter two provinces. The Sadacha section of the Matcha spread from Jibet and Matcha[126] (the westernmost *awaraja* sub-province of Shawa), across Shat, Konch, Ennarya, Bosha, and up to the Gojeb valley. In other words, the Sadacha mainly spread to the Gibe region. Both the Afre and the Sadacha moved across lands that were devastated and depopulated by slave raids conducted by the Christian kings, the lands relatively empty of people, and in most cases the scattered people either fled before them or were adopted and assimilated by them. The Matcha success can be accounted for by the warriors' speed in attack and retreat, by the mobility of their cavalry over long distances, their dependence on cattle, and by their being able to gain knowledge of their enemy. Their bands consisting of six to eight thousand men were mostly "picked young men," skillful in attacks on weak targets, relentless in terrorizing their enemies and resourceful in extricating themselves from the most difficult situation. News of their cruelty spread, causing panic among their thinly spread enemies, and this frequently enabled the Matcha simply to disperse them. The plains, particularly in Shat, Konch, Bosha, and Ennarya, were more affected by depopulation than the highland areas. The general danger encouraged a concentration of population in highland Ennarya. In short, the highlands of southwestern Ennarya were relatively densely populated. After the division and later disintegration of the state of Ennarya, it was mainly the ruling groups who fled across the Gojeb river and took refuge in the kingdom of Kaffa. The bulk of the population of Ennarya remained on their land. This was true of Shat, Konch, and Bosha. Thus in the Gibe region, the two cultures, the agriculturalists of the people of the region and the pastoralists of the Matcha, became mutually dependent on each other. The Matcha came to rely on the

6 Matcha land on the map of modern Ethiopia

people of the area for agricultural products and probably the latter on th
former for their animal products. After almost two centuries of living side b
side and then later together, the Matcha were no longer a threat to the people o
the region. The Matcha settled among the sedentary agricultural populatior
especially in Ennarya, whose people initially may have outnumbered them, bu
through extensive intermarriages and the constant stream of new emigrant:
the Oromo eventually equaled and probably came to outnumber th
Ennaryans. It must be remembered that there was a less dramatic and yet slo
and continuous process of migration into the newly conquered areas, as th
tradition recorded by Lambert Bartels for southern Wallaga and norther
Illubabor clearly shows.

> The eldest son always remained on his father's land; the other sons went in sear
> of new land for themselves; later the sons of those eldest sons, in their turn
> followed their relatives who went before, and joined them in the new country . .
> "It is thus that you find our names everywhere in the country between Ghiml
> and Dembidollo."[127]

In the course of the many decades during the seventeenth century and th
first half of the eighteenth, the ground was prepared and the stage was set fc
the transformation of the Matcha mode of production from a primaril
pastoral way of life to one in which agriculture dominated. This in turn set i

motion a dynamic political process that eventually culminated in the formation of the five Oromo Gibe states around the beginning of the nineteenth
century. The next four chapters will examine the process of state formations,
the political organization, the economic foundation, and ideological orientation of these states.

3

The Gibe states from *c*. 1800 to the 1860s

For this and the following chapters, the major sources[1] are the European travelers of the last century who either visited the Gibe region itself, or gathered information about it in northern Ethiopia from traders coming from the region. The second source of information is Oromo oral traditions re corded by either European travelers and missionaries or the Oromo them selves during the present century. Among the European travelers and missionaries, Antoine d'Abbadie, Charles T. Beke, Cardinal Massaja, An toine Cecchi, and Enrico Cerulli are worthy of mention. D'Abbadie was in the Gibe region between 1843 and 1846.[2] If his stay in the area was brief, the product of that stay was immense.[3] He gathered his information about the geography, history, economy, and politics of the Gibe region from a wide circl of merchants, elders, and political leaders, including Abba Bagibo himself, th famous king of Limmu-Ennarya. An intelligent observer, he kept dated records of everything he heard and so chronicled his own research. It is perhap because of this that one historian describes him as "a giant among all ou informants, whether travellers, missionaries or government agents."[4] Beside the published works, d'Abbadie left behind numerous unpublished materia Altogether there are twenty-seven volumes, most of which deal with Ethiopia though some contain the private papers of d'Abbadie's family. This unpub lished material has provided me with what is truly a mine of informatio without which this study would have remained incomplete. What is more, hi information bears the stamp of authenticity. Dr. C. T. Beke was in Shawa an Gojjam in 1842 and 1843, where he was able to gather from traders certai limited but reliable information about the Gibe region.[5] Guglielmo Massaja the first Catholic bishop of the Oromo territory, was in Ethiopia for thre decades, some of which time he spent in the Gibe region. Three of his twelv volumes[6] contain much useful information about the situation in the Gib region. Antonio Cecchi was in the same area in 1879 and 1880, during whic time he visited and gathered information from almost all the Gibe states.[7] d'Abbadie's information on Limmu-Ennarya is excellent, Cecchi's inform tion on all the Gibe states is highly useful. Finally, in the early part of th century, Cerulli visited the Gibe region, and gathered much useful informatio before the last autonomous Gibe state – Jimma – was annexed by the Amhara administration. Both in his earlier major work,[8] and his later traveler's account,[9] he provides us with useful information especially concerning the spread of Islam in the area. The preceding are the major travelers and missionary sources.[10]

The Oromo sources come essentially from three documents. The first is the manuscript of Abba Jobir Abba Dula, the last king of Jimma. This document contains recent history, oral traditions, as well as fantastic legends of bygone ages. Careful interpretation of this information provides insight into the process of the formation of the state of Jimma Abba Jifar. The second source is the Jimma Interview Programme sponsored by the Addis Ababa University in 1974 and conducted by a group of university students. While the above-mentioned manuscript deals mainly with the history of Jimma, the interview program covers all five Gibe states. Very little could be known about the economic resources of Jimma from Abba Jobir's manuscript, partly because his aim was to refute those who distorted Oromo history, and partly because he did not pay much attention to economic matters. However, the Jimma Interview Programme includes the economic aspect of the Gibe states.

The third Oromo source is the unpublished manuscript of Tasaw Merga,[11] a modern Oromo historian who conducted extensive oral interviews all over Oromo territory, including the Gibe region. The three sources tend to complement each other, and judicious interpretation of them may give a version of history which is the Oromo view of their own past. We have to allow a large measure of truth to these sources, which add a richness and depth to the history of the region but, at the same time, we cannot accept certain parts of these materials, especially those which deal with the introduction of Islam and the formation of states in the area. This is because the first two of these sources push the events back across five hundred years, while in reality both took place only in the early part of the nineteenth century. In short, by careful use of European travelers' accounts and Oromo oral traditions, supplemented by various other sources, which include the recent works of M. Abir on Limmu-Ennarya,[12] and H. S. Lewis on Jimma,[13] it is possible to give a general picture of the process of state formation in the Gibe region.

The previous chapter has shown that political weakness made Ennarya a prize within reach of the Sadacha. The long history of Ennarya gave a special significance to the capture of its highlands. Here was located the capital of Ennarya, at the junction of a series of caravan routes. From here radiated the trade routes leading to Kaffa, the land of coffee, ivory, and slaves; to the western region, the land of gold and other precious commodities. From here, too, originated the trade routes that went northwards to Shawa and beyond, to Gojjam and the Red Sea. Here was located land of unusual fertility, the commercial emporium of the region. This marked Ennarya as an important center of long-distance trade. After the Sadacha captured Ennarya, the old state disintegrated, but this did not directly lead to the emergence of the new Oromo states. Many decades elapsed before the Oromo formed their own states on the ruins of the earlier ones. The formation of the new states has been explained as "borrowing from their neighbors," or as created by leaders who wanted to control trade routes and the lucrative markets, or as a result of the introduction of Islam into the region, or because of the threatening pressure of their Amhara neighbors.[14] Excepting the last point, the consolidation of the Gibe states owed something to all of these factors. But these explanations tend to view the consolidation as a sudden phenomenon, whereas in fact it was a long process. Not a single one of these states sprang into existence all at once, nor were they formed at the same time, but at different times, one after the other. Limmu-Ennarya, the first to be formed, came into existence around 1800, and the last only around 1835. Gumma was formed around 1810, Gomma around 1820, and Jimma in 1830. In short, all the Gibe states developed by internal processes. As examples of state formation from other parts of the world show, "nothing is made of nothing: if a people has not developed to the point of state formation, that formation cannot be superimposed."[15]

Furthermore, judicious interpretation and cautious use of oral history of the Oromo in the Gibe region establishes one fact beyond dispute – that the monarchic institution in the Gibe region was brought about by internal forces.[16] The five states shared similar, if not identical, principles of state organization and common economic practice, state ideology, culture, religion, and defense system. However, this does not mean that these states were not influenced by their Sidama (non-Oromo) neighbors. What we object to here is not the influence, but the assertion which purports to establish that the new Oromo institution was borrowed from their neighbors, as some writers would like us to believe.[17] One must show which typical features were borrowed and which were not. By concentrating on some similarities while ignoring some fundamental differences, some scholars have been able to provide a picture of the supposedly borrowed institution and have believed in their own untenable conclusion.[18] However, we can form a clear picture of the nature of the new Oromo institution only if we analyze both its similarity with and difference from the institutions of its neighbors. As we shall soon see, borrowing was not the decisive factor. What really mattered was not the similarity but the differences in some fundamental aspects between the new institution of the Gibe region and that of their Sidama neighbors, more particularly that of Kaffa.

It would be absurd to deny the Sidama influence (especially that inherited from the old state of Ennarya) on the monarchic institutions among the Oromo. A gold ring as an emblem of authority and an umbrella as a symbol of royalty are two examples which show unmistakable Sidama influence. What scholars generally tend to overlook is that, during the period of Matcha migration and their subsequent settlement among the sedentary agriculturalist population, a fusion took place between Oromo culture and the culture of the assimilated people which resulted in the foundation of a new civilization in the Gibe region. In other words, between the second half of the sixteenth century, when the Matcha first arrived in the Gibe region, and the second half of the

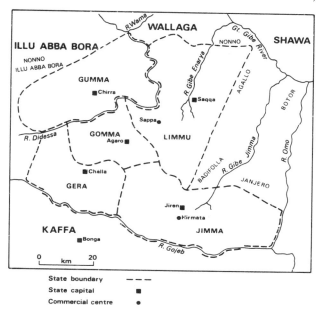

7 The Gibe states in the first half of the nineteenth century

eighteenth century, when the outlines of states in the process of formation became more clearly defined in the Gibe region,[19] the Matcha underwent many transformations, some resulting from the increase in agricultural production, some from the increase in trade, some from the differentiation of the Oromo into classes. Only this accounts for the truly advanced development which the Oromo of the Gibe region achieved in the fields of agriculture, handicrafts, architecture, commercial prosperity,[20] and the generally higher standard of living – all of which matters will be discussed below. Moreover, the cultural fusion between the people of Ennarya and the Matcha, coming from the latter's settlement among the former, had a far-reaching effect on the Matcha, which was also to be seen in the economic sphere. Pastoralism was the most important mode of production for the Oromo during their epoch-making migration. It is no mere chance that the Oromo language is so rich in words which deal with cattle herding and that a number of economic concepts have developed "directed by analogy with the possession of cattle."[21] However, it should be remembered that the Oromo were engaged in mixed farming long before their sixteenth-century migration.[22] During their migration, the Oromo were pastoralists rather than farmers, by necessity and circumstance,[23] but after they had settled in the Gibe region they became by degree more farmers than pastoralists. The intensive agriculture of the people of Ennarya exerted great influence on the Matcha themselves, the majority of whom became settled mixed farmers. The transformation of the Oromo from

87

pastoralism to settled sedentary agricultural life was more profound in the Gibe region,[24] as it also was in the province of Amhara in the north.

An important fact which has relevance to our discussion but which scholars usually tend to overlook concerns the development of various Oromo groups. It is generally assumed that states developed among the Oromo only in the Gibe region. (The outlines of states, still in the process of formation, are not usually mentioned.) States actually developed among the Oromo in three regions, namely, Wollo, the Gibe region, and Wallaga.[25] The last was a development of the second half of the nineteenth century, while the first was a development belonging to the last part of the seventeenth century. In Wollo, the Oromo settled among a large sedentary population whose agricultural practice exerted considerable influence on the newcomers. As a result, in some parts of Wollo, especially northeastern Amhara, mixed farming became a dominant mode of the Oromo economy. It was not by accident that the first recorded account of a local Oromo dynasty, that of Arreloch, was formed in northeastern Amhara.[26] By the beginning of the eighteenth century, almost a century before the formation of states in the Gibe region, another dynasty had already been formed in Wollo. By the second half of the eighteenth century the new dynasty of Warra Himanu, or the Mamadoch, according to local tradition had already overrun the territory of the Arreloch. "Mohammed Ali, otherwise known by the name of his war horse, Aba Jibo, is considered to be the real founder of the Mamadoch dynasty."[27] Abba Jibo died in 1784, but the dynasty he founded dominated the Wollo region up to 1815.[28] We make this brief reference to Wollo for three reasons. First, the Oromo in Wollo were Muslims long before they formed a dynasty. The implication of this will become clear further on in our discussion. Secondly, the control of trade routes and market centers was essential, but not decisive, for the formation of dynasties in Wollo. Thirdly, and more importantly, it was an agricultural peasant economy which formed the material basis of the Oromo dynasty in Wollo. As in the latter, so in the Gibe region, agriculture became the material foundation for the formation of a monarchic institution.

What must be stressed here is that, in different parts of Oromoland, the transition from pastoralism to sedentary agriculture took a longer or shorter period of time depending on the density of the sedentary population among which the Oromo settled and on the resources prevailing in the areas they settled. We have seen above an example of how the Oromo had to adapt themselves quickly to the conditions of the region in which they settled.[29] In the Gibe region, some groups of the Oromo people had already embarked on mixed farming during the second half of the seventeenth century. Mixed farming became particularly important during the eighteenth century, when the Oromo, through division of labor and specialization,[30] produced a relatively improved plough for farming and used their animals to increase the yield on their farms. The success in the field of mixed farming gave impetus to a new branch of the economy – trading. This was a new and remarkable phenomenon of the second half of the eighteenth century. For the first time in the history of the Oromo in the Gibe region there emerged a new Oromo merchant class – the Afkala. What brought about this development is the subject of later discussion.[31] Here it should suffice to say that the transformation of the Oromo mode of production from pastoralism to sedentary agriculture brought in its train social differentiation and class division within the Oromo society in the Gibe region. It changed their economic basis and undermined the egalitarian aspect of the gada system by the formation of class and class relations, and created the material foundation for the new social order, which was a decisive break from the previous Oromo history.

In short, in the course of many decades, out of the masses of the mixed farmers and pastoralists of Matcha, a number of rich families pushed themselves into the foreground, gradually eclipsing the traditional gada leaders. This tendency was observable by the beginning of the eighteenth century,[32] and by the end of the same century a new aristocracy had already been formed. This Matcha aristocracy, distinguished by its influence and wealth of cattle, land, and slaves, was given the name of *sorressa*[33] (i.e., rich, wealthy), in contrast to the pastoral nobility, who were known as Borana. The distinction between the victorious Matcha and the conquered *gabbaro* disappeared and they all became a homogeneous mass of common people, equally subjugated by the new aristocracy. How this new class acquired wealth in land and slaves is the subject of later discussion. Here is should suffice to say that the fundamental reason for the formation of a monarchic institution among the Matcha was the transformation of their mode of production from pastoralism to sedentary agriculture. The agricultural peasant economy furnished bricks and mortar for the formation of the states; thus, the simplistic explanation of "borrowing from their neighbors" overlooks this vital development.

The claim that the Gibe states were created by leaders who wanted "to control the trade routes and lucrative markets"[34] is partly true, because wherever traders found a strong leader who guaranteed safety and security for their persons and property, they traveled frequently, harvesting rich profits for themselves and diffusing substantial benefits to their protector in the form of taxes for protection, customs-dues, and gifts. The protectors, who controlled both caravan routes and market places, were themselves extensive landowners. The rise to power of the family of Gama-Moras in Gudru around the middle of the nineteenth century and his formation of a small state could be taken as a classic example.

According to Massaja, the father of Gama-Moras came to Gudru from Gojjam and was adopted by one of the Borana nobility. Despite the adoption, the Borana nobility in general regarded the son many decades later as a "stranger" and "inferior" because "he had neither wealth in land nor in cattle the two items which brought honour to a family among the Galla."[35] Massaja goes on to say that in the circle of *sorressa* nobility good birth and, more important, wealth were highly regarded, while the poor people were held in contempt. Regardless of birth, he who possessed wealth in land, cattle, and slaves was recognized as a "dignified" man. Then his social standing was elevated to the status of *sorressa* nobility, and his low social origin conveniently forgotten. A good example of this was Gama-Moras, who inherited a large fortune, which his father had made from commerce. Gama-Moras not only bought lands with his money, but he also won friendship among the Borana nobility.

> Mainly because of their manners, generosity, hospitality and talent . . . the greatness of his family spread far and wide, so much so that the most important commercial affairs of the market of Assandabo are concluded in his house, and even that of the remote market of Egibe, so that it could be said that Gama-Moras held in his hand the key to all the market centres [in Gudru].[36]

A few observations could be made on the above. First, wealth in land and cattle was the source of honor and prestige for the Borana nobility. Earlier during the course of the migration, only wealth in cattle had counted, land being the common property of the whole clan. With the transformation of the Matcha mode of production, land not only gained economic value, but also generated struggles among the war leaders for its possession.[37] It was out of this struggle that the new institution was born. Secondly, money was not a source of prestige and honor by itself, but when it was converted into land and cattle it became so. This was a reflection of a peasant economy, in which reciprocal exchange was prominent. Thirdly, those individuals who made good use of their wealth for public relations and for winning friends and supporters had a good chance of making themselves hereditary leaders. In short, along with wealth in terms of cattle, there now appeared wealth in terms of land and slaves. Wealthy men fought for the control of more land, and the control of land made kings.

Massaja's argument that the introduction of Islam led to the formation of the monarchic institution in the Gibe region[38] could be correct only if by this argument it is meant that Islam helped the Oromo kings to consolidate their power and authority,[39] as Massaja himself asserts when referring to Jimma.[40] Without doubt, when the agricultural mode of production was breaking up the traditional political system, Islam not only provided an ideology for the new rulers, but also served as a focus of tribal loyalties. However, two points must be mentioned. First, Islam did not come to the Gibe region at the beginning of the nineteenth century, when these states were formed. Islam had been in the region at least since the sixteenth century. Over and above this fact, some of the Oromo themselves had become Muslims, even as early as the sixteenth century.[41] Secondly, and even more importantly, after the disintegration of the old state of Ennarya in 1710, the commerce of the region had never really died, the adventurous Muslim merchants were still coming to the Gibe region, only probably less frequently.

> The Galla to the south were mostly Mohametans; on the east and west, chiefly pagans . . . The Moors, by courage, patience and attention have found out the means of trading with them in a tolerable degree of safety . . . The Mohametan traders pass through [a number of tribal groups] on their way to Narea, the southernmost country the Abyssinians ever conquered.[42]

Three points could be deduced from the above. First, the disintegration of the state of Ennarya only disrupted, never destroyed, the commercial importance of that region, and slowly trade with Ennarya revived, so that by the 1770s, when Bruce recorded this information, Ennarya was once again a busy trading center. Secondly, neither Islam by itself, nor the continuity of the caravan trade, led immediately to the formation of new states. Both of these factors consolidated the position of the state makers, but were not the fundamental causes for the formation of the new institutions. Thirdly, all five Gibe states had kings before Islam became their official religion. However, once Islam became the religion of the kings, each found in the other what they wanted. Islam found champions and propagators in the kings, while the kings found a powerful ideology, a literate class, and a writing system in Islam, all of which contributed to the consolidation of monarchic power in the Gibe region. In other words, the old religion was incapable of strengthening the new rulers. There remained only Islam with its literate, business-minded preachers, teachers, and traders, and their writing system, which enabled rulers to engage in correspondence with their neighbors.[43] What is more, Islam provided the new rulers with a powerful ideology, one which justified absolute power.[44]

The outward similarity of the symbols of kingship used in Kaffa and the Gibe states seems to have led some writers to assume that the latter borrowed their monarchic institution from the former. The Gibe states did not borrow their symbols of kingship (such as a gold ring, gold bracelet, or an umbrella) from Kaffa. On the contrary, these features, which provided points of contact between the institutions of Kaffa and the Gibe states, had a common origin. This was the historical state of Ennarya. The Matcha who settled in Ennarya and assimilated the Ennaryans adopted a number of things from them, among which the symbols of kingship were probably the most important. As we saw in the previous chapter,[45] during the long period of Matcha attack on Ennarya, a number of ruling groups from Ennarya fled across the Gojeb and took refuge in Kaffa. There is ample evidence to show that Ennarya's symbols of kingship were brought to Kaffa by some of those refugees.[46] In fact, one of the refugee groups, the Minjo, even succeeded in usurping power in Kaffa, where they established the celebrated Minjo dynasty, which dominated that country from the first half of the seventeenth century to 1897 when the Minjo dynasty itself was abolished by the victorious imperial Shawan Amhara soldiers. This historical link between the institutions of Kaffa and the Gibe states is usually overlooked. This may explain why some scholars claim that the Oromo borrowed their monarchic institution from their Sidama neighbors.[47]

Despite the common origin of the symbols of kingship, a comparison of the institution of monarchy in the Gibe region and in Kaffa shows that there were some striking differences between the two institutions. As we shall see further on in the discussion,[48] the Gibe kings had absolute power while the power of a king of Kaffa was limited by the power of the councillors of the state. While the Gibe kings appointed and dismissed their councillors, in Kaffa the seven councillors (*mikrecho*) made and unmade kings. In the Gibe states all government officials were appointed by the kings and offices were not hereditary. The political structure of Kaffa was composed of a series of hierarchically organized clans, at the apex of which stood the royal clan, the Minjo, and under it were the seven most important clans in the kingdom, and the seven councillors of the state were the representatives of the seven clans. As a result, a king of Kaffa did not enjoy a constitutional prerogative which would allow him to decide on the important matters of the state without the consent of the seven councillors.[49] The Gibe kings were accessible to their subjects. They sat in the court of justice in public, received and entertained foreign and local dignitaries both in public and in private, and the range of their daily activities was not limited by taboos. A king of Kaffa was subjected to all sorts of restrictions.

> Because of his semi-divine nature, there were many restrictions surrounding the daily activities of the monarch. No one was allowed to see him (he wore a gown with a veil and he sat behind a curtain); he could not put his feet on the ground and therefore, cotton cloth was always placed where he desired to walk; he was washed and fed, not being allowed to touch his own food; and anyone who was part of an act that caused these restrictions to be violated was put to death.[50]

These few examples (and there are several others) should suffice to show that the monarchic institution in the Gibe region was not a replica of the Kaffa institution.

Finally, Abir's claim that the pressure from the Amhara led to the formation of the new institution[51] among the Matcha is also untenable. First, the Gibe states were formed in the first half of the nineteenth century, while the Amhara pressure was felt in the Gibe region only in the second half of the same century. Secondly, and even more importantly, the Amhara pressure had been deeply felt by the Tulama Oromo in Shawa since the last quarter of the eighteenth century, but they had never formed any state which went beyond the outlines of states in the process of formation. The reason for this is not far to seek. Social stratification based on wealth and privilege and differences in status corresponding to the distribution of power and authority were much less developed among the Tulama than among the Matcha in the Gibe region.[52] By the second half of the eighteenth century the Oromo in the Gibe region were divided into well-defined classes. By their labor on land and engagement in trade they produced adequate surplus which supported the newly emerging ruling class. The new surplus had to be used, and its distribution gave a powerful impetus to the political consolidation of the *sorressa* nobility, which was the new ruling class. The *sorressa* owned most of the land. Below the *sorressa* were the free peasants, who had their own plots of land. Below them were landless tenants, who worked for and lived on the land of the new nobility. Below these tenants were slaves, who were the property of wealthy landowners. There were also artisans and blacksmiths, on whose indispensable skill the economy of the Gibe states depended, but who were despised and ostracized by both the nobility and the rest of the population.[53] This social pyramid had existed before the beginning of the nineteenth century. In other words, among the Matcha the process of class formation and differentiation into rich and poor, rulers and ruled, was much more developed, and by the beginning of the nineteenth century the moment was ripe for the birth of the new order provided by the Gibe states. In the process of formation of class and class stratification into the ruling and the ruled, the old order, its politics, and ideology disintegrated.

> The forces of development of the state are internal to the society; a people increases its resources of wealth by advanced economic organization, technology, and control of natural resources. The economic goods produced are unequally distributed, and one class of the entire society controls a greater amount than any other. More importantly, the ruling class has a greater share of land, cattle, and other means of economic production, and by using its greater part in the economy it is able to assert control over all social classes, which are now inferior to it. The means whereby this control is achieved is political force, including physical power, the highest (that is, most centralized), tightest and most monopolistic control of the political power resides in the state, which is the organ of the ruling class.[54]

The formation of the Gibe states

It is difficult to give the exact date, but sometime after 1800 the new political structure of the Gibe region was framed, and the Oromo society was launched on a course which more or less shaped its development down to the 1880s, when these states were conquered and annexed one after the other by the imperial armies of the Shawan Amharas. Although the existence of these states spanned no more than a few decades, this brief period was packed with events of crucial importance. It witnessed rapid religious, social, cultural, political, industrial, and commercial progress unsurpassed in any of the other Oromo areas in what is today Ethiopia. Although in size the area over which the Gibe states spread was negligible, their achievement in the cultural field was immense. Before the formation and development of these states are described, it is imperative to discuss the features common to them all.

First and foremost, all the Gibe states were the creation of war leaders. War made the Gibe kings, and all of them made war the prime business of their administration. However, it should be noted here that all the early Gibe kings found themselves faced by serious rivals, whom they faced with ruthless cruelty. This perhaps helps explain their excessive cruelty towards opponents, cruelty which included the physical elimination of rivals and the enslavement of all members of their families. This was particularly true of Gumma.[55] Secondly, in all the Gibe states, there was centralization of physical force under the command of the kings. It has been said (and the history of the Gibe states confirms it) that this centralization of force did not precede the state. It was developed within the state and was the sign that the state had been formed.[56] The concentration of power in the hands of a king was the dramatic break with the gada government. As we saw in the Introduction, the power of the gada government was vested in the *chafe* assembly ("meadow assembly"), which met under the shade of a sycamore tree. The various Oromo clans or tribes in the Gibe region had their own independent *chafe* assemblies.[57] Each assembly dealt with matters of supreme importance – making laws, declaring war, concluding peace agreements, electing new officials who would run the government for eight years. However, none of the gada officials had executive power, and the major force behind gada government in the implementation of the assembly decisions was strong public opinion.[58] Leadership within the gada had to be achieved, and achievement was based on social recognition of leadership qualities.[59] The absence of any office with executive power, and the principle of rotation of office, among others, were the distinctive features of gada government. With the formation of the states, the kings became ultimately responsible not only for the defense of the states against internal and external enemies, maintenance of law and order, and dispensation of final justice, but they wielded as well supreme executive authority, against which there was no appeal.[60] With sufficient surplus from their extensive estates, from tribute, taxation, and trade, the Gibe kings were able to maintain permanent military and police forces with which they carried out their will. The kings alone declared war and made peace, and took both the lives and property of their own subjects.[61] The classic example for what had transpired thus far, which is well known and documented, was Gama-Moras, who formed the little kingdom of Gudru. We have seen how he converted his large inherited treasure into land and cattle, thus raising the honor of his name and spreading his prestige far and wide. Now we can observe how he utilized his immense wealth to maintain his own soldiers, through whom he made himself the sole leader of Gudru.

The conquest of his main rival was the object of his hopes and preparation, but he kept his plan secret so as not to provoke him into action before the moment was ripe.[62] All the time Gama-Moras's deepest aim had been to be the king of all Gudru by breaking the power of the nobility. For this purpose, he continued gathering firearms, training his own soldiers, and cultivating friendly relations with all his neighbors. The Gudru nobility's opposition to Gama-Moras's ambition was engineered and led by a certain wealthy man called Fufi, who lived in Assandabo, the capital of Gudru. Fufi's capacity to insult was second only to his followers' exaggeration of their own strength. Fufi promised them that he would expel the "stranger" from the land of Gudru.[63] To Gama-Moras the throne was the main issue. To Fufi, the ambition of the "stranger" was unbearable. To Gama-Moras, the gathering of firearms and the training and the discipline of his crack force were vital.[64] To Fufi, character assassination was part of the psychological warfare. Fufi's supporters were large in number, but it was in number alone that they surpassed their formidable enemy. Gama-Moras perfected his preparation and kept his soldiers with exemplary patience until this was interpreted as cowardice. Insults were imprudently exchanged, a sword was hastily drawn by Fufi's followers, and the first blood that was spilt became a bad omen for their own defeat. They were saved from general rout by the intervention of the elders. Both the victors and the vanquished agreed to take their case to the *chafe* assembly at Qobo in southern Gudru.[65] What followed was very interesting. After many days of deliberation, the *chafe* assembly decided to maintain the status quo. Gama-Moras was left in full control of the market of Assandabo, but he was ordered to pay blood money for the soldiers of Fufi killed by firearms. Fufi was ordered to pay blood money for the soldiers of his enemy who had been wounded. Both men were ordered to fulfil the decision of the assembly, with the proviso that if either failed to implement the decision he was to be declared the enemy of all Gudru.[66] Satisfied with the success of his firearms, which delivered him from the insults of his arrogant enemy, and elated by the decision which favored him, Gama-Moras immediately paid the blood money. What is more, he lavishly feasted the Gudru nobility and honored them with liberal gifts. They were flattered by his hospitality and generosity, and delighted by his political wisdom. They compared Gama-Moras's generosity with Fufi's meanness, and admired the former's willingness to carry out the assembly decision with Fufi's flat refusal to do so. Fufi's refusal to pay compensation demonstrated the helplessness of the *chafe* assembly. Massaja, who was an eyewitness to this drama, states that because the assembly did not have its own army, it could not enforce practically any of its decisions.[67] In the unsettled situation where powerful men fought with each other for supremacy, poor men sought the protection of more powerful ones. The assembly had nothing now but its name and prestige. It was not capable of implementing its own decisions, maintaining peace, or defending the society against the dangers that threatened it. Accordingly, it did not shape important political events. It was only the shell of the *chafe* assembly that continued to exist in the name of the old political institution, but its moral influence, its traditional conception of political thought,[68] and its religious ideas survived for some time to come, and only died out gradually. Gama-Moras, by implementing its decision, was appealing to its moral influence, and on that ground he won a decisive victory.[69] Fufi, by refusing to implement its decision was questioning even its moral influence, and on that ground he earned public outrage.

At this juncture in the discussion about the *chafe* assembly, it is important to make two points very clear. First, even after the transformation of the Oromo mode of production from pastoralism to sedentary agriculture, *chafe* assemblies were still the centers of political actions. The assemblies debated on important issues of the day and made laws but they lacked forces to implement their decisions. Among stateless Oromo tribes, the assemblies were dominated by the war leaders. Secondly, among the Gibe states as regards the function of *chafe* assembly, there was no abrupt break with the past. In all the Gibe states, the assemblies continued to function long after states were formed,[70] but the assemblies no longer decided on the crucial issues of the day. In the Gibe states, the kings alone decided them. The assemblies continued to function, however, because the kings needed their services for settling disputes between clans. In their capacity as leaders, the kings dictated which issues were to be debated on behalf and in the name of the kings and in the interest of the states. Available literature indicates that the kings used the assemblies to consolidate their authorities (a matter not discussed here). It should suffice to say that as "citadel of folk democracy" the assemblies served the kings well.[71] Further in the discussion we shall see that the Gibe kings not only made good use of *chafe* assemblies, but they used the traditional Oromo religion[72] as well as Islam and the institutions of the state for the purpose of consolidating their powers.

Three months of an uneasy lull elapsed, from the day the hostilities stopped by the elders' intervention to the defeat of Fufi, during which time both sides were engaged in frantic preparations. When the hostilities were resumed, Gama-Moras was not again disposed to sacrifice any solid advantage for the elders' call for peace.[73] On the contrary, he ably directed the valor of his soldiers and chased out his enemy. Instead of expelling Gama-Moras from Gudru, as he intended, Fufi had to flee to save himself. His flight betrayed his intention of abandoning everything in the face of danger to his person. Oppressed by firearms and startled by the flight of their leader, Fufi's supporters fled in total disarray. By a single victory, Gama-Moras achieved the ambition of his life. That successful day put an end to the time of uncertainty characterized by anarchy. From that day onward, Gama-Moras abandoned his humble speech of "calling every Gudru my lord."[74] He became their master.

> After becoming victorious he not only confiscated the property of his enemies and distributed it among his soldiers . . . but also became the prince of all Gudru . . . Having achieved his aim, he began to reorganize his little kingdom. First and foremost he thought of the military . . . and adopted a well-known gunner as his son and made him the leader of his soldiers. Secondly, he made a rich merchant a judge of the market place with authority over caravan, over the merchants, and over all that pertains to commerce.[75]

In all the Gibe states the kings were the highest judges. In the field of justice, the law was bent in favor of the wealthy class. A gift of a well-fattened bull (the *natafo*) or some other valuable object to the king or his governors was the key to winning a case. In short, justice was there to be bought in all the Gibe states.[76] In each of them the king was helped by a council of state, usually consisting of three top dignitaries of the state, and while the kings made and unmade the composition of the members of the council of the state,[77] they usually heeded its advice. Below the council of the state came the provincial governors, called Abba Qorros, who in one way or another were related to the kings and exercised administrative, judicial, and military powers in their respective areas.

> . . . Each governor had his own estates and massera or masseras, in which he housed his family, followers and slaves. In time of peace the governor ruled his district, dealt with most of the judicial problems and with the help of an especially appointed administrator collected the taxes from the peasants. In time of war, the governor was the commander of all the able-bodied men in his province and at the head of his contingent took part in the battles under the command of the king.[78]

96

Under the Abba Qorros, came Abba Gandas, governors of villages, and under them came Abba Fuynos ("the fathers of ropes"), who in the name of the king imposed a tribute in kind and in salt, which was levied in relation to a person's possessions. They also arrested offenders, directed corvée labor, and served as messengers between Abba Qorros and the king.[79] This social pyramid was maintained by the labor and produce of the free population of the Gibe region and of the slaves. Thus one obvious economic consequence of the differentiation into classes in the Gibe region was the exploitation of the majority by the minority. This is probably the clearest confirmation of Engels's universal thesis: "Every step forward is relatively a step backward, in which prosperity and development for some is won through the misery and frustration of others."[80]

Each of these states had a defined territory, with defined borders surrounded by strategic lines of defense strengthened by the work of man and fortified by the physical configuration of the land.

> First there was the mogga, a belt of land circumscribing the country and left uncultivated, in which roamed bands of thieves called ketto. The mogga was a battlefield in which all the wars were fought. Next came the lines of the defence proper, made up of palisades, ditches, rivers, swamps and thick forests. Wherever a road from a neighbouring area entered the country, the defences had a gate called kella. Each such gate was guarded by a unit of cavalry commanded by an officer called abba kella. This officer helped a special representative of the king count all incoming or outgoing merchants, inspect their merchandise, and collect the customs. In this way, the king had the strictest control over the people entering his territory, and at the same time could prevent the many thousands of slaves employed by himself and by his subjects from escaping.[81]

Along with defined borders surrounded by strategic lines of defense, the Gibe states had a warning (alarm) system, for which the region was famous.[82] As the following discussion will show, there was a particular demand for alertness against sudden enemy attack in the Gibe region. This led to the development of a sophisticated warning system which also served as a signal for mobilization. The system also skillfully connected the country with the capital, the nerve center, where the decision for war or peace was made. The system was admirably fast and efficient but technically simple. It was based on hitting the *bidru* (a hollowed tree trunk or a drum) suspended from a beam.[83]

> . . . The sound of the Bideru [bidru] could be heard at a distance of several kilometres. Through a system of Bideru placed at appropriate intervals, the news of an approaching enemy could reach the capital in a matter of minutes and every able-bodied man all over the country left the fields and joined the army.[84]

In all the Gibe states, the main residence of the king, the *massera*, represented the most remarkable feature of political as well as commercial development. The main *massera* was the nerve center from which new political ideas radiated. Here questions of war and peace were decided, new proclamations announced. Here was where important political prisoners were kept or executed.[85] Near the main *massera* were located commercial centers of two kinds. The first sector was for local trade, while the second, known as *mandera*, was built by the king for the exclusive use of foreign merchants.

In all the Gibe states, the spirit of independence for the defense of the frontiers of each state was tempered by the mutual dependence and co-operation between them in matters of commerce. As a result, there developed an impressive network of institutionalized trade, in which the markets were named according to the day of the week, and the market-days were arranged in such a way that traders who went from one state to the other were able to buy and sell at different market-places along the route, neither losing a single market-day nor wasting time unnecessarily.[86] Two things are worth noting here regarding trade in the Gibe region. First, trading was controlled by the state legally and organizationally, and on the favorable and unfavorable attitudes of the kings towards the trade depended the prosperity of traders and that of the states.[87] Local trade welded the Gibe region together into one closely knit unit, where the intrepid Oromo traders (the Afkala) were engaged in around-the-year brisk trade. At the same time, the Jabarti, Muslim traders from Gondar, Gojjam, Wollo, Shawa, Harar, and other traders from Kaffa, Majji, Gimira, Kullo, Konta, Walayta, Wallaga, and Illubabor brought their goods to the Gibe region.[88] In exchange the products of the Gibe region radiated in different directions, traveling over great distances. Secondly, the trade within the Gibe region itself led to the development of a relatively efficient and fast system of communications and information networks that welded the region into a single unit. There was regular and constant flow of information between the capitals of the Gibe states. Spies reported to their respective governments of any secret military treaties which were concluded against a third party. Wealthy Abba Qorros (governors) were dispatched as ambassadors to negotiate marriage alliances, to conclude secret military treaties, and to make peace between belligerent states. For the diplomatic relations between the Gibe states and the surrounding non-Oromo areas, interpreters were needed and many of them accompanied official delegations.

In all the Gibe states the kings were well known for giving and taking gifts from each other. *Natafo* (well-fattened bulls), honey, imported luxury goods, and precious commodities were given and received as presents. The Oromo new year in September, the *jarra* ceremony, which took place every eight years in February, and, after the Islamization of the ruling classes, Muslim holidays were times when gifts were exchanged among the rulers. Gift-giving was a mechanism through which marriage connections were consummated, secret military alliances were concluded, and diplomatic arm-twisting was conducted. Another interesting aspect of the politics of the region was that exchange of official state visits was an accepted part of the diplomacy of the Gibe states. Such official state visits were common on occasions of royal weddings or funeral ceremonies. Such visits also took place at the start of the Oromo new year, or at the time of the *butta* celebration, held every eight years, when the Gibe kings met and feasted together, settled their differences, and made treaties. In short, the rulers of the Gibe states maintained extensive contacts with each other via a dynamic network of trade, exchange of messages and messengers, state visits, and "interlocking of ruling families" through political marriages.[89] Such close relationships brought in their trains a new ideological orientation, which explains why Islam so easily won the support of the ruling groups one after the other. It also explains similar, if not identical, principles of state organization and common economic practice, state ideology, religion, and defense system, all of which made the Gibe region a single cultural unit, which may be considered as an expression of Oromo people's capacity to advance to a higher material culture through their labor and interaction with their neighbors.

In all the states, the wedding, birth, or death of a member of the royal family, or a successful hunting expedition of the king, or victory in battle were celebrated by spectacular public processions. On such occasions, the king, surrounded by his elite cavalry, accompanied by the governors and dignitaries, and followed by the infantry, who chanted his praises, led the procession. The infantry was followed by the royal slaves, eunuchs and women, musical bands, and thousands of people who danced to music.[90] These singular conditions, created by the music and the presence of the monarch and high dignitaries, turned the occasion into the manifestation of considerable collective sentiments and pride in belonging to that particular state. The songs of heroes and the boasts of singers about their land fused the emotions of the young and the old into loyalty to the ruling house, the end result developed by mass contact and nourished by the great feasting and drinking which usually consummated the procession. The food and drink from the king's table created among the nobility an unusual mental exhilaration, which expressed itself in blind devotion to, and fear of, their sovereign.[91]

All the Gibe kings had the Oromo title of *moti* ("king" or "conqueror"), and they were known more by the name of their war horses[92] than by their personal names.[93] The queens were addressed by the Oromo title of *genne* ("the lady"), followed by the name of the country of their origin. The princes were called by the names of their war horses, while the crown princes were addressed by the title of *donachaw*, which was again followed by the names of the war horses. Once a prince was made *donachaw*, he was authorized to wear one of the golden bracelets.[94] The Gibe kings had gold rings as the insignia of royal power and gold earrings, silver bracelets, and an umbrella as symbols of royal authority. As the symbol of their Muslim faith, the kings wore black caps made of goat leather, and on special occasions they put an ostrich feather in their hair and held an *alanga* or *licho* (a whip made of hippotamus's hide) in their right hand, both of these being the symbols of traditional gada leaders. Other symbols of royal authority were the crown, the throne, double-bladed spears, which also served as the seal of the king, and two gold arm bracelets.[95] In all the states succession to the throne was in theory hereditary,[96] but more often succession was marked by a power struggle. In the absence of a legitimate successor, a leading member of the *sorressa* (wealthy dignitaries) could be elected by his colleagues to occupy the throne.[97]

In all the states the lion's share of fertile land belonged to the king and the nobility, who spent most of their time either hunting, fighting, or eating and drinking at the main *massera* (royal residence), being supported in these activities by the fruits of the toil of the peasants and slaves. The wealthy landowners used their slaves for cultivating their lands, while those who were short of slaves distributed their land to free tenants who cultivated it in their master's name and interest.[98] The nobility differed from the common people in their increased share of material possessions, their manner of dress, their place of residence, and even in their hair style.[99] Among them luxury had become a necessity and the taste for the products of distant countries, together with their new habits and the acquisition of elite foreign goods,[100] added lustre and glamour to their residences, which were built on the model of the royal *masseras*.

The Gibe kings were constantly engaged in wars with each other, and these wars were a heavy burden on the peasants, who were called upon to fight for their kings at their own expense.[101] Failure to fight with the enemy of the king, at the right time and right place would result in both the confiscation of property and the enslavement of the entire family.[102] Bad as it was, the condition of the free people of the Gibe states was much better than the wretched condition of the slaves.[103] In fact, it seems that one of the main reasons why class antagonism did not develop in the society of the Gibe states was that the ruling classes, instead of exploiting the free population to the maximum, mainly exploited the slaves, who constituted about one third of the entire population.[104] Only the wealthy men had the means to acquire slaves and they alone received slaves as presents from the kings.

Finally, the Gibe states were interlocked through political marriages and secret military alliances. When one state was attacked by another, it called to its assistance certain others and a conflict involving some or all of the states would be provoked in a short time.[105] The spread of the conflict and the diplomatic arm-twisting would be enough sometimes to persuade the two original contenders to stop the hostilities. Thus, political marriages and secret alliances not only guaranteed the survival of every state, but also prevented them from coalescing into one unified political entity. Though these states had cultural homogeneity, common language, common religion, close commercial contacts, similar administrative establishments, similar agricultural practices and land holding systems, they failed to coalesce into one political entity. These then were some of the common features of the Gibe states. A brief discussion of the history of the formation of each of these states now follows.

Limmu-Ennarya

It was the Limmu group of the Sadacha confederacy that formed the first modern Gibe state and gave their name to the new political entity. Their state was better known by the historical name of Ennarya, the best part of the original territory which they had occupied. In order to distinguish the new state from the historical one, and at the same time maintain the popular name of the new state, Limmu-Ennarya, the combination of the two names which the people themselves gave to their state (perhaps to symbolize the unity of the Ennaryans and the Oromo) will be used in this and the next chapters.

Why the Limmu group were the first to form a state is not hard to understand. They were the first whose mode of production was transformed from pastoralism to one in which mixed agriculture was dominant. This was facilitated by the environment in which they settled. The fertile highlands of Ennarya yielded a plentiful cereal crop produced by the labor of the industrious people. Located at the most active center of trade, the Limmu were probably pulled into the trade of the region early on. Without doubt by the second half of the eighteenth century under the relatively improved conditions along caravan routes, Limmu-Ennarya made full use of its geographical advantages, which its location in the Gibe region offered for trade.[106] The Muslim traders from the north intensified their trade with Limmu-Ennarya, with great benefit to the war leaders of that land. James Bruce, the most important literary source on the trade of Ennarya, depicts a lively trade by that land in the last quarter of the eighteenth century.[107] As we have seen above, during their migration to and settlement in the Gibe region, the Oromo were engaged in pastoral economy. They depended on their cattle, supplemented by exchange with the sedentary groups of animal produce and forest products for grain. With the transformation from pastoralism to sedentary agriculture, division of labor deepened. For the first time after the migration, the Oromo were engaged in different aspects of production. Some continued with pastoralism. Others embarked on mixed farming, making it within a short time the dominant part of the economy. Still others embarked on trading, perhaps a new profession for the Oromo.[108] It was in Limmu-Ennarya that the Oromo merchant class, the Afkala, was born, probably during the second half of the eighteenth century. This marked division of labor had tremendous impact on Limmu-Ennarya and hastened the process of state formation. In short, the fertility of the land of Limmu and the labor of its people gave rise to a viable economy, which led to a division of labor and specialization.

> With agriculture as the determinate mode of economic production, the division of labour was also enhanced. The new mode of production required a different technology, new implements and tools were produced. Some of the implements were made by every family for its own use. But the most important ones had to be produced by specialized craftsmen. At this stage, therefore, there were one or more families in every locality engaged in the production of metal tools (tumtu), tanned leather goods (faqi), etc. The cultivation of cotton in the warm river valleys of Dedessa, Gibe, Wama, etc., helped weaving to emerge as a family-based craft. The craftsmen who were collectively known as ogessa (the "skilled ones") exchanged their products with agricultural products at the market places or at their work places.[109]

More than the division of labor, what was perhaps more noticeable was the division of the society into classes of rich and poor. Some wealthy men owned as many as 7,000 head of cattle,[110] extensive land, and a large number of slaves. The wealthy class was not engaged in material production, but only in consumption and in warfare. Perhaps the best example to substantiate this statement comes not from the Limmu, but from their neighbors, the Botor, among whom A. Cecchi stayed for some days in the 1870s.

> The private life of one of these chiefs of Botor can be summed up more or less as "sweet-to-do-nothing". At the break of the day, the chief took his spear and went out of a house, followed by slaves who carried his barchuma (stool) or soft hide, and sat on the hill, located near his residence. Here, wrapped in his beautiful waya (dress) he waited for the arrival of coffee and gaya (pipe), which every wealthy man used. Surrounded by his dependents, he counted his cattle as they came out of their enclosure . . . In the evening he returned to a clean house, where he was served with coffee and a gaya, and discussed tribal affairs with his friends, and contemplated and planned the next raids on their neighbours.[111]

Thus, the nobility of the Botor, who lived in the midst of luxury and idleness, made raiding the consuming passion of their lives. One institution within the disintegrating gada government particularly favored the rise of kingship. This was the office of Abba Dula ("the father of war"). Previously Abba Dula had been an elected officer who led voluntary warriors against an enemy only when the *chafe* assembly declared war. The Abba Dula exercised effective authority only during the course of a campaign. Once hostilities ceased, he was merely one among equals. However, with the disintegration of the gada government, the office of Abba Dula was radically transformed, becoming hereditary. The new generation of hereditary Abba Dulas, who were mainly members of the nobility, struggled with each other for supremacy. Raids formerly conducted for booty, revenge, or to extend tribal territory, were now conducted for bloody plunder, a practice which ruined the poor man for the sake of establishing the authority of the Abba Dulas.[112] Raids conducted by the Abba Dulas became not only a source of wealth and power, but also a means by which free peasants were reduced to the status of tenants on their own lands.[113] The victorious Abba Dulas, besides taking the lion's share of booty of movable property, virtually monopolized the uncultivated arable lands of the vanquished groups, which they distributed among their followers.

It must be emphasized here that by the second half of the eighteenth century, the Gibe region in general and Limmu-Ennarya in particular, had a great deal of wealth and productive capacity tied to land over which the war leaders fought for monopolizing access to those resources. The power of the Gibe states became crystallized around access to the land and the struggle to control more lands. It was out of the struggle for the control of lands that successful war leaders created their permanent military forces. With sufficient surpluses from their extensive estates, from tribute, taxation, trade, and plunder, successful war leaders were able to maintain permanent military forces with which they made themselves kings, consolidated their administrations and monopolized the means of coercion. It was in this manner that the state of Limmu-Ennarya was created. It was in this manner the new ruling class, which had in its hands the surplus produce of Limmu-Ennarya, assumed a position of superiority, which was reinforced and protected by the newly created state machinery.

Bofo (Abba Gomol), *c.* 1800–1825

The state of Limmu-Ennarya was created by Bofo, a famous Abba Dula, who was known popularly by the name of his war horse – Gomol. In dealing with the history of Abba Gomol, one comes up against a difficulty: the records of his rise to power are adequate, but they were all written between 1843[114] and 1879.[115] The oral traditions recorded by travelers and missionaries between these two dates do not give a definite year for any events that took place at the beginning of that century. From internal evidence it would appear, however, that Abba Gomol founded the kingdom of Limmu-Ennarya probably between 1800 and 1802.

> Abba Rebu . . . who is today [1843] an energetic old man was the most important soressa of Ennarya or at least of the Limu tribe. Bofo, the son of bokku [i.e. the son of an Abba Bokku], was a poor nobleman. He worked his land, on the border of Nonno, who often invaded Limu. In one hand, he held his shield and in the other his spear and the plough. From time to time he raided the Nonno country, always returning with booty. Abba Rebu gave his daughter to Bofo and from her Bofo had his son Abba Bagibo, or Ibssa. Young Bofo went on a raid to Nonno riding his famous horse Gomol and he returned with 3,000 head of cattle.[116]

A few important points emerge from the above story. First, Abba Rebu, who was still alive in 1843, was the most important and wealthy man among the Limmu. Secondly, Bofo, the son of a hereditary Abba Bokku, was a self-made successful war leader who expanded his land at the expense of his neighbors, the Nonno. As we shall see below, Bofo, powerful in war, quick to defend his interests, jealous of his power, and suspicious of his rivals, became a formidable war leader. The wealthy Abba Rebu may have tried and failed to defeat him. At least there is internal evidence[117] which seems to suggest this. It is probable that Abba Rebu, having failed to stop Bofo's rise to power, came to terms with the young warrior and cemented their relations with the hand of his daughter. Thirdly, this marriage in or around 1802 produced Ibssa ("the light"), better known by the name of his horse Bagibo, who was to succeed his father in 1825. According to one recently received piece of information, Abba Bagibo came to power at the age of twenty.[118] According to Beke, Abba Bagibo was somewhere between forty and forty-five years old in 1842.[119] Forty would put his date of birth in 1802, while forty-five would place it in the closing years of the eighteenth century. Antonio Cecchi specifically stated that Abba Bagibo came to power at the age of twenty-three.[120] This would also mean that he was born somewhere about 1802. If accepted, this date is important, not only because it establishes the year of the birth of an important figure who dominated the politics of the Gibe region between 1825 and 1861, but also because it indirectly helps to establish the time when the kingdom of Limmu-Ennarya was formed. Fourthly, Abba Bagibo was born at the royal *massera* of Sappa, the capital of his father. Sappa, perhaps an old trading center, appeared as the capital of the kingdom during either the closing years of the eighteenth century or the beginning of the nineteenth. Saqqa, which was also an important trading center, became the capital of the state after 1825.

Both towns began as important trade centers during the second half of the eighteenth century, and probably earlier. It was only after 1825 that Saqqa replaced Sappa as the capital and the main trading center, for reasons to be discussed later. However, during the first quarter of the nineteenth century, Sappa was the most important center in the Gibe region, where all caravan routes met, while between 1825 and 1861, Saqqa became the commercial capital of the southwestern region of what is today Ethiopia.[121] It was in Sappa, the first capital of Limmu-Ennarya, that Abba Bagibo was born, probably in 1802, "educated," and brought up.[122] The implication of the phrase "educated" will be discussed below, but here it should suffice to say that Sappa was already the capital of the kingdom, and by 1802 without doubt Abba Gomol was already a king. This is supported by some written evidence, which categorically states that Limmu-Ennarya became a kingdom at the beginning of the nineteenth century.[123]

The marriage alliance between the wealthy Abba Rebu and the first king of Limmu-Ennarya does not seem to have brought peace between the two rivals. On the contrary, Abba Rebu refused to recognize the supremacy of his son-in-law until he was soundly beaten by the latter. The earlier cited tradition continues to tell the rest of the story in a somewhat confused manner.

> [The tradition] . . . goes on to describe at length how Bofo quarrelled with his father-in-law and was disgraced. Meanwhile, relations with the jealous Gumma neighbours rapidly deteriorated and finally the Gumma invaded Enarea. The Limmu people led by their chief Abba Rebu could not withstand the Gumma attack and they escaped to the mogga. The victorious Gumma who overran the valley of Enarea were celebrating their success when Bofo and a few of his friends penetrated into their midst, took them by surprise, and killed many of them. When the battle was over and the Gumma were completely defeated, the Limmu people returned to Enarea and fell on their knees before Bofo and said, "We do not want any other master but you." Ever after, Abba Rebu was one of Bofo's most devoted subjects.[124]

By connecting Abba Rebu's quarrel with Bofo with Gumma's war against Limmu-Ennarya, this tradition points to a significant event which is implied, but not stated. This was the war fought between Abba Rebu and his son-in-law, in which the Gumma joined with the former against the latter. Encouraged by the Gumma, Abba Rebu seems to have ignored the strength of his son-in-law. The latter, according to the same tradition, possessed genuine courage, and was also an expert horseman who could inspire his followers.[125] Abba Rebu seems to have expected immediate assistance from the Gumma, but that assistance may have been slow in coming and as every day strengthened Bofo's determination to attack, Abba Rebu resolved too hastily to risk an immediate clash with his son-in-law. The war between the two is reported in a confused manner in a recently published document. Here the conflict is presented as one between Abba Rebu and Abba Bagibo.[126] But in reality, it was between Abba Rebu and his son-in-law, and we should read Abba Gomol instead of Abba Bagibo. According to this tradition, Abba Gomol not only defeated his father-in-law, but burned his *massera* at Saqqa as well.[127] Abba Rebu was forced to flee to Gumma, having suffered shame and loss, where he seems to have told the Gumma that his defeat was their own defeat. The Gumma rallied to Abba Rebu's call and invaded Limmu-Ennarya. Abba Gomol, at the head of a small, handpicked cavalry, advanced stealthily towards the valley of Limmu-Ennarya, where he surprised the enemy, killing many and capturing his father-in-law as a valuable prisoner of war.[128] Following this victory, Abba Gomol was ruled by his head rather than his hand, and earned the title of a "wise prince."[129] He was magnanimous towards his father-in-law and forgave him for his rebellion, and Abba Rebu became not only one of his most devoted subjects, but also his principal advisor.[130]

After he made peace with his father-in-law, Abba Gomol stands more clearly as a capable king, strong of will and passionately devoted to the expansion of his kingdom. The same tradition depicts him as a "wise prince," who appeared at a crucial point in the history of his land.[131] While there is an element of exaggeration in this tradition, what is not in dispute is that during his reign Limmu-Ennarya was the cradle of a new dynamic spirit which soon began to shape every material and spiritual aspect of the Oromo society in the Gibe region.[132] His land gave birth to the institution of monarchy, as well as to change in ideology. In short, during the reign of Abba Gomol, Limmu-Ennarya displayed fresh and vital energies which were destined to exert a strong influence on the rest of the Gibe region.

Abba Gomol, the founder of a new dynasty, left his name to posterity as the first Muslim Oromo king in the Gibe region.[133] Today, tradition claims that he was converted by "the miracles of a famous Ashrafi Shaykh (a descendant of the prophet)."[134] In the early 1840s, Captain Harris heard in Shawa that Abba Gomol had been converted to Islam by his uncle.[135] The validity of both claims will be examined in Chapter 5. Here, it is enough to state only a few facts. There is reason to believe that Abba Gomol had a breadth of vision which enabled him to grasp the importance of embracing Islam. He did so only after becoming the king of Limmu-Ennarya. This was shortly before the birth of his son, Ibssa (Abba Bagibo) in 1802. This is supported by four independent sources. First and foremost, the oral tradition collected from the region makes it abundantly clear that Bofo was the first Oromo king who embraced Islam in the Gibe region. This source stresses that the first Muslim king of Limmu-Ennarya gave permission to the Muslim teachers and preachers to teach Islam to the children of the nobility.[136] Secondly, in 1840 Captain Harris heard in Shawa that "prayers are held at the tomb of Bofo the first convert to the faith."[137] Thirdly, in the late 1850s Massaja actually visited the tomb of Bofo,[138] which by then already had taken on the character of a shrine, adding luster to Sappa, which was once the most important market town in the region. Fourthly, in 1879 in Limmu-Ennarya, A. Cecchi wrote that "today after nearly eighty years, Islam is found at full vigour, being already adopted even by the most pauperized classes."[139] In short, there is no doubt that Abba Gomol embraced Islam after becoming the king of Limmu-Ennarya. He accepted Islam for ideological and political purposes. In the state in which the changed mode of production and radically altered political landscape were breaking down the tribal loyalties of the past, the need arose for a unifying ideology which went beyond the narrow limits of old loyalty and welded together the people under a single administration, a new educational system based on reading and writing, and "a power for order and organizing the people." Islam provided him with a focus of unity transcending tribal loyalty, and helped him to justify his ruthless actions. It also created the proper atmosphere for the hundreds of Muslim merchants and preachers to propagate Islam freely.[140] In other words, by accepting Islam, Abba Gomol forged an ideological unity with the many merchants and preachers in his capital, and the latter spread Islam and championed the cause of the king.[141] However, his acceptance of Islam may not have had any profound effect on his spiritual life. On the contrary, the old religion and Islam operated side by side for a long time, and the new religion limited the scope of the old only in the 1860s.[142] There is nothing to show that Abba Gomol himself had ever received any kind of Muslim education. However, his capital at Sappa was teeming with Muslim merchants and teachers at the beginning of the nineteenth century, and some of them were engaged in the teaching of the royal children and those of the nobility.[143] From the way Abba Bagibo compared the illiterate Christian priests and traders with the literate Muslim traders in 1843, his fascination with written words and his exchange of letters with his neighbors, and from his according of special place of honor to literate men, including Catholic missionaries,[144] it appears likely that he had been exposed to some form of education at an early age. It is not possible to say whether he was able to write in either Oromo or Arabic, though he may have been able to read the Quran. Certainly, his correspondence was conducted in both Oromo and Arabic.[145]

Abba Gomol conducted wars against his neighbors, mainly the Gumma, from political and economic motives. Gumma was in the process of state formation and the rival Abba Dulas had brought their conflicts into Limmu-Ennarya, even threatening Sappa, the capital, which was not far from Gumma's frontier. Again, the unsettled situation in Gumma was a menace to Limmu-Ennarya's commercial lifeline to Kaffa. Even after the formation of the Gumma state, Abba Gomol was able to defeat Gumma time and again, but he was never able to take it over completely, probably because he was engaged in expansion against other neighbors such as the Nonno in the north, the Agallo in the west, the Gomma and the Jimma Badi in the south. By launching wars of conquest against his neighbors, Abba Gomol sowed the seeds of future conflict for his successor. What is more, in spite of his strong personal energy, which remained unimpaired up to 1825, when he was deposed,[146] Abba Gomol did not complete the task of enlarging the frontiers of Limmu-Ennarya. This is all that could be said about the history of the formation of Limmu-Ennarya. To summarize what has been described thus far: Abba Gomol (c. 1800–1825) formed the state of Limmu-Ennarya, which became very important between 1825 and 1861 during the reign of Abba Bagibo, the most famous Oromo king of the first half of the nineteenth century. The history of the reign of Abba Bagibo will be discussed in a separate chapter. In the remaining part of this chapter, a brief history of the formation of the rest of the Gibe states will be presented.

Before discussing the formation of the states of Gumma, Gomma, and Gera, it is imperative to say a few words about the paucity of information which we have on these states. First of all, the sources we have for Limmu-Ennarya and Jimma are far richer than what we have for the other three states. Secondly, for Limmu-Ennarya and Jimma the traditions of the original state makers were adequately recorded and written down in the nineteenth century. The written records throw a new light upon the processes of state formation and the stages of economic and cultural development achieved by the two states. Thirdly, the oral history which was recently collected from Limmu-Ennarya and Jimma supplements and further enriches the written records of the nineteenth and early twentieth centuries. Judicious interpretation and cautious use of the available information establish a clear picture and reliable history of the formation of the states of Limmu-Ennarya and Jimma. Unfortunately the same cannot be said about the history of the formation of the other states. This is because the written information on the early history of Gumma, Gomma, and Gera is too sketchy for detailed description. It is extremely difficult to find details about the history of the first kings of these states, and the limited information available is confused and contradictory. In the case of Gera, the scarcity of information compels us to have recourse to conjecture. Moreover, careful and detailed oral history research into the early history of those states has just begun, although the need to undertake such research has become steadily clearer to the scholars in the field.[147] While the Jimma Interview Programme which was conducted in the region in 1974 has produced much information about the history of Gumma, Gomma, and Gera, much remains to be done before knowledge about those states is established on a solid foundation. Consequently, certain aspects of the formation of those states are *terra incognita*. It is therefore important to realize that the following necessarily incomplete picture of the formation of Gumma, Gomma, and Gera is no more than conjecture.

Gumma

Gumma was the second state to be formed in the Gibe region. Like Limmu-Ennarya, the nucleus of the state was formed during the second half of the eighteenth century. However, the process of state formation was completed only around 1810. Accurate description of the process that led to the formation of the state is difficult because information on the early history of Gumma, though relatively rich, is confused and contradictory. According to d'Abbadie, Cecchi, and the "Amharic Short History of the Matcha Kings,"[148] the founder of the dynasty of Gumma was a certain Adam, a Muslim trader from Tigray. The "Chronicle of the Kingdom of Gumma," published by Cerulli, also makes Adam the founder of the state of Gumma.

The Oromo of Ethiopia

However, according to the chronicle, Adam was not a trader from Tigray. On the contrary, Adam was a giant hunter who lived in the forest of Ebbich Talo the wooded region between Gumma and their formidable neighbors, the Nonno, stateless Oromo tribes who lived west of Gumma in what is today the Illubabor region. At that time, Gumma was divided into two parts, namely Dagoye and the area around Chirra. A certain Sarbaroda was the leader of the Dagoye region, while Jilcha was the leader of the Chirra area. According to the chronicle of the kingdom of Gumma, Sarbaroda had tried and failed to capture Adam, who lived in the forest, but Adam was tamed by a daughter of Sarbaroda, who was given in marriage to him. The story goes on to say that Sarbaroda and his "son"-in-law quarreled and in the battle that followed the "father"-in-law was killed by Adam, who made himself the king of Dagoye.[149]

It is tempting, indeed more than tempting, to see in this tradition a power struggle between the leaders of Dagoye and Chirra. The power struggle was between Sarbaroda of Dagoye and Jilcha of Chirra. In the chronicle, Jilcha is presented as the "son" of Adam. But this should not be taken at face value. In the tradition, a Muslim called Adam is made the "father" of Jilcha, so as to Islamize and exalt the origin of the dynasty founded by Jilcha. We say this because the same tradition makes it very clear that Adam in fact was not a historical figure.

> The Man [Adam] was white . . . [He] milks elephants . . . Seizes buffaloes and eats them up . . . Whether Adam was born of the devil or born of human beings, we do not know. There was no flesh that he did not eat; if he hurled a lance, he did not miss the mark; if he spoke he did not err.[150]

The story goes on to say that Adam was a satan and an evil spirit. What is particularly interesting to note here is that the tradition places Gumma's conversion to Islam at the beginning of the nineteenth century, while in reality the ruling house of Gumma did not accept Islam before the 1830s. As we shall see later in the discussion on the spread of Islam in Gumma,[151] Islam did not take deep root there before the 1860s. In the 1880s, Gumma declared jihad in the name of Islam for reasons to be discussed later. It was then that the tradition of Adam was invented so as to Islamize the original founder of the dynasty. What all this amounts to is that the power struggle that raged in Gumma during the first decade of the nineteenth century was between Sarbaroda of Dagoye and Jilcha of Chirra. Sarbaroda may have tried to come to terms with Jilcha by giving his daughter in marriage, but the political marriage seems to have failed to unite the rival contenders to the throne of Gumma. In the battle that followed, Sarbaroda was killed and Jilcha became the first king of all Gumma. Chirra, where the main *massera* (royal residence) of Jilcha was located, became the capital of Gumma. It appears that Jilcha faced serious internal opposition, and his sudden death after becoming the king of Gumma may have been caused by it. Jilcha was succeeded by his son, Oncho (*c.* 1810–1830s). It was Oncho who completed the processes of state formation in Gumma, by mercilessly crushing all internal opposition. He then involved Gumma in a continuous war against its neighbors, mainly

Limmu-Ennarya. It was Oncho's wars against Gumma's neighbors which seem to have earned the people of that land the reputation for being "famous warriors."[152] Without doubt Oncho was a brave warrior who possessed a daring spirit which ignored danger and delighted in war. A leader with a vigorous mind and agile body, he infused his own intrepid spirit into his followers. And yet, his military accomplishments were stained by a licentious indulgence in acts of violence with little regard even for his own people. As we shall soon see, he even treacherously killed the king of Gera. In the sources, Oncho is depicted as a monstrous tyrant, a cruel king who killed or enslaved people for minor offenses.[153] Even in 1879, he was remembered as a callous tyrant who caused untold miseries even to his own people.[154] This is all that can be said about the history of the formation of the state of Gumma.

Gomma

The written information on the early history of Gomma is limited, and confused.[155] A linking thread that runs through this information is that the founder of the dynasty of Gomma was a Muslim "holy" man and the dynasty he founded was known as Awuliani ("the holy one"). On the one hand, Cecchi asserts that a Somali shaykh, Nur Hussein, was the founder of the dynasty of Gomma[156] but this is untenable. As we shall see further in the discussion,[157] Cecchi's Nur Hussein was confused with or developed out of the tradition of Shaykh Hussein, the famous thirteenth-century Muslim religious leader of Bali. On the other hand, the "Amharic History of the Matcha Kings" claims that Awuliani (which is misspelled as Awaleni), the founder of the dynasty, came from Gojjam.[158] What the two sources have in common is that the founder of the dynasty was a non-Oromo Muslim "holy" man. This, however, is historically incorrect, to say the least. It is not difficult to explain why the tradition makes the founder of the dynasty a Muslim "holy" man. This is because Gomma was the first state in the Gibe region where Islam became the religion of the whole people. In other words, the entire people of Gomma were converted to Islam much earlier than the rest of the Gibe states. During the first half of the nineteenth century, while Islam was the religion of the ruling classes in the rest of the Gibe states, it was the religion of the people in Gomma. It was in order to Islamize and exalt the noble origin of the dynasty that did so much to spread Islam in Gomma that the tradition of Awuliani was invented.

We are very fortunate in having the precious information about the early history of Gomma from oral tradition.[159] According to this tradition, the nucleus of the state of Gomma was formed by Abba Boke. He ruled over Gomma, except the region of Qattu.[160] The oral history of Gomma is fascinating both for what it tells us about the early history of Gomma and because it deals with the *chafe* assembly. Careful analysis of this tradition provides us with a clear picture of the way in which the *chafe* assembly lost its traditional power. The tradition makes it clear that settling of disputes by peaceful means was the practice of the assembly. Declaration of war and conclusion of peace were its prerogatives. To command respect and honor and to lead warriors into battle was the task of the leaders elected by the assembly. Abba Boke was such a leader. His power was founded upon the mandate conferred by the assembly.[161] However, he made himself hereditary leader, thus challenging and ignoring the traditional political wisdom of rotating office. What is particularly important to note here is that the tradition depicts Abba Boke's conflict over land with other war leaders. It was out of the struggle over possession and control of lands that Abba Boke gained total control of the land between Yacc and Dogaye.[162] Interestingly, the *chafe* assembly recognized the said land as the property of Abba Boke, who divided and distributed it among his follower and those who sought his protection.[163] So like the other Gibe states, in Gomma also the power of the state became crystallized around access to the land and the struggle to control more lands. What becomes clear from the oral history of Gomma was that the weak feared attack by and sought protection of the strong, while terrorizing the weak into submission became the passion of the strong. In the unfolding drama of anarchy, the protection which the assembly earlier had given to the weak was paralyzed, justice became the monopoly of the strong, and those outside the circle of war leaders and their followers suffered from the lack of safety. In short, Abba Boke effectively controlled the means of protection and offered it in exchange for the appropriation of economic surplus. Nevertheless, Abba Boke died before uniting the region of Qattu with Gomma.[164] He was succeeded by his son, Abba Manno (*c.* 1820–1840), who seems to have gained considerable experience in the army of his father. Abba Manno came to power at a mature age and quickly united the region of Qattu with Gomma, thus completing the process of state formation.[165] Abba Manno is remembered as the first king of Gomma, who introduced Islam to that land. He went further and proclaimed that he was the protector and defender of Islam. He found in Islam an ideological justification for abolishing Oromo traditional celebrations such as *butta* festivals. What is remarkable about Abba Manno was his intense interest in matters of religion. He seems to have believed passionately in the spread of Islam in Gomma and the rest of the Gibe region. He patronized Muslim religious teachers by giving them land and facilitating their missionary activities. As we shall see in the section on the spread of Islam in the Gibe region,[166] Abba Manno enhanced the activities of the Qadiriya order, which furthered in turn the spread of Islam, Muslim teachers, and their missionary activities in Gomma. This had a profound impact on Gomma, so much so that by the 1830s the entire people of that land were already converted to Islam. In short, during the reign of Abba Manno, Islam won the hearts and the minds of the people of Gomma. Furthermore, Abba Manno did much to spread Islam in the Gibe region and that religion in turn strengthened the position of his dynasty in Gomma.[167] It was in the course of the spread of Islam in Gomma that Abba Manno was recognized as "*waliyi*" ("the holy") and his dynasty gained the immortal name of Awuliani ("the holy one"). This is all that can be said about the history of the formation of Gomma.

Jimma

The sources for the history of the state of Jimma Abba Jifar are adequate, and the following brief history of that state does not do justice perhaps to the amount of information at our disposal.[168]

The state of Jimma was born out of the struggle between the two clans: the Badi and the Diggo. The nucleus of the state was created by a Diggo man, named Abba Faro,[169] who was an elected gada official. He was succeeded by his elder son Abba Magal, who was a famous warrior.[170] The Badi group lost in the struggle partly because of the devastating attacks which Abba Bagibo directed against their land, reducing them to the status of tributaries of Limmu-Ennarya, but also partly because the Badi lacked a single leadership. Their war leaders fought more with each other than against their common enemies, exhausting their resources while inflicting real wounds on the Badi group. The Diggo group had an able leader in Abba Magal, who co-ordinated their efforts, marshaled their resources, galvanized them into action, and took advantage of the Badi's double weaknesses. At that time, the region of Jimma-Kakka[171] experienced dramatic conflicts as ten rival Abba Dulas (war leaders) were engaged in the struggle for supremacy. Abba Magal was one of them. Starting from a small area and facing many challenges, he continuously expanded the frontier of his territory. The expansion was a tribute to his leadership and the loyalty and unwavering support of the Diggo group. The history of Abba Magal clearly shows that in the struggle for supremacy the two most important keys to success were a determined leadership and a united people. Abba Magal easily captured from the Badi group the fertile land around the great market of Hirmata. This was the major step on the road to the creation of the kingdom of Jimma. However, Abba Magal was not destined to complete the process, as he was overtaken by death. He left the task of consolidation and the building of the kingdom to his son, Sanna. Sanna was a born warrior, who had gained considerable experience in the wars of his father. After the death of the latter, Sanna had to dispute the succession to his father's authority with his brother Abba Rago.[172] Sanna showed his military abilities by easily defeating Abba Rago, then sound judgment by imprisoning rather than killing him,[173] and diplomatic skill in coming to terms with the king of Gumma. Before embarking on his war of conquest, Sanna created a new army. This army was better than any other in the Gibe region for four reasons. Its discipline and its endurance were better. It effectively employed the element of surprise by attacking suddenly from various unexpected directions. Another reason for its success was its ability to recover quickly, even from a major disaster.[174] Finally, Sanna added to his army's tactical efficiency by his own charismatic personality, and the employment of a strategy of genius which enabled him to galvanize them into action. Tall, well-built, brave, and daring, he infused his men with his intrepid spirit and excited them to action by always being at the forefront of the battle.[175] Such was the army with which he opened the campaign for building a kingdom. Sanna's military ability was matched by his diplomatic skill, which kept his many enemies so divided that he was able to defeat them one after the other.[176] Sanna won his first decisive victory by slaying one of the most important and powerful Abba Dulas of the Badi group, Do-os, who was reputed to have been a hero.[177] The victory assured Sanna of undisputed supremacy in the region of Hirmata. He then took over the *massera* of the defeated Badi leader and made it the seat of his kingdom.[178] From his power base, in the region of Hirmata, Sanna slowly expanded the frontiers of his territory until he had defeated all the rival Abba Dulas one after the other, and by 1830 a new kingdom of Jimma-Kakka had been established. It was in the course of his war of conquest that Sanna earned his immortal name of Jifar, after his famous horse. Gradually, the name of the founder eclipsed that of Jimma-Kakka. Thus, Abba Jifar became both the name of the king and that of the kingdom.

As in the military, so in the political field, Abba Jifar showed "his high intelligence and wisdom."[179] He had created a kingdom, but soon realized that it needed wealth and ideology, which not only nourished the unity of the people, but also consolidated the dynasty's grip on the territory. He wanted wealth from commerce and Islam provided him with the ideology. As we shall see further in the discussion,[180] he embraced Islam for political and economic motives rather than for religious needs.

Before this brief history is concluded it is essential to discuss the economic conflict which developed between Jimma and Limmu-Ennarya after the formation of the former. The formation of the state of Jimma widened the scope of trade and increased opportunities for making a profit in the trade of the Gibe region. This increased the volume of trade and the number of Muslim traders who left Limmu-Ennarya and came to Jimma. The intensification of trade in Jimma at the expense of Limmu-Ennarya not only benefited Abba Jifar, but also angered Abba Bagibo, who was determined to prevent Jimma from crippling the trade of Limmu-Ennarya. As we shall see in the last chapter, the economic conflict between the two states dominated the politics of the region for three decades, thus wasting vital time, much-needed resources, and creative energies required for uniting the Gibe area into a single state. Be that as it may, Abba Jifar ruled up to 1855, and left behind to his successor a powerful kingdom, a new religion, much wealth, and a strong ambition to dominate the politics of the Gibe region.

Gera

The nucleus of the state of Gera was created by Gunji, a successful war leader who made himself king. He is reported to have been a wise leader, who defended and protected his people. However, he died shortly after becoming king and was succeeded by his son, Tullu Gunji (*c.* 1835). According to oral history, Tullu was an intelligent man, a clever politician, a warrior king, and a good administrator.[181] Tullu was popular within Gera and famous in the Gibe region. His popularity excited him into bold adventures of expansion at the expense of his neighbors. He is said to have fought against Kaffa, Gomma, and

Gumma. His relation with Oncho Jilcha, the king of Gumma, was particularly bad. To the border conflict between Gera and Gumma was added Oncho's ambition to place a man of his choice on the throne of Gera. Though popular within Gera, Tullu Gunji seems to have faced a serious challenge from one of his half-brothers, Abba Baso. The mother of Abba Baso was the daughter of Oncho Jilcha. In the struggle between Tullu and Abba Baso, Oncho sided with his grandson. In the battle that followed, it appears that Tullu was captured. The leaders of the surrounding states sent their ambassadors to Gumma to beg Oncho to spare the life of Tullu Gunji. It is said that Oncho treacherously killed the king of Gera.[182] What this treachery involved is not clear from our sources. It appears that when the ambassadors expressed their horror at what happened, Oncho Jilcha brushed aside diplomatic niceties, having them soundly beaten, imprisoned, and forced to grind corn.[183] It was then that Oncho Jilcha earned the dubious reputation for being the exponent and embodiment of cruelty in the Gibe region.[184]

After the death of Tullu Gunji, Abba Baso became the king of Gera. Cecchi claims that Abba Baso was the first king of Gera. However, this is true only in the sense that Abba Baso was the first man to be put on the throne of Gera by the action of Oncho Jilcha. Whether it was because of the way he came to power or not, Abba Baso was an unpopular king. His reign was short-lived. Around 1838, he was overthrown and exiled to Jimma by his brother Abba Rago.[185] Owing to the paucity of information this is all that can be said about the formation of the state of Gera.

To summarize the content of this chapter, all the Gibe states were formed by internal processes. It was Abba Gomol (c. 1800–1825) who formed the state of Limmu-Ennarya. It was Oncho Jilcha (c. 1810–1830) who founded the kingdom of Gumma. It was Abba Manno (c. 1820–1840) who completed the process of state formation in Gomma. It was Abba Jifar I (1830–1855) who created the kingdom of Jimma. It was Tullu Gunji (c. 1835) who formed the state of Gera. There is, however, an enormous disparity between our knowledge of the history of the state makers in the Gibe region. On the one hand, the early history of Limmu-Ennarya and that of Jimma are fairly well documented and therefore we are able to form an accurate picture of the history of Abba Gomol and that of Abba Jifar I. On the other hand, our knowledge about the history of Oncho Jilcha, Abba Manno, and Tullu Gunji is much less satisfactory and necessarily very inadequate.

Finally, the next two chapters will deal with the economic foundation and ideological orientation of the Gibe states: agriculture, commerce, and the spread of Islam in the region.

4

The economic foundation of the Gibe states: agriculture and industry

The most characteristic feature of the Gibe states was the dominating role o
agriculture. However, trade was also promoted; the Gibe states were create
by and in the interests of the landowning class, and trade benefited the rulers
The profession of trading was raised to a status hitherto unknown in th
region, and this provided adventurous traders with the opportunity to amas
wealth, and become prominent politically.[1] As a result, a dynamic indigenou
trading class emerged to dominate the commercial scene in the Gibe region
Moreover, trading influences were accompanied by deeper penetration b
Islam; as elsewhere in Africa, Islam followed in the footsteps of trade.

In the previous chapters, we saw how the settlement of the Oromo in th
Gibe region had a profound impact on their way of life. Of course, when th
Oromo pastoralists first arrived in the region in the 1570s they were unable t
take maximum advantage of the economic potential of their new environment
It was mainly after the transformation of their mode of production fron
pastoralism to sedentary agriculture that they were able to do this. The
changed their political institutions, ideology, and mode of production to mee
the demands of the new conditions. They also transformed the economy of th
region through their labor on the land and their activities in trade an
exchange. In this chapter, I shall attempt to demonstrate that agriculture wa
the material foundation of the Gibe states and to describe the progress o
industry in the region.

Just as it is today, so also in the past,[2] the Gibe region was a very fertile par
of Ethiopia, a great agricultural center and a land of plenty. A Europea
traveler at the beginning of the twentieth century described the fertility of th
region in these terms:

> There are few regions in Africa which are richer than the western and south
> western portions of Abyssinia – generally known as the Galla country. It
> picturesque mountain masses are well wooded and the valleys are regula
> gardens. The climate is ideal, water for irrigation plentiful, and the soil so fertil
> that it will produce anything with the minimum of labour. Two crops a year ca
> be grown without cultivation. All that is necessary is to sow the seeds anyhow; th
> land does the rest.[3]

114

Tasaw Merga, a modern historian, went even further, describing the region as "Africa's paradise."[4] Although this may be an exaggeration, the Gibe region was, and still is, very fertile, offering, by the variety of its natural characteristics, great possibilities for Oromo agricultural activity.

From the Gibe river to the Gojeb, from the Omo to the Didessa, there was a succession of valleys and plains of amazing fertility. Interspersed were areas not quite so productive – hot tracts infested with malaria and tsetse fly, beautiful chains of mountains, and numerous hills. Abundant forests enveloped the whole region. Great rivers – the Gibe, the Gojeb, the Baro and the Didessa – and numerous smaller streams[5] ran swollen by the torrential rains from the middle of June to the end of October,[6] providing opportunities for irrigation. The potentialities and the actual agricultural resources of each state will be described below. What follows is largely based on the works of A. Cecchi, who visited all the Gibe states and gathered invaluable information about their agricultural economy.

In Limmu-Ennarya especially, the plains and valleys were blessed with soil that gave a variety of possibilities for agriculture. Many small rivers cascaded down from the mountains and flowed across the plains to empty into the Omo, the Gibe, or the Didessa. The many plains and valleys were not only endowed with almost inexhaustible pasturage but also yielded plentiful cereal crops produced by the labor of the industrious people. In the northeast, the series of hills which separate the Botor from Limmu-Ennarya provided a contrasting panorama. Even the rocky land in this area was covered with forest. The plain at the foot of the chain was fertile in soil, rich in water, and abundantly cultivated with teff and sorghum.[7] Every kind of grain grew in the central part of Limmu-Ennarya. In the north, in the valley of the Gibe, in addition to cultivated land, pasture, and extensive forests, rich coffee trees took up a considerable area. In the west, the forests in the valleys of the Didessa provided a home for a variety of game. It was also an ideal environment for coffee, which grew there naturally. In the south, sorghum competed with teff, while the Sadacha forest boasted an abundance of game.[8] In the east, on the confines of the mountains overlooking the Gibe Ennarya, barley, wheat, and other highland crops were grown. Even hilltops and mountains yielded abundant products in this part of the country. In short, the land of Limmu-Ennarya produced cereals – teff, sorghum, maize, barley, wheat, finger millet – and oil seeds, a variety of beans, peas and lentils, and vegetables, including onions and garlic. In the lowlands, coffee, cotton, and fruit trees were grown.[9] Root crops such as *ensete*, potatoes, and sweet potatoes were also cultivated. Thus, the economy of Limmu-Ennarya was based on agriculture, and agriculture was the basis of most of the relationships of the people.

The tableland of Gumma, with its cultivated fields interspersed with wooded pasture, was rich in animals.[10] Gumma's abundant grass and well-watered land supported a large number of cows, oxen, sheep, goats, mules, and horses. Gumma was subjected to constant inroads from her pastoral neighbors, the Arjo in the north and the Nonno in the west, and therefore agriculture did not develop along these two boundaries. Here, Gumma's population practiced pastoralism. The economic consequence was that the land under cultivation in Gumma was smaller than in Jimma Abba Jifar and Limmu-Ennarya. However, the central and southern parts of Gumma were intensely cultivated and were very rich in sorghum, wheat, barley, and cotton, but lacked coffee. Thus, the economy of Gumma was based on agriculture and also, to a limited extent, on pastoralism.

Gomma, the smallest of all the Gibe states, was agriculturally a very rich land. According to Cecchi, the wide undulating valley which formed the main part of Gomma produced abundant teff, maize, sorghum, finger millet, cotton, oil seeds, peppers, varieties of beans and peas, coffee, lemons, and vegetables, but it lacked barley and wheat.[11] Grain and coffee were the chief sources of agricultural wealth. No feast and no religious ceremony was complete without coffee. As the most thoroughly Islamized state in the region, Gomma was already substituting coffee for blood in ceremonies.[12] Surrounded by relatively big sister states on all its borders, enclosed by a circle of mountains and blessed with numerous streams, the people of Gomma devoted themselves to farming, earning a reputation for a high degree of civilization.[13] The meadows at the bottoms of the fertile valleys and the uncultivated slopes supported a large cattle population but, as in Limmu-Ennarya, the milieu was overwhelmingly agricultural.

The country where agriculture reached the highest state of development was Jimma Abba Jifar. The main source, Cecchi, names Jimma as the richest of the Gibe states. He attributes its advanced agriculture to the presence of Jabarti traders who were supposed to have transmitted their agricultural skill to the Oromo.[14] The long contact with Jabarti traders may have influenced the development of agriculture in Jimma, but to credit the Jabarti traders with the whole progress of agriculture does not tally with the known facts. In the first place, there were more Jabarti traders in Limmu-Ennarya than in Jimma right up to the time when, in the 1870s, Jimma eclipsed Limmu-Ennarya. Cecchi arrived in the Gibe region in the late 1870s, at the very time when the sun of Limmu-Ennarya was setting and the star of Jimma rising. A large number of Jabarti traders had recently left the declining state and gone to prosper in Jimma. Cecchi's conclusion can be said to reflect merely the unfolding drama of the time. It was not in the 1870s that agriculture developed in Jimma, but in the 1770s and earlier. According to Abba Jobir, a traditional Oromo historian, the forests presented a formidable obstacle to the Oromo when they arrived in the region. However, they soon started massive clearance, towards the end of the seventeenth and beginning of the eighteenth centuries, preparing the way for extensive farming.[15] This would imply that agricultural development preceded the settlement of Jabarti traders in Jimma in the 1830s, perhaps by more than half a century.

Secondly, and more importantly, Jimma Abba Jifar had the largest population in the Gibe region, estimated at 150,000 in the late 1850s.[16] In 1936, the population estimate for Jimma was 300,000.[17] It would seem that, in estimating it at 30,000 to 35,000 in 1879,[18] Cecchi had grossly underestimated the size of Jimma's population. The relatively large population may have contributed to the advancement of agriculture in Jimma. The inhabitants had the reputation of being intelligent and hardworking: they were "possessed of sufficient culture to have made its capital and its land an example of prosperity for all Africa to admire and imitate."[19] In Jimma, the fertility of the soil, combined with the intelligent activity of its inhabitants, made the land of Abba Jifar a country of much greater agricultural wealth than Limmu-Ennarya. The highlands were very rich in wheat and barley, while in valleys there grew maize, teff, sorghum, finger millet, cotton, coffee, lentils, and a variety of forest plants, vegetables, and spices, including several species of *Amomum*.[20]

> Around the edges of the field and in the gardens surrounding their houses, the people of Jimma grow many more plants. Among the many garden crops are [potato]...sweet potato, a number of varieties of beans and peas, a form of yam, a few leafy plants, and gourds. The primary garden crop is ensete...This plant is not as important in Jimma as it is in most of the countries of southwest Ethiopia (Gurage, Sidamo, Gimira, for instance), where it is the staple, but it does fulfill a need during the rainy season and at other periods when few grains are available.[21]

In short, from one end of Jimma to the other, the country was "full of well-cultivated fields, interspersed with wooden pasture and hills with fertile valleys."[22] Thus, even more than Limmu-Ennarya Jimma was a predominantly agricultural land, and agriculture constituted the backbone of the economy.

Finally, we come to the land of Gera, another state with flourishing agriculture. Cecchi described Gera as "a basin surrounded by softly notched hills with gentle slopes."[23] The many beautiful streams cascaded down from the mountains and flowed across the valleys to empty themselves in the Naso river. The valleys yielded abundant teff, maize, sorghum, ensete, finger millet, and several varieties of beans and peas. Wheat and barley were cultivated on the highlands at an altitude of 2,300 meters and above. Teff, barley, and wheat were sown in July and harvested in late November. Unlike Jimma, Gomma, Gumma, and Limmu-Ennarya, where maize was sown in February and harvested in July, in Gera it was sown in April and harvested in August.[24] The forests of Gera competed with those of Limmu-Ennarya in abundance of coffee. It was also the land that boasted the greatest riches in spices.[25] The seven varieties of spices that grew there both sweetened the air and attracted and nourished swarms of bees. Gera was, and still is, the rich land of honey.[26] Beehives were hung on trees all over the land, and caves and hollow tree trunks also yielded their share of honey. There were eight qualities of honey in Gera.[27] Of these, *Ebichaa*, named after the plant from which the bees extracted the nectar, was the most famous of all honeys in the Gibe region. With its excellent flavor, it was known as royal honey, and indeed the famous *dadhi* (mead) was made exclusively from *Ebichaa*. All over the Gibe region the kings and queens and great dignitaries drank the *dadhi* made from this honey. It is not surprising, therefore, that the flavorsome and prestigious *Ebichaa* was a royal monopoly.

Although honey was plentiful throughout the Gibe region, it was Gera honey which enjoyed the reputation of greatest excellence.[28]

From all the sources, it is clear that the economy of the Gibe region was predominantly agricultural. From the valleys of Limmu-Ennarya and Jimma to the mountains of Gomma, from the plains of Gera to the lowlands of Gumma, the land gave forth cereals, root crops, and many varieties of beans, peas and lentils, oil seeds, fruit trees, vegetables, coffee (the main cash crop), cotton, *chat*, and spices. Blessed with fertile soil that needed little irrigation,[29] the Oromo of the Gibe region were engaged in intensive farming, and their relatively developed agriculture produced a large surplus.

Agricultural practice in the Gibe region was very similar to that of the Christian land to the north. The plough used in the Gibe region, however, was somewhat different.[30] Huntingford argues that the Oromo borrowed their plough from the Amharas.[31] This seemingly attractive hypothesis assumes that neither the Oromo nor the people among whom they settled had a plough culture. This is historically incorrect to say the least. We saw above that the Oromo were engaged in mixed farming long before their sixteenth-century migration.[32] This means that the Oromo probably were familiar with plough cultivation even before their migration. In the Gibe region, the Oromo migrated to and settled among people who had a well-developed plough culture. For instance, the indigenous people of historical Ennarya were noted for their prosperous agriculture, which was based on plough cultivation.[33] According to Cecchi, the plough used in the Gibe region was somewhat inferior to that used in Shawa. This may or may not have been the case. What is not in dispute, however, is the fact that the Oromo in the Gibe region did not borrow a plough from the Amhara. They probably acquired it from the indigenous people of Ennarya. As in Shawa, a pair of oxen were used as draught animals and the drawn plough was supplemented by three or four men working with hoes.[34] The plough was the most vital of farm implements in the region and played much the same role in the agricultural economy as it did in Shawa:

> Within the complex of ecological and technological factors, the plough had a central role by working the land better, reducing the amount of human labour needed in agriculture, and freeing individuals for other productive or non-productive activities. The plough also had implications for two very important institutions within the local communities, the household and land tenure; the force needed in ploughing is the ultimate determinant of the strict division of labour between the sexes, and the great capacity of the plough necessitated well-defined rules of land tenure.[35]

This brings us to the difficult question of the landholding system in the Gibe region, difficult because so little was written about it earlier before or after the formation of the Gibe states. As we saw in Chapter 3, the struggle which led to the formation of the Gibe states was over the question of land. It was a struggle which brought about a radical change in the landholding system of the area. Before agriculture became the dominant mode of production for the Oromo in the region, the land and all its resources belonged to the clan as a whole, and conflict over land was settled by the clan assembly, the *chafe*. The landholding system probably differed little from that practiced by other Matcha groups in a similar ecological environment across the Didessa river in Wallaga. A recent study of landholding in Wallaga touches upon the essential features of the system:

> Those who migrated with their cattle into the new territory defeated the original inhabitants, the Gonka, and claimed large areas for themselves and their descendants. They became "fathers of the land," abba lafa, or "possessors of land." abba kabie. The Kabie (Qabie) possession should be confirmed by the ruling gada class at the Caffe (chafe) or gada center, and after such a "registration" no other family could claim that land. Those who in this way took land became founders of localized patrilineages which became associated with certain areas of land. Land was plentiful, and the first immigrants came to be associated with large tracts of land for agriculture and grazing. The country in western Wollega consists of undulating hills with deep valleys in between. The settlements are concentrated on the upper parts of the hills, and each hill is, thus, associated with a certain lineage or sub-lineage. It was usually easy to demarcate the borders between lineage groups and their territory with the help of valleys, creeks and other natural features . . . Every man in the lineage had a right to get a piece of land to build his house on and to get land for agriculture and pasture. Land to which a man could claim such rights was called his Masi. The term refers to the portion of land which is actually under cultivation in the fallow cycle, but it is also used to denote any land a man or his father or grandfather has cultivated previously and to which he could thus claim rights of usufruct.[36]

Two points are worth mentioning here. The conquered people, the *gabbaro*, were not driven off their land, as appears to be implied at the beginning of this long quotation. The *gabbaro* were left on their land and were adopted by, and eventually assimilated into, Oromo clans. Even after the Oromo conquest, the *gabbaro* continued to enjoy ownership of their farms, while their right to the collectively owned clan land was perhaps as good as that of the pastoral conquerors. Since land was plentiful and men few at the time, conflict over ownership was limited. Another reason for leaving the *gabbaro* on the land was that they were engaged in farming and the pastoral Oromo needed their agricultural produce. As we saw in Chapter 2,[37] there was slow but continuous flow of Oromo immigration following the major wave of the sixteenth century. The latecomers were given access to and settled on the land owned by an abba lafa as *qubsisa* on condition that they provided labor for the original possessor of the land. What the *qubsisa* ("late settler" or "tenant") bought with his labor "was the right for him and his descendants to use land and a guarantee that this right would be respected."[38] This is perhaps a good indication that land was passing from the realm of collective ownership and becoming privately owned.

In the Gibe region, the transition from collective ownership to private ownership was a bloody episode in the drama of the struggle between the war leaders. Many examples could be given from all over the region,[39] but perhaps the most vivid is that recorded by Massaja in his account of the struggle between the war leaders of Lagamara and Challa. The land and wealth of their neighbors excited wild ambition in the war leaders of each land, for they had already seen that the acquisition of land and wealth was the surest path to supremacy. The following drama was played before the eyes of the first Italian bishop of Oromoland in the late 1850s. The people of Lagamara and Challa went to war over an incident involving a woman who abandoned an Abba Dula of Lagamara for an Abba Dula of Challa. The true motive for the war, however, went far deeper. It was a question of the political and economic ambitions of the three Abba Dulas of Lagamara and their followers. In the battle following the incident, the Abba Dulas of Lagamara routed those of Challa, who fled to safety in neighboring states. Their followers escaped into the forest but were soon forced by hunger and exposure to return to their land. With tears in their eyes,[40] the unfortunate peasants of Challa begged the victorious Abba Dula for mercy. This was granted, but at a terrible price. The three Abba Dulas divided the land of Challa among themselves and only allowed the vanquished to return to their homes on condition of submission and subservience to the victors.

> The houses and the surrounding farms were given back to the former owners . . . [However,] when the unfortunate people of Challa returned to their houses and farms, they became the tenants of the abba dula in whose district their property was located.[41]

Two conclusions can be drawn from this episode. The free peasants of Challa became tenants of their own land merely through the misfortune that befell them on a single day. The victorious Abba Dulas looted their victims but did not dispossess them of their homes and farms. To do so would have been against tradition and unproductive. It was against tradition because among the sedentary agricultural Oromo, *masi* (cultivated land) was an inalienable right.[42] The position of *masi* among the agriculturalists was perhaps similar to that of the cow among the pastoralists. The cow was the most important animal for pastoral Oromo. Even when neighboring tribes raided and looted each other, cows were returned to their owners.[43] The reason for this is not hard to find. A cow not only provided milk, which sustained life, but also gave birth to another life. It was the concept of fertility, deeply embedded in the psychology of the pastoral Oromo, which led to the belief that there existed a special relationship between a cow and her owner. A cow was considered to be a part of the owner's family: if she fell sick, the owner cared for her just as he would for another member of the family.[44] It was perhaps the same concept of fertility which the agricultural Oromo attributed to their *masi* – it produced food year after year and led to the creation of a special relationship between a man and his land.

> There was, and to some extent still is, a belief that there exists a special relation between the first land occupier (and his lineal descendants) and his land. The Oromo made a distinction between intra-tribal war or feuds, lola, and inter-tribal warfare or war with non-Oromo, dula. In the feuds, lola, it was impossible for the winning side to take land from the defeated; there was a recognition of some sort of mystical bond between man and land and that this could not be changed even by force. In wars with non-Oromo, dula, such a bond was not considered and the territory of the conquered group could be appropriated by the Oromo.[45]

The second point to be noted is that although a victorious group did not expropriate the *masi* of a vanquished group, the victors took over the uncultivated land of the defeated. According to Massaja, the victorious Abba Dulas of Lagamara took all the uncultivated land of Challa and divided it among their followers.[46] It was in this fashion that the war leaders and their followers became the owners of extensive land in the Gibe region. When a successful war leader made himself king, even forests became his property. Besides reducing the peasants of Challa to tenants on their own land and taking over all the uncultivated land, the three Abba Dulas of Lagamara made the public pastures of Challa into the common property of the people of both Lagamara and Challa.[47]

From the limited literature on the subject of the landholding system in the Gibe region, the following necessarily incomplete picture can be formed. Though the kings and the nobility owned the largest areas and most productive parts of the land (including in some cases even forests), generally pastures, mineral water, forest, and forest products were collectively owned. The meadows which dot the Gibe region were left to be used in common for pasture where the herds grazed. The forests, which were famous for their wild animals, became the game areas for the wealthy men, who spent their time hunting big game to prove their courage and marksmanship. The successful hunting expedition of a king was an occasion for official celebration, while its failure caused sadness and sorrow at a royal court.[48] Before the formation of the Gibe states, hunting was mainly undertaken by the young warriors who wanted to earn reputations for bravery by killing big game, or an enemy. After the formation of the states, hunting took on a class character and became a favorite pastime for the wealthy class of Gibe society.

Below the nobility were free peasants who had their small plot of land. The landowning free peasants had neither slaves nor large animal herds, both of which were extensively owned by the nobility. Besides paying tax on their property annually, the landowning peasants had to work on the extensive estates of their kings. They fought for their kings at their own expense and provided hospitality for government officials and guests of the kings. Below these peasants were the *qubsisas* ("the late comers" or "tenants") who had their own plots of land, but who provided labor and services to their land owners. They also performed the same task for the state as the free peasants did. Below the *qubsisa* were landless tenants who worked for and lived on the land of their masters. These tenants were theoretically free to change their masters. Their number continuously fluctuated. Some were given their small plot of land by their masters after years of service. Others bought their own plots of land. However, while some landless tenants elevated their social status and became owners of land, some landowning peasants were forced to become landless tenants by circumstances beyond their control.[49] This applied mainly to the stateless Oromo tribes in which only the powerful had been able to assure themselves of enough wealth and political clout to prevent their being reduced to the status of landless tenants. To recapitulate, in the first half of the nineteenth century, pastures were still common property. The major part of the land was owned by the king and his followers. Free peasants owned their small plots of land. The *qubsisas* ("late comers") also owned land but provided labor and services for the Abba Lafa. Those free peasants who were reduced to the status of tenants on their land as a result of war retained their *masi*, but provided labor and service for the leader under whose jurisdiction they lived.

The landholding system in Jimma can be considered a prototype for the system as it existed in all the Gibe states. The greater part of the land, both cultivated and uncultivated, as well as the forests, belonged to the king. Next came the aristocracy, mainly composed of the Diggo group, who formed the dynasty, and others who collaborated with them.[50]

> As the Diggo began their expansion, they expropriated newly conquered lands for the use of their leaders. When the conquest was over, the Diggo, as a group, owned more land in more places than any other group. Not all private lands belonging to others were confiscated, however, and leaders of important non-Diggo families, successful warriors, and followers and favorites of the kings were given large landholdings in return for services. Landholdings were not frozen at one point in time, nor were they obtainable only through service to the king. A man's skill and luck in farming might force him to sell his Kabiyye [Qabie] or enable him to buy more land. Merchants who made money in trade or craftsmen who got money from the sale of their handiwork could buy and own land. Although a foreigner had to get the king's permission to use or buy land, there was no social bar to purchase by outsiders.[51]

However, it was the existence of the numerous royal estates that gave the agricultural economy of the Gibe region its special character. These were to be found from one end of the region to the other. Every royal *massera* (residence) had its own estate which helped to provision the numerous *massera* personnel. These estates were devoted to the production of cereal, root, and cash crops and to animal husbandry. Coffee was supreme among the cash crops. Coffee production was much more developed in Limmu-Ennarya than in any other state. The forests in the valleys of the Didessa and the Gibe were almost a natural nursery for its production. The royal coffee spread the fame and prestige of Limmu-Ennarya:

> Enarea is principally celebrated for its extensive woods of coffee, the chief locality of which is the valley of the Gibbi [Gibe] . . . These woods are described as containing trees, the trunks of which are from two to three feet in diameter – a size far exceeding anything of the kind elsewhere. They are the property of the king and they are watched by his slaves.[52]

Coffee also held pride of place in the forests of Gera. These forests competed with those of Limmu-Ennarya in abundance of coffee, and the kings of both countries encouraged their people to intensify the cultivation of coffee.[53] Along with Kaffa, Limmu-Ennarya and Gera were famous in what is today the northern Ethiopian region for the good quality of their coffee, which required the minimum of cultivation.[54] The kings of Jimma, Gomma, and Gumma, where coffee did not grow naturally, made it a part of their government policy not only to encourage their peasants to plant coffee, but also to involve themselves in coffee production on their extensive plantations.[55] In this way, for example, Jimma, which lacked coffee in the early 1840s,[56] became a great coffee country, far surpassing Gera by the second half of the nineteenth century. Similarly, the land of Gomma had no coffee around the middle of the nineteenth century, but a few decades later it had become the greatest coffee-producing area in the entire Gibe region,[57] if not in the whole of southwestern Ethiopia.

Interestingly, coffee growing was connected directly with the increase in profit from coffee trade. Before the beginning of the nineteenth century, there is no record either of regular coffee export from the Gibe region or of profits made from it. This indicates that the Muslim traders who visited the Gibe region before the beginning of the nineteenth century mainly traded in other luxury items such as gold, ivory, musk, and slaves. However, we have abundant evidence for the increased demand for coffee during the first half of the century. Under the impetus of the demands for the coffee of the Gibe region, the kings intensified coffee plantations, and cared well for the coffee that grew naturally.[58] They encouraged wealthy men and peasants to plant coffee in the shade of forest trees. The dense forests of the region, coupled with the Oromo religious idea of respect for and honoring of green nature[59] and the practice of not cutting big trees, must have provided an ideal environment for coffee growing. Perhaps that is why the Gibe region became the natural factory for the production of coffee, as it is still today. In short, in the nineteenth century, coffee growing and coffee trade became a profitable means of increasing the wealth of Oromo society in the Gibe region. Under this circumstance it is not an exaggeration to say that the Gibe kings built new wealth for their people in the form of coffee growing.

Although coffee dominated the royal estates everywhere, cotton, oil seeds, *chat*, and spices were not neglected. Bee farming was also an important aspect of the royal estates. Honey was lavishly consumed in the royal *masseras* in the same way as coffee.[60] Coffee seeds fried in clarified butter and mixed with pure honey was a delicacy. *Chat*, chewed and washed down with coffee sweetened by honey, was an excellent stimulant that brought about mental exhilaration. Honey was used both for eating and for making the famous *dadhi* (mead). Bee farming also provided the wax used in lighting the royal *massera*.[61] While most of the produce of the royal estates was for consumption at the *masseras* some, such as coffee and musk, was also sold on a large scale. Finally, civet cat farms were also maintained on the royal estates. Civet cats were captured in the forests of Limmu-Ennarya and Kaffa. The female civet cats were set free and the males, which produced the musk, kept in well-guarded cages. According to A. Cecchi, they were fed with excellent raw or half-cooked meat mixed with butter and flour of teff boiled in the broth of the meat.[62] This food Cecchi wrote "watered the mouth of the guardian slaves who lived on a miserable ration of grain."[63] The cages were regularly cleaned, warmed, and guarded. The cats were milked daily each giving 20 to 25 grams. The civet cat farms were expensive to maintain, but for the kings it was a very profitable business.[64]

The work on the royal estates was done by three groups of people: tenants (*qubsisa*), free peasants, and slaves. The *qubsisa* who lived on the king's land had to provide corvée labor "twice a week, every Monday and Friday."[65] The free peasants had also to provide labor for the king, whenever he demanded it of them. Thus, the free peasants might have to work on the royal estate in their times of sowing and harvesting. The major part of the work on the royal estates, however, was done by the king's slaves.[66]

This brings us to the question of slavery in the Gibe region. Domestic slavery became economically important to the wealthy cattle owners mainly after the settlement of the Oromo in the region. When the Oromo were migrating, especially when pastoralism was the dominant mode of production, they perhaps needed only a limited expenditure of labor to tend their cattle, which provided them with food (milk, butter, blood, and meat) and clothing (i.e., leather dress). Pasturage was abundant and water plentiful. The region was, and still is, famous for mineral water, which the cattle needed from time to time. The size of the animal population rapidly increased and the wealth of their owners expanded, which in turn created marked differences in wealth and social class.[67] Among pastoral Oromo wealth was measured by the heads of cattle an individual had. Perhaps wealthy cattle owners needed extra hands to look after their cattle. We saw above how some wealthy Matcha individuals enslaved the *gabbaro*, provoking the celebrated rebellion of the conquered people during the second decade of the seventeenth century.[68] What remains to be added here, however, is the fact that slaves became of great value for the wealthy cattle owners and slavery became an important economic institution because of the increasing demand for domestic service and for work in the fields and because of the profit which was made from the slave trade. The social differentiation within previously more or less egalitarian society brought in its train the increased demand for slaves. The wealthy cattle owners conducted raids against their neighbors for booty in cattle and for capture of prisoners of war, who were used as slaves.[69] By the beginning of the nineteenth century domestic slavery had become an important institution in the economic landscape of the Gibe region and, after land and cattle, slaves were the most important economic possession for the wealthy class. In short, by the first half of the nineteenth century, slavery was as rampant in the Gibe region as it was in Kaffa to the south and in the Christian area to the north.[70] In the late 1870s Cecchi estimated that about one third of the population of the area was composed of slaves of both sexes.[71] Tasaw Merga went even further, claiming that in Jimma the slaves outnumbered the free population.[72] He said much the same about the rest of the Gibe region, but does not base his claim on evidence. His argument rests on this assertion:

> The slave population in Jimma was probably larger than the free population of that state. Abba Jifar II alone owned ten thousand slaves. The wealthy men of Jimma owned a thousand or more each. Even peasants who only had a small plot of land may have owned one or two slaves.[73]

These conclusions are untenable on two counts. First, while it is true that Abba Jifar was notorious both for trade in and ownership of many thousands of slaves[74] and that the wealthy and some rich peasants owned slaves, the small peasant with a small plot of land certainly did not have any slaves. This will be discussed further below; here, suffice it to say that not everyone, from king to poor peasant, owned slaves in Jimma. What is certain, however, is that among the nobility "slaves were the most sought after commodity in the Gibe region."[75] They were exchanged for horses, mules, guns, beautiful clothes, paid as a price for medicine, and given as gifts.[76] The nobility owned slaves as they owned cattle. Slaves were to be found in the royal residences, in the army, in the residences of wealthy men, and in their fields. The wealthy landowners used their slaves to cultivate their lands, "while those who were short of slaves distributed their land to tenants, who cultivated it in their master's name and interest."[77] Thus, though slaves were highly desirable, they were an expensive commodity quite beyond the means of poor peasants. The second point is that the Gibe region was an important center from which slaves were sent to Gojjam, Gondar, Massawa, and the Red Sea, as well as to Shawa, Harar, and beyond. This export of slaves militated against any large increase of the settled slave population in the Gibe region. Thus, it would seem that Tasaw's assertion remains an unsupported assertion.[78]

Tasaw stands on firmer ground, however, when he states that slaves were massively oppressed in the Gibe region. Slavery and oppression appear to have been as much a part of the history of the region as they were in Kaffa to the south and the Christian state to the north. To gloss over this oppression by designating it as a benign form of domestic slavery[79] is both to ignore the data and to mask the magnitude of the oppression. Cecchi had the opportunity to observe the oppression of slaves at very close range and what he has to say amply supports Tasaw's statement. He gives horrifying examples of what some slaves were subjected to.[80] Where the accounts differ is that Tasaw ignores the diversity of conditions among slaves and presents the case as if they were all equally oppressed:

> The slaves had neither the right to take to court their masters if they were unjustly treated nor to own property ... The slaves were considered not as human beings but as talking animals. These oppressed slaves, however, formed the major work force that cultivated the estates of the kings, the nobles and wealthy men. In other words, the slaves were the pillar of the economy of the region.[81]

Where Tasaw makes slaves talking animals, Cecchi maintains that a slave was a human being who had no legal personality. Where Tasaw claims that a slave owned no property of his own, Cecchi maintains that a slave retained control of property he had acquired, although on his death it was inherited by his master.[82] Cecchi's most positive contribution to our understanding of the institution of slavery in the area, however, is his picture of the diversity in the conditions of the slaves themselves:[83]

> The slaves who have the favour of the queen or the king are raised to some position of authority at the court. There are slaves of pleasure and luxury, and there are also slaves who are destined to teach the Quran . . . There are slaves whose duty is to introduce guests to the royal house and to maintain discipline by whipping other slaves. The eunuchs watched over the wives of the king, guarded the gates of the royal massera, and performed many other functions. All court personnel is composed of slaves who sometimes number three thousand.[84]

Though some slaves enjoyed a position of authority at the royal residence,[85] and others gained prestige and honor by valor in war, the vast majority of them were grossly oppressed. Their persons, their labor, and their property were at the disposal of their owners. This can be plainly seen in cases of homicide involving a free man and a slave or two slaves:

> A free man who killed a slave had to pay five head of cattle or had to give another slave of the same value to the owner . . . A slave who killed a free man was tied by the owner in front of his own door, where the relatives of the deceased killed him in a revolting manner. If a slave who killed a free man had escaped, the owner and his family had to hide so that the relatives of the deceased could not take revenge upon them. When a slave killed another slave, the owner of the killer had to pay five head of cattle or give a slave of the same value to the owner of the deceased.[86]

With regional variation and diversity in the condition of slaves, the universality of their oppression would seem to be an established fact. The myth of a benign domestic slavery in the Ethiopian region conceals much more misery and oppression than has hitherto been acknowledged. A comparison of the above quotation with what Marc Bloch had to say on the historical contrast between slavery and serfdom helps to make this plain:

> The servus was the object of a master who disposed arbitrarily of his person, his work and his property . . . The servus was not truly a part of the mass of free men, he was like a foreigner deprived of all rights. Should he be killed or wounded the master received the compensation. Should he commit a crime against his own master, the latter was allowed to judge and penalize as he saw fit. Should he injure a third party, the master again took up the responsibility. The latter could sometimes even rid himself of that burden by handing over the guilty person or occasionally even by fleeing.[87]

There were many sources of slaves in the Gibe region. The first and most important source was warfare against neighboring peoples and the subsequent plunder of the disorganized losers.[88] Here it is important to make clear distinction. Prisoners of war taken in a conflict between Oromo states were not sold as slaves. They were returned to their country of origin as a part of the peace agreement.[89] Sometimes important prisoners of war were kept in the capital of the state that captured them as a guarantee for the good neighborliness of their country of origin,[90] but this was the exception rather than the rule. Since almost every conflict among the Oromo states was concluded by a peace agreement, the prisoners of war from these states were neither sold nor reduced to domestic slavery. However, prisoners of war from among the surrounding stateless Oromo suffered the same fate as non-Oromo prisoners of war. A victorious king had the power to make the vanquished people his slaves:

> In this case the entire population are considered as the slaves of the king, in which case he had the right to transfer part of these people to another territory, or he could make them his own slaves on his own estates.[91]

Warfare was accompanied and followed by famine and poverty, which forced the victims to volunteer to become slaves in order to escape from their wretched conditions. This was more common among the stateless tribal groups:

> The worst thing is that these chiefs are jealous of each other, greedy for power and pleasure . . . keeping the country in a permanent civil war. Because of this, the poor people . . . continuously pass from one master to the other depending on the fortune of the day. In addition to this, often terrible punishment is inflicted on them by the fact that a party that lost could appeal to its neighbour for military assistance. When "foreign" soldiers enter a country nothing is spared, families, villages, agriculture, cattle and everything disappears in a few days.[92]

Under these circumstances it was not uncommon for a father to sell his children for food. Because of man-made disaster and general insecurity, men and women also had to "volunteer to become slaves."[93] These unfortunates volunteered to be the slaves of kings and wealthy men, under whom they had security for their person, protection from hunger, and exemption from taxation. In 1843, Antoine d'Abbadie recorded a sad story of a family of three generations that was brought to market for sale. The circumstance which led to this event is not clear, but what is certain is that the incident was so moving that it forced Abba Bagibo into action.

> In September 1843, they displayed at the market of Saqqa, exposed for sale, a mother, her daughter, and her grand daughter, not to mention the other children. The grand daughter kept kissing her mother and each time she saw a buyer approach she would cry out, "By the power of God I beg you to buy me along with my mother or leave me here." The mother was crying as one has never seen any crying in Abyssinia. No one dared buy a single member of this family, that the king probably gave [them] to some favourites, because they never more appeared at the market.[94]

The neighboring state of Kaffa was a reservoir of slaves for the Gibe region. According to the reports of Catholic missionaries who lived in Kaffa between 1859 to 1861, it was in that country more than anywhere else that the poor volunteered to be slaves.[95] The reason for this is not far to seek. Taxation was heavy in Kaffa. "The great devour the small"[96] was the phrase by which the Catholic missionaries expressed the wretched condition of the poor peasants in that country. It is not surprising, then, that the king of Kaffa received tribute in slaves from his subjects.[97] The slaves of Kaffa were brought to the Gibe region by slave traders, who also gave slaves as gifts to the kings of the Gibe states. The Gibe kings themselves reduced to slavery thieves who stole royal cattle, enslaving their family and relatives along with them.[98] The fact that slaves were an important item of bridewealth in royal marriages led to large numbers of slaves exchanging masters.[99]

Finally, there was the politically inspired slavery which was imposed on the families of political offenders. This form of slavery was distinguished from others: it was known as *hari* ("sweep away" or "throw away"). The political offender himself was eliminated either by drowning or being left to rot to death in the *gindo* (state prison).[100] His property was confiscated and his wife and family declared *hari* ("those to be swept away"). Then they were sold publicly to the slave traders, and the proceeds of the sale went to the treasury of the king.[101] This inhuman method of destroying political opponents without trace was practiced widely in Janjero and Kaffa as well.[102] In the Gibe states it was a common practice in their early history at a time when the new rulers had a number of political opponents. The horror of those old cruelties was long remembered in the region. Magnified and embroidered with the passing of time, many a nasty tale was told of cruelties committed by those early kings. One of these, Oncho, the founder of the state of Gumma, was even accused of desiring to eat human flesh.[103] Even in 1842, the king of Gumma was known as the most cruel of all the Gibe kings:

> The inhabitants of Gumma were more than those of any other country doomed to slavery, as their sovereign, who has a character of extreme severity, is in the habit of selling whole families for offences – sometimes of the most trifling nature – committed even by a single individual.[104]

Following the consolidation of each ruling house, and above all the adoption of Islam as the official religion of the rulers, the practice of *hari* was gradually abandoned. Antoine d'Abbadie, who gathered the traditions about *hari* in Limmu-Ennarya, recorded the following in Saqqa in 1843:

> The hari or sweeping, is [enslavement] confiscation formerly practiced in Limmu, Jimma, Gumma, Gomma and Gera. [It] was abolished after the Gallas adopted or pretended to adopt Islam. While it existed people [were enslaved and] confiscated for the slightest fine.[105]

Antoine d'Abbadie makes it clear that *hari* was a political weapon that was used for destroying political enemies and punishing those who stole royal property. It was a practice that was much abused by the Gibe kings and intensely feared and hated by the people. Perhaps the fear of *hari* may have encouraged the people to embrace Islam. At any rate, the adoption of Islam not only undermined the *hari* institution, but also seems to have facilitated the process of manumission on the same scale. In this it was Gomma (for reasons to be discussed in the next chapter)[106] which led the way. Gomma intensified the process of manumission, abolished the *hari* institution and called on the rest of the Gibe kings to do likewise. Other Gibe kings followed the example of Gomma and abolished the *hari* institution. According to d'Abbadie, Muslims freed their slaves when they were satisfied with their performance. The freed slaves usually fell within the age bracket of 36 to 55.[107] Two other ways by which slaves gained their freedom were by being adopted into the family of the owner and by obtaining enough money to purchase liberty.[108] Such methods were exceptional. Slavery remained a common feature of the Gibe states, and slave labor constituted the principal work force on the royal estates.

Slaves of both sexes worked on the royal estates. In Limmu-Ennarya women were actively involved in the coffee harvest. They picked coffee berries and carried them to the royal store, just as the men did.[109] The slaves also guarded the royal coffee in Limmu-Ennarya. But in Gera the tasks of guarding, picking, and carrying the coffee to the royal treasury were performed by the free population. This difference in the type of labor employed was due to the number of slaves available at the two courts. In Limmu-Ennarya, the royal court owned a far greater number of slaves than the mere three thousand at the court of Gera.[110] Generally speaking, the women slaves performed the numerous household duties in the *massera*. They also fetched water, carried wood, and even helped the men with the weeding in the fields. The men tilled the royal estates, manured the soil, and harvested the crops. The production on the royal estates was immense, and it was this which gave the agricultural economy of the Gibe region its special character. The royal estates formed an economic pillar of the monarch. Consequently, the tax burden on the peasants was not too high in the Gibe region.[111] According to the information gathered from the region, the *busi* (tribute) to the king was paid both in kind and in *amole* (block of salt).[112] Wealthy men paid five *amoles*, while peasants paid either one or two *amoles*, depending on their economic status.[113]

After agriculture, the second major economic activity in the Gibe states was cattle-raising (stock-breeding).[114] An additional source of wealth and part of the cultural heritage, cattle-rearing was very widely practiced. Among the agricultural Oromo it was not as developed as it was among the pastoralists, however. There were individual pastoralists who owned as many as 7,000 head of cattle.[115] In the Gibe region, some rich peasants owned 400 to 500 head while wealthy dignitaries often possessed 2,000 to 3,000 head of cattle.[116] The kings owned a large number of animals. The meadows which dotted the fertile valleys, the untilled plains, the hillsides, and the forest glades were covered with abundant grass that supported a large number of oxen, cows, goats, sheep, horses, and mules. The fattened oxen of Limmu-Ennarya, the beautiful cows of Gera, the goats of Gumma, the sheep of Gomma, and the cattle and fowl of Jimma were especially celebrated.[117] Oxen for ploughing, cows for milk, and goats and sheep for meat constituted the wealth of a peasant.[118] There were two types of oxen: those used for ploughing and those fattened for sale, tribute, or gifts to the king, known as *natafo*. Domestic animals were plentiful and very cheap. Even the best *natafo* was sold for two or three thalers.[119] It was by head of cattle, the number of slaves, and the size of the cultivated land that the wealth of the great dignitaries was reckoned at the time.

Right to the end of our period, internal stability was the essential and effective factor for the prosperity of the Gibe region. On the military strength and political ability of the king depended the internal stability and hence the economic well-being of the people. Military defeats and natural disasters, on the other hand, caused great difficulties for the people. Not even Abba Jifar I could avert a military disaster in 1843 in Jimma, nor could Abba Bagibo mitigate the effects of the great plague of 1849.[120] But Jimma and Limmu-Ennarya successfully weathered those storms and soon recovered an even greater vigor and vitality. Such recovery was made possible by two conditions which existed in the Gibe states but were lacking among the surrounding Oromo tribes: unity of the people and central authority. Thus, while the cattle of their stateless neighbors was looted and their agriculture destroyed under the feet of raiding war leaders, the Gibe states enjoyed amazing prosperity.

While the full effect of this prosperity did not reach beyond the landowning class, the poor peasants in the Gibe region probably enjoyed a higher standard of living than any peasants in the Ethiopian region. The abundance of cereal crops, supplemented by root crops, guaranteed their safety from famine. Cattle provided them with milk. The light burden of taxation and the possibility of earning more and buying land also contributed to the better standard of living of the ordinary peasant. Though modest, the level of the living standard of the Gibe peasant had some impact on the increase in industrial production, growth in trade, and a change in ideology.[121]

Antoine Cecchi, who traveled all over the Gibe states and was also a prisoner in 1880 at the royal court of Gera, described and expressed his admiration for the stage reached by industry in the area.[122] Of course, when compared with agriculture and cattle-rearing, industry had only a small place in the economic life of the people. Here I use the word industry in its meaning of the transformation of raw materials into useful objects that met the needs of the peasants and provided luxuries for the wealthy class. Industry outside the *massera* was materially inferior to that inside, which catered to the needs of the royal court. The last chapter[123] will demonstrate that the royal *masseras* were the busiest industrial centers in every state. Inasmuch as the artisans and craftsmen of the local industry paid their tribute in kind to the king, the *massera* industry was supplemented by the local industry, but the *massera* industry was somewhat superior in that it was better equipped and had a more skilled workforce, which included Jabarti and Arab traders.[124] Precious metals – gold and silver – only were used in the *massera* industry.

The artisans and craftsmen of the local industry were collectively known as *ogessa* (skilled ones). To the category of *ogessa* belonged the blacksmiths, *tumtu*, the carpenters and the tanners, *faqi*, the potters, *fuga*,[125] "the beehive makers and bee keepers, *gagurtu*, and the hunters and foragers, *watta*."[126] These artisans and craftsmen, whose skill and products were so vital to the agricultural economy of the Gibe region, were distinguished in three ways from the society among whom they lived.

First, all artisans and craftsmen belonged to a low social caste known as *hiru* ("those shared-out"). The term describes the historical evolution of this minority low-status group among the Oromo of the region. At a time when pastoralism was predominant, there was only a limited need for the products of the *ogessa*. However, once the Oromo embarked on agriculture on a large scale, the demand for *ogessa* products rapidly increased. Since the *ogessa* were in short supply, the Oromo clans "shared them out." But these "shared-out" skilled minorities were not adopted and assimilated into the Oromo clans, for reasons to be explained.[127] Secondly, the artisans and craftsmen did not have the *qabie* right, the right to the communal ownership of land. The reason for this was that while they lived under the protection of each clan, they were not part of any one clan. The *qabie* right was for those who were part of the clan. Because they were not entitled to *qabie*, the artisans and craftsmen were given land by the clan leaders, the wealthy *sorressa* and the kings.[128] Thirdly, the artisans and craftsmen were feared and stigmatized because they were thought to possess fantastic supernatural powers which enabled them to harm others. Their members were thought of "as ritually impure, were hyenas, bearers of the evil eye, and eaters of impure meat."[129] They were not allowed to give testimony in court. Younger children were hidden from their eyes, while older folks dreaded eating in their presence. Though many of them were of Oromo origin, they were endogamous groups who remained outside the main stream of Oromo society.

The industry of the Gibe region depended on the skill and labor of the very people who were feared and stigmatized by the majority. This attitude had negative consequences. It did not allow the majority of the people to aspire to the acquisition of craft skills. These skills were proscribed and remained within the confines of the minority belonging to a low social caste. Nevertheless, within these confines, Cecchi thought that "the industry had reached a certain degree of civilization."[130]

The technology of iron-mining was very similar to that in Shawa. Local mining was sufficient for the needs of the industry.[131] The blacksmiths made spears, knives, axes, hoes, sickles, and ploughshares from locally mined iron.[132] Work was also done with copper. Weaving was perhaps the most flourishing industry. The weaving industry developed because its product was demanded by the vast majority of the population. It must be remembered that during their sixteenth-century migration, pastoral Oromo mainly used leather dress. Even then, the changeover from leather dress to cotton cloth was far more apparent among men than among women.[133] By the beginning of the nineteenth century only female slaves were still using leather, while others had replaced it by cotton cloth. This may have given impetus to the expansion of the weaving industry, which was also engaged in export business. For instance, four types of colored cloth were produced and exported to the surrounding areas.[134] Tanners produced good quality leather goods, chief among which were leather clothes. Hides were plentiful and leather dress was worn exclusively by female slaves.[135] The rest of the population wore cotton clothes of local manufacture, supplemented by the clothes imported from the surrounding lands, while the wealthy wore expensive imported clothes from America, Egypt, Europe, and India. As already indicated, leather had previously been used as the national dress of the Oromo, but by the nineteenth century even the most pauperized class in the Gibe region avoided it, despising and stigmatizing it as "the dress of slaves."[136] Tanners also made strong shields and good *licho* or *alanga* (whip) from buffalo hide. Leather was made into containers such as *qanqallo* (a small sack which can hold up to 25 kilograms of grain), *gorbotta* (a big sack which holds up to 100 kilograms of grain), and *qarbata* (a honey and butter container). Leather was also made into *kophe* (footwear), *sirre* (bed), *sijaja* (prayer mat), and *tepha* (a long strip used for measuring land and for tying goods on the back of pack animals). Coffee cups were made from buffalo horns. Quality saddles and beautiful wooden containers for milk and butter were also produced.[137] Within narrow technological limits, the building industry also made some progress. The royal *masseras* were the product of that industry,[138] as were the few bridges thrown across some rivers.[139] Pottery was the exclusive domain of women. Crockery of every dimension and shape was produced with such precision and elegance that they "appeared to have been made by well-qualified artists."[140]

Industrial products of the Gibe region were exported in almost every direction and were highly sought after even among the Christians to the north.[141] However, most of the industrial products of the region were made for the local and neighboring markets. The artisans and craftsmen exchanged their products for the agricultural produce of the peasants in the market places, and also paid them as tax to the kings and as land rent to their landlords. The scale of industrial production was greatly limited by the low level of technology used, coupled with the socio-political environment which militated against its growth. Thus, though active, the output of the industry of the Gibe region was small and its capacity for expansion negligible; consequently, its impact on the social structure was insignificant. The society of the Gibe region remained overwhelmingly that of a community of mixed farmers.

5

Trade and the spread of Islam in the Gibe region

The trade of the Gibe region was famous from early times. It appears that the Muslim state of Shawa, which was replaced by Ifat in 1285, and the Amahara dynasty, established in Shawa by Yikuno-Amlak in 1270, traded with the Gibe region. From early times the region was the economic center, as it lay on the main caravan routes from east to west, from north to south. The importance of the region was all the greater because it produced vital luxury goods. Both the Christians and the Muslims were dazzled by gold from the region,[1] and both endeavored to bring the trade and economic resources under their control. In this the Christian kingdom met with spectacular success. By the sixteenth century, the region was the main economic center as it lay on the main route from the gold-producing southwestern area to the central, northern, and eastern parts of the Ethiopian region, the locality of gold consumption. Moreover, the Gibe region was itself a gold-producer. It became one of the wealthiest trading centers of the Horn of Africa, famous for its slaves, ivory, and musk. Even before the days when Imam Ahmad sought to add to his triumphs the conquest of the Gibe region, the products of the area constituted a vital part of the export items for the international trade of the Christian kingdom. Of all the products of the region, the most coveted was gold. The lure of gold urged the conquering Muslim leaders to cross the Gibe river, and it was gold that saved Ennarya from the devouring sword of the Muslims.[2] The Muslim historian of the time described the Gibe region as a highly prosperous area, blessed with abundance of gold,[3] and the evidence of trade proved the correctness of his observation. Once the jihad had run its course and a weakened Christian authority had been restored to the region, it was trade with Ennarya and gold tribute from Ennarya that became the mainstay of the Christian kingdom. Gold tribute from Ennarya reached its zenith during the reign of Sarsa Dengel,[4] who is said to have once received "five thousand Oqueas of gold."[5] This large figure speaks eloquently for the abundance of gold in Ennarya. Some gold was mined in Ennarya itself, while a large part was brought to that country by traders from the surrounding gold-producing areas. By the first quarter of the seventeenth century, Ennarya's trade with the Christian kingdom benefited both countries, while the amicable relationship between the Christian leaders and the governor of Ennarya had reached an all-time record.[6] By this time also, the inhabitants of Ennarya had made considerable cultural progress, whose dazzling impression we can still glimpse in the writings of the Portuguese historian, Almeida. The indigenous people of Ennarya were celebrated for their agriculture, trade, trustworthiness, and the politeness of their manners. Their fertile land, blessed with a fruitful soil and abundant water, produced the things that were needed. In short, the Ennaryans were very industrious people and their land enjoyed flourishing trade and agricultural prosperity. In the words of Almeida, "The natives of Narea are the best in the whole of Ethiopia, as all the Abyssinians admit."[7] Almeida's information on the products and trade of Ennarya are among the most important data for the history of the Gibe region during the first half of the seventeenth century. Its chief importance lies in the fact that the author rightly attributes the advanced material culture of the inhabitants of Ennarya to their industry, to the fertility of their land, and above all to their prosperous trade. The amazing prosperity of Ennarya created a special relationship between the Christian rulers and the ruling house of Ennarya. As an educated foreigner having access to the court of Susenyos (1607–1632),[8] Almeida was probably expressing the estimation in which the Christian court held the rulers of Ennarya and its people.

We saw earlier that the Oromo conquest and settlement in the Gibe region did not stop trade altogether.[9] It is true, however, that trade was disrupted for a while. In fact, traders were attacked and looted by some Amhara leaders[10] and Oromo warriors. Without the security of trading centers and in the absence of safety for the traders and their goods while *en route*, trading could not flourish. The Oromo needed trading during their migration. However, once they settled in the Gibe region and embarked on mixed farming, they needed market centers even more, for they had to sell their agricultural produce and animal products and to buy necessary commodities such as salt and clothes there. This new need and dependence on trading centers and caravan routes led to greater safety for traders. In short, as soon as relative safety was restored, long-distance caravan trade to and from the Gibe region was resumed. This was facilitated by a number of factors. The caravans that passed through the Oromo territory benefited the Oromo themselves, who were slowly but surely pulled into the trade of the region. The commercial interests of the Oromo leader and those of the northern Muslim traders, the Jabarti, coincided: so long as the Jabarti gave gifts to the Oromo leaders, they were provided with hospitality and safety along the caravan routes.[11] Safety would have been impossible had the caravans not protected themselves from the robbers. The success of a caravan depended upon its strength and its ability to negotiate and pay for safe conduct in hostile territory. Protected by Oromo leaders, for the benefit of the traders and themselves, the caravan routes to and from the Gibe region once again became the principal arteries along which gold, slaves, ivory, musk, and spices flowed to the outside world. By the second half of the eighteenth century, new desires and increasing ardor for commercial enterprise enabled the Gibe region to boast of a new commercial revival, which brought about the birth of a new social order by the beginning of the next century.

It was in Limmu-Ennarya that this revival first consolidated itself through the formation of a state. The new state promoted trade and protected the interests of the traders. The discussion of trade in the Gibe region will concentrate mainly on Limmu-Ennarya (though other states are also covered) mainly because its capital, Saqqa, was the greatest emporium in the region up to the 1850s.[12] In the second half of the nineteenth century, when Jimma eclipsed politically Limmu-Ennarya, Hirmata, Jimma's famous market town, also eclipsed Saqqa's commercial importance. By then the Thursday market of Hirmata was "the greatest in all southern Abyssinia."[13] That development had its own momentum, but it is beyond the scope of our discussion here. Limmu-Ennarya was already the major commercial center during the reign of Abba Gomol (1800–1825). It became even more eminent during the reign of his successor, Abba Bagibo (1825–1861). Abba Gomol is remembered for having encouraged Muslim Jabarti traders to settle in his capital, Sappa, where they intermarried with the Oromo women, thus increasing the Muslim population in the capital.[14] Abba Gomol is also said to have had very good relationships with the governor of Gojjam and the king of Kaffa. During the 1810s and the 1820s, the relation between the governor of Gojjam and the king of Limmu-Ennarya underwent a transformation. For instance, the caravan route between the two countries, which was important even in the eighteenth century, became the main artery for the trade of the two lands. As a result, trade between the two countries became regular and faster, and increased in volume. Luxury goods from Limmu-Ennarya such as the best quality ivory, musk, spices, precious skins, slaves, and above all, gold, built a bridge of understanding and good relations between the governor of Gojjam and the king of Limmu-Ennarya. Abba Gomol depended on the governor, for cooperation in maintaining the safety of the caravan route between the two countries, while the governor depended on the ruler of Limmu-Ennarya for the rich gifts which the latter sent from time to time to the former. In short, the good relations between Gojjam and Limmu-Ennarya were the result of an agreement between the two rulers brought about by mutual commercial interests cemented by exchange of gifts. In a sense the exchange of gifts between the governor and the king on one hand and between the latter and the king of Kaffa on the other was an important feature in the circulation of luxury goods within and beyond the Gibe region. An English traveler of the early nineteenth century who lived in Tigray between 1810 and 1819 was struck by the flow of trade which sprang from Limmu-Ennarya and the surrounding region.[15] By the second quarter of the same century, the trade of Limmu-Ennarya and the surrounding region had become so important and vital, even to the Christians in the north, that the gold, slaves, ivory, musk, and spices of the Gibe region were the most sought-after items exported from Massawa. Another English traveler, Beke, who stayed at the entrepôt of Baso in Gojjam in 1842, was impressed by the trade of the area. He made clear that the market of Baso was the most important commercial place in northern Ethiopia, where the traders from the Red Sea coast met their counterparts from the Gibe region and beyond.[16] In fact, it was the Gibe trade which made Baso famous, where imported foreign goods were exchanged for the products of southwestern Ethiopia. Beke adds that the distinguishing feature of the market of Baso was the trade in the produce of Limmu-Ennarya and the surrounding countries, which was brought by Oromo traders and exchanged for European manufactures.[17] Baso was Limmu-Ennarya's commercial outlet in southern Gojjam. All roads led to Baso, but Baso and northern Ethiopia depended on the trade with Limmu-Ennarya in more than one sense:

> Baso . . . is the grand focus of the trade with Enarea and the countries to the south and west, and in fact the sole source of the foreign trade of Abessinia; . . . the gold, ivory, coffee, spices and civet which, independently of slaves, may be said to form the only articles given in return for the manufactures of Europe, which find their way into Africa by this road.[18]

How did Limmu-Ennarya come to play such a dominating and decisive role in the trade of the Ethiopian region in the first half of the nineteenth century? As the discussion on the political history of Limmu-Ennarya will show in the next chapter, there is no simple answer to this question. Success in trade depended on the military strength of the kingdom, the political wisdom and diplomatic skills of its rulers, and above all, sound commercial policies, all of which will be discussed in the next chapter.[19] Four factors, taken together, attempt to answer the above question. These factors are: the strategic position of Limmu-Ennarya in the trade of the Gibe region; the emergence of a dynamic Oromo merchant class; the Afkala; the organization of trade; and the abundance of trading goods in the region.

The Gibe region, as we have seen, was very fertile and productive. Over this region ran many caravan routes, large and small, which connected Kaffa and the southern region with Gojjam and beyond, and Wallaga and the western region with Shawa and Harar. Owing to the unique advantage conferred upon it by its geography,[20] Limmu-Ennarya constituted the nexus of these routes. All trade routes in the region, whatever their direction, led to Saqqa, the capital. One major route went from Saqqa to Bonga, the capital of Kaffa. Kaffa, the legendary land of coffee,[21] the reservoir for slaves, the famous land of ivory, civet, and spices,[22] fed the trade of Limmu-Ennarya with a great variety of goods. From Bonga, a number of small routes branched off in different directions, all facilitating the flow of goods into Bonga, from whence the fast-moving Afkala merchants brought them to Saqqa.

A number of routes ran from Saqqa to Jimma, Gera, Gomma, and Gumma, along which the various products of these countries were brought to the commercial capital of the Gibe region.[23] Other caravan routes from Saqqa went to Janjero with its slaves and ivory and to Kullo, which, in addition to slaves and ivory, provided Saqqa with mules and cotton.[24] There were routes to Walayata, bringing precious skins, and to Gurage, Hadiya, Gimira,

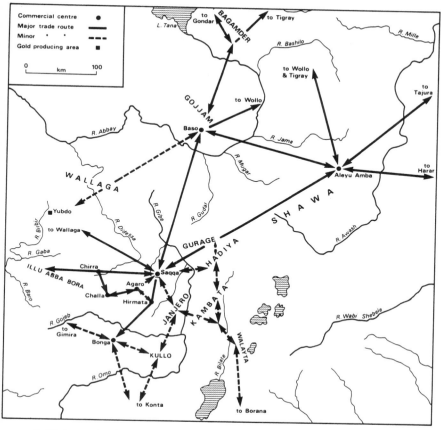

8 Major and minor routes which linked the Gibe region with surrounding lands in the first half of the nineteenth century

Kambata, Meji, Konta, Tambaro, Gamo, and Gardo.[25] Another major route led to Wallaga, whence came most of the gold and where the Gibe merchants met with the Arab merchants from the Sennar.[26] Slaves and ivory were brought to Saqqa along the route from Illubabor. There was still another caravan route that went from Limmu-Ennarya across the Gibe river to Agabaja in Shawa, from whence it went to Wollo and beyond. This was the main route along which the rich coffee of the Gibe region went to Wollo, where it met the needs of the Muslim population in that land.

The most important of all routes leading out of Saqqa was that which went to Baso, along which traders came from Gojjam, Gondar, Wollo, and Tigray. This was the main artery for the commercial activities of the Gibe region in general and Limmu-Ennarya in particular. Most of Limmu-Ennarya's exports and imported foreign goods traveled along this route. If Baso was Limmu-Ennarya's major commercial outlet, the prosperity of Baso depended entirely

137

on its trade with Limmu-Ennarya. "A very considerable portion of the revenue of the province of Gojjam is levied at Baso in the form of duties or market dues."[27] Still another caravan route ran from Saqqa across the Gibe into the Tulama land and on to Aleyu Amba, "the great central market"[28] of Shawa. There it joined another major caravan route that went through the semi-desert of Awash, along the plains of Charchar to Harar and beyond. Along the route to Aleyu Amba went the portion of Limmu-Ennarya's trade goods which were exported to Shawa[29] and exchanged for foreign goods imported by Harari, Somali, and Afar traders. Thus, all the caravan routes between the northern and the southern, the eastern and the western parts of the Ethiopian region led to Saqqa. With its strategic position within the Gibe region itself, Saqqa soon became the converging point for the Jabarti traders from the north, a springboard for Oromo traders journeying in all directions.

The whirlwind of trading activities in the Gibe region gave birth to an aggressive and dynamic merchant class, the Afkala. The Oromo merchant class made its appearance probably during the last quarter of the eighteenth century, when the revival of long-distance trade registered itself in the region. Before the appearance of the Afkala, trade was dominated by the Jabarti, the Muslim traders from the northern Ethiopian region, who intensified trade with Limmu-Ennarya at this time.[30] By intensifying this trade, the Jabarti unconsciously gave birth to their counterparts and rivals – the Afkala. The reason for the appearance of the Afkala lay in the condition of Oromo society in the Gibe region. Some of the Afkala were ex-slaves, or ex-servants of the Jabarti traders,[31] but most of them were younger sons, who according to customs in the Sidama and Oromo areas, "did not share the inheritance of their fathers."[32] The evidence from oral tradition stresses that during the period when land was plentiful, the eldest son remained on his father's land, while younger sons went in search of new land.[33] Younger sons who did not have the prospect of opening up new land for themselves seem to have turned to trade, which became very important to the economy of the Gibe region during the nineteenth century. Thus, it was not members of the wealthy landowning class that turned to trade, but landless young men who ventured to live by trade and thereby created new wealth for themselves. In their regular marches up and down in the Gibe region and beyond, the Afkala traders used to sing songs in praise of trade along the way. The following song depicts how the Afkala viewed poverty.

In summer they even make the dust rise;
in winter they even trample the mud!
If they talk with the dark maiden,
and smile upon the red maiden,
poverty will never leave them.
Poverty is a terrible disease;
it penetrates the sides,
it bends the vertebrae,

138

it dresses one in rags,
it makes people stupid;
it makes every desire remain in the breast;
those who are long it shortens;
those who are short it destroys wholly.
Not even the mother that has borne [the poor man] loves him any longer!
Not even the father who has begotten him any longer esteems him![34]

The Afkala provide us with a good example of young Oromo entrepreneurs, who occupied a new niche that made trading so important. They had very little capital behind them. And yet by their activity and dynamism they infused new life into trade in the Gibe region, making it an important branch of the economy of the area. The Afkala marched like *gero* ("young soldiers") and traveled as many as twenty miles a day.[35] They depended on speed for their survival in the business. According to Antoine d'Abbadie, the Afkala traveled fast and with surprising energy. In a week, they went from Saqqa to Baso, a distance of about 150 miles.[36] It took them four days to reach Bonga from Saqqa and three days to Wallaga.[37] The reason why the Afkala traveled so fast, putting both themselves and their pack animals at risk, appears to be that it was their method of beating the stiff competition they faced from the Jabarti traders, who were richer than they were. The Afkala possessed little capital,[38] while that of the Jabarti was relatively large. The Afkala had to travel fast in order to survive, and they hoped by so doing to win success. Survive they did, but success was a scarce commodity. Although it took the Jabarti traders three to four weeks, and sometimes even longer,[39] to cover the distance between Baso and Saqqa, this was because a Jabarti caravan was like a moving market; they bought and sold wherever they went. They had large caravans with quantities of goods. The Afkala caravans were small[40] and had few goods. Because they traveled fast, they bought in haste, often at a high price, and then sold at a low price; they probably made marginal profit, or sold at the same price as they had paid. According to Antoine d'Abbadie:

> The continuous complaint of the merchants of Enarya is that the Afkala destroyed their profits while giving prices that were too high. They are not happy to take one trip a year but go and come incessantly, for the activity of the Gallas causes them to resemble the Europeans in that respect. It follows that since they sell quickly they can content themselves with a slight profit.[41]

The Jarbarti traders traveled between the Gibe and the northern region once or twice a year. They limited their trading activities to eight months of the year, from November to June, their travel to and from the Gibe region ceasing completely during the long rains.[42] The Afkala traders, however, engaged in trade all the year round in the Gibe region itself, and traveled to the surrounding countries even during the long rains, as long as the rivers such as Gojeb, Omo, Gibe, Didessa, and Abbay were passable. However, at the end of the day their profit was not perhaps commensurate with their industrious trading activities. To make reasonable profit, the Afkala needed more capital than

139

what was at their disposal. It is not clear from the literature or oral tradition whether or not the Afkala could borrow capital from Abba Gomol. Perhaps they did not. Even if they did they probably could not find sufficient capital from him alone.[43] After all, Abba Gomol was not as wealthy as his successor, Abba Bagibo. Unable to compete with Jabarti traders because of the small size of their capital and their small turnover, the Afkala genius had never been greater than when they sought a political solution to their commercial problem. In other words, after proceeding by trial and error for perhaps a decade or two, the Afkala concentrated on finding a political solution to their problem. They seem to have appealed to Abba Gomol, the first king of Limmu-Ennarya, to prohibit the Jabarti traders from going to Kaffa. The issue was crucial; the choice of Kaffa gave economic meaning to the Afkala request. It was from Kaffa that the largest number of slaves, sometimes as many as 8,000 in a year, were exported.[44] From Kaffa also came the best ivory, musk, and spices as well as a large quantity of coffee.[45] The Afkala traders wanted Abba Gomol to prevent the Jabarti traders from going beyond Limmu-Ennarya, thus removing competition and preserving the lucrative trade with Kaffa for themselves. Overwhelmed by internal crises,[46] however, Abba Gomol lacked the political will for decisive action. On the contrary, he seems to have granted the Jabarti traders permission to go to Kaffa. This policy was dramatically reversed by his successor, who forbade[47] the Jabarti traders to go beyond Saqqa, the new capital. In 1825 the newly emerging merchant class of Limmu-Ennarya may have supported the overthrow of Abba Gomol by Abba Bagibo (see Chapter 6). This was because the latter represented the interest of the Afkala, while the former favored a "free-for-all" commercial policy. We do not know exactly when Abba Bagibo first implemented the policy of prohibiting the Jabarti traders from going beyond Saqqa, but it is known with certainty that in the 1830s the new policy was in operation and the Jabarti traders were affected by it.[48]

> In the early ninteenth century . . . Abba Bagibo, fully conscious of the advantages of the trade, accorded the merchants every protection provided that they traded exclusively in his territory, but if they sought to visit other lands, they could count on his hostility. Caravans from Kaffa and the north were likewise liable to be pillaged if they tried to trade direct without meeting at Ennarya.[49]

While the Jabarti traders from the north and the Sidama traders from the south were restricted and forced to trade only in Limmu-Ennarya, the local Afkala traders were free to trade up in the north and down in the south. They not only dominated the local trade of the Gibe region, but also traveled to Illubabor, Wallaga, Gojjam and beyond, Shawa and a number of surrounding lands. Though less frequently, some Afkala traders even went to the port of Massawa on the Red Sea coast.[50] This gave them great advantages and a monopoly of the trade beyond the Gojeb. The Jabarti traders found the luxury goods from beyond the Gojeb already gathered in Saqqa. The Jabarti traders were angered by the ban since their profit was affected by the monopoly of the Afkala over the Kaffa trade. From 1830 onwards, the energy and subtlety of the Jabarti raders was called into action against the monopoly of the Afkala. The Jabarti raders influenced the rival king, Abba Jifar of Jimma, to adopt a "free-for-all" commercial policy against Abba Bagibo's restrictive one (see Chapter 6). At first, Abba Jifar's pragmatic policy did not succeed because Jimma herself was dependent on the caravan route that passed through Limmu-Ennarya. Abba Bagibo's policy became obsolete and unproductive only in the 1840s, for reasons to be discussed shortly.

Until 1847, Abba Bagibo's restrictive policy contributed to the growth of his capital, his own prosperity, and that of the Afkala. Saqqa became the major emporium in the region. Here the products of Kaffa and all the surrounding countries were collected, to be funneled mainly to Baso, Limmu-Ennarya's commercial outlet in Gojjam.[51] A smaller proportion[52] of these goods also found their way to the kingdom of Shawa and beyond. The transit trade that entered and left Limmu-Ennarya benefited the kings in the form of gifts and customs duties.

Abba Bagibo owed his great wealth partly to the benefits of trade and partly to his extensive estates and the tribute and taxes paid by the peasants.[53] He dominated the political scene of the Gibe region up to 1861, not only through his sophisticated policy of "divide and rule,"[54] reinforced by political marriages and generous gifts, but also as a result of the fact that his capital was the headquarters for commercial exchange. In Saqqa, the Jabarti traders from the north, the Afkala traders from the Gibe region and others from Gurage, Hadiya, Kullo, Konta, Kaffa, Janjero, Gamo, Gardo, Tambaro, Walayeta, Wallaga, Illubabor, and many other places met[55] while engaged in buying and selling. Saqqa's population included Muslim traders from the north (both Oromo and non-Oromo), Arabs, Hararis,[56] a few Christian traders from Gojjam, Gondar, Tigray, together with mercenaries from the latter,[57] and traders from the surrounding kingdoms. It already had that cosmopolitan atmosphere which later characterized Hirmata (near Jiren), the capital of Jimma Abba Jifar.[58]

However, by 1847 Abba Bagibo's restrictive policy had become counter-productive, mainly because of the military weakness of Limmu-Ennarya.[59] Not satisfied with prohibiting the Jabarti traders from going beyond Saqqa, Abba Bagibo had imposed other restrictions[60] on the traders, which added to the bitterness they felt. Abba Bagibo may have justified his actions on the grounds that he wanted to protect the interests of the Afkala,[61] whose small capital could not compete with that of the Jabarti. The Afkala apparently tolerated the presence of the Jabarti traders in Saqqa, but wanted to preserve for themselves the commerce beyond the Gojeb, which supplied the best quality ivory, musk, spices, and slaves to the ever-expanding market of Saqqa. They probably regarded this as their prerogative, and one which Abba Bagibo zealously guarded for them. Upon this trade the Afkala prospered, as did Saqqa, while the Jabarti traders were deprived of this source for luxury products. The Afkala traders enjoyed other advantages over the Jabarti traders:

141

Their most important asset was that they belonged to the country and had relatives or other connections in the surrounding areas. They could travel swiftly from one place to another and reach the remote markets. While travelling they stayed with their kinsmen and were protected by them . . . In fact the limited scale of their commerce enabled the Afkala to terminate their affairs quickly in each market and, when they exhausted their stock of goods, to travel quickly to one of the main commercial centres of the south or to the markets on the verges of the Amhara areas. Whereas Jabarti merchants could only undertake one trip to the south-western markets each season, or if they brought a large quantity of goods might take even two or three seasons to dispose of their merchandise, the Afkala could travel several times a year to the northern markets and back.[62]

The Jabarti traders did not accept the Afkala monopoly without resistance. In fact, even in the 1830s their energy and subtlety in finding an alternative route to Kaffa became apparent. The formation of the state of Jimma Abba Jifar provided them with the opportunity they sought. The new state did not impose any restrictions on the Jabarti traders. The plentiful profits from trade in Kaffa excited and animated them and they soon flocked to the capital of Abba Jifar. Thus, the competition between the Afkala and the Jabarti traders became a characteristic of the trade of the Gibe region. This in turn seems to have led to an increase not only in volume, but also in the commodities that were exchanged. Large quantities of goods were assembled in the Gibe region, thus enabling the Jabarti and the Afkala traders to build up a profitable system of local and long-distance trade. As already indicated, the Jabarti traders were quick to impress upon the king of Jimma the necessity of converting his military superiority into commercial benefit. Encouraged by their advice, and motivated with the prospect of success, Abba Jifar devoted some years to the conquest of the land between the Great Gibe and his own country. In this region, he conquered Janjero, Botor, and Badi Folla.[63] Thus by 1847, Abba Jifar had expanded the frontiers of his state at the expense of his neighbors and freed his country from dependence on Limmu-Ennarya's route to the northern markets. An independent route between Jimma and the northern market rendered meaningless Abba Bagibo's ban on movements beyond Saqqa. I also diverted the flow of trade from Limmu-Ennarya's territory. Gradually the center of exchange shifted from Saqqa to Hirmata in Jimma. However, for the next fourteen years Saqqa remained the center of commercial exchange in the Gibe region for two main reasons. Firstly, as we shall see in the next chapter,[64] Abba Bagibo overhauled and reinforced the efficiency of his administration by injecting fresh blood into it in 1847. Among the new top appointees was one Abba Shamal, a very capable and energetic trader: he was appointed Abba Mizan, the official responsible for all business affairs. The diplomatic skill of the king and the vigorous ability of his new Abba Mizan soon restored the confidence of the Jabarti traders. Secondly, and even more importantly, Abba Bagibo carried out a decisive and far-sighted economic measure in 1848. This step shows his perspicacity in economic matters and his concern for the commercial prosperity of his land.

We saw above that Abba Bagibo banned the Jabarti traders from going beyond Saqqa and imposed a number of irritating restrictions upon them. After Abba Jifar opened an independent caravan route to the north, Limmu-Ennarya's commercial prosperity rapidly dwindled. The king realized that it was not in his power to stop Abba Jifar from undermining his country's monopoly of commercial profit. He knew perfectly well that his own policy had embittered the traders to such an extent that they were avoiding his country. He knew well, too, that he could attract the Jabarti traders back by following a generous policy and treating them well. He not only abolished the prohibition on trading beyond Saqqa,[65] but went much further to win their hearts and minds. Antoine d'Abbadie received the following valuable information in northern Ethiopia from Ibssa, an Oromo trader, who was delighted with Abba Bagibo's change of policy.

> Abba Bagibo became charming. He permitted trading in all liberty in red cloth, thaler, etc. And the only prohibition left is for gold. He even allowed his slaves to offer their favors to merchants because the latter went into Guma and Jimma to seek mistresses there.[66]

If the change of policy came a little too late, it nonetheless produced the desired effect. For the first time, we find both the king and his slaves ready to help traders in every way. This was remarkable. Prompted by the desire to attract the Jabarti traders, he acknowledged his past mistakes, reversed his former policy and declared that he was the friend and protector of traders. This liberal policy did not fail to impress the Jabarti traders, who came flocking back to Limmu-Ennarya. Ibssa, an Oromo trader from the region and a beneficiary of the change of policy himself, was one of those whom the new measure delighted.

As a result of the change of policy, commerce flourished in Limmu-Ennarya, and Saqqa remained the seat of wealth and luxury[67] up to 1861. By then Limmu-Ennarya was militarily a spent force. Only very skillful leadership at the center could maintain that country's commercial preeminence: through ingenious diplomacy supported by secret military alliances, political marriages, and lavish gifts for the ruling families of the neighboring states, Abba Bagibo was able to continue.[68] His successor, Abba Bulgu, did not have his supreme diplomatic skill, and his mistakes hastened the commercial ruin of his country.

> It was not long before the star of Ennarya began to be eclipsed and that flourishing and powerful kingdom returned to the early miserable condition. The merchants, angered by unbearable vexations, abandoned the route to that country.[69]

The reasons for the rapid disintegration of the prosperous trade of Limmu-Ennarya are beyond the scope of this chapter. During the period that concerns us, Limmu-Ennarya enjoyed unparalleled commercial superiority in the region; this is our main concern here.

In Limmu-Ennarya, as in all the Gibe states, trading was a highly organized business, in which government played a key role. The whole business of trade was under the jurisdiction of an important official named Abba Mizan (the father of the balance). This official was a member of the Council of State and one of the most powerful men in the kingdom. According to Tasaw Merga, the criteria for appointment to the office of Abba Mizan were a thorough knowl edge of business matters, strength of character, organizational capacity, and the ability to handle traders and deal with their problems.[70] More than wealth in land, it was knowledge of trade and experience in business matters which were considered by the Gibe kings as best qualification for the office of Abba Mizan. His office demanded sensitivity to the needs of traders and adaptability to the change in trade situation. An able Abba Mizan had to join the commercial interest of his king with warm hospitality to traders.[71] From oral tradition it appears that trade in the eyes of the Gibe kings was not just one branch of the economy; it was a part of the fabric of their luxurious life.[72] Consequently, the king appointed an Abba Mizan only from among successful and able traders. While all other important government offices were filled by the landed aristocracy, the office of Abba Mizan was filled by a meticulous and capable trader, whether he had landed property or not.[73] Knowledge of business and business matters was all that counted. Even successful foreign traders, the Jabarti, were appointed by some Gibe kings to this important office.[74] This shows the significance which Gibe kings attached to matters of trade, so important that only a capable and successful trader was entrusted with the responsibility of the office of the Abba Mizan. An Abba Mizan had many functions, which could be executed effectively only by a mature and experienced trader who had traveled widely and was broadly acquainted with the workings of government and its relation to business matters.

> This official had the combined functions of treasurer and minister for foreign affairs. He supervised the king's treasury, accounts, store houses, private domains and royal workshops. He was responsible for relations with foreigners and foreign merchants and he supervised the markets and merchant villages.[75]

As the foreign minister, the Abba Mizan received and presented foreign visitors and dignitaries to the king. He was, in effect, "the right hand of the king."[76] He was also the "right hand" of the traders, for he looked after their interests. In short, he was the channel of communications between the king and foreign merchants. As such, he had to join the commercial interest of his king with the well-being of and hospitality for the traders. There were two groups of officials who functioned under the authority of the Abba Mizan, maintaining law and order in the market places and collecting customs dues at the entrance gates. They were the Abba Gaba (father of the market) and the Abba Kella (father of the entrance gate). The Abba Gabas were appointed by either the king or the Abba Mizan himself. These "fathers of the markets"[77] were responsible for collecting market dues and maintaining law and order in the market places. They were also responsible for assigning places to the traders to set up their stalls or lay out their goods on the ground, "or for assigning different sections of the market to different products, and expanding or contracting these sections as the needs demanded."[78] On a market day, the Abba Gaba combined the role of police officer, judge, and governor.

The Abba Gaba sat in the market on a raised platform surrounded by a few armed men. It was his job to see that stealing was punished, fights were stopped, and that disputes arising in the market were judged. If a man found a debtor in the market he would haul him before the Abba Gaba. If two men fought over the possession of an animal or other goods they went to see the Abba Gaba. The Abba Gaba could levy fines, have thieves flogged by his men, and order a man to pay his creditor. When one man accused another they went before a market judge; the loser had to pay a fee to the king.[79]

The Abba Kellas were the second group of officials who were under the authority of the Abba Mizan.[80] The Abba Kellas were appointed by the king himself,[81] and they were responsible for guarding the entrance gates day and night.[82] They counted all incoming and outgoing merchants, inspected their merchandise and collected the customs from them.[83]

From the entrance gate to the capital of the kingdom, trade was efficiently organized, hospitality was guaranteed to the foreign traders, who upon arrival in the capital were received by the Abba Mizan. The latter in turn presented the foreign traders to the king, who received them warmly and ordered the Abba Mizan to assign quarters for their pack animals and hostels for the traders themselves.[84] This was done the very day traders arrived in the capital. All foreign merchants, both the Muslim Jabarti traders from the north and the Idama traders from the surrounding lands, were the guests of the king. As such, they were provided with accommodation in the king's hostels. For this purpose, all the Gibe kings built merchants' villages known as *mandera*, sited near their main *masseras* in their capitals. Accordingly, there were merchant villages in Saqqa, Limmu-Ennarya, Hirmata near Jiren in Jimma, Agaro in Gomma, Challa in Gera, and Chirra in Gumma.[85] Merchants were provided also with food from the king's kitchen for the first night. The next day, important merchants were formally invited to the *massera*, where they were entertained in the presence of the king. He questioned them at length about security along the caravan routes and about the general situation in the country from which they came. This having been done, the merchants gave their gifts to the king,[86] and went back to their hostels. The presents they gave the king were known as *harka fudha*[87] ("hand-shake"). Gift-giving took two forms. The first was the gifts given to the king in return for his hospitality and for providing the traders with accommodation in the merchant villages. The second was known as *gumatta*, a "special gift," given to the king on special occasions by all important men of the kingdom, including foreign traders.

In the capital of every Gibe state there were commercial centers of two kinds. The first and smaller one was at the *mandera*, where all luxury foreign goods were sold to the king and the aristocracy. The second and more important was the main market for local trade in the capital. The two centers served two different groups and interests. In the first center the king himself sold many commodities and bought luxury foreign goods, some of which he then distributed among his top officials.[88] The second center, the market for local trade, was the meeting-place for the multitude, who bought and sold and bartered or exchanged their goods against local or imported goods. This was not a place for diplomatic niceties: here wrongdoers were punished on the spot. In thi market there was no limit to prestige goods: both foreign and local product intermingled and changed hands. The mode of exchange here was not primar ily through the medium of money – Maria Theresa thaler,[89] gold and colore cloth, and other traditional money – here, barter was the predominant mode o exchange.[90] The literature is silent on the difference between the two markets Perhaps it was the dominance of the reciprocal exchange of goods at one cente and the use of traditional money at the *mandera* which made the two market different. Coupled with this, there was also the involvement of the kings i trade. In fact, all the Gibe kings were wealthy traders who monopolized certai luxury goods such as gold and musk, which were sold to the traders at th *mandera*. In short, the wealthy class bought imported luxury goods at th *mandera* and they sold luxury local products at the same place.

Several large caravans visited Saqqa annually. Among them, two fron Gondar were noted for their riches. The arrival of a Gondar caravan i Limmu-Ennarya and the commercial prosperity of that country are describe by Pankhurst in the following extract:

> Ennarya . . . enjoyed a considerable trade between Gondar and Kaffa and othe lands to the south which supplied slaves and cotton cloth, civet, ivory, gold coreander, and horses in exchange for salt, copper, horses, cows, coloure clothing, stuffs, guns, and other articles from Gondar market. The arrival of th Gondar caravans was a time of popular rejoicing. When the celebrations wer over . . . Abba Bagibo would call the leaders of the richest caravans, examine thei merchandise, purchase some of it on his own account or accept some as gifts, an then order trade to begin. The articles most prized were blue and red cloth, silk and velvets, copper, sal ammoniac, glass bottles, tobacco, black pepper, sal iron, gears, trinkets, mirrors, knives, scissors and kitchenware. Swords and gun were also in demand.[91]

In addition to the two from Gondar, various other caravans arrived annuall from the north – from Baso and some from Shawa – bringing foreign manufac tures to the Gibe region, mainly to Limmu-Ennarya. Every caravan from th north brought one item which was highly desired, both in the Gibe region an beyond. This was salt money, the *amole*.

> The amoleh could be considered to have been the official currency all over th highlands from Tigre to Kaffa and from Wollaga to Argoba. In many cases tax and tribute were paid in amoleh . . . It was indispensable to the long-rang caravan trade, because the further the merchants penetrated into the interior, th less ready were people to accept thalers, while the amoleh was always welcome.[9]

There were various other types of traditional money used as a medium c exchange in the Ethiopian region[93] – colored cloth, iron, beads, bracelets, gol – but the *amole* was an important medium of exchange in the Gibe regior

> The rate of exchange of amoleh for the thaler, at any trading or administrativ centre, differed according to its distance from Agame and Enderta. This resulte mainly from the cost of transportation and the unavoidable damage to the fragi amoleh on the road; but also from the heavy taxes laid upon the amole

merchants by governors and by customs authorities all along the caravan routes. Therefore, while at Ficho up to 120 amoleh were received per thaler, at Sokota in Lasta or Adowa in Tigre, fifty to seventy were given per thaler, in Begemder thirty to forty, in Gojjam and Shawa about twenty and in Enarea ten to twelve.[94]

Though an *amole* was expensive in the Gibe region, it was widely circulated, eclipsing all other traditional forms of money, even the thaler, which was also used in the region. In fact, for all the Gibe kings and especially for Abba Bagibo, the *amole* seems to have performed all three functions of money: as a medium of payment, as a measure of wealth, and as a store of value. Abba Bagibo had a large amount of *amole* money, with which he paid for some of the luxury goods he acquired. According to the information gathered from the region, all the Gibe kings received tribute in kind and in *amole*,[95] and they all had stores for *amole* in their treasury, where this brittle wealth was preserved by suspending it above a fire. "The amoles of the treasures of Abba Bagibo are completely black; the fear of seeing salt fall causes it to be placed on top of the hut where it absorbes smoke."[96]

Some imported luxury goods were sold at the *mandera*. Other less expensive ones, such as poor-quality clothes, varieties of beads, and cheap metalware, were sold at the local market. Although imported luxury goods had the reputation of being a concomitant of social status and prestige, no differential protection circumscribed trade in them; nor, with the exception of gold, were the common people excluded from their possession. However, the unusually high cost of imported elite goods made them to all intents and purposes prestigious possessions enjoyed only by the wealthy class. The reason for this is clear. To begin with, imported luxury goods were bought at a high price even in Massawa. By the time they reached Gondar, their price had doubled or tripled.[97] In Limmu-Ennarya their price would have increased still further. Such a large increase in the price of luxury imported goods was due to the difficulty involved in traveling and, above all, to the many customs posts along the route, at each of which the caravans were taxed. It is said that there were some twenty-eight such customs posts between Massawa and Limmu-Ennarya,[98] which means that these goods had been taxed at least twenty-eight times by the time they arrived in Saqqa. Thus they were very expensive and remained beyond the means of the common people. It was these expensive commodities which were sold at the *mandera*.

The local market of Saqqa was held on Sundays in an open field which was large enough to accommodate several thousand people. Among the commodities sold, exchanged, or bartered here were:[99] livestock, including cows, oxen, fattened bulls (*natafo*), goats, sheep, horses, mules, donkeys and chickens, eggs, butter, honey, cereal grains, including teff, wheat, barley, sorghum, finger millet, and maize, root crops including *ensete*, potatoes, sweet potatoes, onions and garlic, varieties of beans and peas, oil seeds, ivory, musk, coffee, raw cotton, and precious skins. Here also were to be found the products of local industry such as ploughshares, knives, spears, sickles, wooden goods, leather goods, hides, and skins, articles of pottery of various kinds, cotton clothes, saddles, and coffee cups. It was this market that met the needs of the common people, a type of market to be found all over the Gibe states.

> As a rule no single market place is used more than one day a week, each one having its own special day. These market days are staggered so that there will be no conflict within a region. The whole countryside is connected by this web of markets and on each day of the week a person in any spot in the country can walk to some market. Similarly, market days along the caravan routes are so coordinated that long-distance merchants can attend different markets on almost every day of their march.[100]

As a result there developed an impressive network of institutionalized trade within the Gibe region itself and across the Gojeb to Kaffa and across the Didessa to Wallaga, which enabled the Afkala traders to engage in a brisk trade all the year round.[101] The well-organized web of markets linking the Gibe region with Kaffa not only facilitated the flow of commerce between the two regions but also enabled the intrepid Afkala traders to buy and sell at different places along the route without missing a single market day or wasting unnecessary time.

> Merchants going from Jiren to Anderaca in Kafa could stop at the Sunday market in Saka, the Monday market in Sombo, the Tuesday market in Sebe. On their return from Kafa they once again stopped at Sebe on Tuesday, at Ule Waka on Wednesday, and arrived in Hirmata for the great Thursday market.[102]

Thus, besides the Oromo products of the region and the imported foreign manufactured goods which we have described above, the markets of the Gibe region were fed by products from Kaffa – coffee, slaves, ivory, musk, and spices, from Janjero – slaves, cotton, and ivory, from Walayita – precious skins, and from Wallaga – slaves, ivory, and, above all, that most precious of commodities, gold.

The caravan routes which criss-crossed the Gibe region and interwove it with the surrounding lands provided the trade of the area with an amazingly co-ordinated all-the-year-round communications system, facilitating the creation of a series of well-attended markets all over the Gibe states. However, it was Limmu-Ennarya which was at the hub, and which was the nerve center for the trade of the region. During our period, Saqqa was the major emporium in southwestern Ethiopia. Saqqa was both the headquarters of the Afkala traders[103] and the meeting-ground for the Jabarti traders from the north, the Afkala traders from the area, and the Sidama traders from the surrounding regions. Saqqa was also the great commercial entrepôt, the store town for the goods to be sent to Baso in Gojjam, to Gondar, Wollo, Tigray, Massawa, and beyond, and to Shawa, Tajura, Harar, and Berbera, everywhere feeding the revival of trade in the Red Sea Basin.[104]

It is possible that the very revival of the Red Sea trade, and certainly its prosperity, depended to a large extent on the availability of luxury products from the Gibe region. These products, which so enriched the Oromo rulers of the Gibe region and easily dominated the export lists of Red Sea trade, were slaves, gold, ivory, musk, spices, and coffee, the latter also being consumed by the Muslim population in the northern Ethiopian region.[105] Both for the

148

Jabarti traders on their return journey from the Gibe region and for the Afkala traders on their frequent trips to Baso, slaves were one of the most important commodities in their caravans. Slaves were assets to the traders. The strong ones carried goods for them. They also cooked food for them. Women were used as concubines. Young girls were well looked after and beautiful ones were often married by the slave dealers.[106] One important consideration was that because slaves were mobile they were "little affected by the difficulties of transport which affected other trade."[107] The prices of slaves varied, depending on their sex and age. Eunuchs were the most expensive, followed by young girls. Young men and old women fetched the lowest price.[108] The slaves from the Gibe region were generally known as "Gallas," although the majority of them were not actually Oromo. "When they reach the Red Sea, these 'Gallas' ... pass by the yet more incorrect denomination of 'Abessinians,' by which name they are commonly known in Egypt."[109]

Gold played the greatest role in the trade of the Gibe region from early times. In fact, the profit to be made in gold trade seems to have been a major factor stimulating caravan expeditions to the Gibe region during the eighteenth century. After the formation of the Gibe states gold continued playing an important role in the trade of the region. Of course, gold was a royal monopoly, and the trade in musk was also dominated by the king and the wealthy class. Gold came mainly from Wallaga, while musk came from the Gibe region itself and from Kaffa. Trade in gold and musk was a privilege limited to the wealthy and to certain well-known traders. They had unique value as commodities because they were easy to transport, duty free at Baso[110] and highly sought after, fetching a high profit. The international trade of Limmu-Ennarya was famous not only for slaves, gold, and musk, but also for ivory. The tusks from Limmu-Ennarya were famous for being "large, soft and white."[111] The trade in ivory was dominated by the kings themselves, in two ways. First, all the Gibe kings received one tusk for every elephant killed in their territory.[112] Secondly, the kings were themselves the biggest tusk merchants.

The trade in precious skins was also dominated by the kings. Two other commodities were also important: spices for international trade and coffee for consumption within the Ethiopian region itself. There was also a huge consumption of coffee inside the Gibe region. Abba Bagibo was the biggest coffee trader. Both the Jabarti traders and the Afkala bought a lot of coffee from him. It is said that in the 1840s the Jabarti traders annually bought about 40,000 kilograms of coffee from Limmu-Ennarya, while the Afkala traders sold about 80,000 kilograms at Baso. Altogether about 160,000[113] kilograms of coffee was sold at Baso, a large part of it going to Wollo and the northern region. Just as coffee from the Gibe region met the needs of the Muslim population in the northern part of the country, it was the luxury products of the region which financed the imports of northern Ethiopia.

The slaves, gold, ivory, musk, coffee and other items exported annually from southern and western Ethiopia fetched on the coast twice or three times their original cost. As the central and northern plateau hardly produced any exportable

149

items, it might be said that exports of southern and western Ethiopia paid not only for the imported goods brought to the Galla Sidama countries, but they also financed to a large extent the imports of northern Ethiopia, and contributed greatly to Ethiopia's favourable "balance of trade" with the outside world.[114]

The spread of Islam in the Gibe region

As with the formation of the states, the spread of Islam among the Oromo in the Gibe region was a phenomenon of the nineteenth century. This does not mean, of course, that the Oromo were not exposed to Islamic influence before that time. As we have shown earlier, contact between Islam and some Oromo groups spanned six or seven centuries.[115] Perhaps as early as the fourteenth century, and certainly by the fifteenth, the influence of the two universal religions in the Horn of Africa was filtering through contemporaneously into the area of the original home of the Oromo. Of the two religions, it was Islam which left a lasting mark on some aspects of Oromo culture, especially the Qallu institution.[116] While the previous radiation out of the Muslim principalities under the Christian administration may have kindled a spark of Islam among some sedentary Oromo groups within or on the periphery of the Christian kingdom – a spark which may have burst into flame during the short lived jihad of Imam Ahmad – the pastoral Oromo on the whole retained their traditional religion. During their migration, they moved across land where there were Muslim populations, such as the Hadiya, whom they adopted and who were eventually assimilated. In the process of the migration, the Hadiyas,[117] and perhaps also some Muslim Oromo, lost their Islamic religion but retained their Muslim names. It was because of this phenomenon that we find Muslim names in the genealogies of the various Oromo groups. In the Gibe region itself, there were a number of groups who traced their genealogies back to the sixteenth century, to the time when they lived in Bali: they took pride in the Muslim names in their genealogy after they had accepted Islam in the nineteenth century.[118] After the Oromo conquest and settlement in the Gibe region, the Muslim traders continued coming to the area, though less frequently. The commercial interests of the itinerant Muslim traders from the north and of the local clan leaders coincided. As long as the Muslim traders gave gifts, the Oromo leaders protected them and extended hospitality to them. However, at this stage in their relations, the Muslim traders did not find the time propitious for both marketing and preaching: the ground was not sufficiently prepared. Falling short of their traditional role as the ideological arm of Islam in the Horn of Africa, they do not seem to have engaged overtly in religious propaganda, perhaps for fear of alienating gada officials.[119] With the decline of the power of the gada officials and the rise of war leaders, the Muslim traders were encouraged to settle in the Gibe region itself.[120] It was in Limmu Ennarya that they first settled, perhaps in the second half of the eighteenth century. That was the turning-point in the spread of Islam in the Gibe region. It only remained for the first king of Limmu-Ennarya to discover that it was both

150

simpler and more politic to enlist the Muslim traders in his capital, together with their religion, on his side and for his cause.

Before we embark upon a brief description of the conversion of each ruling house and their people to the new religion, it is vital to mention three points which have a bearing on our subsequent presentation of the story. First and foremost, the Jabarti traders from northern Ethiopia, who included Oromo traders from Shawa and Wollo, played a very prominent role in the conversion of the nobility in the Gibe region. In their capacity as traders, the Jabarti established a good relationship with the Gibe nobility – a relationship cemented by mutual commercial interest. Initially, the Jabarti traders seem to have assumed responsibility for the teaching of Islam and for the education of the children of the nobility.[121] By the beginning of the nineteenth century, Muslim teachers already were engaged in the cultivation of the minds of the future leaders of the region. According to Trimingham, education for children came at a fairly late stage in the process of Islamization.[122] This, together with the two stages in the spread of Islam, which will be discussed shortly, seems to suggest that Islam had a foothold at least in Limmu-Ennarya and Gomma decades before the beginning of the nineteenth century.[123] In short, there are reasons to believe that Abba Bagibo, the king of Limmu-Ennarya (1825–1861), and Abba Manno, the king of Gommo (1820–1840), may have been exposed to Islamic education while young.

Secondly, Islam spread in the Gibe region in two stages. During the first, which lasted up to the 1840s, Islam was the religion of the kings and the nobility in all the Gibe states except Gomma. During the second stage, Islam gradually became the religion of the people, mainly as a result of ardent kings who made it their duty to spread it to the people. In the first half of the nineteenth century, all the Gibe kings (except those of Gomma) were indifferent in matters of religion: European travelers and missionaries admired their tolerance. In the 1860s that tolerant generation was replaced by intolerant zealot leaders, mainly as a response to the threat from the Christians to the north, coupled with their internal difficulties. Since this period is beyond the scope of this study, only a few salient points will be mentioned so as to show the fortunes of Islam in the region.

Thirdly, during the first stage of the spread of Islam in the area, all the Gibe states exhibited a dual character. The majority of the common people retained their traditional religion, the belief in Waqa, the sky god, while the wealthy class became Muslims and championed Islam.[124] The nobility's contact with the better informed and more active Muslim merchants not only created a favorable climate among this class for the spread of Islam, but also demonstrated to the ruling class that the traditional Oromo religion was inadequate.[125] The Gibe kings quickly realized the advantages to be derived from acceptance of the new religion. In matters of politics and administration, the Muslim traders were consulted while the traditional Oromo priests were ignored. The rivalry between the Oromo priests and the Muslims represented two views of politics and two political systems. The Muslim teachers ex-

The Oromo of Ethiopia

pounded the necessity of having a permanent central authority, while the Oromo priests probably enumerated the virtues of the *chafe* assembly and the dignity and advantage of having a new government every eight years. Marriages of convenience between the Muslim merchants and preachers and the new nobility sealed the success of Islam and ensured the slow disintegration of the old religion. It seems that for the nobility it was not so much that Islam attracted them more than the traditional religion; it was not Islam which was at stake, but the interests Islam represented.[126]

However, it would not be correct to assume that the traditional Oromo religion failed to put up any resistance, since many decades were necessary to overcome it. In the end Islam replaced the old religion mainly because it had the full support of the state, while the old religion lacked a literate class, organized preachers, and the ideological strength of Islam. The Oromo believed in Waqa (sky-god), the creator of the universe. To pass from believing in Waqa to accepting Allah as the creator of the universe was not a formidable transition.

> It was a simple process to change their conception of the sky-god to Allah because, He is a remote conception to begin with, and popular Islam in its accommodation with animism, whilst avoiding the sin of shirk [polytheism] was ready to accept all the subsidiary realm of spirits as well. In so far as Islam offered something akin to animism the new religion could easily become the spiritual possession of the animistic Muslim. Once it has been accepted the new doctrine has the opportunity to gain greater hold and gradually influence the inner life.[127]

It must be said that the spread of Islam among the Oromo was a slow process. Islam had the advantage of contact with the Oromo in the market centers, through traders along caravan routes, and most importantly the Oromo settled among the relatively large Muslim population in historical Ennarya.[128] Furthermore, the Islam that was presented to the Oromo was already peculiarly adopted to their condition.[129] What all this amounts to is that there was a series of gradations in the conversion of the Oromo to Islam, which acted as an insulator absorbing Islamic radiation without violently uprooting their traditional values. "The psychological shock involved in the change of religion is thus reduced to the minimum. Islam does no violent uprooting, but shades off into a long series of gradations and . . . the new culture gives immediate values without displacing the old."[130]

It was easy for the kings to replace non-Muslim by Muslim governors.[131] However, it was much more difficult for the kings to rid themselves of habits which were rooted deeply in the soil of the traditional religion.[132] Thus these Muslim kings not only acted as the leaders of the *butta* ceremony in their respective states, but they also danced together with the people in the ceremony.[133] Thus, though Muslim, they performed the role of the gada leader in the traditional religion, for the *butta* ceremony was pivotal to the traditional religious cycle.[134] This does not mean that there were no changes made in the *butta* ceremony. The themes of the *gerarsa* poems recited at this time were altered. Before the formation of the kingdoms, individual heroes, their fam-

152

ilies, and their clans were the principal themes of *gerarsa*. Now the kings themselves were the heroes and their respective dynasties the sole theme of *gerarsa*. Previously *butta* was a time of solemn prayer. Now it became a time of marriage for the young men and women.[135] *Butta* had been the time when the people met and settled their differences peacefully; now it became the time when the Gibe kings met and settled their disputes peacefully.[136] This means that no more of the traditional religion was given up than was necessary, while the new religion was colored by the background of the old. It has been said rightly that "the old beliefs do not lose all their validity to African Muslim's life; on the contrary, certain beliefs gain a renewed vitality by acquiring an Islamic orientation."[137] This was particularly true of *wadaja* – Oromo traditional prayer. After Islamization, *wadaja* continued to be the chief religious act among the Oromo. But the traditional prayers were changed to Muslim prayers and the whole purpose of *wadaja* therefore acquired a new Islamic orientation.[138] Furthermore, after the Oromo accepted Islam, the Muslim Shaykh took the place of Qallu – the traditional Oromo priest. In some parts of Oromo areas, especially in Wollo, the Muslim Shaykh was often called Qallu. "The transference of the name was natural since there would at first seem to be little different in their functions, for both were the repositories of religious knowledge among . . . people."[139]

At this juncture, it must be said that the decisive factor in the history of Islam in the Gibe region was undoubtedly the kings' concern for its spread. In almost all cases the success of Muslim teachers and preachers in spreading Islam depended on the support they got from the kings. In some cases, as in Limmu-Ennarya during the reign of Abba Gomol (1800–1825), in Gomma during the reign of Abba Manno (1820–1840), in Jimma during the reigns of Abba Boka (1859–1861) and Abba Jifar II (1878–1932), and in Gumma during the reign of Abba Dula (1854–1879), the kings were able continually to enlarge and regenerate the ranks of Muslim preachers and teachers by welcoming Islamic scholars from different parts of north east Africa.[140] The kings encouraged the Muslim teachers to establish Muslim schools, to teach children, and lead the people in prayer. Interestingly, however, the Gibe kings championed and propagated Islam while offering sacrifices to Waqa,[141] and without stopping the famous pilgrimage to the land of Abba Muda, the spiritual head of the Oromo religion. What is more, the kings not only sent gifts to Abba Muda, by the hand of the *jila* (pilgrims), but also regarded the presence of the *jila* in their states as conferring a blessing.[142] In 1846 Antoine d'Abbadie saw the *jila* from Limmu-Ennarya, Gumma, Jimma, and Gera gathered in Limmu-Ennarya before their departure on the long journey to the land of Abba Muda.[143] Only Gomma did not send any pilgrims on this pilgrimage, for alone of all the states at that time, it had been thoroughly Islamized. How Islam spread in each state is discussed briefly below.

In Limmu-Ennarya, Abba Gomol was not only the founder of a new dynasty, but he also left his name to posterity as the first Muslim Oromo king in the Gibe region.[144] Like the rest of the Gibe kings after him, Abba Gomol accepted Islam for ideological and political purposes. As already indicated, Islam provided him with a focus of unity transcending tribal loyalty and helped him to justify his ruthless actions. His acceptance of Islam created conditions in which the hundreds of Muslim merchants and preachers could propagate Islam freely.[145] Thus, Abba Gomol forged an ideological unity with the many Muslim traders and preachers in his capital, who in turn championed the cause of the king. It is unlikely, however, that his acceptance of Islam had any profound effect on the king's spiritual life. The old religion and Islam operated side by side for a long time, and it was only in the second half of the nineteenth century that the new religion limited the scope of the old.[146]

It was reported in Shawa in 1841 that Abba Gomol was converted to Islam by his uncle, Mukhtar.[147] This report is important, not for what it tells us, but for what it implies: it gives a Muslim name to the uncle of the king. This was not an attempt to Islamize the distant members of the dynasty who lived in the eighteenth century. Perhaps it was a genuine reflection of the fact that the barrier against the use of Muslim names had been broken and that the first stage, the preparatory conditioning for the acceptance of the new religion, had already been passed. According to J. S. Trimingham, "three stages mark the process of conversion: germination, crisis, and gradual reorientation."[148]

> The first stage is preparatory, the infiltration of elements of Islamic culture into animist life. The second is the conversion, characterized more by the break with the old order than the adoption of the new. The third is the gradual process by which Islam changes the life of the community.[149]

Today, Oromo traditions in the Gibe claim that Abba Gomol was converted by "the miracles of a famous Shaykh" and his descendants.[150] The name of this shaykh was Sayid Nassrullah, and the traders called him Abba Yo ("our father"), implying that he was holy. The phrase "his descendants" implies two things: first, that this shaykh was in the Gibe region for a long time and second, that the actual conversion of Abba Gomol took place at the time of his descendants. Perhaps Nassrullah was among the first generation of Muslim traders who settled in Limmu-Ennarya. Tradition has it that the shaykh was an Ashrafi[151] (descendant of the prophet). This should not be taken too literally, however. He probably was of Arab origin and with a good Islamic education, which would have raised his prestige among the first generation of traders who settled in Limmu-Ennarya. It probably was these traders who elevated his social status to the point where his Ashrafi ancestry was accepted (either during his lifetime or in retrospect after his death). Sayid Nassrullah was a distinguished counselor and an accomplished teacher. He may have started some form of Islamic education, first for the benefit of the children of the Muslim traders and later for the children of the nobility. His literacy in Arabic probably impressed the Oromo nobility, who attached unusually great importance to the ability to communicate in writing. For whatever reason, he was and still is universally regarded as a saint and as the first standard bearer of Islam in the Gibe region; thousands of believers visit his shrine every year.[152]

Notwithstanding the conversion of the king and the religious activities of the

Muslim traders and preachers, there was no mosque in the country during the reign of Abba Gomol, or even during the reign of his successor. In 1841, it was reported in Shawa that there were no mosques in the country: "prayers are held at the tomb of Bofo (Abba Gomol), the first convert to the faith."[153] In the late 1850s Massaja actually visited the tomb of Abba Gomol, which by then had already taken on the character of a shrine. In 1861 a fanatical new king, who gave himself the title of King of Limmu-Ennarya and "the father of the Muslims,"[154] put a stop to the activities of the Catholic missionaries and expelled them from his country. And yet even he did not build mosques in his territory. When Cecchi visited him in the late 1870s there was only one mosque and that was in his *massera*. Nevertheless, by that time, Islam had won the struggle and the entire population of Limmu-Ennarya were Muslims. He writes: "Today, after nearly eighty years, Islam is found at full vigor, being already adopted even by the most pauperized classes."[155] The reason for the conspicuous absence of mosques in Limmu-Ennarya and in the Gibe region in general is well put by J. S. Trimingham: "Naturally the mosque of the people was then as it still is under a village tree at some spot hallowed by tradition."[156]

The ruling house of Gomma was the second to accept Islam in the Gibe region. According to Cecchi, and accepted by Trimingham and others, Gomma was the first state in the region to have accepted Islam.[157] This is true in the sense that Gomma was the first of the Gibe states where the entire population embraced Islam. The ruling house of Limmu-Ennarya, however, accepted Islam before that of Gomma. The ruling dynasty of Gomma, known as Awuliani ("the holy"), claimed descent from Nur Hussein of Bali.[158] In narrating this tradition, Cecchi seems to have confused it with the story of a Somali shaykh, who around the beginning of the nineteenth century, was the guardian of the tomb of Shaykh Hussein. According to Cecchi's version, a Somali named Nur Husain emigrated from Mogadisho in 1780 and settled among the Oromo, where he showed himself to be a worker of marvelous miracles.

> This man, Nur Husain, otherwise known as Wariko, was a worker of miracles. He could fly like an eagle, and could change men into animals. He first settled in Kafa, but was forced to flee and took refuge in Gomma, crossing the flooded Gojeb by striking the waters with his staff and dividing them.[159]

There is good reason to believe that the above tradition developed out of the tradition of Shaykh Hussein of Bali, whom the Oromo called Nur Hussein. In the first place, these miracles are almost the same as those attributed to Shaykh Hussein of Bali by the *Rabi-al-Qulub*.[160] Secondly, according to Oromo traditions gathered from the Gibe region, Shaykh Hussein of Bali had two sons, named Muhammed Aman, who went to Harar, and Awuliani, who came to the Gibe region and settled in Gomma, the Gomma dynasty being descended from him.[161] Such a claim is untenable historically, of course, since Shaykh Hussein lived in the thirteenth century. The claim was simply made in order to Islamize and exalt the saintly origin of the dynasty. However, there does lie a concrete historical reality behind the tradition connecting a Somali shaykh, Nur Hussein of Bali, and the Awuliani of Gomma. Amir Abd al-Shakur (1783–94), the famous ruler of Harar, is known to have built a mosque on the holy site of Shaykh Hussein and to have dedicated it to Abd al-Qadir al-Jilani.[162] A Somali shaykh was in charge of that mosque, which became the center of diffusion of the Qadiriya order to the Gibe region.[163] In fact, the Somali shaykh himself is reported to have brought the Qadiriya order to the Gibe region, to Gomma itself. The establishment of the Qadiriya and other orders in the Gibe region in the nineteenth century was the key to the spread of Islam among the people.[164] These orders established themselves in the countryside, where they opened Quranic schools.[165] It was in Gomma that the Qadiriya order was first established and where many *fuqaha* (legal scholars) and shaykhs zealously spread Islam. This explains the connection between the tradition of Awuliani and Shaykh Hussein of Bali, whom the Oromo call Nur Hussein of Bali. More importantly, it explains the rapid spread of Islam in the little state of Gomma. In terms of the spread of Islam in Gomma, a revolution took place during the reign of Abba Manno (1820–1840). The Qadiriya order, which arrived in Gomma in the last quarter of the eighteenth century,[166] reached its full development during his reign. Another order, Tijaniya,[167] also established itself in Gomma at this time. Abba Manno provided the orders with land and encouraged them to intensify proselytization. The result was dramatic. By 1841, according to what Harris had heard in Shawa, "in Gomma the Moslem faith is universal."[168] The rapid spread of Islam among the people of Gomma had some consequences, for both Gomma itself and others in the region. First, the rapid spread of Islam was accompanied by mushrooming Muslim education, which marked the definite transition to an Islamized society.

> It is at this level that the education of children to prepare in them a collective mentality and introduction to the worship technique of the dervish orders begin to play a part in providing the Muslim neophyte with a spiritual home. He thus gains a wide outlook, a new self-assurance, and a feeling of religious and social solidarity, with which comes a readiness to distinguish between insiders and outsiders (dar al-Islam and dar al-harb) and the feeling of belonging to the favoured, the umma of God.[169]

Muslim education in Gomma (as in the rest of the Gibe states) consisted of learning the Arabic alphabet and the memorization of the Quran. In this, Gomma made a considerable achievement. By the late 1870s, "both the old and the young always memorize the Quran, which is taught by migrant Muslims."[170] Secondly, it was in Gomma that the notorious practice of enslaving their own people was first abolished. While the rest of the Gibe kings were still selling their own people, one of the kings of Gomma, when asked why he did not, is reported to have said, "But if I sell my subjects, whose king do I remain? Perhaps of the monkeys?"[171] Though the kings of Gomma continued selling their non-Muslim slaves, they decisively ended *hari*, the practice of selling their subjects on various pretexts. This may reflect the strong impact

Islam had on the rulers of Gomma. To the credit of the new religion, one must say that where compassion and political expediency failed to stop the *hari* institution, Islam succeeded in bringing to an end the infamous practice.

Emulating the example of the Gomma king, all the Gibe kings came to abandon the practice. They also slowly encouraged serious proselytization among their people. Even the most indifferent and tolerant of all the Gibe kings, Abba Bagibo, was compelled to encourage proselytization in his country.[172] It was also at this time that some aspects of Islamic law, the Sharia, started to influence the lives of the people. In matters of marriage and inheritance, Islamic law slowly replaced traditional Oromo law.[173] It is not possible to say how much of the five pillars of Islam – Shahada,[174] Salat,[175] Sawm,[176] Zakat,[177] and Haji,[178] – were rigorously upheld by the people at large. "These five pillars are the kernel of Ebadat, regulations relating to worship, on which the foundation of Islam rests, and which constitutes one of the three broad classifications of Sharia (the Muslim law)." Of the five, fasting seems to have been well observed. Zakat was also introduced by the kings.[179] Some Oromo went on pilgrimage to Mecca and Medina. In the 1840s d'Abbadie met several Muslims from the region who had gone to Mecca and Medina a number of times.[180] The pilgrimage to Mecca indicates that Islam was making progress in the Gibe region. It may have also enriched and broadened their knowledge of the Muslim world. Be that as it may, while Muslim Oromo went on pilgrimage to Mecca, the *jila*, Oromo pilgrims from the Gibe region continued going to Abba Muda, the spiritual father of traditional religion.[181] Nevertheless, by the 1840s, Islam had already started making a real impact even beyond Gomma. For instance, circumcision, which previously took place late in life, was now carried out early on. Even the Muslim calendar started to be used alongside the Oromo oral calendar.[182]

Abba Jifar, the first king of Jimma, was converted to Islam by Shaykh Abdul Hakim,[183] who is known to have been a trader and preacher who came from Gondar.[184] Another famous religious leader in Jimma was Abba Arabo.[185] He seems to have been of Arab origin. Today both Shaykh Abdul Hakim and Abba Arabo are considered as saints and annually thousands of believers visit their shrines.[186] However, it was the former who seems to have been the standard bearer in the spread of Islam in Jimma. Abdul Hakim seems to have found the ground prepared for his missionary work in Jimma in 1830. Muslim traders already had cultivated friendly relations with Abba Magal, the father of Abba Jifar, in the first quarter of the nineteenth century. When Abba Jifar created the kingdom, he soon realized[187] that it needed wealth and an ideology, which not only would nourish the unity of the people but also would consolidate the dynasty's grip on the territory. According to Massaja, Abba Jifar embraced Islam for political and economic motives rather than for religious needs.

> Abba Jifar . . . thought that for reasons of stability and the future of his country, in addition to the material unity, it is essential to have religious unity as well. He chose Islam not only because it was comfortable, but because it favoured the idea

157

of an absolute king. Having embraced Islam, and declared it the religion of the court, he invited to the kingdom a number of Muslim saints [teachers] to preach and spread the new religion.[188]

Despite this, it was only after 1860 that Islam won any considerable ground in Jimma. There were three main reasons for this. The first two kings of Jimma were more interested in expanding the frontiers of their state than in spreading Islam among their people. It was only the third king, Abba Boka (1859–61), who devoted his short reign to the cause of Islam, thus earning the title of Al-Mahadi, the reformer.[189] The title is perhaps an exaggeration of the achievements of Abba Boka. However, what he did within that short span of time was indeed remarkable.[190]

> He built many mosques and ordered that mosques be built in each of the sixty provinces. He sent learned Muslims to proselytize and teach in the provinces. Abba Boka instituted the collection of the poor tax (Zaka) and set aside land (Wakfi) near Jiren, to be used by Muslim merchants (Negade) from the north who would settle there, pray at the Jiren mosques for the health of the king and the realm, and teach those who wanted to learn about Islam.[191]

Secondly, in the second half of the nineteenth century, Limmu-Ennarya declined militarily, politically, and commercially, and as a result a large number of Muslim traders abandoned Saqqa in favor of Hirmata near Jiren. Jiren became the leading Muslim capital, famous for the learning of its scholars. Rising to importance three decades after Saqqa, Jiren outshone Saqqa, becoming the major center of Islamic learning in the whole of southwestern Ethiopia.

In this, Jiren was helped by the third factor. As a result of the persecution of the Muslim Oromo in Wollo, first under Tewodros (1855–67) and then under Yohannes, a number of Muslims were forced to flee from Wollo. Some of these refugees seem to have come to Jimma. According to Abbar Jobir, "Wollo was the land of Muslim saints, who were the mountain of knowledge."[192] Certainly, some learned men among the immigrants to Jimma increased the number of Muslim teachers in the capital and gave Jiren added luster. The other king who did a great deal for the spread of Muslim education in Jimma was Abba Jifar II (1878–1932). During his long reign many orders flourished there. The orders were established in the countryside, where they were supported by land grants from the king and gifts from wealthy Muslims. The orders did not have political clout, but they became centers of Islamic learning and religious culture.[193] Moreover, as the commercial emporium of the southwestern region of what is today Ethiopia and a famous center of learning, it attracted talented individuals from different parts of Oromoland. Consequently, "all the most celebrated Galla minstrels gathered at the court of Abba Jifar II to produce their songs in this literary and commercial centre of the Gibe region."[194] In short, there is reason to believe that Abba Jifar II contributed to the growth of Islamic education in his land. This is because by the 1880s Jimma claimed to have sixty *madras* (schools of higher education).[195] If this claim is true, it is an amazing achievement for Jimma. Perhaps this explains why Jimma became the most famous center of Islamic learning for all Oromo in the Horn of Africa. Even today, along with Daawwe in Wollo, Jimma is regarded as the best center of Islamic learning in the Horn of Africa. Despite such enviable and deserved fame, Oromo scholars in Jimma produced only a modest amount of religious literature in their own language.[196] Inspired by the desire to communicate their spiritual fervor and their love of saints, such as Shaykh Hussein of Bali and Abd al-Qadir al-Jilani, few Oromo scholars produced religious poetry in their own language. According to Cerulli, this poetry is similar to the Muslim literature found in East Africa.[197] Perhaps the difficulty involved in writing Oromo in Arabic orthography,[198] coupled with the scholars' exaggerated reverence of Arabic as the language of the Quran and the mother tongue of the Prophet,[199] hindered the flourishing of religious poems in the Oromo language. The following song, which depicts death and the grave in lugubrious pictures, is an example of religious poetry that was produced.

> When my soul will . . . depart from my body,
> and the angel looks at her
> and will say to her "turn to your path"
> when my fate will be discussed
> Mercy! Oh Nur Hussein!
> When I will be wrapped with funeral sheet
> when they transport me [to my grave]
> when I will be separated from my friends
> when I will be thrown away alone
> Mercy! Oh Nur Hussein.[200]

In this song, Shaykh Hussein, whom the Oromo call Nur Hussein, the famous thirteenth-century Islamic standard-bearer in Bali, is not only venerated but almost deified. The reason for this is not difficult to understand. First, Shaykh Hussein was and still is a saint of great importance in the Ethiopian region and beyond. Secondly, and equally important, it was the Ahamadiya Order which had its headquarters at the shrine of Shaykh Hussein in Bali that established itself in Jimma and promoted the veneration of that saint in the Gibe region. In short, together with the immigrants from Wollo, the orders in Jimma made that land the most important center of Islamic learning in the Gibe region.

Gumma was the second state to be formed, the fourth to accept Islam, and the first to declare a jihad in the name of that religion. Islam became the religion of the ruling dynasty of Gumma only in the 1830.[201] It has been said that Abba Manno, the king of Gomma, played a role in the spread of Islam in Gumma. It appears that it was Abba Manno who persuaded Jawe Oncho (1840–1854), the king of Gumma, to abolish the festival of *butta*.[202] It was also Abba Manno who seems to have encouraged the Qadiriya order to establish itself and spread Islam in Gumma. Nevertheless, Islam took deep roots in Gumma during the reign of Abba Dula (1854–1879), who seems to have believed passionately in the spread of Islam in his country. It was in the 1860s

159

that Gumma experienced intense Islamic fervor. This was brought about by three interrelated factors. First, besides Qadiriya, other orders also established themselves in Gumma in the 1860s. Secondly, Abba Boka (1859–1861), the religious-minded king of Jimma, sent Muslim teachers and preachers to Gumma. Thirdly and even more importantly, Abba Dula received a letter written by Shaykh Said Ahmad, the custodian of the tomb of the Prophet at Al-Medina. The letter reached Abba Dula either in late 1865 or early 1866. It urged all the believers that the "end" of the world was coming and that they should fortify themselves in their faith.[203] It had its desired impact on Abba Dula and his son and successor, Abba Jobir. Perhaps it was in response to this letter that Abba Dula and his successor declared a jihad in the name of Islam – although it was also in their own territorial interest. The first jihad was against their non-Muslim stateless Oromo neighbors, who lived between the rivers Didessa and Baro. Gumma even succeeded in forming a Muslim League, which included other Gibe states, except Gera, but before the Muslim League had time to impose its will on its non-Muslim Oromo neighbors, Menelik's invasion of the Gibe region changed the course of history. However, even after the Amhara occupation of the Gibe region, Gumma remained the hotbed of rebellion and Muslim fanaticism against alien colonial administration. Gumma's resistance was inspired, organized, and led by Firrisa, the heir to the throne of Gumma. After the occupation of Gumma, Firrisa fled to Massawa. There he met with Shaykh Abdurahman, a scholar fugitive from Gomma. The two men made several pilgrimages to Mecca and Medina. Inflamed by the jihadic idea Firrisa went to the Sudan, where he assembled his followers and returned to the western Oromoland in 1899. He soon proclaimed himself king of Gumma "independent of the Amhara."[204] Although support for his call was not lacking, his jihad was short-lived, as the Amhara force which had superiority in firearms defeated his followers and captured Firrisa and Shaykh Abdurahman in 1902. The latter managed to escape, while the former was condemned to death together with many of his followers.

> Firrisa demanded to be executed holding the Koran in his hands, and before the hanging he cried out that he would be buried outside Ethiopia . . . The tragic death of the last prince of Gumma made a great and painful impression on the Galla. Even today, all the Mussulmen of these lands consider Firrisa a saint (wali).[205]

Gera was the last state to be formed, and the last to accept Islam, in the late 1840s. The death of Abba Rago,[206] around 1848, was followed by a bloody power struggle between Abba Magal on the one hand and his brothers and cousins on the other. Abba Magal was a formidable and cunning individual who saw his own salvation in an alliance with Abba Bagibo, the king of Limmu-Ennarya. The latter was even more cunning, an expert in subjugating his own passions, as well as those of the zealous Muslims at this court, to the interest of his ambition, an ambition which he colored with the cause of Islam. When Abba Magal appealed to him for military assistance, Abba Bagibo promised to help him on the condition that, in the event of victory, Abba

Magal would embrace Islam. As soon as Abba Bagibo's support put him on the throne of Gera, Abba Magal fulfilled his promise, yet he remained uncircumcised.[207] This would seem to indicate that his acceptance of Islam did not bring about any profound change in his life. Abba Magal reigned for the next two decades.

> The most notorious of the kings of Gera was Abba Magal, a cruel man who was suspicious of everybody. He surrounded his house with thick banana plantations in which he hid and listened to the conversation of people who went there, in case anyone should try to plot against him. Near his house he made two cabins in which he confined his personal enemies shackled to heavy logs; in wet and dry weather alike they lay there half naked and starving in a most pitiable state.[208]

According to Cecchi, Abba Magal became a zealous Muslim towards the end of his life as a result of a circular letter from the guardian of the tomb of the Prophet in Al-Medina which was brought to Gera in 1866 by Abba Jobir, the son of the king of Gumma.[209] Perhaps it was this message which inspired and intoxicated the leadership in Gumma to embark on the jihad against the non-Muslim Oromo. The circular letter failed to provoke a similar response in Gera, but it may have contributed to the process of proselytization, which was in full swing by 1870. By 1879, when Cecchi was in Gera, the court was thoroughly Islamized and several *fuqahas* and shaykhs taught and prayed at the tomb of Abba Magal. The reigning queen was noted for buying hundreds of copies of the Quran, which she distributed amongst the nobility.[210] Because of the lack of written evidence, we do not know much about the spread of Islam and the growth of Muslim education in Gera. The one thing that can be said with certainty is that it was the religious orders that spread Islam and established Islamic education in Gera.

To conclude, the spread of Islam in the Gibe region was preceded by commerce, and its agents were the Muslim Jabarti traders from the north, mainly from Gondar, the Muslim Oromo traders from Shawa, and Wollo, and some from Harar. The Jabarti traders brought to the Gibe region not only imported luxury foreign goods but also a non-purchasable commodity, Islam, which eventually was to change the ideological orientation of the Oromo society in the Gibe region. The Oromo language was the *lingua franca* of trade at the time, and the majority of the agents of Islamic radiation were Oromo speakers. This may have facilitated the spread of Islam by overcoming the difficult problem of communication. It was the kings who first accepted Islam, and they imposed it on the ruling class.[211] Their conversion ensured the gradual spread of Islam among the people in the region. After 1861, all the thrones of the Gibe states were occupied by zealous Muslim rulers. The existence of rival centers of power may have contributed to the spread of Islam and the growth of Islamic learning, since the kings may have vied[212] with one another in attracting Muslim preachers and teachers to enhance the luster of their capitals.

6

The era of Abba Bagibo in the politics of the Gibe region, 1825–1861

I have devoted a chapter to the era of Abba Bagibo in the politics of the Gibe region, because that era marks the Golden Age of the Gibe states. Abba Bagibo tried to unite the region through diplomacy and it was his political strategies which have given his reign a special fascination. It was one of the greatest strokes of good fortune for Limmu-Ennarya that Abba Bagibo was an exceptionally able leader and consummate politician and that his reign spanned thirty-six years during which time he built up her power to its highest point and made her famous across what is today southwestern Ethiopia and beyond. During his long reign Limmu-Ennarya was the economic center and political powerhouse of the Gibe region. This chapter documents the history of Limmu-Ennarya and that of her most famous king between 1825 and 1861.

Background to Abba Bagibo's rise to power

Abba Bagibo was born in 1802. He was educated and brought up in Sappa, the first capital of Limmu-Ennarya. We do not know how much Islamic education he received, but one thing is certain: Muslim religious teachers seem to have influenced the mind of the Abba Bagibo while he was still young.

Abba Bagibo was generally described both in oral tradition and by foreign travelers as "white,"[1] a notion which gives credibility to the legend of the "Portuguese" origin of his dynastic line. The dynasty founded by his father was known as Sapera, based on a famous historical name. Sapera was the name of the mythical father of the Borana.[2] Even towards the end of the sixteenth century, when the Tulama and the Matcha fought together against a common enemy, they called themselves Sapera[3] in memory of their mythical ancestry. In order to glorify the origin of the family, a legend was invented,[4] probably during the reign of Abba Gomol, and later elaborated under his successor, in order to connect the dynasty with two "white men," named Sapera and Sigaro. As Sapera was a historical name, so was Sigaro. When the legend was recorded by the European travelers and missionaries, who knew about the Portuguese assistance to the Ethiopian Christian kingdom in the 1540s, the two "white men" became Portuguese, adding additional credibility to the legend. These two, it is said, "had come to Abyssinia with Cristovao da Gama, who brought help to Galawdewos against Gran."[5] The legend goes on to say that the two men were later expelled by Galawdewos and that they escaped into Ennarya, where with their fantastic skills and courage they earned a great reputation among the people. Sigaro fixed his residence in the northern part of Ennarya near Saqqa, while Sapera settled further south near Sappa. The two eventually became the founders of dynasties.[6] The legend reflected, of course, the reality of the struggle between two clans; the one settled near Saqqa and the other settled near Sappa. Abba Rebu, the wealthy man in Limmu, was the leader of the clan around Saqqa, while Bofo was the war leader of the clan around Sappa, and when the latter established a new dynasty it was called Sapera. The founder of the dynasty may have not believed in the legend, though his two successors believed in it passionately, referring to European travelers and missionaries as "our white brothers."[7]

The young, handsome,[8] eloquent, and promising Ibssa, who is said to have possessed a considerable share of his father's vigor, though lacking his courage,[9] had spent his early years in learning the art of war in his father's army. He had probably been engaged with his father in subjugating the surrounding tribes through war and diplomacy. It was during those years of training and ideological preparation for the leadership, that Ibssa acquired his popular name from that of his horse Bagibo. In those early years, the young Abba Bagibo does not seem to have ventured to advance any independent claim to the leadership, and apparently his father was not frightened by his rising popularity. On the contrary, Abba Gomol seems to have trusted his son and rewarded him by making him *donachaw*,[10] the heir apparent to the throne. It also seems that it was his father who arranged Abba Bagibo's marriage to the daughter of the king of Kaffa.[11] Abba Bagibo's first wife, Genne Minjoti ("the lady" from the kingdom of Kaffa) remained his principal wife, until her death. Abba Bagibo's connection with Abba Rebu, through his mother, his marriage link with the powerful kingdom of Kaffa, his association with the Muslim traders and preachers in Sappa, must all have contributed to his rising popularity. His long training in the army, his exceptional qualities of leadership and "cunning and crafty diplomacy,"[12] together with his organizational ability, may have won him widespread support among his father's soldiers. While the popularity of the son was rising, that of the father was declining, and this may at last have aroused the jealousy of the father. What probably brought the matter to a head was the beginning of discontent and revolt in various areas, more particularly near Saqqa, the old power base of Abba Rebu. Previously, Abba Gomol appeared to have dealt very ruthlessly[13] with every rebellion, but now adopted a policy of moderation, perhaps suggested by the fear that something was in the air. Before going on to describe the power struggle between the father and his son, it is necessary to mention a few vital points. First, our information on this episode is very slight, and some of our conclusions about it are no more than conjecture. Secondly, we saw that Abba Gomol had a very good relationship with the governor of Gojjam.[14] This was brought about by mutual commercial interests. The governor of Gojjam and Abba Gomol cooperated in maintaining the safety of the caravan route within the two countries.

Limmu-Ennarya depended on Kaffa, no less than it depended on Gojjam. Kaffa was the source of many of the luxury goods which Limmu-Ennarya exported through Gojjam. For this and probably for security reasons as well, Abba Gomol cultivated a good relation with the king of Kaffa. The marriage bridge between the two states had clearly been generated by the desire to maintain good relations. What is interesting to note here is that Abba Gomol did not interfere with the flow of trade between the two countries. On the contrary, he seems to have permitted the northern Muslim merchants, the Jabarti, to go as far as Kaffa. This policy was dramatically reversed by his successor, who banned the Jabarti traders from going beyond Saqqa, the new capital of Limmu-Ennarya, after 1825.[15] In fact, it is suspected that the overthrow of Abba Gomol by his son may have been supported by the newly emerging merchant class of Limmu-Ennarya, the Afkala.

The aristocracy of Limmu-Ennarya itself had its own stake in the affair and the king himself was among the biggest of the merchants. It should be noted here that Abba Gomol was the builder of a state rather than the defender of the interest of the Afkala. He followed a policy which favored the Jabarti traders. As we saw above,[16] the Jabarti were far superior to the Afkala because of their bigger captial (i.e., the variety and large size of their goods), their experience in long-distance trade, and their organizational skill. The Afkala required more capital than they had at their disposal. As a result, they were not in a position to compete successfully with Jabarti traders. To remain in business the Afkala needed the support of the state. It is reasonable to assume that the Afkala support for Abba Bagibo was an expression of their disapproval of Abba Gomol's commercial policy and it seems to have been motivated by desire for profit and success. It is not clear from the sources whether or not the Afkala support tipped the balance in favor of Abba Bagibo. What is certain, however, is that Abba Bagibo appears to have understood the plight of the Afkala and consequently he banned Jabarti traders from going to Kaffa, the rich source of gold, ivory, musk, and slaves. This provided the Afkala with a golden opportunity to monopolize the trade between Limmu-Ennarya and Kaffa. Without doubt, the prosperity of the Afkala traders depended on the support of Abba Bagibo. Therefore, it is not unreasonable to assume that the change of rulers was the outcome, not merely of political struggle between the father and the son, but also of a class interest, in which the son represented the interest of the Afkala, while the father represented a "free-for-all" policy. Abba Gomol was aware of the rising fame of his son, but was probably unable to devise effective measures for curbing his popularity. His kingdom lacked unity, because he alienated even members of his own family by threatening them with death. He also failed to protect the interests of the newly emerging class, by following an open-door policy towards the northern traders. Even the Jabarti traders, whose interest was threatened by the weakness of his government, may have betrayed him. Isolated and frightened, Abba Gomol adopted a policy of moderation, but by then it was already too late.

Abba Bagibo was probably twenty-three years old before he felt himself strong enough to challenge his father and stage a *coup d'état*. Having built up a solid basis of political and military support, he decided to take over the government and dictated the conditions for his father's abdication. Each condition was an insult to the pride of the aging father. "My father, please, eat and drink and I will reign for you,"[17] was the declaration with which he surprised his father. Abba Gomol was shocked by the rebellion of his son, but he was not prepared to step down without drawing sword so that, by 1825, Abba Gomol was faced with two parallel crises. There was a rebellion of a sort around Saqqa, based essentially on an old problem, but looking for a new catalyst; and there was Abba Bagibo's threat to overthrow him, essentially a new crisis looking for a detonator. This it found in the Saqqa rebellion. Abba Gomol seems to have thought that only the punishment of his son could restore the confidence of his soldiers, and restore his honor and prestige. He forgot about the popularity and strength of his son and remembered only his own old military exploits. In a moment of uncontrolled wrath, fueled with bitterness and a sense of lost pride, he even sought to destroy his sons and brothers, who probably supported the cause of his rebellious son.[18] Deserted by his own sons, brothers, slaves,[19] and soldiers, Abba Gomol found that the remnant of his supporters was hopelessly inadequate in the face of the increasing numbers of the enemy, so that eventually his determination to fight to the bitter end had to yield to the suggestion of an honorable peace formula. Abba Bagibo's close supporters, being desirous of legalizing his seizure of power, supported a peaceful resolution of the event. Besides the motives of political expediency which might have prompted Abba Bagibo to come to terms, there was the experience of the settlement which Abba Gomol had reached with his father-in-law, two decades before. Abba Gomol handed over the gold ring to Abba Bagibo, signaling not only the transfer of power, but also marking the end of one reign and the beginning of another. Abba Bagibo was magnanimous to his father, as his father had been magnanimous to his father-in-law. Abba Gomol was left in his *massera* at Sappa, with some control over the surrounding district.[20] Abba Gomol died in 1837, twelve years after he was deposed. He was an energetic king while on the throne, and an affable father-figure after he was removed from power. He was buried in Sappa, where his tomb became a shrine, adding spiritual luster and glamour to the first capital of Limmu-Ennarya.

In his struggle for power, Abba Bagibo was said to have been helped by his brothers and two cousins.[21] Unfortunately, we know neither the names of the brothers who helped him nor the role they played in Abba Bagibo's administration, but we do know that Abba Bagibo was embroiled in political dispute with his two cousins and two of his sons at different times, and that three of them became his victims.[22] This brings us to an important point. Although we have much more information on his reign than on any of the contemporary rulers of the Gibe states, the otherwise adequate sources of information paint two contradictory portraits of Abba Bagibo. On the one hand, some oral traditions recorded by Cecchi and others depict him as a hot-tempered, and superstitious man, who enslaved or killed people for minor offenses; as a dandy, who squandered his wealth on clothes; as cruel, even killing his own son.[23] On the other hand, he is generally depicted as an extraordinary king, endowed with a liberal and generous hand, a consummate and accomplished politician, a patient and exceedingly tolerant father-figure, and a man of peace.[24] There are elements of truth in both aspects of the above description. Without doubt, he was one of the outstanding politicians of his time; but his achievements were stained by bouts of licentious passion, during which he indulged in acts of cruelty with too little regard even for his own flesh and blood. The character of the real Abba Bagibo may be understood if his long reign is divided into two periods. During the first part of his reign he was cruel and impatient, while during the second part he ruled by his head and patience rather than by his hand and passion, thus becoming a statesman who dominated the Gibe region by political marriage and diplomacy, rather than by the sword.

The reign of Abba Bagibo, 1825–1841

Probably the first task Abba Bagibo had to face after accession to the throne was the suppression of the rebellion around Saqqa. The evidence from limited literary sources and oral tradition is in amazing agreement that Abba Bagibo did not act hastily. He "consolidated his power considerably and made certain the readiness of his soldiers."[25] The time so consumed enabled him to win fresh political grounds. At the same time, he took great care to involve an important political figure, whose power base was Saqqa itself, for weakening and defeating the rebellion at and around Saqqa. In other words, he sought the support of his grandfather, Abba Rebu, for settling the Saqqa rebellion. This was perhaps intended to divide and weaken the opposition. In short, Abba Bagibo did everything with the full knowledge and support of Abba Rebu.[26] As a result the resistance put up by his enemies did not match the amount of effort Abba Bagibo had put into the preparation. His easy victory in Saqqa opened the way for his long and continuous wars against his neighbors, the Nonno and the Agallo, at whose expense he expanded his territory.[27]

At Saqqa, Abba Bagibo found a commercial town surrounded by a land of uncommon fertility, which probably surpassed even his own expectations. Along with his wars against his neighbors (which will be discussed later),[28] Abba Bagibo built a new capital at Saqqa. The transformation of Saqqa into a new capital was naturally connected with the implementation of a new commercial policy. Sappa had been the capital of the kingdom of Limmu-Ennarya, during the reign of his father. Probably as part of the peace formula, Abba Bagibo left Sappa under his father's hand and founded a new capital. Saqqa, favored by a most fortunate geographical position and the fertility of its surroundings, was a flourishing commercial town. The policy which had the most fruitful influence in the short run was that of banning the Jabarti traders from going beyond Saqqa. This gave the Afkala the monopoly of the trade beyond the Gojeb. It also contributed to the growth of his capital and to the king's own prosperity. It is worth noting here that, starting early in his reign, Abba Bagibo not only made all crucial decisions on trade, but he was also economically the center point from which significant quantities of luxury commodities radiated in different directions. The immense importance of Limmu-Ennarya in the trade of the southwestern region reached its climax in the 1840s, but the groundwork for this development was laid in the 1820s and early 1830s. The flourishing trade made Saqqa a unique commercial capital in the Gibe region, where all the caravan routes met, and traders from various nationalities rubbed shoulders while buying and selling.[29] In short, the growth of trade in Limmu-Ennarya directly contributed to the growth of Saqqa, the capital.

By 1840, Saqqa had a population of about twelve thousand.[30] This constituted ten to twelve percent of the entire population of Limmu-Ennarya, since her population at the height of her power was said to have been just over 100,000.[31] Such a concentration of population in the capital was probably preceded or accompanied by remarkable progress in the division of labor and a specialization of workers, not witnessed anywhere up to that time among the Oromo, if not among the sedentary agricultural population of the Ethiopian region. This was not without far-reaching consequences for the development of art and industry in Limmu-Ennarya.

> The inhabitants of Enarea enjoy the reputation of being the most civilized of all the Gallas and manufactures flourish here in a higher degree than anywhere else in this quarter of Africa.[32]

Nothing could give a better idea of the wealth of Abba Bagibo and his firm grip on his subjects than his many *masseras*, which spread all over the country and included "Sapa, Garuqqe, Saqa, ... Uga, Darru, Kocaw, Gena, Gu-ujujo, Du-ujuma, Tuniqe, Tora, Kusae, and Laga Sombo."[33] All the fifteen *masseras*[34] (royal residences) were built on the tops of hills wide enough to accommodate many huts, but high enough also to dominate the surrounding areas. Of his many *masseras* the most beautiful, and the largest one was that of Garuqqe near Saqqa, the capital.[35] This is also the *massera* about which we have the fullest information. It was the heart of the kingdom, where the king lived most of his time, the political nerve center from which orders radiated to all corners of the country, and the commercial capital of the region, where the largest concentration of Jabarti traders was found. This *massera* of Garuqqe can be considered as a prototype for the *masseras* of other states of the Gibe region. Apart from size and beauty, the *masseras* of the Gibe states were very similar in their layouts, structure, composition, and activities.[36] Furthermore, the artists and the builders of the Gibe states were able to produce elegant, relatively splendid, well-designed and artistically executed *masseras*. Some of the *masseras*, especially that of Jiren in Jimma had the capacity to accommodate thousands.[37] The building of such spacious residences needed the power of the states and the organizational skills of the kings.

The *massera* of Garuqqe was a large village, built to accommodate the king, his family, his bodyguards, his wives, numerous concubines, and slaves. Such a complex and sophisticated settlement could not have been built without the organization of a massive labor force, and the involvement of architects,

167

artists, and craftsmen of all kinds. The labor force was composed of three elements: the king's ever-expanding slave population, the free peasants of Limmu-Ennarya who had to work for the king whenever he demanded their labor, and the *qubsisa*, that is the king's tenants who had to work "twice a week each Monday and Friday"[38] either on the royal residence, the royal estates, the building of bridges across rivers, or on the maintenance of roads. Judging by the nature of the construction, the unskilled labor force provided the building materials, prepared the ground, built the walls, and constructed the fences. The specialist craftsmen handled the roofs, the doors, and internal decorations, and furnished the houses with the necessary utensils. The organization of such a co-ordinated labor force would have needed a vigorous man of action and indeed Abba Bagibo was not only such a man, but also had an insatiable appetite for refined things. His interest in the expansion of industry and arts enabled him to build an elegant and splendid *massera* at Garuqqe.

> When we arrived near to the first entrance gate we were ordered to descend from the mules for the respect of the royal residence. The more we advanced towards the massera, the greater our admiration increased, because despite previous descriptions by our men, about the beauty of the court, we had not expected to see so much luxury and so much elegance in the construction of various huts, some of which for their architecture, and internal decoration would have deeply impressed our own engineers . . . Cleanliness and order which excited our curiosity dominated every corner.[39]

The Garuqqe *massera* was a large compound surrounded by a high fence made of interwoven boughs in the midst of which were found at equal distances from each other trees[40] whose branches, leaves, and flowers, added their own share of beauty to what was already elegant. What particularly added special beauty and elegance to the Garuqqe *massera* was the unique environment in which it was located. It was built on the edge of the largest coffee forest of Limmu-Ennarya, which was the property of Abba Bagibo.

> In the middle of this thick green forest [of coffee] . . . comes up with sudden roaring of sound a majestic white mantle of Hursa Mandio [Fall], which the Gibe forms here in the forest, almost to complete the wonderful landscape. Few countries in Western Ethiopia can be compared in beauty to this which has surprising effect and tells the traveller with charms of its unforgettable colours . . . I admired the fall and the beauty that no artist has thought of and no poet has chanted. And which hides its kingdom in this wild forest almost jealous of itself and its force.[41]

As with all other *masseras* in the region, the Garuqqe *massera* had three large fences, and at the main gate of the outer fence was a high tower, upon which stood guards who were intended to observe any suspicious movement. As in Jiren, the gates of the first and second fences were guarded by armed men.[42] Within the outer fence lived the elite troops, the bodyguard of the king, numbering around 200 cavalry and the same number of infantry.[43] Within the second fence were found many huts, destined for the use of the king's guests, and for the court of justice. Here the beautiful reception hall was located. This hall, where foreign guests and ambassadors were received and entertained, was also the place where great banquets were offered to the dignitaries of the land on many occasions. The reception hall was surrounded by a wide and elegant fence, whose entrance gate was decorated with designs of a Chinese fashion, which had produced a strong impact on the minds of his subjects.[44]

> I found the king seated in the middle of [c. 50] great dignitaries of the kingdom and the top officials of his residence. I have seen many princes during my many years stay in Ethiopia, but none had made so much impression upon me like Abba Bagibo . . . He sat on the throne, . . . and had such majesty in posture, to which at the first sight the imagination resorted to fly to what was used to be said of King Solomon. The fruits of the royal residence, the walls built with such magnificence and skills could not find a match in the whole of Ethiopia.[45]

As the beneficiary of Abba Bagibo's moral and material support (not to mention his protection and liberal tolerance of the activities of the Catholic missionaries), Massaja may have exaggerated the wisdom of Abba Bagibo and the greatness of his *massera* at Garuqqe. No louder praise of Limmu-Ennarya under Abba Bagibo can be found than in Massaja's writings. It was thanks to the administration of Abba Bagibo, Massaja maintains, that prosperity flourished and peace was established in the kingdom.[46] Massaja finds nothing blameworthy in Abba Bagibo. To him the king was an exceptional person, and he adds that if Abba Bagibo had received a European education he would have been a great philosopher and the leader of a great nation.[47] Be that as it may, on the question of elegance of the *massera* of Garuqqe, other sources also agree.[48]

The gate of the third fence was guarded by eunuchs and no one was allowed to go beyond it, especially during the night, without permission from the king.[49] This section of the *massera* contained three courtyards – for the king, his wives and other personnel of the royal house, including the concubines, the slaves, and the eunuchs, who watched over the king's women. In this section of the *massera*, the king built a stone house where he deposited his riches and clothes.[50] Probably here, too, he kept his few firearms. It was also in this section of the royal residence that the notorious state prison, the so-called *gindo*, was located. The term *gindo* had two meanings. First, it signified the huge tree to which the prisoners were chained. Secondly, a heavy log weighing as much as 60 kilograms[51] and shackled to one leg of a prisoner was also known as *gindo*. In short, the *gindo* was the state prison and a unique place of torture. Prisoners who were sent to the *gindo* were as good as dead. There was no way of escaping from it, because the prisoners with the heavy logs attached to their feet were chained to the huge tree. Political prisoners and recaptured runaway slaves were imprisoned at the *gindo*, where their feet would rot and they would suffer until death freed them. Governors who failed to carry out their duties also received a "short sharp shock" treatment at the *gindo*.[52] The *gindo* was one of the best indications that Limmu-Ennarya's governmental system had already developed such judicial sanctions as torture, mutilation, and slow killing, the use of which was intended to serve as an example for others. Rebellious members of the royal family, too, were subjected to the torture at the *gindo* before they were banished to one of the surrounding kingdoms.[53]

The presence of the *gindo* inside the third fence of the *massera* of Abba Bagibo reminds one that he was a tyrannical ruler, while the presence of the reception hall within the second fence remains suggestive of his majesty, wealth, generosity, and magnanimity. The negative aspects of his reign were overshadowed by the positive ones, and the wealth which he spent lavishly on feeding his dignitaries or presenting them with precious gifts covered more miseries than was usually recognized.

One important aspect of the Garuqqe *massera* which has so far remained unmentioned is that it was the busiest industrial center in the kingdom. Though active and skilled, this industry worked only to provide the necessities of the *massera*, as well as to furnish those items wanted for gift-giving. As with Jiren,[54] among the buildings within the *massera* were workshops for the various artisans, goldsmiths, carpenters, armorers, weavers, tanners, and artists. The king had a total monopoly of gold, and the work performed on it was in the hands of the king's goldsmiths, who made rings or eardrops only to his order.[55] The carpenters made beds, doors, windows, and above all else stools, for which the Gibe region is still famous. The armorers produced both weapons for war and farm implements, which were needed on the king's estates. Weavers made various types of cotton clothes, some of which were of excellent quality.[56] Tanners produced leather clothes for many hundreds of female slaves who lived in the *massera* and were distinguished by their noisiness and leather dresses.[57] Leather working was highly developed. Shields were made from buffalo skin, and excellent drinking cups were made from buffalo horns. Leather saddles, jackets, and bags were also produced.[58] Over and above this self-sufficient, *massera*-based industry, the king also received tribute in kind from many artisans all over his country. Abba Bagibo was justifiably praised[59] for encouraging art and industry.

> I have seen daggers and well-wrought blades and ivory handles very elegantly inlaid with silver as well as clothes with ornamental borders, brought from Enarea, such as would in vain be looked for in Abessinia.[60]

What gave this *massera* a special character was the conspicuous demonstration of wealth, which was meant to impress both the local people and foreigners alike. Abba Bagibo was not only the wealthiest king in the region, but also he knew how to use that wealth to impress outsiders with his power and the greatness of his country. In this, he must have met with success after success. By his diplomacy[61] he divided and dominated his neighbors;[62] by the generous use of wealth he won many friends and neutralized enemies. Nothing can give a better idea of how he used his wealth to further his cause than this letter of 1840 to the governor of Gojjam. This interesting letter will be analyzed further in the discussion,[63] but here it should suffice to say that Abba Bagibo seems to have believed that, if he opened his hand in generosity, men from far and near would love, adore, and praise him. He knew he was blessed with wealth and that for

170

his kingdom to endure and increase from age to age and for him to enjoy power and respectability in the Gibe region and beyond, he had to use his wealth. Gift-giving was the mechanism with which he redistributed to the privileged few what he received from traders in taxation and from his subjects in tribute. Gift-giving and political marriage were the cornerstones of his diplomacy. In short, each of Abba Bagibo's favorite ways (creative policies) of spreading his fame and popularity – liberality towards the nobility, diplomacy of "divide and dominate," political marriage, hospitality towards traders, and conquest – involved large expenses which he alone could afford and knew how to use effectively.

Abba Bagibo knew how to make good use not only of his wealth, but also of the faith of his subjects as well. In other words, the religious arts of Abba Bagibo were skillfully adapted to the faith of his people. As a Muslim king, he was the champion of Islam in his country, and the presence of a large number of Muslim people in Saqqa added spiritual luster and glamour to his capital. Notwithstanding the fact of being a Muslim king, Abba Bagibo remained a believer in traditional Oromo religion. In the 1840s, Antoine d'Abbadie recorded the following under the title of "the Oromo sacrifice."

> The great priest was Abba Bagibo, in person and the God was good old mount Agamsa. The king himself walked towards the sacrificial animal pronouncing loudly; Oh God [Qallo Agamsa] where the goats are fed, I give you a bull, so that you favour us, protect our country, guide our soldiers, prosper our country side, and multiply our cows: I give you a bull, I give you a bull. This done the animal was knocked down and the king cut its throat with a sabre, without stooping to do so. A small piece of meat was cut from above the eye and it was thrown into the fire together with myrrh and incense. Then all the courtiers returned to the palace. Someone told me that the slaves of the king would eat the flesh of the sacrificed animal.[64]

From start to finish, this had nothing to do with Islam. It was pure and simple Oromo religious practice. There is no Islamic influence even in the prayer uttered by the king. By such a performance the Muslim king was fulfilling the double role of an Oromo priest (Qallu) and a political leader Abba Gada. Before the formation of the state of Limmu-Ennarya, it was an Abba Gada (the leader) who led the *chafe* assembly in prayer for peace, rain, plenty, and fertility. Now Abba Bagibo prayed to the traditional god for the same results on behalf of his people, his country, and his soldiers. In this sense, he was the symbol for the close bond which linked together the function of a political leader and a spiritual father. In fact according to one source, Abba Bagibo considered himself as the chief Qallu of his kingdom.[65] As such he practiced and protected the old religion. Thus, even in the 1840s "notwithstanding the conversion to [Islam] of so large a portion of the population"[66] of his country, Abba Bagibo was still making sacrifices to Waqa (the Oromo god). What is more, he continued to treat kindly not only the *jila*, the Oromo pilgrims to the land of his spiritual father, but he also sent gifts to the Abba Muda himself.[67] We saw above that the two main tasks of the *jila* were to maintain the link between the spiritual father(s) and the various Oromo groups, and also to try to make peace among the competing Oromo groups.[68] During the reign of Abba Bagibo the *jila* continued performing their traditional tasks, but with one important difference. Now they maintained the peace of the king, in his name and for his benefit. They made peace between him and his subjects and among the people themselves.[69]

Abba Bagibo was particularly generous towards European missionaries. In the 1840s he persisted in regarding Antoine d'Abbadie as a priest and offered to build him a church if he wanted to stay in his country.[70] The king admired and respected Cardinal Massaja, the first Catholic bishop of Oromoland, and he treated him with the greatest courtesy. Massaja was impressed by the kindness which he received from Abba Bagibo. The king's considerable charm, hospitality, kindness, and support for the Catholic mission can be seen again and again in Massaja's writings.[71]

In short, it was with the help of Abba Bagibo that the Catholic missionaries were able to propagate their faith in the Gibe region as well as in Kaffa. Under this circumstance, it is not surprising that Massaja believed that, had his mission arrived three decades earlier, Abba Bagibo would have been converted to the Catholic faith. Massaja went further and stated that "30 years ago the Catholic mission would have converted all of these Oromo kings, who today are Muslims."[72]

He wrote these words in 1859. But even in the 1820s and 1830s, a considerable part of the population of Limmu-Ennarya was already Muslim,[73] and it is unimaginable that Abba Bagibo could have entertained the idea of converting his people to Catholicism even in the 1820s. It is likely that his support for the Catholic missionaries was derived from his respect and admiration for Cardinal Massaja. What is not in doubt is the fact that, being nominally a Muslim king[74] Abba Bagibo may have raised the morale of his Muslim population. By continuing to practice the traditional religion he may have allayed the anxieties of traditional believers. By tolerating the Orthodox Christian traders and others in Saqqa to propagate their faith freely, by allowing the Catholic missionaries to establish their center of operations in his country, Abba Bagibo raised the morale of his Christian subjects and foreign guests, and earned the reputation of being the most liberal of all the Gibe kings, the protector of the Christians in the region.[75]

Abba Bagibo was also reported to have been fair in his administration of justice. In 1841, the missionary Krapf recorded the following in Shawa:

> Abba Bagibo [is] good ruler, who administers justice publicly in his capital, and to whom every one has easy access. On such occasions he sits on a wooden throne over which skin is spread. His people do not bow the upper portions of the body, nor prostrate themselves to the ground, as is the custom of the Abessinians in their intercourse with kings and great men; they simply kiss his hand after the fashion of the Mohammedans.[76]

Like the rest of the Gibe kings, Abba Bagibo was accessible to his people. He held secular power which was not shrouded in mysteries and circumvented by taboos.

172

Outside the main fence of the *massera* lived several important officials of the kingdom. Among them three members of the council of state were the most noticeable. In 1843, the council of state included important persons such as Abba Rebu, the grandfather of the king, Abba Jobir, and one unnamed uncle of the king. Abba Rebu was an energetic old politician, while Abba Jobir, a brother of the king, was the Abba Mizan (treasurer and minister for foreign affairs). Unfortunately, we do not know the name of the third most important personality in the council of state, but we do know a few important facts about him. First, he was one of the uncles of Abba Bagibo, who had helped the king to seize power in 1825. Secondly, he had been involved in the conspiracy against Abba Bagibo in 1835, which had been quickly crushed. After the failure of the conspiracy he fled to Jimma Abba Jifar, where he lived in exile for seven years. Following the conclusion of peace between the kings of Jimma and Limmu-Ennarya in 1842[77] this uncle made peace with Abba Bagibo and returned to Saqqa, where the king made him one of his confidants and a member of the council of state.[78] As in Jiren,[79] several important governors and the wealthy men of the kingdom probably had their houses just outside the main fence of the Garuqqe *massera*. In short, this *massera* was the nerve center of the kingdom.

Attached to the court were a number of courtiers called dagno, who carried the royal insignia, usually double-bladed spears, and were known to every official in the country. These were in fact the immigration and custom officials who were entrusted with the inspection and counting of those entering the country, and who accompanied all those permitted to leave the country. The very extensive political life, the intrigue and the negotiation of treaties with the neighbouring countries necessitated a large number of messengers and ambassadors called lemi. The importance of lemi varied according to the duties they were entrusted with. For minor affairs, the king employed less important personalities, where for treaty-making and important messages he would employ a well-known dignitary (sorressa) or even an abba koro. A number of translators of the different languages in use in the surrounding kingdoms were also employed in the court of Abba Bagibo.[80]

According to a recently collected tradition from the Gibe region, it is claimed that political offenders of royal blood were neither subjected to the *gindo* nor eliminated, but were punished by honorable banishment to one of the surrounding kingdoms.[81] This claim is contradicted, however, by accounts of many irrefutable cases from all the Gibe states, which show beyond any shadow of doubt that members of the royal family who lost in the power struggle were punished by death just as other political offenders were. Many examples could be given from these states, but here it is enough to give a few examples only from Limmu-Ennarya. When Abba Bagibo seized power in 1825 he was helped by his brothers and two of his cousins. It is reported that Abba Bagibo had two sons at that time. One of these sons probably was his first born. It was said that Abba Bagibo ordered him to be drowned in the river Didessa, where the young man was treated as food for the crocodiles.[82] The king justified this cruel action on the grounds that his son did not look like him.

While it is not possible to establish the date of this event, it can be said that it took place before the conspiracy of 1835. Coming at a time when the king was preoccupied with rebellion and intrigues,[83] the elimination was probably politically motivated. This harsh action was perhaps justified in the eyes of the king as a measure not only to remove the opposition of a political leader capable of uniting his enemies but also to prove to them that he would not show mercy to rebels even if they were his own flesh and blood. Abba Bagibo was unmoved by the pleas and tears of his wife begging for the life of her son. The distress of the mother was alleviated only by the promise of the king to make her second son the next heir apparent to the throne.[84] She later found good reason to distrust her cruel and hot-tempered husband,[85] whose treatment of the second son turned out to be no better than that of the first.[86] If Abba Bagibo had sacrificed his first-born son to deprive the opposition of an effective leader, he must have been disappointed to discover a new conspiracy to unseat him organized by his uncles around 1835. As with his son, so with his uncles, the king took immediate and decisive action.

> Abba Bagibo had drowned and buried with two sons, one of his [uncles] who wanted to seize power. The other [uncle] then succeeded in escaping and stayed in Jimma for seven years. He subsequently made peace and today (1843), he is one of the confidants of the king, and takes care of state affairs, with Abba Bagibo Abba Rebu and Abba Jobir.[87]

From what has transpired thus far, it is apparent that the paradoxical character of Abba Bagibo, which was mentioned at the start of the discussion of his reign, was a real one. On the one hand, his cruelty extended even to his relatives, and on the other hand we have noted the magnificence of his *massera* at Garuqqe and his generosity. However, there is another aspect of his generosity, which has not yet been described. The wealth radiating from the *massera* of Garuqqe benefited only the wealthy class of Limmu-Ennarya and the rulers of the neighboring states. Only the wealthy dignitaries were entertained at his lavish feasts and received his gifts. The luxurious tastes which were gradually spreading to the wealthy class made Saqqa a center of attraction for manufactured foreign goods, which the king distributed to his officials from time to time. He even distributed to them the gifts and tributes which the Jabarti traders had to present to him on their arrival in his capital.[88] The consequence was foreseeable. The wealthy class developed to a hitherto unknown extent a taste for luxury. Thus, the luxurious and costly articles which were mainly imported, became necessary to feed the pleasures and maintain the grandeur of a small minority in the kingdom. At this time imported foreign goods were mainly commodities meeting the requirements of the wealthy class, consisting mainly of silk, colored clothes, wines, mirrors, beads, and similar items. The wealthy had exchanged the ferocity and simplicity of their national character for pride and vanity.[89] It was this class, headed by Abba Bagibo, which ruled Limmu-Ennarya in its own interest. The vast majority of the people of Limmu-Ennarya probably were content with the local products and bartered their goods with those of their neighbors. Limmu

Ennarya, therefore, was a class society in which the fruits of the labor of the majority went to benefit the minority. However, this does not mean that the people of Limmu-Ennarya did not enjoy a better life under Abba Bagibo. On the contrary, they did achieve higher standards of living, from which there was a gradual decline only in the 1860s during the reign of his successor.[90] This aspect will be discussed later.

Abba Bagibo continued with the wars which his father had initiated, with much more vigor and success. During the first few years of his reign, the thrust of his campaigns was directed against Gumma. It soon became apparent that while he, like his father, was able to defeat Gumma time and time again, he was not able to reduce it to a tributary status. It was not long before he abandoned the idea of making Gumma tributary to Limmu-Ennarya. While this was a wise decision, it was an admission that the energies which he and his father had expended on Gumma had been wasted. He soon replaced his losses in Gumma by the gains he made against Jimma Badi. The latter was an unorganized group which was unable to resist Abba Bagibo's assaults and was subsequently reduced to the status of a tributary to Limmu-Ennarya. This success assured the safety of the caravan route between Limmu-Ennarya and Kaffa. It seems that Abba Bagibo even extended an olive branch to the ruling house of Gumma, but his policy of peaceful coexistence foundered on the solid rock which had come into being by the formation of the state of Jimma Abba Jifar in 1830. The latter state expanded at the considerable expense of Limmu-Ennarya.[91] Moreover, Jimma Badi, the tributary of Limmu-Ennarya, became part of the new state, thus depriving Limmu-Ennarya of a common border with Kaffa. What is more, Gumma and Jimma formed an alliance against their common enemy, Limmu-Ennarya. Thus, by the middle 1830s, it became apparent that Abba Bagibo had to cut his losses on the western and southern fronts and to replace them from somewhere else. This he did on the eastern and northern borders. On both fronts he expanded his territory and influence over the disorganized Agallo, Botor, Badi Folla, Nonno, and even the Janjero[92] (the Yamma of Antoine d'Abbadie)[93] became a tributary to Limmu-Ennarya.

> Twice during each year great military expeditions are undertaken which rarely extend beyond eight or ten days. Every soldier carries a small supply of bread and trusts for further subsistence to pillage and plunder. Many bloody battles are annually fought with the surrounding tribes and wide tracts of country thus annexed to the royal possessions. The Agallo, Yello, Betcho, Sudecha, Chora and Nono are all subjects to the Suppera, or king of Enarea, whose sway extends to the Soddo and Maleem Galla, about the sources of the Hawash, which rises in Adda-Berga.[94]

Two points are worth mentioning here. It is very clear from the above that Abba Bagibo's influence and political control extended beyond the Gibe river to the famous market of Soddo in what is today the administrative region of Shawa. This was at the time when King Sahle Sellassie of Shawa was at the height of his power. As we shall see later,[95] his influence and political control of the Soddo area lasted to the end of this reign. Secondly, Abba Bagibo's expansion and ambition were not limited to the direction of Soddo. He had also a strong desire to expand the frontier of his kingdom towards the Abbay as well as towards what is today western Wallaga. However, he succeeded only on the eastern and northern fronts, the two fronts of his highest military achievement, and he reaped the economic benefits that flowed from this success. The caravan route to the famous market of Soddo and the "coffee route" that passed through the market of Agabja to the Muslim land of Wollo came under Abba Bagibo's jurisdiction.[96] Thus, besides Baso, which was Limmu-Ennarya's commercial outlet in Gojjam, Agabja and Soddo[97] now became not only Limmu-Ennarya's commercial outlets, but also sources of revenue, which may have increased the wealth of the king. At this time, Limmu-Ennarya was militarily at its zenith and commercial prosperity at its height. Encouraged by this happy turn of events and intoxicated by the widespread fame of his name which had made him almost a legendary figure in the Ethiopian region by 1840 Abba Bagibo aspired to conquer the land of Torban Gudru in the same year

> The province of Goodroo is the high road between Gondar and Enarea, though there are several others, and is divided into seven districts . . . The inhabitants can scarcely be numbered but taking the area at forty by thirty miles, I should calculate them at from 100,000 to 120,000. Of these, the greater portion, being accustomed to trade with Baso, are unwarlike, but those on the frontiers, from their numerous enemies, are brave warriors and have no occupation but battle and scarcely a home but the saddle.[98]

Besides the political and military motives, which might have prompted Abba Bagibo to embark on the conquest of Torban Gudru ("the seven houses of Gudru"), who were probably equal in number[99] to the population of Limmu-Ennarya, he was attracted by the wealth of the Gudru and encouraged by their division. The Gudru at this time were deliberately endeavoring to create a state. This was almost fifteen years before Gamma-Moras formed the little state of the Gudru.[100] The Gudru war leaders had shown time and again that they had been singularly unsuccessful in forming a common front even in the face of a common danger. The Gudru Abba Dulas had nothing much to look back on except a history of internal struggle and chaos. With their reputation for disunity and anarchy, the Gudru Abba Dulas were not in a position to set their house in order and face the common enemy. The greatest stimulus for Abba Bagibo's ambition for the land of the Gudru, however arose out of its fertility and wealth.

> The salubrity of the climate and fertility of the soil of Goodroo is perhaps scarcely equalled in the many fertile provinces that Galla prowess and Abyssinian feuds and misgovernment have thrown under the sway of pagans or Mohamedans . . . The productions of the soil include almost everything that Abyssinia produces on its various elevations – barley, wheat, . . . millet, beans nook . . . potato . . . are found growing in neighbouring fields, their sheep and cattle are celebrated . . . And horses are bred in numbers . . . The highlands are so well cultivated.[101]

The experience of fifteen years on the throne had enabled Abba Bagibo to resist being provoked into immediate action by sight of the wealth and the anarchy of the Gudru. His caution was not without reason nor his precaution without effect. He knew that, though divided and disunited, the Gudru, who were reported to have had 15,000 cavalry, were not easy opponents.[102] At the same time, the combined force of Gumma and Jimma were attacking Limmu-Ennarya, and Abba Bagibo probably thought that it was dangerous to embark on the conquest of the Gudru at such a time. Two factors, namely the maintenance of the safety of his gains on the northern and eastern fronts, and the realization of the rising power of Jimma Abba Jifar, caused him fear and anxiety. His strategy for tackling the situation and sharing in the spoils of the Gudru was to form a grand alliance with Goshu, the governor of Damot, "Gojjam-proper" and Agaw-medir, from 1823 to 1840.[103] Goshu had his own axe to grind with regard to the Gudru. He wanted to share in the spoils of that land. However, the idea of the alliance originated with Abba Bagibo.

> Abba Bagibo, desirous of subjugating Gooderoo, and the countries to the north as far as the Nile, sent to propose an alliance with Dedjasmach Goshoo, the ruler of Gojjam . . . One hundred horns of civet and fifty female slaves which had been sent by the Suppira, were . . . accepted, and thirty matchlocks, with the persons versed in the use of the firearms, were forwarded in return.[104]

Captain Harris heard the above story in Shawa, probably from traders from Limmu-Ennarya. This story is substantiated and further elaborated by Abba Bagibo's letter to Dajazmach Goshu in 1840. This letter is not only an important historical document which has survived out of Abba Bagibo's prolific correspondence with his neighbors, but it also sheds a new light on Abba Bagibo's view of wealth and how it should be used to strengthen his position and to benefit his country. Moreover, the letter shows the direction which Abba Bagibo's new policy was taking during the second part of his reign. Before presenting the letter itself, it is necessary to mention a few cautionary notes concerning it. It was written in Oromo[105] and then translated into Arabic. Unfortunately only the Arabic version has survived. But it was written in "an archaic style, which cannot be translated directly as they are couched in the language which was itself common to Arabic."[106] This letter was given to Arnauld d'Abbadie by Dajazmach Goshu in Gojjam, and the French missionary in turn sent it to Berbera on January 14, 1841. It was then translated into French, but unfortunately not standard French.[107] These two inadequacies have rendered some parts of the letter unclear and incomplete, though its general message is clear.

> [Submission] to the only God: Peace and salvation on the envoy of God, Muhammad, after whom there is no other prophet. And next, perfect salvation to his presence General Goshu Gana, son of Zawidy. O thou who will read this letter, tell him: Be, O my brother [during two decades], speaking with your tongue as if it were mine, like the waves and the sea. Now you have sent me a message, and I have taken it in my hand. Ask me, O my friend, the same thing I ask you, O my friend, O freshness of my eye. Now I am like you! If you love me, I love you, and heed my words: [Travellers heading to the country of Gudru are treated badly. But they should be treated nicely in Gudru as they are treated] in your

country as in my country. And renew your promise. Now love me and grant me
(let it be) between you and me as it was with my father and as it will be among our
children. Now this is what I ask of you: Grant me your daughter; I am rich in
horses, excellent mules, excellent war clothing, lion skins, considerable lands.
Now all that is in my hand is the same as in yours, if you wish it in your heart. And
if you give me your daughter, you will have at your disposal my lands and all the
rest, if you desire in your heart some money, (I shall give you some) just as much
(as you want) even though you should count by the thousands and I would have
sent you some, if our roads had been safe. But I feared the perils of the road. Keep
your word: I ask for your friendship, and if you say: "all that is welcome"
certainly I am willing (then) I shall have found happiness through you".

On that note,
farewell!

I, the writer of the letter, may God save him, . . . may this sheet reach Dajazmach
Goshu son of Zawidy. I have sent the letter to the hands of Bokschy son of
Goromy: now the individual named Bokschy is on the way. I love you, O my
father, as you love me: now the travellers (messengers) between you and me, treat
them as your friend is treated in your country.

On that note,
farewell[108]

This long letter is interesting for several reasons. Firstly, with the opening
formula of the letter, Abba Bagibo declares his Muslim faith, but beyond this
he is not obsessed with any religious differences between Goshu and himself.
Notwithstanding the opening sentence, there is nothing that would show us
what his faith was. For him, religious faith was secondary and what counted
was the friendship between the two. It was in this spirit, without due regard to
the religious difference, that he asked for the hand of the daughter of the
Christian governor of Gojjam. He may have been liberal in religious matters
but the ruler on the other side of the Abbay was not. Secondly, the style of the
letter is more reminiscent of the spoken language, which would mean that it
probably was dictated by the king in Oromo to a scribe who wrote it down
using the Arabic script, from which it was then translated into the Arabic
language. In the process of translation into Arabic a few words may have been
omitted, thus creating some gaps in the text. Thirdly, it is self-evident that only
the essentials were committed to writing and the details were left to the
ambassadors to explain. For instance, the letter mentions a treaty to be
concluded with Goshu, which in fact had yet to be negotiated and agreed upon
in Gojjam. Fourthly, Arabic and Oromo were the official languages of correspondence for Abba Bagibo. Notwithstanding letter writing in Oromo, literary output in that language never went beyond a few poems which expressed
religious exhortations.

More importantly, the letter contains two messages in order of their significance. The first was the question of the Gudru, which remains elliptical, at least
as it stands in the letter. The gap in the text may have been created by the fact
that the issue was too sensitive to be written and, therefore, the king left it to his
ambassadors to confide it to Goshu, or the scribe may have omitted some
words in the process of translation. The letter implies that Abba Bagibo

previously had asked Goshu for some joint action against the Gudru, but to no avail. Accordingly, he asked Goshu again to act immediately. He wanted two things with regard to the Gudru: to maintain the safety of the caravan route between Gojjam and Limmu-Ennarya, which had to pass through the Gudru, and also to form an alliance directed against that country.[109]

The second and equally important message of the letter was Abba Bagibo's request for a marriage alliance. This was a politically motivated marriage, by means of which he wanted to establish a lasting relationship with the governor of Gojjam. There is reason to believe that Abba Bagibo's request for the daughter of Goshu itself was inspired by his desire to control the land of the Gudru. In 1840, Arnauld d'Abbadie reported that "the king of Ennarya flatters himself that he would hold all the Gudru together by this marriage."[110] Abba Bagibo believed and acted as if marriage was the key to politics, and in fact during the second part of his reign, political marriages became the kernel of his foreign policy and a powerful weapon in the arsenal of his diplomacy. As it is clear from the letter, Abba Bagibo was willing to pay any price for such a political marriage, and it is no exaggeration to say that he laid out part of his wealth on such marriages.

Another interesting aspect of this letter was the message from Dajazmach Goshu, of which Abba Bagibo said, "I have taken it into my hand." From the content of the letter it appears that the message was important but Abba Bagibo did not specify what it was. It remained unmentioned, again most probably because it was too sensitive to be written. The letter also implies that there was a good relationship between the fathers of Abba Bagibo and Goshu, which is supported by what we saw above about Abba Gomol's relationship with the governor of Gojjam.[111] Finally, from the last part of the letter, which seems to have been added as an afterthought, it is apparent that Abba Bagibo was engaged in an active correspondence with his neighbors.

Abba Bagibo expected an immediate response from Dajazmach Goshu, but the logic of history has its own course to follow. By 1840, Goshu was engulfed in his own external and internal crises. He quarreled with Ras Ali (the *de facto* power behind the throne in Gondar), who devastated his territory and forced him into submission. By swearing allegiance to the *ras*, Goshu maintained himself in power, but at a considerable price to his own prestige and territory. Goshu's son, Birru, was outraged at the terms his father concluded with Ras Ali.

> The relation between the father and son progressively deteriorated until 1841, when they fought at the battle of Ingatta. Defeated and dispossessed of his territory, matchlocks and horses, Goshu became his son's prisoner. But soon father and son were reconciled: after 1841 we find Goshu ruling over Damot and Birru over "Gojjam-proper."[112]

Goshu's defeat, at the hands of both Ras Ali and his own son not only shattered his prestige, but also cost him the territory of Agaw Midir and "Gojjam-proper." Goshu's loss of territory had an immediate impact on Abba Bagibo's grand design on the Gudru. With regard to that land, his hope was pinned on the military alliance with Goshu, but the latter abandoned th project and confined all his efforts to devising ways of regaining his ol territory. Nevertheless, Abba Bagibo's friendly letter excited his compassio and the generous gift stirred him into action. Goshu sent Abba Bagibo th already-mentioned thirty matchlocks with persons versed in the use of fire arms.[113] Compared to what Abba Bagibo expected, the gift probably was to small, but it was a token of good will which was intended to communicat politely to Abba Bagibo that neither a military alliance nor a marriag connection was feasible, the former on account of Goshu's difficulties, th latter because of the religious difference between them, which wa unbridgeable in the eyes of Goshu.[114] It was Abba Bagibo's grand design o the Gudru which had lured him in to extending the relationship to the highe level of a political marriage with the intention of converting the weddin ceremony into a Christian–Muslim alliance. Had it happened, it would hav been an event of the utmost importance which might have opened a new era o relationship and set a pattern for the future co-operation of the Amhara an Oromo rulers. The much hoped-for alliance foundered on the solid rock o Goshu's political problems. Abba Bagibo's failure persuaded him to re evaluate his entire policy in the region.

1841 was also a year which saw many negative developments on th southern and western borders of Limmu-Ennarya. Jimma Abba Jifar ex panded at considerable expense to Limmu-Ennarya.[115] In fact, Abba Jifa had emerged from the war of 1841 with military strength greater than that o Limmu-Ennarya and political prestige equal to that of that state. This was turning-point in the short history of the Gibe region, which brought to a clos the phase of Abba Bagibo's military offensives. His military drive had failed o two fronts despite earlier successes on the northern and eastern borders. I other words, by 1841 Abba Bagibo's ambition to expand his territory, whicl started in 1825, came to an abrupt end on two fronts and was reversed on th other two. Over that period of sixteen years, he had achieved success whicl almost brought him close to realizing his deepest ambition. At that moment h seemed on the threshold of the great historical opportunity of uniting the Gib region and the surrounding Oromo tribes in what are today the provinces o Wallaga and Illubabor. Furthermore, his control and influence even extendec across the Gibe river into the region which today constitutes a significant par of Shawa province.[116] He was the first Gibe king who had the means and th ambition to unite the Oromo from Shawa in the east to Wallaga and Illubabo in the west, from the Abbay in the north to the Gojeb river in the south. In othe words, he wanted to unite the vast land over which the Matcha had spread Had it happened, it would have been an event of the utmost importance, whicl might have changed the course of the history of the Oromo and that o Ethiopia. However, that opportunity was missed, fundamentally becaus Abba Bagibo failed to understand what the Christian princes to the north hac come to understand much earlier: the importance of the acquisition of fire arms. While the Christian rulers (including those of Oromo origin) made th acquisition of firearms their top priority and the object of their raids on their neighbors, Abba Bagibo failed not only to invest his wealth in acquiring an arsenal of modern weapons, but also failed even to appreciate their value. Other Oromo rulers of the Gibe region followed the example of Abba Bagibo, and they were slower to adjust themselves to the effective use of modern European weapons of destruction, for which mistake both the rulers and people of the Gibe region paid a terrible price in the 1880s.[117] Nevertheless, the conflict between Jimma and Limmu-Ennarya forced Abba Bagibo to adopt a pragmatic and realistic policy.

At this juncture, it is important to discuss briefly the history of the state of Jimma. This digression is unavoidable and essential because for the next three decades the history of the Gibe region was dominated by the struggle between the two states, which prevented the region from developing into a unified state.

History of Jimma 1830–1861

It has already been demonstrated that Abba Jifar I (1830–1855) established the kingdom of Jimma. Abba Jifar, who was referred to as a sultan, was also the first Muslim king of Jimma.[118] He was reported to have invited to the kingdom a number of Muslim teachers and preachers to spread their religion. By inviting the Muslim teachers to spread their religion freely, Sultan Abba Jifar wanted to win over the Jabarti traders, who had their own reasons for being hostile to Abba Bagibo.[119] His immediate aim was to share in the profit bonanza of the commerce of the Gibe region. His long-term aim was to change the center of commercial exchange from Saqqa to Hirmata. It was a splendid economic strategy, with which he sought to weaken Limmu-Ennarya by drying up the source of her prosperity. The ruling class of Limmu-Ennarya, whose wealth was mainly derived from commerce, and who were notoriously addicted to refined foreign luxuries, could by no means dispense with the privilege its merchant class had enjoyed, and their king was determined to resist Abba Jifar's threat aimed at its arterial supply of his own luxurious life and his country's prosperity. Thus, the economic motive was the underlying factor which generated and sustained the struggle between the two states. The peace agreement of 1842[120] failed to reconcile the economic interests of the two states, and by the beginning of 1843 Abba Jifar, taking advantage of Abba Bagibo's embroilment with the Badi Folla,[121] occupied the land between the Gibe region and the famous market of Soddo. This was Abba Jifar's first major step towards opening an independent caravan route to the northern markets. It also enabled him to surround the territory of the rebellious Badi Folla.[122] What is more, this sudden success brought Abba Jifar to the frontier of Janjero, which was said to have been a tributary to Limmu-Ennarya during the 1830s.[123] The king of the latter country, who soon realized that he could not stop Abba Jifar's expansion, turned a blind eye to the loss of territories at the periphery of his country. Abba Bagibo's attitude encouraged Abba Jifar to overreach himself. On September 18, 1843, a delegation from Abba Jifar was in

Saqqa negotiating some agreement with Abba Bagibo[124] concerning the Janjero. What is fascinating to note here is Abba Bagibo's double dealing and diplomatic skill in maneuvering the situation. At the very time when Abba Jifar's delegation was in Saqqa, perhaps seeking reassurance that Limmu-Ennarya would not attack Jimma while the latter was at war with the Janjero there was another delegation from the king of Kullo in Saqqa,[125] to conclude a secret mutual defense pact directly against Jimma. Abba Bagibo's promise to remain neutral in the conflict between Jimma and Janjero seems to have persuaded Abba Jifar to venture on the conquest of Janjero. Encouraged by Abba Bagibo's neutrality, intoxicated by the supposed panic of the Janjero and entirely unsuspecting of a trap, Abba Jifar sent a strong force into Janjero through the gates by which they were never to return. In the trap, the men of Jimma, united by danger and animated by despair, fought bravely before they were overwhelmed by numbers and destroyed.

> On 27 September (1843) a messenger from Jimma arrived at Saqqa to inform about the disaster that had come upon the troops of his country, who were going to attack the Janjero or Yamma. The country was defended on the border by ditches and fortifications of palisades. There were six to eight gates of entrance The Janjero opened them and said to the men of Jimma, that their own forces were in a state of panic and had run away to a certain massera (a fortified house). Full of confidence, the Jimma advanced. A good number of their troops entered into the massera and then the Janjero closed all the gates. Then they jumped on the men inside and started the carnage which went on for a long time. 307 cavalry with red shirts were cut down. The number of soldiers of lesser rank who were killed were so great that . . . they could not be counted. Jimma had lost all her brave warriors in this single encounter alone . . . The men of Jimma abandoned ten leagues of the countryside having lost (many warriors). At this time, Jimma was seeking an agreement with Limmu, Gomma, Gumma, and Gera, for revenge and to drive the Janjero from the land. The Gallas estimated the loss of Jimma at ten thousand.[126]

This disaster had overtaken Abba Jifar's troops when, under the influence of an exaggerated sense of self-confidence, they had underestimated their enemy's determination to resist. Jimma's loss of ten thousand men may have been exaggerated. Nevertheless, the loss must have been a shattering disaster to Jimma. The loss of ten thousand, if true, might have been almost impossible to replace in a land numbering 150,000 people.[127] Fortunately for Abba Jifar, the fabric of the state which had been enriched by the experience of thirteen years, was not destroyed by the misfortune of a single day. However, the psychological impact of the victory on Janjero and the effects of the loss on Jimma went beyond the limits of a single day. The Janjero were jubilant and their pride was elated by the victory, which perhaps surpassed their own expectations. It gave them a self-confidence and an undying spirit of resistance which sustained them in the struggle with Jimma for the next four decades in spite of considerable devastation.

The news of the disaster must have caused as much panic in the capital of Abba Jifar as it had caused along the borders of Jimma with Janjero.[128] Abba

Jifar was left with the task of restoring the wrecked morale of his army, and of building a new force, which would restore the honor of his name and avenge Jimma's humiliation. His appeal for assistance was part of the strategy with which he hoped to revive the courage of his remaining troops, restore the morale of his officials, and replace the loss. Neither the disaster which had fallen upon Jimma no Abba Jifar's appeal excited Abba Bagibo into action. On the contrary, he remained indifferent, even after he had learned about the outrages which the Janjero had committed.[129] Towards the end of October 1843, he was still unwilling either to fix the time for his action, or even to express his readiness to send his troops.[130] Abba Jifar threatened to break diplomatic relations with Abba Bagibo. In order to appease him, Abba Bagibo decided to have a conference with him on November 4, 1843. However, the conference was not intended to help Abba Jifar, but to silence his supporters in the court of Abba Bagibo. Abba Bagibo's son, the heir apparent to the throne, was married to a daughter of Abba Jifar.[131] Abba Bagibo's uncle, who was a member of the council of state, was also a good friend of Abba Jifar. These top men in the government of Limmu-Ennarya seem to have urged Abba Bagibo to help Abba Jifar. However, Abba Bagibo remained adamant. The conference was held on neutral territory between the two states, but nothing concrete came out of it. Unable to undertake immediate revenge, Abba Jifar embarked on massive preparations to fight alone. By now honor had been added to a strong desire for revenge as an incentive for victory over the enemy, with the recapture of the land Jimma lost to Janjero. Abba Jifar's military genius, combined with the eagerness of his army to win the battle, proved too much for the leadership of the Janjero. His fortune was improved by the willingness of the Janjero to fight outside their own fortifications. For this overconfidence the Janjero paid dearly; they met with resistance more obstinate than they had reason to expect from an enemy they had previously routed. Pressed on every side and hotly pursued by an enemy aflame with the desire for revenge and intoxicated by the fortune of the day, the Janjero were soundly beaten. Among the prisoners of war who fell into the hands of Abba Jifar was the king of Janjero. Many of his relatives were sold into slavery by Abba Jifar.[132] Notwithstanding Janjero's spirit of resistance, the capture of their king marked their submission. However, this apparent submission lasted no more than three years: as soon as their king made some agreement with Abba Jifar, who set him free, he returned to his land planning to avenge the humiliation and degradation he had suffered in the prison of Abba Jifar.[133] Thus the struggle between Janjero and Jimma continued for the next four decades.[134] Whether the conquest of the Janjero or territorial expansion was the goal of Abba Jifar, he pursued that goal with an indefatigable ardor which could be neither satiated by victory nor quelled by difficulties. No sooner had he defeated the Janjero than he turned to expansion, but only as a first step in diverting the trade of the Gibe region towards his capital.

Abba Jifar's success against Janjero in 1844 was followed by that against Badi Folla in 1847.[135] The conquest of Badi Folla was important for Abba

Jifar in two ways. First, it assured him of an independent caravan route between his country and the northern markets. This was a victory for the commerce of Jimma, but a setback to that of Limmu-Ennarya. The latter could no longer enjoy its virtual monopoly over trade in the Gibe region. Secondly the victory brought to its climax Jimma's expansion during the reign of Abba Jifar. For the next eight years he fought time and again against Limmu Ennarya, Gomma, Gumma, and Gera, but almost every conflict was concluded by a peace treaty that maintained the status quo. In 1855, while he was on his way to Janjero, he suddenly died.[136] In the words of Abba Jobir Abba Dula, "He was the man who reformed the constitution of Jimma and its laws. He increased the size of the kingdom, systematized the administration of the country and built the palace of Jiren, his capital."[137] After an energetic reign of a quarter of a century, the founder of the new state bequeathed to his successor the inheritance of a new kingdom, a new capital, a new religion, and many "administrative and political innovations."[138]

> A short dispute over the succession developed between his oldest son, Abba Gomol, the legitimate heir to the throne, and a younger (and more vigorous) son Abba Rebu. Abba Jifar died in a palace east of Jiren. Abba Rebu was with him at the time, while Abba Gomol was at a palace southwest of Jiren. Abba Rebu was therefore able to gain possession of the gold ring of kingship. With his followers he reached Jiren before his brother and seized the throne. Abba Gomol was then exiled to Kafa.[139]

A young man of powerful physique, handsome, and a brave soldier, Abba Rebu was only twenty years of age when he seized power. He has been described by one source as "a lion and a hero,"[140] and by another as "the Galla Napoleon."[141] There is an element of exaggeration in both comparisons. Nevertheless, Abba Rebu was a brave, strong man who truly wanted to conquer all the Gibe states one after the other. In fact, he defeated some of them and his exploits frightened and threatened all of them so much that they formed a secret alliance to come to the assistance of each other in the event of his attack.[142] Abba Rebu had no strategy for dividing his enemies, either turning them against each other or neutralizing them in conflict. In fact, one of his major weaknesses was his inability to combine military activities with secret diplomacy. The main threat to his life came not from defeat by the enemy, but as a result of the political cunning of his main rival. Abba Bagibo, with his devious talent for intrigue, more subtly infiltrated the nobility of Jimma and turned them against Abba Rebu's war of conquest. According to the oral history of Jimma, Abba Rebu was disliked by the *sorressa* (wealthy men) of that land. He confiscated the property of those wealthy men who opposed his wars against the neighboring states, and killed many of them.[143] By so doing, he alienated the elite of his country, who may have conspired with his external enemies to get rid of him. The difference between Abba Bagibo's policy and that of Abba Rebu was that the former dominated the politics of the Gibe region through diplomacy and political marriage, while the latter wanted to unify and dominate the region solely by means of conquest. The taste for conquest ultimately became his nemesis, as it had been his strength. In short, Abba Rebu's classic error was that he wanted to conquer all of his enemies too soon and too quickly, and by so doing he shortened his life.[144] Abba Bagibo, with his diplomatic skill, formed a solid alliance against this threat, and turned the elite of Abba Rebu's own court against him as well. At the head of an army, the unsuspecting Abba Rebu advanced rapidly towards Gomma, expecting victory in a day.[145] He was surprised to discover that he was surrounded and set upon by an enemy whose force was continually being renewed and increased. Instead of facing only the men of Gomma, he was met by the combined forces of the four states. To fight was suicidal and only flight held some hope of survival. He chose to fight, and fought bravely, killing many of his enemies. He was able to withstand the formidable enemy for a day, but fell at the hand of an internal enemy who had decided to buy peace with his life.[146] He was mortally wounded by one of his men and died the following day in 1859. Such was the fate of Abba Rebu in his twenty-fifth year.[147] He had been a prince who had a burning desire to unify the region by means of conquest, but sank under the weight of the intrigues of the Gibe states.

After the untimely death of Abba Rebu, his infant son was bypassed in favor of an old man named Abba Boka, a brother of Abba Jifar I. Abba Boka (1859–1861) was a man of peace, who was more interested in the spread of Islam within Jimma than in conquest of his neighbors. As soon as Abba Boka renounced his predecessor's aggressive policy of conquest, the Gibe kings made peace with him without inflicting any punishment on Jimma. Abba Boka cemented his relationship with the king of Gumma by effecting a marriage alliance. This marriage seems to have been inspired by religious considerations rather than by political calculation. As the section on the spread of Islam in Jimma showed (pp. 157–9),[148] Abba Boka did a great deal to extend that religion in both Jimma and Gumma. At that time Gumma was experiencing Islamic fervor for the first time. Accordingly, a daughter of Abba Dula (the king of Gumma from c. 1854 to 1879) was given in marriage to Abba Gomol, the son and successor of Abba Boka. It was out of this marriage that the most famous king of Jimma, Abba Jifar II (1878–1932), was born in 1861.

The reign of Abba Bagibo, 1841–1861

The general picture which Abba Bagibo presented during the last twenty years of his reign was one of defender rather than aggressor. Instead of aspiring to continue with the war against the combined force of Gumma and Jimma, he confined his attention to diplomatic ways of stopping the expansion of an enemy whose strength was on the increase. Thus, after 1841, his hot temper and his notoriety as a cruel king were profitably exchanged for the image of a patient and wise peacemaker, "the new Solomon of the Galla."[149] In other words, after 1841, the character of Abba Bagibo stands more clearly as that of an exceptionally peace-loving king, strong-willed, passionately devoted to the maintenance of peace and order in the Gibe region.[150] Such a character, combined with his long political experience and effective use of wealth, must have created a profound impression of his political wisdom on his people and his neighbors as well as on his foreign admirers. The first major success of his new policy was the peace agreement reached with his main rival, Abba Jifar I. More than anything else, commercial considerations forced Abba Bagibo to come to this agreement with Abba Jifar. Limmu-Ennarya's commerce with Gojjam through Baso, with Wollo and beyond through Agabaja, and with Shawa and Harar through Soddo, increased in volume. This flourishing trade which was a never-failing source of wealth to the Gibe region, did not spread its beneficial effects in a way which was commensurate with the military strength and size of the territory of Jimma Abba Jifar. This was for two main reasons. First, only a fraction of the profit of the trade in the region went to Jimma. Secondly, Jimma lacked certain vital commodities, such as coffee and musk.[151] Above all, Jimma had little gold within its borders, while Limmu-Ennarya owed much of its wealth and fame to its own gold as well as to that found in the neighboring lands of Kaffa and Wallaga. Abba Jifar decided to strengthen and maintain caravan routes to and from gold-producing lands. Without a doubt, control of caravan routes and access to the gold-producing lands played a significant role and even may have been one of the causes of economic conflict between the two states. Abba Bagibo sought ways and means of maintaining his country's commercial advantages. The peace agreement with Abba Jifar, albeit temporary, brought commercial success; as a result, Limmu-Ennarya continued to enjoy a near-monopoly of commerce[152] in the Gibe region up to 1847.

Abba Jifar had devoted himself to conquest and expansion between 1830 and 1841; now he needed to consolidate his gains before embarking on the next phase of his expansion. Thus the desire for peace was probably mutual, and the peace agreement was cemented by the marriage of Abba Bagibo's son to a daughter of Abba Jifar.[153] The peace treaty and the wedding festivities which followed raised hopes that the era of conflict was now over and a new era of unity had at last dawned, but Abba Bagibo had his own motives for using the wedding festival as the hope of a new beginning. For neither the first nor the last time[154] was hope for unity raised, but to no avail. For Limmu-Ennarya, the peace agreement and the marriage union with Jimma were events of the utmost importance. In the first place, the marriage of Abba Dula, Limmu-Ennarya's heir to the throne, to the daughter of Abba Jifar[155] seemed to have provided the basis for the continuity of peace between the two states. Secondly, the peace agreement with Jimma strengthened the internal unity of the ruling house of Limmu-Ennarya. For Abba Jifar, the peace agreement was only a temporary lull, providing the time necessary for his men to recuperate and for him to replace his losses prior to the next phase of the conflict.

It is important to note here that, after 1841, political marriage became an important strategy in the diplomacy of Abba Bagibo. He himself married wives from all the ruling houses of Gibe, as well as from Kaffa. His marriage link with Kaffa was unique in a double sense. First, his principal wife, who had the right to wear a golden bracelet, was the daughter of the reigning king of Kaffa. In 1843, Abba Bagibo decided to marry a sister of the reigning king of Kaffa as his twelfth wife.[156] Among the distinguished men who were sent to Kaffa as elders to negotiate that marriage was the French traveler Antoine d'Abbadie.[157] Around 1846, at the age of forty-four, Abba Bagibo married a fifteen-year-old daughter of the king of Kullo. Interestingly, Antoine d'Abbadie's brother, Arnauld, was selected to be among the distinguished elders who were to negotiate this marriage. For d'Abbadie, Abba Bagibo appeared to live for his aspiration to govern the Gibe region through political marriages.

> Abba Bagibo who seemed to live only for women, to whose numerous concubines he has already given 27 sons and 45 daughters claimed especially to extend his influence through marriages. He was a blue beard of rare kind, he already had 12 queens and approximately 300 concubines . . . His thirteenth queen, a daughter of the king of Kullo, was the most beautiful of many others, who had entered in the care of the eunuchs of Limmu-Ennarya.[158]

Like his contemporary rulers in the Ethiopian region (both Muslims and Christians) Abba Bagibo had hundreds of concubines. But of all his contemporaries, only Sahle Sellassie, the Amhara king of Shawa who was reported to have had "300 concubines of the royal harem,"[159] equaled Abba Bagibo in that respect.

Of Abba Bagibo's sons, more than twenty[160] married women from either the ruling houses of the surrounding countries or from the *sorressa* (wealthy men) of their own country. The numerous daughters born to his wives and concubines were given in marriage to wealthy men of the surrounding countries. Thus, Abba Bagibo held together his own country through political marriages.[161] It is possible, too, that all his Abba Qorros (provincial governors) may have had marriage links with the royal house of Limmu-Ennarya. As with his own country, Abba Bagibo sought to hold together the surrounding countries through political marriage.[162] However, the marriage union between Limmu-Ennarya and Jimma Abba Jifar did not bring lasting peace between the two states. The economic and political interests that produced conflict between them were too wide and too deep to be closed by marriage alone. The hostility generated by the conflicts increased, being freshly fueled by the intrigues of the Jabarti traders and the ambition of Abba Jifar to expand the frontiers of his state at the expense of Limmu-Ennarya.

The economic motive behind Abba Bagibo's decision to prevent the Jabarti traders from going beyond Saqqa has been examined in Chapter 5,[163] and here it suffices to say that the Jabarti traders did not accept this ban on their movement. On the contrary, they tried to find an alternative route to Kaffa. The formation of the state of Jimma Abba Jifar in 1830 provided them with the unique opportunity they sought. The new state did not impose any restrictions on the Jabarti traders who, without going to Limmu-Ennarya, braved the difficult and dangerous route through the tribes on the eastern periphery of that country, who were only nominally under the control of Abba Bagibo.[164]

The Oromo of Ethiopia

The Jabarti traders who came to the capital of Abba Jifar impressed upon the king the need to convert his military superiority into commercial benefit. They advised Abba Jifar to free himself from dependence on Limmu-Ennarya's route to the north.[165] In other words, the Jabarti traders urged Abba Jifar to open an independent route between his country and the northern markets. His iron determination to do just that was a powerful threat to Limmu-Ennarya's territory on the eastern front. The loss of Limmu-Ennarya's territory was hastened by two interconnected factors – its internal problems and Abba Jifar's expansion.

The territory of Badi Folla, which came under the nominal control of Abba Bagibo in the 1830s, had been involved in rebellion around 1842. Badi Folla was different from all the surrounding Oromo countries in one respect. It was the land where prisoners of war and captives were castrated,[166] to become eunuchs in the homes of the great.[167] Badi Folla was heavily forested, and this enabled the inhabitants to repulse Abba Bagibo's attack.[168] The inhabitants of Badi Folla, who seem to have trusted more to their notorious practices than to their discipline, and more to their forest cover than to their fighting qualities, dispersed before the cavalry of Abba Bagibo, which proceeded to devastate the lowland of Badi Folla, forcing the survivors to desert their land for almost a year.[169] Abba Bagibo probably was less worried about the loss of poor-quality cotton from the lowland of Badi Folla[170] than about the constant disruption its inhabitants caused to Limmu-Ennarya's caravans, which had to pass through their territory *en route* to the market of Soddo. Unable to restore his authority in Badi Folla, Abba Bagibo cut his losses by admitting its independence from his control.[171] This was his first major loss; more were soon to follow. The most dramatic reversal of Abba Bagibo's gain came from the direction of the market of Soddo. While the Gibe states were fighting among themselves, embroiled in a conflict which made the possibility of presenting a common front against a common enemy remote, Sahle Sellassie, the king of Shawa, was gathering firearms which were to bring near destruction of the once invincible Tulama cavalry in Shawa.[172] So it was that in the early 1840s Sahle Sellassie, with an army of between 30,000 and 50,000,[173] armed with a relatively large stock of firearms, suddenly became a real menace to Abba Bagibo's possessions. What is more, Sahle Sellassie's drive to the west and south deprived Limmu-Ennarya of control of or direct access to the markets of Agabaja and Soddo.

> Shawan raids to the west and southwest devastated the area and stopped Limmu-Enarea's expansion in this direction. The coffee route to Warra Himenu also fell into Shawan hands when the Christian armies conquered Agabaja. Moreover, as a result of Shawa's southward drive the Galla tribes to the south of Shawa came under its sway and Enarea lost its influence over, and even more important its access to, the important Soddo markets. Consequently, Enarea was cut off from the Harar, Zeila and Tajura outlets and became much more dependent on the northern outlet through Gojjam.[174]

Such a sudden reversal of fortunes disrupted commerce and inflicted a severe blow on the commercial prosperity of Limmu-Ennarya, from which it

188

recovered only after 1848.[175] Despite the recovery of five years later, however, Limmu-Ennarya never regained her political control over the outlet to the market of Agabaja. Thus her territorial loss became permanent, not because of Shawa's strength after the death of Sahle Sellassie,[176] but because of the military weakness of Limmu-Ennarya herself. By 1846 that weakness was apparent and soon led to further loss of territory.

For Abba Bagibo, 1847 proved a difficult year. It seems to have started with the rebellion of the Agallo, and was followed by that of the crown prince. The rebellion of the Agallo, who had been incorporated into Limmu-Ennarya early in the reign of Abba Bagibo, was not sudden. The discontent which may have been simmering for some time persuaded Abba Bagibo to build a new *massera* at a strategic place called Tinnqe, from where he may have hoped to control them. The Agallo, agitated by the desire to free themselves from the control of Abba Bagibo, and attracted perhaps by the wealth of the new *massera*, surrounded it and set it alight. The fire, which consumed one part of the royal residence,[177] also destroyed the attackers themselves. The accidental destruction of this invading party did not put an end to the rebellion, however, which continued for some time. Peace was eventually restored when the majority of the Agallo submitted voluntarily to Abba Bagibo. They were allowed to go back to their homes with all the cattle they had looted from Limmu-Ennarya.[178] Abba Bagibo's political moderation in handling the rebellion of the Agallo seems to have been a policy generated by the internal crisis which was afflicting the ruling house of Limmu-Ennarya at this time.

This brings us to what was perhaps the most serious political challenge Abba Bagibo had to face during his long reign. This conspiracy, which broke out into the open some time in 1847, was aimed at removing him from power. It was engineered by his son, the heir apparent. Abba Bagibo had already eliminated his first son for reasons which remain obscure. The one thing which is known with certainty is that the second son was not implicated in the conspiracy of 1835. On the contrary, he seems to have been very close to his father, who trusted him with the gold ring and made him *donachaw* (the crown prince). By 1841, the *donachaw* had also been made Abba Dula ("the minister of war"), and the following year Limmu-Ennarya celebrated his wedding to the daughter of Abba Jifar. As heir to the throne, he seems to have enjoyed widespread popularity. As the minister of war, he may have had support among the soldiers. The marriage union with the ruling house of Jimma Abba Jifar may have suggested that he was an important figure who was destined to outshine even his illustrious father. It did not take long before his popularity excited the ambition of the son and aroused the anxieties of the father.[179] The *donachaw*, who was unaware of his father's suspicions, nevertheless continued with his secret preparations and expanded the circle of his supporters, who included among others a shaykh[180] and a famous non-Muslim wealthy Oromo magician.[181] The Muslim shaykh may have been agitated into action by the Jabarti traders, who hated Abba Bagibo's ban on their movements beyond Saqqa. What is difficult perhaps to understand, let alone explain, is the involvement of the wealthy magician in the conspiracy. It is said that this man was highly respected and honored by the king.[182] These two men, from two widely differing backgrounds, combined to make Abba Dula the man he was. His thinking was an amalgam of Islamic teaching and exaggerated belief in magical power. Abba Dula's tragedy was that he wanted to be the king too much and too quickly, so he repeated the history of his father's rise to power. He wanted to force his father to abdicate.[183] He had a considerable share of his father's ambition, but lacked his mental resources. Worse still, he was incapable of conducting the conspiracy with sufficient skill and secrecy. Abba Bagibo, who knew about the preparations of his son, carefully and secretly watched every step of the conspirators.[184] Matters came to a head with two interconnected mysterious tragedies in late 1847. "Many people came from Kaffa to offer their condolences to Abba Bagibo who lost two of his wives and one of his sons."[185] The circumstances which had led to these sudden deaths are not clear. However, a recent publication suggests that at least one of the deaths was caused by a politically motivated killing. "The crown prince had suffocated to death one of his father's wives in order to immerse the king in deep sorrow."[186] From the intensity of Abba Bagibo's grief, it seems that the woman was probably his favorite wife, and she may have been the mother of the dead son. This mysterious death was soon followed by another equally mysterious one. "Abba Dula, the successor to the throne lost his wife, the daughter of Abba Jifar, and his only son."[187] If the ungrateful son was the author of at least one of the deaths, the role of the cunning and crafty king[188] cannot be precisely connected with the death of his son's wife and her only son.[189]

Abba Dula, who probably counted on Abba Jifar's support in his struggle for power, immediately went to Jimma after the death of his wife and "asked for the hand of one of the sisters of his wife, who was promised to him."[190] To complete the tragedy, Abba Dula wanted to make his wedding-day the occasion for the elimination of his father. The preparation of this latter event became the object of Abba Dula's boundless desire for revenge. On the flimsy pretext of improving the *massera* at Daga, Abba Dula prepared his trap,[191] but Abba Bagibo knew all about it through his network of spies. His calculated and relaxed way of letting this develop was to give the appearance of ignorance about the plot, while developing three strategies to tackle it. These were, first, readiness to crush the plot, second, offering a reward for loyalty to himself, and third, mercilessness to the conspirators. The father surprised his unsuspecting son on the morning of the wedding-day, when he ordered his offspring to come immediately to the main royal residence. For Abba Dula to refuse the order would have been tantamount to a declaration of open rebellion, and to delay in its implementation was to alert the king of what had been prepared for him. The crown prince, who lacked his father's political acumen, had neither the time to think, nor the farsightedness to suspect his father's order. At the head of a large number of his soldiers,[192] he arrived at his father's *massera* where he found himself in a trap from which escape was well-nigh impossible. There was an extraordinarily tense atmosphere inside the *massera* which alarmed Abba

Dula and frightened his men. It was a humiliating moment for the Abba Dula, who was capable neither of inspiring his followers in the face of danger nor of decisive action at the critical moment. He wasted time in hesitation and confusion. The king stunned the startled soldiers with the exposure of the treachery of his son, and relieved their anxiety by the promise of safety. "You have to choose between your old king, who had brought you victories and happiness and the ambitious inexperienced and ill-advised son."[193] The troops seem to have compared the courage of the father with the cowardice of the son, the glory of the father with the ignominy of the son. Reassured by the promise of safety and attracted perhaps by the reward of liberty for loyalty, the soldiers claimed ignorance of the treason and declared their decision to abandon the son for the cause of the father. Abandoned by the majority of his troops, the crown prince and a few of his staunch supporters were soon overpowered, disarmed, and imprisoned. On the very day which was supposed to be his wedding-day and that for the political elimination of his father, Abba Dula was humiliated, tortured, and imprisoned at the *gindo*. Later, he was exiled to Gera,[194] but drowned in the Didessa river[195] while on his way there. Abba Dula's supporters, some of whom were even accompanied by their relations, were fed to the crocodiles[196] in the same river. The famous magician, who had nothing to gain but everything to lose by his involvement in the conspiracy, was himself humiliated and tortured at the *gindo* before he too was drowned. His great wealth was confiscated and his numerous cattle were distributed among the poor.[197] It was probably with the confiscated property that Abba Bagibo fulfilled his promise of liberality to the deserters. The elimination of the conspirators closed this short chapter of serious crisis that threatened the life of Abba Bagibo. It was the saddest episode of his reign, but it is a tribute to his good judgment that the conspiracy ended with comparatively little bloodshed.

Though the political wound of this crisis appeared to have been healed, and while Abba Bagibo continued to enjoy wide popularity in the Gibe region, its effect was to poison his attitude towards his sons for the next thirteen years. He never trusted any one of them with the golden ring or the title of *donachaw*. Abba Bulgu, his third son, was different from the unfortunate crown prince in that he was very timid and docile. In spite of this, Abba Bulgu was insulted and hated by everyone at the court. His father even prohibited him from eating the best quality teff bread.[198] Though Abba Bulgu was an unambitious man who was dominated by the fear of his father, the king never trusted him with the golden ring until three days before his death. Nevertheless, the conclusion of this sad drama must have brought everyone in Limmu-Ennarya relief. After indulging his officials with lavish feasts, the king one again showed his capacity to deal with reality with unique political wisdom. Instead of continuing his old policy, he sought to reverse it and to repair the damage it had caused. Abba Bagibo took two immediate measures – one political and the other economic – with which he intended to revitalize his administration. The stability, tranquility, and prosperity at home and the relative peace which he maintained abroad for the last twelve years of his reign stemmed from these two measures.

First, he injected fresh vitality into his administration by replacing old by young and vigorous men. We no longer hear of such men as Abba Rebu, his old grandfather, Abba Jobir, and his uncle (all members of the council of state). Among the new appointees was Abba Shamal, who became the new Abba Mizan. According to Antonio Cecchi, who had met this official in the same capacity in 1879, Abba Shamal "seems to have been gifted with uncommon intelligence."[199] The business-minded Abba Shamal was knowledgeable on matters of internal administration, articulate in language, discreet in judgment, decisive in taking action, and impressive in convincing the king. It is said that Abba Bagibo readily listened to the opinions of Abba Shamal and made him his first advisor. He was in his sixties when Cecchi met him in 1879, and over a glass of special wine he boasted to the Italian traveler "now . . . I am old and no more capable to go to war, but I have an intelligent head, and the king who knows this loves me as his father, and asks advice from me on every matter and nobody is listened to as I am."[200] Though there may be an element of self-aggrandisement in this statement, it does not alter the fact that he was a very capable right-hand man for Abba Bagibo. In fact, it was the same official who protected Abba Bulgu, the third son of Abba Bagibo, from the wrath and suspicion of his father by vouching for the loyalty of the son. Abba Bulgu, after succeeding to the throne, rewarded the worthy Abba Shamal by maintaining him in the same office for many years.

Besides appointing new men to the council of state, Abba Bagibo also dismissed some of his provincial governors and replaced them by more energetic ones. "The lieutenant who commanded between Koma and the Ulmaya was replaced because he abused the poor people a great deal."[201] It is important to note that the region of Ulmaya, which includes the famous market of Soddo, was still under the firm political control of Abba Bagibo. This is shown by the fact that Abba Bagibo was still appointing the commander of the region. By appointing energetic and intelligent men to the council of state and replacing governors, Abba Bagibo overhauled and reinforced his administration, which thereby continued to be efficient to the end of his reign. The diplomatic skill of the king and the vigor and abilities of his officers restored Limmu-Ennarya's former glory. With advancing age, Abba Bagibo began to lose his belligerence of spirit, and also became fat and less agile,[202] concentrating more on calls for peace than on preparations for war. Ever after, he fought only when forced to because his vital interests were at stake. For instance, in either late 1847 or early 1848, Limmu-Ennarya and Jimma Abba Jifar went to war for a short time. "Limmu and Jimma had quarreled and the king of Kullo had advanced as far as Gojeb to attack Jimma but withdrew at the news about the peace that the king of Ennarya hastened to send to him."[203] The cause for the dispute between the two states must have been the internal crisis of Limmu-Ennarya, which may have agitated Abba Jifar because of the loss of his daughter and son-in-law. It was he who opened hostilities, but Abba Bagibo who made peace. Again in 1848, when the troops of Abba Jifar were badly beaten by the people of Botor,[204] Abba Bagibo did not take advantage of the weakness of his old adversary. In the same year, when Abba Magal (the crown prince) was in dispute concerning the crown of Gera, with his brothers and cousins, Abba Bagibo supported the former, apparently on ideological grounds. Abba Magal promised to accept Islam if he could seize power, and Abba Bagibo fought on his side. The reason behind this decision seems to have been Abba Bagibo's desire to win the sympathy and support of the Muslim shaykhs and *fuqahas* in Saqqa. The new king of Gera fulfilled his promise by embracing Islam,[205] and Abba Bagibo may have enjoyed the admiration of the Muslims in the Gibe region. Again in the same year, when Limmu-Ennarya and Gumma quarreled, Abba Bagibo averted war by a generous offer of peace, a peace agreement which was cemented by a political marriage. "Peace was declared and the king of Gumma had just sent 200 cows and 200 pails of honey to request the hand of the daughter of the king of Limmu." [206] In the same year Abba Bagibo made peace also with the Buno, a peace which brought a sense of relief to merchants traveling from Gojjam to Gumma. The merchants were no longer molested by the *ketto* (robbers) on the short route via the desert, since they were now escorted by the border guards of Limmu-Ennarya.[207] Numerous examples of Abba Bagibo's peaceful gestures during the last part of his reign could be given, but these above suffice to show that he had become truly a man of peace. It was during this period that he earned the reputation of being the arbitrator of peace and war. His European guest of honor in 1859 described his reputation in these glowing terms:

> Though lord of a small state he dominated by his esteem and authority not only the surrounding states, but also that of Kafa and other Galla countries. His words have so much weight to those princes and tribal leaders, so much so that he was the arbiter for war and peace.[208]

Secondly, it is no exaggeration to say that Abba Bagibo was one of the rare Oromo kings who understood the importance of changing outdated and counterproductive policies. In 1848, the king took a very decisive and far-sighted economic measure. This step shows the depth of his understanding of economic matters and his real concern for the commercial prosperity of his land. Although Abba Bagibo had banned the Jabarti traders from going beyond Saqqa, by 1848 he realized that this policy had embittered the Jabarti traders to the extent that they were avoiding his country. He not only abolished the prohibition on trading beyond Saqqa, but also removed many restrictions on trade and traders.[209] He even lifted the monopoly on some important commodities. Only the royal monopoly on gold was maintained.

Abba Bagibo could not and would not have lifted the monopoly on gold because it was not only a royal monopoly, but was also the universal symbol of royal authority in the region. To try to lift it would have been to undermine his own legitimate authority by depreciating the value of the precious metal. The king reversed his earlier discriminatory policy and replaced it by a pragmatic policy of gold for the king and the rest free for all. He had sufficient breadth of vision to enable him to perceive the direction in which events were moving; the change in policy did not fail to produce the desired effect.

However, by this time Limmu-Ennarya was in decline; indeed the decline had already begun in 1841. The second part of Abba Bagibo's reign was a period of political splendor rather than military strength, and this did not encourage growth. The decline was hastened and aggravated by the terrible plague which decimated a large portion of the population of Limmu-Ennarya in the late 1840s.[210] While the decline had already begun, it was overshadowed by the personality of the king, and there was little consciousness that this small domain was falling apart bit by bit. According to an eyewitness, who was in the country towards the end of the reign of Abba Bagibo, Limmu-Ennarya was prosperous, relatively stable internally, and respected in the courts of the surrounding countries, and the people led a relatively happy life.[211]

Finally, before this long discussion on the reign of Abba Bagibo is closed, it is not out of place to comment on his last attempt to unite the Gibe region, not for unity *per se*, but against a common enemy. By 1858, Tewodros's governor of Shawa, Bazabeh, had expanded his territory up to the Gurageland, and demanded tributes from some Oromo tribes who were under the influence and political control of Abba Bagibo. The threatened groups appealed to Abba Bagibo for help. Moreover, Tewodros's threat to the Gibe region itself acted as a catalyst for common action. It was reported that Abba Bagibo regarded the payment of tribute to Tewodros as a confirmation of slavery and called on all of the Oromo of the Gibe region to unite and face the common enemy. It is not possible to say whether all the Oromo kings participated in the extraordinary gathering held in Limmu-Ennarya, at which it was decided that:

> All the Galla will unite as one man and they will repay Tewodros's threat with their spears and cavalry at any time, at any place, and on any front. And that their . . . common resolution and common shout should reach the ears of Tewodros and the Amharas.[212]

Massaja, the author of the idea of unity against Tewodros, and the man who drafted the letter to that end, claims that this resolution sufficed to stop Tewodros from pursuing his ambitious plan against the Gibe region. Massaja may have overstated Abba Bagibo's determination to unite the Oromo against the common enemy. However, what is not in doubt is that Abba Bagibo's inspiring leadership stirred the spirit of resistance among the Oromo in the region.[213]

The year 1861 was noted in the Gibe region for two phenomena: the first was the extraordinary rains of that year, with raging thunder and lightning which frightened the people. The lightning struck the houses of the king (or near them), killing many people.[214] The sudden illness of the king which followed this event may have been interpreted by the Muslim fanatics as Allah's anger against Abba Bagibo's religious laxity. It probably provided them with ideological justification for whipping up fanaticism, never seen before in Limmu-Ennarya.[215] The second phenomenon was the death of Abba Bagibo, which occurred after a reign of thirty-six years,[216] when he had reached the mature age of fifty-nine. When Abba Bagibo was suddenly taken ill, he realized that the end was coming and called together all his sons and the three members of the council of state. He gave his gold ring to Abba Bulgu saying, "Here is the successor after my death." [217] By so doing, he averted a possible power struggle. He died at midday on September 24, 1861, after a short illness of five days.

> His death was a great misfortune not only for the Catholic mission but also for the kingdom of Ennarya, for all Galla principalities of the south, who gained in him skilled counselor and a very valid protector. Even European science . . . lost a true and sincere friend, because he opened the road for the first explorer Antoine de'Abbadie . . . up to Kaffa. In fact, it can be said in part that he was the founder of the Catholic mission of Ennarya, of Gera, and of Kaffa, and without his favour, I should never have been able to put my feet in the latter kingdom. [218]

No other Oromo king had had longer or closer relations with the Christian princes to the north than Abba Bagibo. He had come to power in the days of Sahle Sellassie of Shawa and died in the days of Tewodros. He had known the leaders of all the surrounding states, with whom he had fought and made peace and with whom he had arranged political marriages. He symbolized the hope for unity, which died with him.

> Abba Bagibo's inspiring leadership prevented Tewodros from pursuing his design in the Gibe region in 1858. However, after his death, the absence of the mind that led and directed them, the Galla unity was broken. Instead of preparing to form one front against the enemy, the various kingdoms began to fight among themselves . . . Their disunity not only undermined their strength, but also invited and facilitated the coming of the invaders who devastated their land. [219]

Epilogue

The history of the Oromo in the Gibe region in the 1570s to 1860s, which has been reconstructed in the foregoing chapters, is the story of their migration. During the pastoral Oromo migration to and the settlement in the Gibe region, the indigenous people were mainly absorbed and assimilated, and in the process the Oromo population expanded rapidly. It is the story of the transformation of the Oromo mode of production from pastoralism to sedentary agriculture combined with cattle keeping. It is the story of the formation of the Gibe states, their political organization, economic foundation, and ideological orientation. This history reached its climax around 1800 when the new political structure of the Gibe region was mapped, and Oromo society was launched on a course which more or less shaped its development down to the 1880s, when these states were annexed by King Menelik of Shawa (and after 1889 the emperor of Ethiopia). Though the existence of these states spanned less than a century, this brief period was packed with events of crucial importance. It witnessed a flourishing of trade, the spread of Islam, the flowering of culture, and the achievement of social and economic progress unsurpassed in any of the other Oromo areas in Ethiopia. In the field of religion, the Gibe region became the most famous center of Islamic learning for all the Oromo of Ethiopia. Even today, along with Daawwe in Wollo, the Gibe region is regarded as the most important center of Islamic learning in the Horn of Africa. In the field of commerce the whirlwind of trading activities in the Gibe region gave birth to an aggressive and dynamic Oromo merchant class, the Afkala. In all these states, trading was a highly organized business, in which government played a key role. This led to the development of an impressive network of institutionalized trade, which enabled the Afkala traders to engage in a brisk trade all the year round. The caravan routes which crisscrossed the Gibe region and interwove it with the surrounding lands made the area the major emporium of what today is southwestern Ethiopia, where the products of the surrounding lands were collected and funneled to the north through Gojjam, or to the east through Shawa. The transit trade that entered and left the Gibe region supplied the kings with gifts and customs duties. Indeed, the Gibe states enjoyed prosperity. While the full effect of this prosperity did not reach beyond

196

the landowning class, the poorer peasants probably enjoyed a higher standard of living than other peasants in the Ethiopian region. The abundance of cereal crops, supplemented by root crops, guaranteed their safety from famine. The light burden of taxation and the possibility of earning more and buying land also contributed to a better standard of living for the ordinary peasant.

From the 1840s, the leaders of the Gibe states were becoming conscious of unity among the Oromo in general, of the unity of the Gibe region in particular, and of its place in the Ethiopian region as a whole. For two decades Abba Bagibo sought to unify the Gibe region through diplomacy and political marriage. The great leader died in 1861 and was succeeded by Abba Bulgu (1861–1883), who immediately set about reorganizing his father's tolerant and liberal administration to his own fancy. His obsession with Islam turned the business of administration into an elaborate fanaticism. Abba Bulgu not only lacked the supreme diplomatic skill of his father, but also made mistakes which hastened the commercial ruin of his land. The merchants, angered by the unbearable vexation of his administration, left Limmu-Ennarya to prosper in Jimma.[1] It was during this period that Jimma emerged as the most powerful of all Gibe states. The rulers of Jimma, driven by the desire to attract traders to their country and urged on by the need to maintain the safety of caravan routes to and from their land, made their country the commercial capital of south-western Ethiopia.[2] Jimma eclipsed Limmu-Ennarya commercially, politically, culturally, and militarily. Yet Jimma was not able to unify the Gibe region. In short, both Limmu-Ennarya and Jimma failed to unify the region into a single political unit. They failed for two reasons. First, the rivalry among the Gibe rulers consumed their creative energy and diverted their attention from the common danger that was to ruin all of them. This was also true of the Oromo leaders in Wallaga, who were engaged in constant struggles for supremacy.[3] While Oromo strength was consumed in their quarrels, their enemies rejoiced in the important discovery that Oromo leaders were unsuccessful in forming a common front even in the face of a common enemy. It was Takla Haymanot of Gojjam who, as a neighbor of the Oromo of Wallaga, made the discovery and tried to turn it to his own advantage. In the 1870s, when the clouds had already gathered thick and low over the Oromo of the southwestern region, Takla Haymanot crossed the Abbay and established his authority in Horro-Gudru in northern Wallaga.

Secondly, the weakness of the defense system was reflected in the absence of firearms in the Gibe region and Wallaga and the slowness of the landlocked Oromo leaders to adjust themselves to the use of such weapons. This weakness was apparent in the 1840s. During the second half of the nineteenth century, the Amhara polity to the north had access to a large quantity of modern European weapons of destruction which drastically tipped the balance of power in its favor. Never since the first half of the sixteenth century had such a radical change in the balance of power occurred in the Horn of Africa and with such speed as it did during the second half of the nineteenth century. The new weapons not only made victories easier for the Amhara, but also enabled their

197

leaders to set up administrative and military colonies in Oromo territory at a long distance from their home base. What the Oromo leaders of the southwestern region did not realize was that, by the 1870s, the Amhara leaders of Gojjam and Shawa, whom they were to face now, had strong territorial ambitions, political motivation, centralized administration, relatively large quantities of firearms, and a detailed understanding of the divisions within Oromo society. By 1880 Takla Haymanot and Menelik were scrambling for the conquest and colonization of the Oromo of the southwestern region.[4] The scramble stemmed from the intensified competition between the two political rivals. Of the two, it was Menelik who had European-trained and well-armed soldiers,[5] and political ambition to conquer all the Oromo from Wallaga in the west to Hararghe in the east, from Wollo in the north to Borana in the south. In this Menelik met with success as the various Oromo leaders were forced to fight for his interest and in his cause against their own people. This is not surprising "for it is a characteristic of empires that they turn their victims into their defenders."[6] The driving social force behind Menelik's conquest was economic. ". . . the green and lush Oromo lands and their boundless commodities (gold, civet, ivory, coffee), and [their] prosperous markets"[7] were the economic motives. We may add that the search for new sources of food for Menelik's soldiers, the plunder of Oromo property, free Oromo labor, and the expropriation of Oromo land were the primary economic motives.[8] Menelik's conquest of the Oromo of southwestern parts of what is today Ethiopia was accomplished by Gobana, who was himself of Oromo origin. At this point, it is pertinent to state briefly the role Gobana played in the conquest of the Oromo.

Gobana Dacche was born in Shawa in 1821 to a princely Christian Oromo family. When Menelik escaped from Tewodros's prison[9] in 1865 and returned to Shawa, Gobana submitted to and put his wealth and experience at the disposal of the young king.[10] In return Menelik invested Gobana with the title of Abagaz, chief of the palace guard. This was the beginning of Gobana's spectacular rise to power. Menelik, perceiving Gobana's talent, promoted him to the rank of *dajazmach*, commander of the armed forces. By 1878 Gobana was made *ras* (literally head). He was probably the first Christianized and Amharized Shawan Oromo to receive this highest title.[11] Intoxicated by his promotion to the title of *ras*, and probably elated at the prospect of a more illustrious title of *negus* (king), Gobana took upon himself the conquest of his own people.[12] Gobana was an excellent horseman, a brave warrior, an able strategist, and an accomplished expert in the knowledge of Oromo warfare and psychology. He was Menelik's ablest general and the greatest empire-builder. However, for the Oromo, Gobana was a traitor. In the following poem, Gobana, the son of Dacche, is referred to as strange dog, who betrayed and worked against the interests of his own people:

> It is strange, it is strange, it is strange,
> women do not raid houses:
> she who gives birth to a dog is strange.

Relatives do not hurt each other,
the haft of an axe is strange
people of one stock do not sell each other
that of the son of Dacche is strange.[13]

The scramble for the conquest of Oromo territory which started in 1880
between Takla Haymanot of Gojjam and Menelik of Shawa culminated on
June 6, 1882, at the Battle of Embabo, where the former was routed and
dramatically knocked out of the contest by the latter. The battle was the
turning-point in the conquest of the Oromo of southwestern parts of Ethiopia.
It was also decisive for Oromo history. It was Ras Gobana who won the Battle
of Embabo for Menelik.[14] It was also the same Gobana who won the Gibe
region, where four Oromo kings and a queen-regent submitted to him without
a blow being struck. It appears that the Oromo leaders of the Gibe states found
justification for their peaceful submission in Gobana's promise of local autonomy,[15] and in their belief that whatever they did, the well-armed and ruthless
Gobana would force them into submission. Within a few years Ras Gobana
successively and successfully brought under Menelik's administration the
Oromo of Wallaga, the Gibe region, and Illubabor – the three richest regions
which henceforth economically became the backbone of Menelik's empire.
"This formidable Oromo warlord brought southern Oromo . . . under the
Amhara in five years, a mission that Amhara kings and warlords tried and
failed in 400 years." [16] For his victory at the battle of Embabo and spectacular
success in obtaining the peaceful submission of various Oromo leaders, Menelik rewarded Gobana by entrusting him with the administration of the Gibe
region, which now was united under a single authority. Menelik also appointed
Gobana as the *negus* (king) of Kaffa, a province which was not yet conquered.
However, this appointment backfired and eclipsed his illustrious political
career.

> The popularity of Gobana and the high title he received aroused envy and
> perhaps the jealousy of officials surrounding Menelik. The possibility that
> Gobana backed by the various Galla chiefs, would defy Menelik's authority and
> set up a federated empire of Galla territories seemed to many imminent.[17]

Menelik not only withdrew the title of *negus* from Gobana but also removed
him from the administration of the Gibe region, after which Gobana's influence in Menelik's government diminished as rapidly as it had risen. Interestingly, Menelik disgraced Gobana only after the latter had almost accomplished the conquest of the Oromo of the central and southwestern parts of
Ethiopia. Probably like several other Oromo leaders, who only realized what
had happened too late, Gobana must have been disappointed and dissatisfied
by the loss of the title of *negus* and the administration of the Gibe region, the
richest part of Menelik's empire. It was too late to rebel: Menelik was
powerful[18] and Gobana was too old for rebellion. Outwardly, he must have
shown satisfaction, on the marriage of his son Wadajo to the daughter of
Menelik; so he may have concealed his feelings about his appointment to a

narrow corridor along the Sudanese border from the emperor and just lived out the next few years, until he died suddenly and mysteriously in 1889.[19]

Perhaps in an attempt to fulfill his own secret personal plan,[20] Gobana facilitated and completed the conquest of the Oromo of the southwestern region, without himself understanding what the future had in store for him. Shortly after his removal from the administration of the Gibe region, the latter was aflame with rebellion. The Oromo leaders of the Gibe region paid dearly for their rebellion. Of the five states, only the kingdom of Jimma survived. The thrones of Limmu-Ennarya, Gomma, Gumma, and Gera lay in dust. The remaining members of the ruling houses spent their last days in the dungeons of Abbar Jifar II of Jimma. The common people did not fare any better. Oromo peasants were reduced to landless, rightless, second-class subjects, who suffered much under the deadly weight of Menelik's empire, "of which all the members were subjects rather than citizens, but in which almost all the Oromo were colonial subjects."[21] It is this situation which is one of the root causes of the current tragic conflict in Ethiopia. It is hoped that Ethiopia will one day be able to transform itself radically and create a democratic system which will right the old wrongs, redress the old injustice, heal old wounds and, more importantly, ensure the genuine equality of all Ethiopians in every facet of life – political, economic, social, cultural, and religious, which in turn will guarantee its survival. In the unity and equality of the Oromo and other people of Ethiopia lies the future of their country.

Notes

Preface

1 Taddesse Tamrat, *Church and State in Ethiopia, 1270–1527* (Oxford: 1972).

2 U. Braukamper, "Islamic principalities in southeast Ethiopia between the thirteenth and sixteenth centuries," *Ethiopianist Notes*, 1 (2) (1977): 30–5.

3 E. Cerulli, *Studi Etiopici II: La Lingua e la Storia dei Sidamo* (Rome: 1938), p. 32. See also Taddesse Tamrat, *Church and State*, p. 6.

4 Merid Wolde Aregay, "Southern Ethiopia and the Christian kingdom, 1508–1708, with special reference to the Galla migration and their consequences," Ph.D. thesis, University of London, 1971, pp. 44–5.

5 Braukamper, "Islamic principalities in southeast Ethiopia between the thirteenth and sixteenth centuries," *Ethiopianist Notes*, 1 (1): 17–47; Braukamper, *ibid.*, 1 (2): 1–30. See also his *Geschicte der Hadiya Süd-Athiopiens* (Wiesbaden: 1980), pp. 97–130.

6 See, for instance, Mohammed Hassen, "The Oromo of Ethiopia, 1500–1850: with special emphasis on the Gibe region," Ph.D. thesis, University of London, 1983, pp. 50, 57, 61, and 64.

7 *Ibid.*, pp. 38–68.

8 Darrel Bates, *The Abyssinian Difficulty: The Emperor Theodorus and the Magdala Campaign, 1867–68* (Oxford: 1979), p. 7.

9 E. Haberland, *Galla Süd-Athiopiens* (Stuttgart: 1963), p. 772.

10 See p. 4.

11 Haberland, *Galla Süd-Athiopiens*, p. 774.

12 See, for instance, Arab Faqih, *Futuh Al-Habasha*, trans. and ed. by R. Basset (Paris: 1897), pp. 135–7.

13 *Ibid.*, pp. 269, 291, 298, 355, 361, 382. See also Mohammed Hassen, "The Oromo of Ethiopia," pp. 53–8.

14 Arab Faqih, *Futuh Al-Habasha*, Arabic text (Cairo, edn.: 1974), pp. 254–5.

15 Hassen, "The Oromo of Ethiopia," pp. 63–8.

16 M. Abir, *Ethiopia and the Red Sea* (Frank Cass, London: 1980), see Chapter VII.

17 U. Braukamper, *Geschichte der Hadiya Süd-Athiopiens*, pp. 97–130.

18 Aregay, "Southern Ethiopia," pp. 150, 156 *passim*.

19 Hassen, "The Oromo of Ethiopia," pp. 220–30.

20 *See below*, pp. 69–71.

21 Of which *Chronica de Susenyos, Rei de Ethiopia*, trans. and ed. by F. M. E. Pereira, Lisbon, 1892–1900, is the most important. Its chief importance lies in the fact that it contains the most detailed account of campaigns against the Oromo.

201

22 To this category belongs Bahrey's "History of the Galla." His information on the gada system and on other aspects of Oromo life provides the most important data to students of Oromo history.

23 This includes Arab Faqih's monumental book, *Futuh Al-Habasha*, which makes it abundantly clear that some sections of the Oromo people who lived in the hotly contested areas suffered during the jihadic war of Imam Ahamad (1529–1543).

Introduction

1 Bairu Tafla, ed., *Asma Giyorgis and His Work, "History of the Galla and the Kingdom of Sawa."* (Franz Steiner Verlag, Wiesbaden GMBH, Stuttgart: 1987), pp. 48–9.

2 Bahrey, "History of the Galla" in *Some Records of Ethiopia*, trans. and eds., C. F. Beckingham and G. W. B. Huntingford (The Hakluyt Society, London: 1954), p. 111.

3 W. C. Harris, *The Highlands of Ethiopia* (London: 1844), vol. III, pp. 72–3.

4 Bogumil Jewsiewicki and David Newbury, eds., *African Historiographies: What History for Which Africa?* (Sage Publications, Beverly Hills, California: 1986), p. 17.

5 Abir, *Ethiopia and the Red Sea*, Preface, p. xix.

6 Among others, see Taddesse Tamrat, *Church and State in Ethiopia*. See also his "Ethiopia, the Red Sea and the Horn" in *The Cambridge History of Africa, 3 c. 1050–1600* (Cambridge University Press, New York: 1977), pp. 98–182. See also his "The Horn of Africa: the Solomonids in Ethiopia and the states of the Horn of Africa" in UNESCO, *General History of Africa – IV Africa from the Twelfth to the Sixteenth Century* (Heinemann, California: 1984), pp. 423–58. In the above three works, Dr. Taddesse does not mention Oromo history. Equally Professor S. Rubenson, *The Survival of Ethiopia's Independence* (London: 1976) has totally ignored Oromo history.

7 E. Ullendorf, *The Ethiopians: An Introduction to Country and People* (London: 1960), p. 76.

8a Among others see, for instance, Donald Levine, *Greater Ethiopia: The Evolution of a Multi-Ethnic Society* (The University of Chicago Press: 1974), p. 88 and S. Pankhurst, *Ethiopia: A Cultural History* (London: 1955), p. 387. See also Mesfin Woldemariam, *An Introductory Geography of Ethiopia* (Addis Abebe: 1972), p. 16.

8b I am deeply indebted to Dr. Paul Baxter for his practical suggestion concerning this section.

9 Bahrey, the author of the "History of the Galla" produced his manuscript in 1593. It contains the first detailed account of Oromo history and social organization, not to mention the history of their migration.

10 Bahrey, "History of the Galla," p. 112.

11 Antoine d'Abbadie, Bibliothèque Nationale (Paris) Nouvelles Acquisitions Françaises, no. 21300, folios 731, 788.

12 Haberland, *Galla Süd-Athiopiens*, p. 772. See also Hassen, "The Oromo of Ethiopia," pp. 84–8.

13 Negaso Gidada, "History of the Sayyoo Oromoo of south western Wallaga, Ethiopia, from about 1730 to 1886," Inaugural dissertation zur Erlangung des Grades eines Doktors der Philosophie im Fachbereich Geschichtswissenschaften der Johann Wolfgang Goeth-Universitat zu Frankfurt am Main, 1984, pp. 46–8.

14 E. Cerulli, *Somalia: scritti vari editi ed inediti* (Rome: 1957), vol I, pp. 70–1; I. M. Lewis, *A Pastoral Democracy: A Study of Pastoralism and Politics among the Northern Somali of the Horn of Africa* (Oxford University Press: 1960), pp. 23–6; Haberland, *Galla Süd–Athiopiens*, p. 772; H. S. Lewis, "The origin of the Galla and the Somali," *Journal of African History*, 7 (1966): 27–46; U. Braukamper, "Oromo country of origin: a reconsideration of hypothesis" in *Ethiopian Studies Proceedings of the Sixth International Conference*, Tel-Aviv, 14–17 April 1980, ed. Gideon Goldenberg (offprint), pp. 25–40. See also his *Geschichte der Hadiya Süd Athiopiens* (Wiesbaden: 1980), pp. 136–9.

15 Hassen, "The Oromo of Ethiopia," pp. 84–8.
16 Haberland, *Galla Süd-Athiopiens*, p. 772.
17 Hassen, "The Oromo of Ethiopia," pp. 85–6.
18 Martial de Salviac, *Un peuple antique au pays de Menelik: les Galla, grande nation Africaine* (Paris: 1905), pp. 167–8.
19 Haberland, *Galla Süd–Athiopiens*, p. 774.
20 Hassen, "The Oromo of Ethiopia," p. 38.
21 *Ibid.*, pp. 16–17 and 49–51. See also Gidada, "History of the Sayyoo Oromoo," pp. 57–8.
22 Hassen, "The Oromo of Ethiopia," p. 73.
23 Haberland, *Galla Süd-Athiopiens*, p. 277, reports a Gujji Oromo legend which claims that the Borana came from Gujji herdsmen "who wandered off" (wronite in boronte), went on something, and did not come back. In Oromiffa (the Oromo language), the term Borana conveys a very strong concept of a "wanderer" who moves from place to place sticking to the simple but noble tradition of pastoral life. Probably the term Borana developed to express the concept of those who "wandered off" and did not return. That must have been the reason why the term Barentu was an old Cushitic name, while Borana was an Oromo term of later origin.
24 Martial de Salviac, *Les Galla*, pp. 20–36. See also E. Cerulli, *Etiopia occidentale* (Rome: 1933), vols. I and II, pp. 139–43.
25 Antoine d'Abbadie, Nouvelles Acquisitions Françaises no. 21300, folio 717.
26 The term Qallu stands both for the institution and the high priest who performed rituals.
27 *Bokku* was a wooden scepter which was used as a symbol of authority. It was a multi-purpose ceremonial emblem, whose importance will be discussed later.
28 The karrayu Qallu of the Borana is said to have fallen from heaven itself. The first Qallu of the Gujji is said to have been the son of Waqa, who fell from heaven. See also K. Knutsson, *Authority and Change: A Study of the Kallu Institution among the Matcha Galla of Ethiopia* (Goteborg: 1967), pp. 145–7.
29 Paul Baxter, "Social organization of the Galla of northern Kenya," D. Phil. thesis, Oxford University, 1954, pp. 156–92. See also Haberland, *Galla Süd-Athiopiens*, pp. 475, 537.
30 Angelo Mizzi, *Cenni etnografici Galla ossia organizzazione civile use e costumi Oromonici* (Malta: 1935), p. 9. See also de Salviac, *Les Galla*, pp. 152, 155–6.
31 Baxter, "Social organization of the Galla," p. 48. See also Asmarom Legesse, *Gada: Three Approaches to the Study of African Society* (London: 1973), p. 216.
32 Legesse, *ibid.*, p. 10. See also G. W. B. Huntingford, *The Galla of Ethiopia: The Kingdoms of Kafa and Janjero* (London: 1955), p. 83.
33 F. M. Pereira, *Chronica de Susenyos*, p. 214.
34 A. Cecchi, *Da Zeila alle frontiere dell Caffa* (Roma: 1886), vol. II, p. 30, trans. by K. Knutsson, *Authority and Change*, p. 148.
35 According to Professor Asmarom, "The term jila does not refer to people but to an event. It means ceremony or ritual: the celebrants are usually referred to as warra jila." Asmarom Legesse, unpublished MS "The Oromo cradle land and polity: comments on the introduction to Mohammed Hassen's Book on Oromo history," p. 7. However, according to many other sources, the term *jila* refers to the celebrants.
36 Angelo Mizzi, *Cenni etnografici Galla*, p. 9. See also de Salviac, *Les Galla*, pp. 155–6.
37 de Salviac, *ibid.*, p. 159. Translation by G. W. B. Huntingford, *The Galla of Ethiopia*, pp. 83–4.
38 K. Knutsson, *Authority and Change*, p. 155. See also Huntingford, *The Galla of Ethiopia*, p. 83 and Haberland, *Galla Süd–Athiopiens*, p. 776.
39 Cerulli, *Etiopia occidentale*, vol. I, pp. 139–43, 172. See also Paul Soleillet, *Voyages en Ethiopie, Janvier 1882 – Octobre 1884, notes, lettres et documents divers* (Rouen: 1886), p. 261 and de Salviac, *Les Galla*, pp. 154–5.
40 Baxter, "Social organization of the Galla," p. 157.
41 de Salviac, *Les Galla*, p. 104.
42 K. Knutsson, *Authority and Change*, pp. 147–55.

43 *Ibid.*, p. 67. See also Cerulli, "Folk literature of the Galla of southern Abyssinia," *Harvard African Studies*, 3 (1922): 178–80.
44 Jan Vansina, *Oral Tradition: A Study in Historical Methodology*, trans. by H. M. Wright (Routledge & Kegan Paul, London: 1961), p. 66.
45 Asmarom Legesse, *Gada: Three Approaches*, p. 81.
46 Angelo Mizzi, *Cenni etnografici Galla*, pp. 53–60. See also his *Semplici constatazioni felologico-etnologiche Galla* (Malta: 1935), pp. 64–5.
47 Asmarom Legesse, *Gada: Three Approaches*, p. 8.
48 *Ibid.*, p. 51.
49 There is variation from region to region in the names of the grades.
50 There is also variation from region to region on the names of the gada in power, as footnote 54 indicates.
51 Yelma Deressa, *Ya Ityopya Tarik Ba' asra Sedestannaw Kefla Zaman In Amharic (History of Ethiopia in the Sixteenth Century)* (Addis Ababa: 1957; Ethiopian Calendar: 1965), pp. 217–20.
52 Cerulli, *Etiopia occidentale*, vol. II, p. 124.
53 Asmarom Legesse, *Gada: Three Approaches*, p. 124.
54 d'Abbadie, 1880:   Fathers: Birmaji, Malba, Mudana, Robale, Dulo
                     Sons: Aldada, Horata, Bifole, Sabaqa, Kilrole
   Cerulli, 1920s: Fathers: Horata, Robale, Dulo, Melba, Holcisa
                     Sons: Michelle, Birmaji, Bifole, Mudana, Kilole
   Yelma Deressa, 1960s: Fathers: Michelle, Mudana, Robale, Melba, Birmaji
                     Sons: Kilole, Mulata, Bifole, Dulo, Horata

   Various other gada names are given by Huntingford in *Some Records of Ethiopia*, pp. 206–8. However, what is important to note here is that in the above three examples almost all Bahrey's gada names are repeated. These were the most important gada names.
55 Bahrey, who wrote his "History of the Galla" in 1593, did not write the name of the gada who came to power in 1594.
56 Cerulli, "Folk literature of the Galla," pp. 167–80. See also Deressa, *Ya Itopya Tarik*, pp. 212–27; de Salviac, *Les Galla*, pp. 184–95; Legesse, *Gada: Three Approaches*, chapter 8; and Mohammed Hassen, "The relation between Harar and the surrounding Oromo 1800–1887," unpublished manuscript, 1973, pp. 23–6.
57 P. T. W. Baxter, "Boran age-sets and generation-sets: gada, a puzzle or a maze" in *Age, Generation and Time Some Features of East African Age Organization*, eds. P. T. W. Baxter and Ulri Almagor (C. Hurst and Comi .ny, London: 1978), pp. 151–82. In the same book see also John Hinnant, "The Guji: gada as a ritual system," pp. 207–43.
58 de Salviac, *Les Galla*, pp. 184–95. See also G. Massaja, *I miei trentacinque anni di missione nell'alta etiopia* (Rome: 1886), vol. III, pp. 172–7 and *passim*.
59 Legesse, *Gada: Three Approaches*, p. 73.
60 Bahrey, "History of the Galla," p. 122.
61 E. Cerulli, "Folk literature of the Galla," p. 68.
62 Haberland, *Galla Süd–Athiopiens*, p. 394.
63 Deressa, *Ya Itopya Tarik*, pp. 219–20.
64 E. Cerulli, "Folk literature of the Galla," p. 58.
65 Gucci (guchi) has double meaning: It means ostrich. It also means an ostrich feather which a valiant warrior put in his hair.
66 Cerulli, "Folk literature of the Galla," p. 102.
67 Bahrey, "History of the Galla," p. 122.
68 Legesse, *Gada: Three Approaches*, p. 81.
69 *Ibid.*, p. 83.
70 See below, pp. 60-3.

71 All the major sources I am using in this introduction underline that there were election campaigns.
72 de Salviac, *Les Galla*, pp. 190–1.
73 *Ibid.*, p. 184.
74 For detailed analysis of the gada system and election refer to Asmarom Legesse's excellent book *Gada: Three Approaches to the Study of African Society*, Chapter 8, pp. 202–32.
75 de Salviac, *Les Galla*, pp. 182–90.
76 *Ibid.*, pp. 188–9.
77 Cerulli, "Folk literature of the Galla," p. 179.
78 For further information on the *bokku*, see below.
79 Some authors seem to consider Abba Bokku as an official different from Abba Gada.
80 Everyone in the Gada grade (VI) had to slaughter a bull for his *butta*, the feast mentioned earlier.
81 de Salviac, *Les Galla*, p. 191.
82 *Ibid.*, p. 196. See also Legesse, *Gada: Three Approaches*, pp. 215–20 and Maurice Bloch, ed., *Political Language and Oratory in Traditional Society* (London: 1975), pp. 50–3.
83 de Salviac, *Les Galla*, pp. 196–7.
84 See for instance, Haberland, *Galla Süd–Athiopiens*, p. 204.
85 Baxter, "Social organization of the Galla," Preface, p. iii.
86 Virginia Luling, "Government and social control among some peoples of the Horn of Africa," a thesis submitted for the Master of Arts degree at the University of London, 1966, p. 87.
87 Legesse, *Gada: Three Approaches*, p. 101.
88 Luling, "Government and social control," p. 89.
89 For instance C. T. Beke, "On the countries south of Abyssinia," *Journal of the Royal Geographical Society*, 13 (1843): 255.

1 The migration of pastoral Oromo

1 As can be seen, Borana was both the name of the major section that spread to the north (Matcha-Tulama) as well as the name of the group that spread over southern Ethiopia and northern Kenya. The one difference is that the Matcha-Tulama section used the term Borana as the name of their common "father" in relation to the Barentu Oromo, while the southern group still use the term Borana as their own national name.
2 C. F. Beckingham and G. W. B. Huntingford, *Some Records of Ethiopia*, p. 112.
3 Bahrey, "History of the Galla," p. 112.
4 *Ibid.*, p. 114.
5 Mohammed Hassen, "The Oromo of Ethiopia, 1500–1850: with special emphasis on the Gibe Region," p. 154.
6 J. A. Davis, "The sixteenth century jihad in Ethiopia and the impact on its culture," *Journal of the Historical Society of Nigeria* 3 (1964): 113.
7 Arab Faqih, *Futuh al-Habasha*, pp. 135–7.
8 Hassen, "The Oromo of Ethiopia," pp. 53–67.
9 Unfortunately, tradition speaks only of males within the category of those adopted. It appears as if girls were not adopted, but this is not true; girls and women, too, were adopted.
10 Tasaw Merga, "Senna Ummatta Oromo: jalqaba Jarra Kudha Jahafti hama dhumiti Jarra Kudha Sagalafanti," ("History of the Oromo people: from the beginning of the sixteenth century to the end of the nineteenth century"), MS. (Addis Ababa: 1976), p. 78.
11 Apart from these two forms of adoption, there was also another form, which was more of protection:

There was also a form of adoption called kolu, which only applied to Oromo. Those wh
were adopted by kolu were men who deliberately left their home and went to a man i
another lineage and demanded to be adopted . . . When the run-away had chosen such
man he went to his house and kneeled in front of him and said "kolu," save me, help me
keep me, and the other man had to give him full protection and keep him in his house

Jan Hultin, "Man and land in Wallega, Ethiopia," *Working Papers of the Department c
Social Anthropology, University of Gothenburg* (1977), no. 10, pp. 19–20.

12 E.g. *The Journal of C. W. Isenberg and J. L. Krapf Detailing Their Proceedings in the Kingdo*
of Shoa and Journeys in Other Parts of Abyssinia in the Years 1839–1842* (London: 1968), p
256.

13 Merga, "Senna Umatta Oromo," p. 78.

14 *Ibid.* See also Mizzi, *Cenni etnografici Galla*, p. 82; *idem, Semplici constatazioni filologico*
etnologiche Galla, pp. 62–3.

15 I have drawn on D. W. Cohen, "Lwo speakers" in *Zamani: A Survey of East African History*
ed. B. A. Ogot (Nairobi: 1974), pp. 136–49.

16 The adopted members fully participated in the gada assembly as well as in other ritua
activities.

17 Huntingford, in *Some Records of Ethiopia*, Preface, pp. lxxiv–lxxv.

18 Arab Faqih, *Futuh al-Habasha*, pp. 380–1, 390 *et passim.*

19 Bahrey, "History of the Galla," pp. 116–17.

20 These three stages seem to form the general pattern, especially during the early phase of th
migration.

21 Bahrey, "History of the Galla," p. 115. See also Hassen, "The Oromo of Ethiopia," p. 162

22 Bahrey, "History of the Galla," p. 116.

23 Hassen, "The Oromo of Ethiopia," pp. 169–70.

24 Bahrey, "History of the Galla," pp. 116–17.

25 See, for instance, Taddesse Tamrat, *Church and State in Ethiopia 1270–1527*, pp. 152, 276, 29
and *passim.*

26 Hassen, "The Oromo of Ethiopia," pp. 182, 223.

27 F. M. E. Pereira, *Historia de Minas* (Lisbon: 1886), p. 17.

28 *Ibid.*, p. 27.

29 Richard Pankhurst, *History of Ethiopian Towns* (Wiesbaden: 1982), p. 94.

30 Factors that contributed to the development of this situation are beyond the scope of thi
study.

31 Ennarya has been spelled variously as Enarya, Inarya, Innarya, Narea, and Hinnario. Th
latter is based on the pronunciation of the indigenous people. However, Ennarya is th
standard spelling that I use in this study.

32 Hassen, "The Oromo of Ethiopia," pp. 186–7.

33 Mohammed Hassen, "Menelik's conquest of Harar, 1887 and its effects on the politica
organization of the surrounding Oromos up to 1900," in *Working Papers on Society an
History in Imperial Ethiopia: The Southern Periphery from the 1880s to 1974*, eds. D. L
Donham and Wendy James (African Studies Centre, Cambridge University: 1975), p. 228

34 Conti Rossini, ed., "Historia regis Sarsa Dengel (Malak Sagad)" 2 vols. *Corpus Scriptorun
Christianorum Orientalium scriptores Aethiopici*, III (1907), pp. 44, 48–9, 51, 96 and *passim*

35 Arab Faqih, *Futuh al-Habasha*, Arabic text, p. 209.

36 In this sense what made Ennarya different from all her neighbors was the size neither of he
territory nor her population. It was her pragmatic policy of self-preservation based o
neutrality and caution.

37 W. E. Conzelman, trans. and ed., *La Chronique de Galawdewos, rai d'Ethiopie* (Paris: 1895)
pp. 37–8.

38 R. W. Whiteway, trans. and ed., *The Portuguese Expedition to Abyssinia in 1541–1543 as Narrated by Castanhaso with Some Contemporary Letters; the Short Account of Bermudes, and Certain Extracts from Correa* (The Hakluyt Society: 1902), pp. 237–8.

39 Aregay, "Southern Ethiopia," p. 161.

40 The Jesuit Goncalo Rodrigues in a letter of December 1556, cited in Aregay, "Southern Ethiopia," p. 104.

41 Aregay, *ibid.*, p. 371.

42 *Ibid.*, p. 213.

43 Hassen, "The Oromo of Ethiopia," pp. 230–1, 233.

44 Conti Rossini, *Historia regis Sarsa Dengel*, pp. 25–6.

45 *Ibid.*, p. 30.

46 Like several other minority groups, the Gafat people were reduced to an insignificant number by the events of the sixteenth and seventeenth centuries.

47 It was at this time that the tax on cattle was introduced for the first time. This new tax seems to have proved a timely pretext for impoverishing the Gafat pastoralists as well as the farmers. On this tax, see M. de Almeida, "The history of High Ethiopia or Abassia, p. 88.

48 Conti Rossini, *Historia regis Sarsa Dengel*, pp. 19, 27.

49 *Ibid.*, p. 35.

50 e.g. F. Alvares, *The Prester John of the Indies*, vol. II, p. 455.

51 See p. 35.

52 Conti Rossini, *Historia regis Sarsa Dengel*, p. 44.

53 Hassen, "The Oromo of Ethiopia," pp. 237–40.

54 On *malasay*, see Arab Faqih, *Futuh al-Habasha*, pp. 84, 111, 130, 185, 207, 466.

55 These were part of the Muslim force left behind by Amir Nur in Waj in 1559.

56 Conti Rossini, *Historia regis Sarsa Dengel*, pp. 48–9.

57 Perhaps Sarsa Dengel did this in gratitude for the help of Asma-ad-Din, whose support won him the throne in 1563 to strengthen the defence of Waj against the Borana.

58 Aregay, "Southern Ethiopia," pp. 234–5. See also Conti Rossini, *Historia regis Sarsa Dengel*, pp. 48–9.

59 From the records it is difficult to tell whether Fanuel was made *dajazmach* at the time of his appointment. *La Chronique de Galawdewos*, p. 144, only says that Galawdewos deputed Fanuel in his place, while he himself went to Damot. As a deputy of the emperor with authority over Dawaro and a number of other provinces, Fanuel may have had a title higher than *dajazmach*. See, for instance, Aregay, "Southern Ethiopia," pp. 268–9.

60 Hassen, "The Oromo of Ethiopia," pp. 184, 220–2.

61 Bahrey, "History of the Galla," p. 119.

62 *Ibid.*

63 James Bruce, *Travels to Discover the Source of the Nile in the Years 1768–1773*, vol. III (Edinburgh: 1805), p. 249.

64 Conti Rossini, *Historia regis Sarsa Dengel*, pp. 60–1.

65 *Hega Waser'ata Mangest*, cited in Aregay, "Southern Ethiopia," pp. 269–70.

66 Bahrey, "History of the Galla," p. 120.

67 *Ibid.*, p. 117.

68 *Ibid.*, p. 120.

69 Aregay, "Southern Ethiopia," p. 335.

70 James Bruce, *Travels to Discover*, vol. III, pp. 249–50.

71 See below, p. 49.

72 On the *jarra* ceremony, *supra*, p. 15.

73 Bahrey, "History of the Galla," p. 122.

74 *Ibid.*, p. 123.

75 James Bruce, *Travels to Discover*, vol. III, p. 250.

76 It seems that Christian influence started penetrating Ennarya after the middle of the thirteenth century. See Tamrat, *Church and State in Ethiopia*, pp. 35, 88, 122, 176, 182. See also Werner J. Lange, *History of the Southern Gona (Southwestern Ethiopia)* (Franz Steiner Verlag GMBH, Wiesbaden: 1982), p. 17.
77 Aregay, "Southern Ethiopia," pp. 298–9.
78 Conti Rossini, *Historia regis Sarsa Dengel*, pp. 136–7.
79 *Ibid.*, p. 180. This highly useful piece of information is found in the variant of the long chronicle.
80 Werner J. Lange, *History of the Southern Gona*, p. 26.
81 *Ibid*, citing Conti Rossini, *Historia regis Sarsa Dengel*, p. 181.
82 Conti Rossini, *ibid.*, p. 136.
83 *Ibid.*
84 *Ibid.*, p. 138.
85 *Ibid.*, p. 141.
86 *Ibid.*, p. 144.
87 Almeida, "The history of High Ethiopia," p. 78. See also Alvares, *The Prester John of the Indies*, vol. I, p. 320.
88 Bahrey, "History of the Galla," p. 123. Bahrey claimed that *dawe* (Jawe) in the Oromo language "has the meaning of those who stay behind." Rather it means snake.
89 The main residence of Sarsa Dengel.
90 Conti Rossini, *Historia regis Sarsa Dengel*, pp. 144–5.
91 See above, p. 36.
92 This province was bordered by Waj in the east and Gamo in the south. In the west it was separated from Kambatta by the Bilate river, and from Hadiya by the Barbare river in the northwest.
93 I.e. Bahrey himself.
94 Bahrey, "History of the Galla," p. 114.
95 Conti Rossini, *Historia Regis Sarsa Dengel*, pp. 154–5.
96 *Ibid.*
97 *Ibid.*, p. 145.
98 Bahrey, "History of the Galla," p. 127. See also Hassen, "The Oromo of Ethiopia," pp. 252–3.
99 On *chafe* assembly (meadow assembly), see above, p. 14.
100 Bahrey, "History of the Galla," pp. 112–13.
101 Knutsson, *Authority and Change*, pp. 176–81.
102 Deressa, *Ya Ityopya Tarik*, p. 236.
103 Cerulli, *Etiopia occidentale*, vol. II, p. 170.
104 Shaykh Bakri Sapalo, "Kitāb irsāl al-sawarikh ilā samā al-tawarikh" (56 pp. Arabic manuscript which deals with the history of the Oromo nation), p. 44.
105 The loot gained from the raids enabled and encouraged further raids, while personal glory which individuals gained from warfare in enemy territory attracted their attention.
106 Shaykh Bakri Sapalo was a remarkable Muslim Oromo intellectual, who, during his 50 years of teaching all-around Islamic education, gained considerable popularity, for three main reasons. First, he was a prolific writer. He produced eight major works on history, geography, culture, society, and Islamic religion, all of which were written in Arabic. Secondly, he was an outstanding Oromo poet, who won immense popularity by his poems in the Oromo language, short enough for the people to learn by heart. He also produced a quantity of religious poetry in Arabic. Thirdly and equally importantly, he was the man who first invented an indigenous Oromo alphabet. On the latter, see "The Oromo orthography of Shaykh Bakri Sapalo" by R. J. Hayward and Mohammed Hassen in *Bulletin of the School of Oriental and African Studies*, 44 (3) (1981): 550–66. I am greatly indebted to Shaykh Muhammed Rashad, a student of Shaykh Bakri Sapalo, who not only gave me copious information about the life of his teacher

but generously provided me with copies of a number of his manuscripts, which are otherwise inaccessible. I am likewise indebted to Dima Yonis, who took great trouble in interviewing former students and friends of Shaykh Bakri on my behalf. Shaykh Bakri Sapalo died in April 1980, at the age of 83, in a refugee camp in northern Somalia.

107 Shaykh Bakri Sapalo, "Kitab irsāl," pp. 44–5. See also the manuscript of Abba Jobir Abba Dula, p. 9.
108 See above, p. 42.
109 MS Abba Jobir Abba Dula, p. 9.
110 Shaykh Bakri Sapalo, "Kitab irsāl," pp. 44–5.
111 MS Abba Jobir Abba Dula, p. 9.
112 M. Fortes and E. E. Evans-Pritchard, eds., *African Political Systems* (London: 1961), p. 17.
113 Cerulli, *Etiopia occidentale*, vol. II, p. 170.
114 Shaykh Bakra Sapalo, "Kitab irsāl," pp. 44–5.
115 See below, p. 84.
116 Antoine d'Abbadie, Nouv. Acq. Fr., no. 21300, folio 719–21.
117 Hassen, "The Oromo of Ethiopia," pp. 94–5.
118 Lambert Bartels, *Oromo Religion Myths and Rites of the Western Oromo of Ethiopia: An Attempt to Understand* (Dietrich Reimer Verlag, Berlin: 1983), p. 60.
119 Gidada, "History of the Sayyoo Oromoo," pp. 49–51.
120 Bartels, *Oromo Religion*, p. 60.
121 *Ibid.* See also his "The concept of 'saffu' among the Matcha Oromo of Ethiopia," a paper presented at the Conference on Ethiopian Feudalism, Addis Ababa University, 1976, cited in Gidada, "History of the Sayyoo Oromoo," p. 51.
122 Bartels, *Oromo Religion*, p. 248.
123 *Ibid.*, p. 339.
124 *Ibid.*, pp. 336–7.
125 Second interview with Ato Na'a Bassa (a well-known traditional historian). Place: Naqamte, Wallaga; date: 27.1.1973, p. 29. I am deeply indebted to A. Triulzi for providing me with a long and immensely rich oral tradition which he gathered from Wallaga, Ethiopia.
126 On *gabbaro*, the conquered people who were adopted *en masse* by the Matcha, see below pp. 63–5.
127 Interview with Ato Na'a Bassa, *ibid.*, pp. 27–9. If we trust this tradition Makko is reported to have opened negotiations with the Gabbaro on their own terms. During the night, he advised his followers to start up fires everywhere, and while the startled Gabbaro were watching what was happening, the Matcha observed a weak point in their siege and dashed at it with full speed, thus forcing the enemy to give way.
128 Makko Billi seems to have accomplished probably three tasks: he contributed to the foundation of the new strategically located central *chafe*, he successfully led Matcha at a difficult time, and he set a pattern for Matcha conquest in the southwestern region.
129 Aregay, "Southern Ethiopia," pp. 329–30.
130 Conti Rossini, *Historia regis Sarsa Dengel*, p. 159. See also G. W. B. Huntingford, "Historical geography of Ethiopia from 1st century A.D. to 1701" (1969), unpublished MS at School of Oriental and African Studies, p. 151.
131 See, for instance, Ullendorf, *The Ethiopians*, p. 76.
132 See above, pp. 30, 37.
133 See below, pp. 70–1.
134 Aregay, "Southern Ethiopia," pp. 282, 321.
135 See below, pp. 69–71.
136 See below, pp. 63–4.

2 Ennarya and the Sadacha

1 Huntingford, "Historical geography," p. 152, citing the Cambridge MS. Oriental, 1873
2 Bruce, *Travels to Discover*, vol. III, p. 253.
3 This information is summarized from the manuscript of Abba Jobir Abba Dula, pp. 13–1
4 In 1604, armed with the content and spirit of Bahrey's "History of the Galla," King Z
Dengel raised a huge army with which he intended to rescue at least some of the lost province
See, for instance, Hassen, "The Oromo of Ethiopia," pp. 264–8. See also S. B. Chernetso
"The History of the Gallas and the death of Za-Dengel King of Ethiopia (1603–4)," *I
Congresso internazionale di studi etiopici* (Rome: 1974), pp. 803–8.
5 See above, p. 22.
6 During the reign of Ya'eqob (1597–1603) the trimvirate (consisting of the queen mother ar
her two sons-in-law) dominated the political scene of the Christian kingdom. In 1603 at tl
age of 14, Ya'eqob decided to take the reins of power into his own hands. For this prematu
move the triumvirate deposed him and placed Za Dengel on the throne.
7 Bruce, *Travels to Discover*, vol. III, p. 260.
8 Susenyos, the son of the cousin of Sarsa Dengel, was captured by the Oromo around 1585. F
was adopted as a "son" and lived among the Oromo for more than two years, during whic
time he learned their language and manners, and acquired their fighting skill. Again betwee
1597 and 1607 he lived as a bandit, mainly among the Oromo. See, for instance, Hassen, "Tl
Oromo of Ethiopia," pp. 268–71, 279–95. See also Pereira, *Chronica de Susenyos*, pp. 4–5 .
passim.
9 Susenyos had already distinguished himself by his services to the Afre and the Warantisha i
their attacks on Gojjam.
10 Pereira, *Chronica de Susenyos*, pp. 16–24 *et passim.*
11 Asma Giyorgis, "Ya Galla Tarik" (MS Ethiop, 302, Bibliothèque Nationale, Paris), p. 5.
12 Pereira, *Chronica de Susenyos*, p. 49.
13 *Ibid.*
14 From the chronicle's description of this episode, it appears that Susenyos was routed and h
followers suffered real carnage. See also Aregay, "Southern Ethiopia," p. 409.
15 Interestingly, it was with the help of his Oromo followers that Susenyos was able to captur
the throne in 1607. However, ironically he conducted an extensive campaign against th
Oromo.
16 Hiob Ludolf, *A New History of Ethiopia: Being a Full and Accurate Description of th
Kingdom of Abyssinia, Vulgarly though Erroneously Called the Empire of Prester Joh*
(London: 1682), pp. 179–80.
17 Aregay, "Southern Ethiopia," p. 408.
18 Bruce, *Travels to Discover*, vol. III, pp. 267–8.
19 Pereira, *Chronica de Susenyos*, pp. 105–6.
20 Hassen, "The Oromo of Ethiopia," pp. 276–81.
21 Huntingford, "Historical geography," pp. 145–6
22 Almeida, "The history of High Ethiopia," p. 153.
23 Werner Lange, *Domination and Resistance Narrative Songs of the Kaffa Highlands* (Michigan
1979), p. 18.
24 Aregay, "Southern Ethiopia," p. 517.
25 Lange, *Domination and Resistance.*
26 See below, pp. 75–6.
27 His cruelty towards his enemies suggests that Banaro probably did not come to power legally
There is also some internal evidence to be discussed later on which shows that Banaro was no
from the old ruling house of Ennarya.
28 Almeida, "The history of High Ethiopia," p. 148.

29 *Ibid.*
30 See below, pp. 71–2.
31 Almeida, "The history of High Ethiopia," pp. 149–51.
32 *Ibid.*
33 *Ibid.*, p. 152.
34 Pereira, *Chronica de Susenyos*, p. 156.
35 See below, pp. 75–8.
36 Ludolf, *A New History of Ethiopia*, pp. 83–4.
37 Almeida, "The history of High Ethiopia," p. 135.
38 Susenyos's long experience with the Oromo enabled him not only to exploit their political weakness, but also he adopted their effective *chiffra* fighting system, which improved his soldiers' speed, the co-ordination and the capacity to attack rapidly, or retreat in time. See, for instance, Pereira, *Chronica de Susenyos*, p. 79.
39 Cited in Aregay, "Southern Ethiopia," p. 404 (see note).
40 Pereira, *Chronica de Susenyos*, pp. 139–42.
41 Knutsson, *Authority and Change*, p. 181.
42 W. C. Plowden, *Travels in Abyssinia and the Galla Countries* (London: 1868), p. 310.
43 Those Matcha individuals who protected merchants and defended caravan routes were perhaps already themselves engaged in trading. This cannot be verified by written evidence. However, there is adequate evidence within the Christian sources, which show beyond any doubt that during the seventeenth century some families among the Matcha had accumulated so much wealth that they started to emerge as influential members of society. These wealthy men, some of them very rich in cattle and slaves, not only eclipsed the elected gada leaders, but also became *de facto* rulers. Among others, see I. Guidi, *Annales Yohannis I Iyasu I, Bakaffa*, (4 vols.), *Corpus Scriptorum Christianorum Orientalium* (1903–1905), p. 245.
44 By Hadiya is meant here the small Muslim state (which bore the historical name of Hadiya) located between the Bilate river and the Gurage highlands and inhabited by the people who called themselves Hadiya.
45 Almeida, "The history of High Ethiopia," p. 170.
46 Aregay, "Southern Ethiopia," p. 427.
47 *Ibid.*, p. 525.
48 Iyasu's battle against the Liban took place at the beginning of the eighteenth century.
49 Guidi, *Annales Yohannis*, pp. 238–46.
50 J. S. Trimingham, *Islam in Ethiopia* (London: 1952), p. 94.
51 Deressa, *Ya Ityopya Tarik*, p. 242.
52 The old Oromo saying "nine are Borana ('pure Oromo') and ninety the Gabbaro" (the conquered people) expresses the disparity between the two groups.
53 Knutsson, *Authority and Change*, pp. 180–1.
54 Second interview with Ato Na'a Bassa, Naqamte, Wallaga, January 27, 1973, p. 26. See also Bakri's manuscript, pp. 4–5. This ms., which is fifty pages long, deals mainly with the ninteenth-century history of Wallaga. It depicts the struggle for state formation and traces the rise to power and the prominence of the Bakre family in Wallaga. I am deeply indebted to A. Triulzi for allowing me to photocopy the translated version of this ms.
55 Deressa, *Ya Ityopya Tarik*, pp. 234–41.
56 *Ibid.*
57 Bahrey, "History of the Galla," p. 116.
58 See above, pp. 21–2.
59 *The Journal of C. W. Isenberg and J. L. Krapf*, p. 256.
60 E.g., Aregay, "Southern Ethiopia," pp. 422–4.
61 d'Abbadie, Nouv. Acq. Fran. no. 21300, folio 763.
62 Pereira, *Chronica de Susenyos*, p. 191.

63 d'Abbadie, Nouv. Acq. Fran. no. 21300, folio 763.

64 *Ibid.*

65 *Ibid.*

66 According to Na'a Bassa, a well-known Matcha traditional historian, there were two assemblies. One was called Oda Borana (the Borana assembly) and the other Oda Gabbara (the Gabbora assembly). In this context the term *oda* (sycamore tree) has a double meaning. It means the meeting-place, and it also means that assembly itself.

67 After their separation in the late 1580s, the Matcha and the Tulama began to turn militarily against each other, the pretext being the daily dispute over pasturage in the no-man's land between them.

68 See below, p. 74.

69 Pereira, *Chronica de Susenyos*, p. 191. Translation by Aregay "Southern Ethiopia," pp. 420–1.

70 Pereira, *Chronica de Susenyos.*

71 *Ibid.*

72 *Ibid.*, p. 192.

73 *Ibid.*, p. 191.

74 The feasts were intended to prepare the soldiers for assault as well as to create understanding between the *gabbaro* and the Christian force.

75 Pereira, *Chronica de Susenyos*, pp. 191–3.

76 *Ibid.*

77 *Ibid.*, p. 194.

78 *Ibid.*

79 Almeida, "The history of High Ethiopia," p. 136.

80 The availability of food, and not the morale to fight, seems to have been the most important factor with the Christian army. The desire to loot the weak, the fear of hunger, the uncertainty of finding the enemy if they followed them into the deep forest, the fatigue of the chase, and the willingness to take risks in unknown land seem to have been sufficient excuse for his soldiers. As they came in haste with euphoria, they wanted to leave without despair.

81 Pereira, *Chronica de Susenyos*, p. 195.

82 *Ibid.*, pp. 195–7.

83 See above, pp. 12–15.

84 Deressa, *Ya Ityopya Tarik*, pp. 218–19.

85 Pereira, *Chronica de Susenyos*, see Chapter XLV. According to what is contained in this chapter, Susenyos stayed for a month (1614) in Agaw land, during which time the Agaw were exterminated and their land became a desert. Those who survived the slaughter were sold into slavery.

86 Susenyos came to the throne for the first time in 1604. However, when King Ya'eqob suddenly returned from his exile in Ennarya, Susenyos was deserted by his Amhara supporters and Ya'eqob was put on the throne for the second time. It was only after Susenyos defeated and killed Ya'eqob in 1607 that he made himself emperor for the second time.

87 By 1608, Susenyos had an army of 25,000 fighting men, while by 1622 this had grown to around 40,000 strong. See for instance, Aregay, "Southern Ethiopia," pp. 475–6. See also Almeida, "The history of High Ethiopia," pp. 77–8.

88 Aregay, "Southern Ethiopia," pp. 479–80.

89 Pereira, *Chronica de Susenyos*, p. 194.

90 *Ibid.*

91 *Ibid.*, p. 209.

92 *Ibid.*

93 It may be that the spectre of previous defeats inhibited the people from endorsing the new aggressive policy, beyond highland Ennarya. The security of highland Ennarya may have

weighed more with the people than the exploitation of the new opportunity with which the Sadacha weakness provided them.
94 See below, pp. 75–6.
95 Aregay, "Southern Ethiopia," p. 519.
96 Pereira, *Chronica de Susenyos*, pp. 239–40.
97 *Ibid.*
98 Aregay, "Southern Ethiopia," p. 519.
99 See below, pp. 74–6.
100 Pereira, *Chronica de Susenyos*, p. 217.
101 *Ibid.*, p. 220.
102 Almeida, "The history of High Ethiopia," p. 137.
103 Pereira, *Chronica de Susenyos*, pp. 220–1.
104 Bruce, *Travels to Discover*, vol. III, p. 238.
105 Pereira, *Chronica de Susenyos*, p. 222.
106 *Ibid.*, pp. 223–44.
107 Almeida, "The history of High Ethiopia," p. 150.
108 Pereira, *Chronica de Susenyos*, pp. 239–40.
109 *Ibid.*, p. 240.
110 Aregay, "Southern Ethiopia," p. 491.
111 Almeida, "The history of High Ethiopia," p. 150.
112 In 1632 after Susenyos was removed from power, his son and successor Fasiladas (1632–1667) restored the Orthodox church and banned Catholicism.
113 Almeida, "The history of High Ethiopia," p. 150.
114 According to some sources, Yaman Christos is reported to have once come to Fasiladas "laden with gold." See, for instance, R. Pankhurst, *An Introduction to the Economic History of Ethiopia from Early Times to 1800* (London: 1961), p. 185. No date is given for this event. In all likelihood it must have taken place at the earliest before the re-establishment of the old church, and at the latest before Sela Christos (the father-in-law of Yaman Christos) was removed from power and executed.
115 Lange, *Domination and Resistance*, p. 18.
116 Lange, *History of Southern Gonga*, p. 17.
117 *Ibid.*, pp. 35–7.
118 Lange, *Domination and Resistance*, p. 18. I am indebted to the author for the information on the closing years of Ennarya's history.
119 *Ibid.*
120 Lange, *History of Southern Gongo*, p. 30.
121 Lange, *Domination and Resistance*, p. 18.
122 Aregay, "Southern Ethiopia," p. 592. See also Guidi, *Annales Yohannis*, pp. 245–6.
123 Lange, *Domination and Resistance*, pp. 21–2.
124 Max Grühl, *The Citadel of Ethiopia: The Empire of the Divine Emperor*, translated from the German by Ian F. D. Marron and L. M. Sieveking (London: 1932), p. 207.
125 *Ibid.*, pp. 170, 205–12. See also Cecchi, *Da Zeila*, vol. II, p. 484.
126 e.g. Daba Hunde, "A portrait of social organization and institutions of the Oromo of Jibat and Machcha in the nineteenth century till the conquest of Menelik II," B. A. thesis, Haile Sellassie I University, Addis Ababa, 1972, p. 14.
127 Lambert Bartels, "Studies of the Galla in Wallaga: their own view of the past," *Journal of Ethiopian Studies* 3 (1) (1970): 139.

3 The Gibe states

1 In the previous two chapters I have made extensive use of Ethiopian Christian sources as well as a few Muslim ones. These sources now dry up for the period under discussion. At first glance, it seems that to pass from the use of those sources to new ones is "to bid good-bye to the waters where every detail of navigation is well-known and to embark upon an uncharted sea." However, it soon becomes very apparent that there is another rich source of information. It is for this reason that I briefly say something about these sources right from the start.

2 The following are among the published works of Antoine d'Abbadie:
> (a) 1877, "Les causes actuelles de l'esclavage en Ethiopie," extract *La Revue des Questions Scientifiques* (Loubsin), pp. 409–34.
> (b) 1880, 'Sur les Oromos, grande nation Africaine," *Annales de la Société Scientifique de Bruxelles*, vol. IV, pp. 167–92.
> (c) 1890, *Géographie de l'Ethiopie* (Paris).

3 d'Abbadie's unpublished materials are found at the Bibliothèque Nationale of Paris.
4 M. Abir, "Trade and politics in the Ethiopian region 1830–1855," Ph.D. thesis, School of Oriental and African Studies, London, 1964, preface, pp. x–xi.
5 The following are only a few examples from among the published works of C. T. Beke:
> (a) 1843, "On the countries south of Abyssinia," *Journal of Royal Geographical Society*, 3: 254–69.
> (b) 1852, *Letters on the Commerce and Politics of Abyssinia and Other Parts of Eastern Africa* (London).

6 Massaja, 1885–1895, *I miei trentacinque anni di missione nell' alta Etiopia* (12 vols.).
7 Cecchi, *Da Zeila* (3 vols.).
8 Cerulli, "Folk literature of the Galla."
9 Cerulli, *Etiopia occidentale* (1933), 2 vols.
10 The Catholic mission in the Gibe region did send many letters and reports to their headquarters in Europe and those letters and reports were recently published in G. Massaja, *Lettere e scritti minori* (6 vols., Rome: 1978). Vols. II and III are useful.
11 Merga, "Senna Umatta Oromo."
12 M. Abir, *Ethiopia: The Era of the Princes 1796–1855* (London: 1968); *idem*, "The emergence and consolidation of the monarchies of Enarea and Jimma in the first half of the nineteenth century," *Journal of African History*, 6 (1965): 205–19.
13 H. S. Lewis, *A Galla Monarchy: Jimma Abba Jiffar, Ethiopia 1830–1932* (Madison: 1965). *Idem*, "Reconsideration of the socio-political system of the western Galla," *Journal of Semitic Studies*, 9 (1964): 139–43.
14 Abir, *Ethiopia*, p. 93. See also his "Trade and politics in the Ethiopian region," pp. 109–10; Huntingford, *The Galla*, p. 55; and G. Massaja, *In Abissinia e fra i Galla* (Roma: 1895), p. 279.
15 Lawrence Krader, *Formation of the State* (New Jersey: 1968), p. 74. See also Fortes and Evans-Pritchard, eds., *African Political Systems*, Preface, pp. xii, xiii, and also the Introduction, pp. 1–23.
16 The Jimma Interview Programme, folios 5, 7, 17–18, 28–9 *et passim*.
17 Huntingford, *The Galla*, p. 55.
18 Cerulli, *Etiopia occidentale*, vols. I and II, pp. 100–1.
19 e.g., Beckingham and Huntingford, *Some Records of Ethiopia*, pp. lxxx, lxxxvi.
20 See below, pp. 134–8.
21 See for instance, *Siyaasa Dinagdee* (Political Economy) 1983, Oromo Liberation Front Publication.
22 Haberland, *Galla Süd–Athiopiens*, p. 772.
23 It seems that pastoralism was a profession that suited their movement and was more compatible with their warrior tradition.
24 Huntingford, in *Some Records of Ethiopia*, Preface, p. lxxviii.

25 The Afre section of the Matcha who mainly spread to the region of Wallaga remained pastoralists much longer than the Sadacha. This may account for the delay in the formation of states in Wallaga.

26 Zergaw Asfera, "Some aspects of historical development in Amhara (Wallo) *c*. 1700–1815," B. A. Thesis, Addis Ababa University, 1973, pp. 10–16. Zergaw does not clearly state that the Arreloch was an Oromo dynasty, but the names of all the principal actors in the Arreloch are of Oromo origin. Furthermore, Zergaw does not dispute the fact that the Oromo element constituted a considerable number of the population in northeast Amhara.

27 *Ibid.*, p. 20.

28 *Ibid.*

29 See above, pp. 60–1.

30 See below, pp. 101–2.

31 See below, pp. 138–9.

32 E.g., Guidi, *Annales Yohannis*, pp. 238–46.

33 See below, p. 92.

34 Abir, "Trade and politics," pp. 109–11.

35 Massaja, *I miei trentacinque anni*, vol. III, pp. 52–3.

36 *Ibid.*

37 See below, pp. 118–21.

38 Massaja, *In Abissinia e fra i Galla*, p. 279.

39 The Jimma Interview Programme, folio 5.

40 Massaja, *I miei trentacinque anni*, vol. VI, p. 10.

41 See below, p. 150.

42 Bruce, *Travels to Discover*, vol. III, pp. 243–5.

43 See below, pp. 177–9.

44 Massaja, *I miei trentacinque anni*, vol. VI, p. 10.

45 See above, p. 79.

46 Amnon Orent, "Lineage structure and the supernatural: the Kaffa of southwestern Ethiopia," Ph.D. thesis, University of Boston, 1969, pp. 59–62. See also Cecchi, *Da Zeila*, vol. II, p. 489.

47 Huntingford, *The Galla*, p. 55. See also Abir, *Ethiopia*, p. 93.

48 See below, p. 94.

49 Among others see, Cecchi, *Da Zeila*, vol. II, pp. 487–8; Massaja, *Lettere e scritti minori*, vol. II, p. 360; Grühl, *The Citadel*, pp. 219, 282–300; F. J. Bieber, *Kaffa: Ein Alt Kuschitisches Volkstum Inner-Afrika* (Wien: 1923), vol. II, pp. 170–9, 290; Lewis, *A Galla Monarchy*, pp. 123–5.

50 Orent, "Lineage structure," p. 84, citing. Cerulli, *Etiopia occidentale*, vol. II, p. 184; Lewis Krapf, *Travels, Researches and Missionary Labours during an Eighteen Years Residence in Eastern Africa* (London: 1860), p. 48; F. J. Bieber, *Kaffa*, p. 133; Soleillet, *Voyages en Ethiopie*, p. 192.

51 Abir, *Ethiopia*, pp. 93–4.

52 e.g., Svein Ege, "Chiefs and peasants: the socio-political structure of the kingdom of Shawa about 1840," M.Phil. thesis, Havedoppgave i historie, ved universitetet e Bergen Hasten, 1978, pp. 130–1.

53 See below, pp. 130–1.

54 Krader, *Formation of the State*, pp. 44–5. This is a summary of the Marxist literature on the formation of the state. See also Frederick Engels, *The Origin of the Family, Private Property and the State* (Peking: 1974), pp. 205–6.

55 See below, p. 128.

56 Krader, *Formation of the State*, p. 102.

57 Antoine d'Abbadie, Nouv. Acq. Fran. no. 21300, folio 797. The Jimma Interview Programme, folio 18.

58 Luling, "Government and social control," pp. 145–52.

59 Lewis, *A Galla Monarchy*, pp. 127–8. See also his "Reconsideration of the socio-politic system of the western Galla," *JSS*, p. 140.
60 Cecchi, *Da Zeila*, vol. II, p. 151.
61 *Ibid.*
62 Massaja, *I miei trentacinque anni*, vol. IV, pp. 53–4.
63 *Ibid.*, p. 170.
64 Donald E. Crummey, "European religious missions in Ethiopia, 1830–1868," Ph.I dissertation, London University, 1967, p. 349.
65 Massaja, *I miei trentacinque anni*, vol. IV, pp. 171–2.
66 *Ibid.*
67 *Ibid.*
68 The Jimma Interview Programme, folio 21.
69 Massaja, *I miei trentacinque anni*, vol. IV, pp. 171–2.
70 The Jimma Interview Programme, folio 21.
71 *Ibid.*
72 See below, pp. 170–1.
73 Massaja, *I miei trentacinque anni*, vol. IV, pp. 171–2.
74 *Ibid.*, p. 174.
75 *Ibid.*, p. 179. Translation by Lewis, *A Galla Monarchy*, p. 128.
76 Cecchi, *Da Zeila*, vol. II, p. 164.
77 *Ibid.*, pp. 151, 270.
78 Abir, *Ethiopia*, p. 83. See also Lewis, *A Galla Monarchy*, p. 80; Cerulli, *Etiopia occidentale* vol. II, p. 76.
79 Cecchi, *Da Zeila*, vol. II, p. 166; see also Jimma Interview, folios 12, 26.
80 Engels, *The Origin of the Family*, p. 75.
81 Abir, *Ethiopia*, p. 81. Abir's description was meant for Limmu-Ennarya, but it could equall apply to all the Gibe states. See for example, Cecchi, *Da Zeila*, vol. II, pp. 233–4 and th Jimma Interviews, folios 5, 9.
82 The Jimma Interview Programme, folios 4, 31.
83 Cecchi, *Da Zeila*, vol. II, p. 327. See also Cerulli, *Etiopia occidentale*, vols. I and II, p. 172
84 Abir, *Ethiopia*, p. 82.
85 Cecchi, *Da Zeila*, vol. II, pp. 163, 206, 272.
86 See below, p. 148.
87 The Jimma Interview Programme, folio 33.
88 d'Abbadie, Nouv. Acq. Fran. no. 21300, folios 357, 314, 349. See also Merga, "Senna Umatt Oromo," p. 143.
89 See below, pp. 186–7.
90 Cecchi, *Da Zeila*, vol. II, pp. 238–9.
91 *Ibid.*, p. 262.
92 *Ibid.*, p. 137. See also A. d'Abbadie, Nouv. Acq. Fran. no. 21300, folio 753.
93 All the kings had at least three names: their personal names, which were seldom used; thei Muslim names, which were not used at all; and their war-horse names, which were generally used.
94 Cecchi, *Da Zeila*, vol. II, p. 165.
95 *Ibid.*, p. 197.
96 The Jimma Interview Programme, folios 27–9.
97 Cecchi, *Da Zeila*, vol. II, p. 165–6.
98 *Ibid.*, p. 277.
99 The manuscript of Abba Jobir Abba Dula, p. 14.
100 Cecchi, *Da Zeila*, vol. II, p. 174.
101 *Ibid.*, p. 317. See also d'Abbadie, Nouv. Acq. Fran. no. 21303, folio 496.

02 According to the Jimma Interview Programme, folios 4, 21, alarm about an approaching enemy was sounded by hitting *bedru* or *gonno* (drums). Through a system of *gonno* placed at appropriate intervals, the news of an imminent enemy attack could spread all over a country within a short time and every able-bodied man had to leave his field to join the army of his Abba Qorro. Those who failed to do so were enslaved and their property confiscated.

03 To the category of slaves also belonged the eunuchs, who guarded the wives and numerous concubines of the kings.

04 Cecchi, *Da Zeila*, vol. II, p. 289.

05 See below, pp. 184–5.

06 Beke, "On the countries south of Abyssinia," p. 260.

07 Bruce, *Travels to Discover*, vol. III, pp. 243–5.

08 M. Abir, "Southern Ethiopia" in *Pre-colonial African Trade: Essays on Trade in Central and Eastern Africa before 1900*, eds. R. Gray and D. Birmingham (London: 1970), p. 122.

09 Mekuria Bulcha, "Land ownership and social class formation among the Matcha of south-western Oromia-Ethiopia," unpublished paper presented to the Institute of Sociology, University of Stockholm, 1980, p. 28. I am indebted to the author for sending me a copy of his useful paper.

10 d'Abbadie, Nouv. Acq. Fran. no. 21300, folio 797.

11 Cecchi, *Da Zeila*, vol. II, pp. 131–4.

12 Massaja, *I miei trentacinque anni*, vol. IV, pp. 55–6.

13 *Ibid.*, pp. 68–9.

14 In 1843, Antoine d'Abbadie was in Saqqa, the capital of Limmu-Ennarya, where he recorded the history of Bofo's rise to power from many elders, including the father-in-law of Abba Gomol himself. See also the Jimma Interview Programme, folio 50.

15 In 1879, A. Cecchi recorded a version of another tradition which depicts the history of Bofo's rise to power.

16 Antoine d'Abbadie, Nouv. Acq. Fran. no.21300, folios 569–72. Translated by Abir, "The emergence and Islamisation of the Galla kingdoms of the Gibe and north Ethiopian trade with these kingdoms 1800–1850," unpublished African History Seminar paper, SOAS (1962–1963), p. 2.

17 See below, pp. 104–5.

18 Massaja, *Lettere e scritti minori*, vol. II, p. 372.

19 Beke, "On the countries south of Abessinia," p. 259.

20 Cecchi, *Da Zeila*, vol. II, p. 157.

21 See below, pp. 136–8.

22 Massaja, *In Abissinia*, p. 165.

23 A. d'Abbadie, Nouv. Acq. Fran. no. 23851, folio 34.

24 *Idem*, Nouv. Acq. Fran. no. 21300, folios 569–72. Translation by Abir, *Ethiopia*, pp. 78–9; see also Massaji, *I miei trentacinque anni*, vol. IV, p. 144; Harris, *The Highlands of Aethiopia*, vol. III, pp. 53–4; Cecchi, *Da Zeila*, vol. II, p. 157.

25 d'Abbadie, Nouv. Acq. Fran. no. 21300, folios 571–2.

26 Massaji, *Lettere e scritti minori*, vol. II, p. 372.

127 *Ibid.*

128 *Ibid.*

129 *Ibid.*, p. 371.

130 d'Abbadie, Nouv. Acq. Fran. no. 21300, folios 26–7.

131 The Jimma Interview Programme, folios 16, 29.

132 *Ibid.*, folios 26–7.

133 *Ibid.*

134 *Ibid.*

135 Harris, *The Highlands of Aethiopia*, vol. III, p. 54.

136 The Jimma Interview Programme, folios 8, 16.
137 Harris, *The Highlands of Aethiopia*, vol. III, p. 53.
138 Massaja, *In Abissinia*, p. 165.
139 Cecchi, *Da Zeila*, vol. II, p. 160.
140 The Jimma Interview Programme, folios 6, 8, 35.
141 *Ibid.*, folio 5.
142 See below, pp. 151–3.
143 The Jimma Interview Programme, folios 6, 8, 16.
144 Massaja, *In Abissinia*, p. 283; see also Crummey, "European religious mission in Ethiopia 1830–1868," p. 361.
145 See below, pp. 177–8.
146 See below, pp. 164–5.
147 It was in this spirit that the Jimma Interview Programme was sponsored by the History Department of Addis Ababa University in 1974.
148 A. d'Abbadie, *Géographie d'Ethiopie* (Paris: 1890), p. [Page no.]; Cecchi, *De Zeila*, vol. II, p 541; I. Guidi, "Storia dei Loro regni (dei Mec'c'a)" in *Mitteilungen des Seminars für Orientalische Sprachen*, 10 (1907), p. 181.
149 Cerulli, "Folk literature of the Galla," pp. 152–4.
150 *Ibid.*
151 See below, pp. 159–60.
152 Cerulli, "Folk literature of the Galla," pp. 18–19, 40, 154.
153 Beke, "On the countries south of Abyssinia," p. 259.
154 Cecchi, *Da Zeila*, vol. II, pp. 541–2.
155 Guidi, "Storia dei Loro regni (dei Mec'c'a)," p. 181. See also Cecchi, *Da Zeila*, vol. II, pp. 239–40.
156 Cecchi, *ibid.*
157 See below, pp. 155–6.
158 Guidi, "Storia dei Loro regni (dei Mec'c'a)," p. 181.
159 The Jimma Interview Programme, folios 2–3, 34, 59.
160 *Ibid.*, folio 2.
161 *Ibid.*
162 *Ibid.*
163 *Ibid.*, folios 17, 35.
164 *Ibid.*, folios 2, 17.
165 *Ibid.*, folio 3.
166 See below, pp. 156–7.
167 The Jimma Interview Programme, folios 5, 17–18.
168 What is intended here is only to give a brief sketch of the history of the formation of the kingdom of Jimma.
169 Tesema Ta'a, "The political economy of western central Ethiopia: From the mid-16th to the early 20th centuries," Ph.D. dissertation, Michigan State University, 1986, pp. 87–8.
170 Massaja, *I miei trentacinque anni*, vol. VI, pp. 5–6.
171 The Manuscript of Abba Jobir, p. 33.
172 *Ibid.*
173 Massaja, *I miei trentacinque anni*, vol. VI, pp. 5–6.
174 See below, pp. 182–3.
175 Massaja, *I miei trentacinque anni*, vol. VI, p. 6.
176 The Manuscript of Abba Jobir, *ibid.*
177 *Ibid.*
178 Masseja, *I miei trentacinque anni*, vol. VI, p. 6.
179 *Ibid.*
180 See below, pp. 157–8.

81 The Jimma Interview Programme, folio 7.
82 Guidi, "Storia dei Loro regni (dei Mec'c'a)," p. 181. See also Cerulli, "Folk literature of the Galla," p. 161.
83 Guidi, "Storia dei Loro regni (dei Mec'c'a)," p. 181. See also Cerulli, *ibid.*
84 Beke, "On the countries south of Abyssinia," p. 259; see also Cecchi, *Da Zeila*, vol. II, pp. 541–2.
85 Cecchi, *ibid.*, p. 266.

The economic foundation of the Gibe states

1 See below, pp. 143–5.
2 For history, see Almeida, "The history of High Ethiopia," pp. 149–52.
3 A. H. S. Landor, *Across Widest Africa: An Account of the Country and the People of Eastern, Central and Western Africa, as Seen During a Twelve-months Journey from Djibouti to Cape Verde* (London: 1907), pp. 120–1.
4 Merga, "Senna Umatta Oromo," p. 136.
5 *Ibid.*
6 Cecchi, *Da Zeila*, vol. II, p. 162.
7 *Ibid.*, p. 146.
8 Grühl, *The Citadel*, p. 127.
9 Cecchi, *Da Zeila*, vol. II, p. 541.
10 *Ibid.*
11 *Ibid.*, pp. 238–9.
12 *Ibid.*
13 *Ibid.*
14 *Ibid.*, pp. 537–8.
15 The Manuscript of Abba Jobir Abba Dula, p. 13.
16 Massaja, *I miei trentacinque anni*, vol. VI, p. 6.
17 *Consociazione Turistica Italiana: guida dell'Africa orientale Italiana* (Milan: 1938), p. 528.
18 Cecchi, *Da Zeila*, vol. II, p. 540.
19 Grühl, *The Citadel*, p. 166.
20 Cecchi, *Da Zeila*, vol. II, pp. 537–8.
21 Lewis, *A Galla Monarchy*, p. 52.
22 Beckingham and Huntingford, in *Some Records of Ethiopia*, Preface, p. lxxxix.
23 Cecchi, *Da Zeila*, vol. II, p. 263.
24 *Ibid.*, p. 278.
25 *Ibid.*, pp. 280–1. The seven varieties of spices: Ginger, Ogghio, Sunco, Abessud, Chefa, Dembla, Marga-orga.
26 The Jimma Interview Programme, folio 27.
27 Cecchi, *Da Zeila*, vol. II, pp. 281–2. These were: *Buto* (whitish), *Bila* (red), *Gumaria* (dark), *Ebichaa* (dark), *Dommisa* (white and pure), *Maccannisa* (reddish-white), *Qeto* (red), *Tufa* (pale reddish).
28 *Ibid.* See also Landor, *Across Widest Africa*, p. 189; the Jimma Interview Programme, folios 4, 27, 52–3.
29 Landor, *ibid.*, pp. 120–1.
30 Cecchi, *Da Zeila*, vol. II, p. 164.
31 Huntingford, *The Galla of Ethiopia*, p. 73.
32 Haberland, *Galla Süd–Athiopiens*, p. 772.
33 Almeida, "The history of High Ethiopia," pp. 149–50.
34 Cecchi, *Da Zeila*, vol. II, p. 164.
35 Ege, "Chiefs and peasants," p. 53.
36 Hultin, "Man and land in Wollega," pp. 1–3.

37 See above, p. 82.
38 Hultin, "Man and land in Wollega," p. 12.
39 e.g. Lewis, *A Galla Monarchy*, pp. 49–50.
40 Massaja, *I miei trentacinqu anni*, vol. IV, 68–9.
41 *Ibid.*
42 Hultin, "Man and land in Wollega," p. 8. The author conducted extensive field work among the Oromo peasants in Wollega in the 1970s.
43 Merga, "Senna Umatta Oromo," p. 14.
44 Cecchi, *Da Zeila*, vol. II, p. 132.
45 Hultin, "Man and land in Wollega," p. 8.
46 Massaja, *I miei trentacinque anni*, vol. IV, p. 68.
47 Massaja, *ibid.*
48 Cecchi, *Da Zeila*, vol. II, pp. 328–30.
49 Massaja, *I miei trentacinque anni*, vol. IV, pp. 68–9.
50 Merga, "Senna Umatta Oromo," p. 140.
51 Lewis, *A Galla Monarchy*, p. 50. The author conducted field work in Jimma in the late 1950s
52 Beke, "On the countries south of Abyssinia," p. 257.
53 Cecchi, *Da Zeila*, vol. II, p. 164.
54 Abir, *Ethiopia*, p. 86. Here the author's reference is to the situation that existed in the Gibe region in the 1840s and 1850s.
55 The Jimma Interview Programme, folios 13, 53.
56 Beke, "On the countries south of Abyssinia," p. 260. See also Antoine d'Abbadie, Nouv. Acq Fran. no. 21300, folio 673.
57 Beckingham and Huntingford, in *Some Records of Ethiopia*, p. lxxxix
58 Beke, "On the countries south of Abyssinia," pp. 257–8. See also Cecchi, *Da Zeila*, vol. II, p 164.
59 Among others see de Salviac, *Les Gallas*, p. 191; Shaykh Bakri Sapalo, "Kitāb irsāl," unpublished MS, pp. 44–5; Trimingham, *Islam in Ethiopia*, p. 261; *Journal of Isenberg and Krapf*, pp. 39–40; Bartels, *Oromo Religion*, p. 240.
60 L. Traversi, "Escursione nel Gimma," *Bolletina della Società Geografica Italiana*, 6, 1: (1888), p. 914; see also the Jimma Interview Programme, folios 4, 27, 52–3.
61 Cecchi, *Da Zeila*, vol. II, p. 206.
62 *Ibid.*, p. 515.
63 *Ibid.*
64 e.g., Abir, *Ethiopia*, p. 86. "A wakia of musk (about thirty-two grammes) was sold in Enarea for one-fifth of a thaler, fetched over a thaler in Massaw and two thalers in Cairo." According to Antoine d'Abbadie, Nouv. Acq. Fran. no. 21300, folio 572, "Even during the rainy season. when commercial activities were at their lowest in the Gibe region, up to 4,000 wakia of musk was sold in Saqqa, the capital of Limmu-Ennarya."
65 Merga, "Senna Umatta Oromo," pp. 140–1. See also the Jimma Interview Programme, folio 24.
66 Cecchi, *Da Zeila*, vol. II, p. 277.
67 *Ibid.*; see also the Manuscript of Abba Jobir Abba Dula, p. 14.
68 See above, p. 64.
69 I have drawn on Fritz M. Heichelheim, *An Ancient Economic History*, vol. I, trans. Joyce Stevens and A. W. Sijthoff (Leyden: 1968), pp. 52–3.
70 For a general description of slavery in the Ethiopian region, see Richard Pankhurst, *Economic History of Ethiopia 1800–1935* (Addis Ababa: 1968), pp. 73–93.
71 Cecchi, *Da Zeila*, vol. II, p. 289.
72 Merga, "Senna Umatta Oromo," pp. 140–1.
73 *Ibid.*
74 The Jimma Interview Programme, folio 35.

75 Cecchi, *Da Zeila*, vol. II, pp. 291–2.

76 *Ibid.*

77 *Ibid.*, p. 277.

78 Tasaw Merga seems to have been greatly influenced by F. Engels's book, *The Origin of the Family*.

79 See, for instance, R. Pankhurst, *Economic History*, pp. 73–93.

80 Cecchi, *Da Zeila*, vol. II, p. 276.

81 Merga, "Senna Umatta Oromo," pp. 140–1.

82 Cecchi, *Da Zeila*, vol. II, pp. 273–4, 292–3. See also the Jimma Interview Programme, folios 5, 8, 35, 53.

83 Cecchi, *Da Zeila*, vol. II, p. 292.

84 *Ibid.* Here Cecchi was referring to the condition of the slaves in the royal court of Gera, but it can be taken as representative of the general condition of slaves in the Gibe region. This is because he said more or less the same thing about the condition of slaves in Gomma, Gumma, Jimma, and Limmu-Ennarya. See, for instance, pp. 271–2, 276–7, 292–3.

85 According to the Jimma Interview Programme, folio 35, the royal slaves seem to have lived better lives than some poor peasants.

86 Cecchi, *Da Zeila*, vol. II, pp. 273–4.

87 Marc Bloch, *Slavery and Serfdom in the Middle Ages*, trans. by William R. Beer (London: 1975), p. 35.

88 Antoine d'Abbadie, "Les causes actuelles de l'esclavage en Ethiopie," *Revue des Questions Scientifiques* (1877), p. 410.

89 The Jimma Interview Programme, folios 34, 53.

90 Cecchi, *Da Zeila*, vol. II, p. 321.

91 Cerulli, *Etiopia occidentale*, vol. II, p. 77.

92 Massaja, *I miei trentacinque anni*, vol. IV, p. 151.

93 Antoine d'Abbadie, Nouv. Acq. Fran. no. 21300, folios 227–8.

94 *Ibid.*, folio 223.

95 *Ibid.*, folio 235.

96 Massaja, *Lettere e scritti minori*, vol. II, p. 360.

97 Cecchi, *Da Zeila*, vol. II, p. 517.

98 *Ibid.*, pp. 423–4.

99 *Ibid.*, p. 292

100 On the *gindo*, see pp. 169–70.

101 d'Abbadie, Nouv. Acq. Fran. no. 21300, folios 218–19, 710. *Idem*, "Causes actuelles de l'esclavage," pp. 413–14.

102 d'Abbadie, Nouv. Acq. Fran. no. 21300, folios 267–8. See also Massaja, *Lettere e scritti minori*, vol. II, p. 360.

103 Cerulli, "Folk literature of the Galla," p. 154.

104 Beke, "On the countries south of Abyssinia," p. 259.

105 Antoine d'Abbadie, Nouv. Acq. Fran. no. 21300, folios 218–19, 710. See also his "Causes actuelles de l'esclavage," pp. 414–15; Beke, "On the countries south of Abyssinia," p. 259.

106 See below, pp. 155–7.

107 d'Abbadie, Nouv. Acq. Fran. no. 21300, folio 233.

108 *Ibid.*, folio 225.

109 Beke, "On the countries south of Abyssinia," pp. 257–8.

110 Cecchi, *Da Zeila*, vol. II, p. 292.

111 The Jimma Interview Programme, folio 24.

112 *Ibid.*, folio 10. According to the same source, folios 1–2, tax was also paid in Maria Theresa thaler.

113 *Ibid.*, folios 2, 10, 21.

114 Cecchi, *Da Zeila*, vol. II, p. 282.

115 Antoine d'Abbadie, Nouv. Acq. Fran. no. 21300, folio 797.
116 Cecchi, *Da Zeila*, vol. II, p. 283.
117 The Jimma Interview Programme, folios 2, 27, 52–3.
118 Cecchi, *Da Zeila*, vol. II, pp. 282–3.
119 *Ibid.*
120 See below, p. 194.
121 The rest of the chapter will deal with the increase in industrial production, while the next chapter will be devoted to growth in trade and the spread of Islam.
122 Cecchi, *Da Zeila*, vol. II, p. 287.
123 See below, p. 170.
124 Cecchi, *Da Zeila*, vol. II, p. 289.
125 Bulcha, "Land ownership and social class formation among the Matcha," p. 28.
126 Lewis, *A Galla Monarchy*, p. 53. See also the Jimma Interview Programme, folio 2.
127 Our information on the artisans and craftsmen in the Gibe region mainly comes from the Oromo data which was gathered in the area.
128 The Jimma Interview Programme, folio 2; see also Merga, "Senna Umatta Oromo," pp. 140–1.
129 Lewis, *A Galla Monarchy*, p. 53.
130 Cecchi, *Da Zeila*, vol. II, pp. 287–8.
131 According to the Jimma Interview Programme, folio 54, "All land where iron was mined belonged either to the king or his provincial governors, or wealthy dignitaries."
132 Cecchi, *Da Zeila*, vol. II, pp. 287–8. See also the Jimma Interview Programme, *ibid.*
133 Hassen, "The Oromo of Ethiopia," pp. 197–8.
134 The Jimma Interview Programme, folio 54.
135 Female slaves wore only leather dress, while male slaves wore either leather dress or cheap quality locally manufactured cotton clothes.
136 Cecchi, *Da Zeila*, vol. II, p. 289.
137 *Ibid.*, pp. 289–90. See also Antoine d'Abbadie, *The Athenaeum: Journal of Literature, Science and the Fine Arts* no. 1042 (1847), pp. 1077–8.
138 See below, pp. 167–70.
139 Massaja, *In Abissinia*, p. 188.
140 Cecchi, *Da Zeila*, vol. II, pp. 290–1.
141 Beke, "On the countries south of Abyssinia," pp. 258–9.

5 Trade and the spread of Islam

1 See for instance, Tamrat, *Church and State in Ethiopia*, p. 88.
2 Arab Faqih, *Futuh al-Habasha* (Arabic text), p. 209.
3 *Ibid.* (Arabic text), p. 309.
4 Sarsa Dengel ruled from 1563 to 1597.
5 Almeida, "The history of High Ethiopia," p. 85.
6 E.g. Pereira, *Chronica de Susenyos*, p. 209.
7 Almeida, "The history of High Ethiopia," p. 149.
8 Susenyos was converted to Catholicism in 1622, thus cementing his amicable relationship with the Portuguese missionaries at his court.
9 See above, pp. 90–1.
10 Pereira, *Chronica de Susenyos*, pp. 38–9.
11 The Jimma Interview Programme, folios 8, 33.
12 Beke, "On the countries south of Abyssinia," p. 259.
13 Grühl, *The Citadel*, p. 146.
14 The Jimma Interview Programme, folio 55.

15 N. Pearce, *Life and Adventures in Abyssinia*, Introduction by Dr. R. Pankhurst (London: 1980), vol. II, pp. 8–9.
16 Beke, *Letters on the Commerce*, p. 15.
17 *Ibid.*, p. 16.
18 Beke, *Letters on the Commerce*, p. 15.
19 See below, pp. 185–7, 192–3.
20 Beke, "On the countries south of Abyssinia," p. 260.
21 Grühl, *The Citadel*, pp. 171–3.
22 Cecchi, *Da Zeila*, vol. II, pp. 507–19.
23 Antoine d'Abbadie, Nouv. Acq. Fran. no. 21300, folio 357.
24 *Ibid.*
25 Merga, "Senna Umatta Oromo," p. 143. See also the Jimma Interview Programme, folio 33.
26 Antoine d'Abbadie, Nouv. Acq. Fran. no. 21300, folios 314, 349.
27 Beke, *Letters on the Commerce*, p. 21.
28 Ege, "Chiefs and peasants," p. 49.
29 Beke, "On the countries south of Abyssinia," p. 259.
30 Bruce, *Travels to Discover*, vol. III, pp. 243–5.
31 Abir, "Southern Ethiopia," p. 126.
32 d' Abbadie, Nouv. Acq. Fran. no. 21300, folio 633.
33 Bartels, "Studies of the Galla in Wallaga," p. 139.
34 Cerulli, "Folk literature of the Galla," p. 146.
35 Antoine d'Abbadie, Nouv. Acq. Fran no. 21303, folio 360.
36 *Ibid.*, folio 254.
37 *Ibid.*, folios 360, 363.
38 Abir, "Southern Ethiopia," p. 127.
39 Antoine d'Abbadie, *The Athenaeum*, no. 1041 (1847), pp. 1056–8. According to this source caravan traveling sometimes took more than eight weeks.
40 The Jimma Interview Programme, folios 52–3.
41 Antoine d'Abbadie, *The Athenaeum*, no. 21300, folio 386.
42 Beke, *Letters on the Commerce*, pp. 24–5.
43 Oral literature is silent on this aspect.
44 de Salviac, *Les Galla*, p. 314. See also the Jimma Interview Programme, folio 56.
45 Cecchi, *Da Zeila*, vol. II, pp. 507–19.
46 See below, pp. 164–5.
47 *The Journal of Isenburg and Krapf*, p. 14.
48 *Ibid.*
49 R. Pankhurst, *Economic History of Ethiopia*, p. 445.
50 e.g. d'Abbadie, Nouv. Acq. Fran. no. 21303, folio 287.
51 Beke, *Letters on the Commerce*, pp. 15–16.
52 *Idem*, "On the countries south of Abyssinia," p. 259.
53 Abir, *Ethiopia*, p. 85. See also the Jimma Interview Programme, folios 10, 57–8.
54 Massaja, *Lettere e scritti minori*, vol. II, p. 372.
55 Merga, "Senna Umatta Oromo," pp. 143–4. See also Antoine d'Abbadie, Nouv. Acq. Fran. no. 21300, folio 205.
56 d'Abbadie, Nouv. Acq. Fran. no. 21303, folios 287, 317, 357.
57 *Ibid.*, folios 219, 393. See also his no. 21300, folios 797–800; Beke, "On the countries south of Abyssinia," pp. 257–9.
58 Grühl, *The Citadel*, p. 146.
59 See below, pp. 188–9.
60 d'Abbadie, Nouv. Acq. Fran., no. 21300, folio 589.
61 Abir, "Southern Ethiopia," p. 127.

62 *Ibid.*

63 Abir, *Ethiopia*, p. 91.

64 See below, pp. 191–2.

65 Abir, *Ethiopia*, p. 92.

66 d'Abbadie, Nouv. Acq. Fran. no. 21300, folios 799–800.

67 Massaja, *Lettere e scritti minori*, vol. II, p. 372.

68 See below, pp. 186–7.

69 Massaja, *In Abissinia*, pp. 283–4.

70 Merga, "Senna Umatta Oromo," p. 144.

71 *Ibid.*, pp. 144–5.

72 *Ibid.* See also Jimma Interview Programme, folios 6, 14, 22, 33–4.

73 Merga, "Senna Umatta Oromo," p. 144.

74 Cerulli, *Ethiopia occidentale*, vol. II, pp. 78–9.

75 Abir, *Ethiopia*, p. 83. See also Cecchi, *De Zeila*, vol. II, pp. 256, 259, 412–13, 527.

76 *Ibid.*, p. 167.

77 Merga, "Senna Umatta Oromo," p. 144.

78 Lewis, *A Galla Monarchy*, p. 95.

79 *Ibid.*; see also Merga, "Senna Umatta Oromo," pp. 145–6.

80 The Jimma Interview Programme, folios 9, 52.

81 Merga, "Senna Umatta Oromo," p. 145.

82 The Jimma Interview Programme, folio 56.

83 Abir, *Ethiopia*, p. 81, citing Cecchi, *Da Zeila*, vol. II, p. 228, footnote 1; Antoine d'Abbadie, Nouv. Acq. Fran. no. 21302, folios 389–90, 411–12. *Idem*, no. 21303, folios 112–13. *Idem, Geographie de l'Ethiopie*, p. 22 (Preface). See also Lewis, *A Galla Monarchy*, pp. 108–9; Merga, "Senna Umatta Oromo," p. 145.

84 d'Abbadie, Nouv. Acq. Fran. no. 21300, folio 189.

85 Merga, "Senna Umatta Oromo," p. 136. See also d'Abbadie, Nouv. Acq. Fran. no. 21302, folios 420, 425; Massaja, *I miei trentacinque anni*, vol. IV, p. 145; Abir, *Ethiopia*, p. 84.

86 d'Abbadie, Nouv. Acq. Fran. no. 21300, folios 189–90.

87 Merga, "Senna Umatta Oromo," pp. 143–4.

88 d'Abbadie, Nouv. Acq. Fran. no. 21300, folios 189–90.

89 Cecchi, *Da Zeila*, vol. II, p. 298.

90 The two centers of trade in the capitals of the Gibe states, one for elite goods and the other for ordinary goods, had some similarity with the market of Whydah in Dahomey, which was beautifully described by Rosemary Arnold in the article "A port of trade: Whydah on the Guinea coast," in *Trade and Market in the Early Empires; Economics in History and Theory*, eds. K. Polanyi, C. M. Arensberg and H. W. Pearson (Illinois: 1957), pp. 155–85.

91 R. Pankhurst, *Economic History of Ethiopia*, p. 351.

92 Abir, *Ethiopia*, pp. 44–6, citing Rochet d'Héricourt, *Second Voyage* (Paris: 1846), p. 261 Harris, *The Highlands of Aethiopia*, vol. II, p. 170.

93 R. Pankhurst, *Economic History of Ethiopia*, pp. 445–6. *Idem*, "Primitive money in Ethiopia," *Journal de la Société des Africanistes* (1963): 213–47. See also his *Introduction to the Economic History of Ethiopia*, pp. 260–6.

94 Abir, *Ethiopia*, p. 48; see also P. V. A. Ferret and J. G. Galinier, *Voyage en Abyssinie* (Paris: 1847), vol. I, p. 453, vol. II, p. 9; Harris, *The Highlands of Aethiopia*, vol. I, pp. 376–7, 379; C Johnston, *Travels in Southern Abyssinia* (London: 1844), vol. II, p. 248; C. T. Lefebvre *Voyage en Abyssinie executé pendant les annees 1839, 1840, 1841, 1842, 1843* (Paris: 1845–51) vol. II, Appendix Mer Rouge, p. 82.

95 The Jimma Interview Programme, folios 10, 21, 58.

96 d'Abbadie, Nouv. Acq. Fran. no. 21303, folio 357.

97 d'Abbadie, Nouv. Acq. Fran. no. 21301, folios 116–17.

98 R. Pankhurst, *Economic History of Ethiopia*, p. 521.
99 The Jimma Interview Programme, folios 52, 56.
100 Lewis, *A Galla Monarchy*, p. 55.
101 For a description of similar markets, see Francisco Benet, "Explosive markets: the Berber highlands," in *Trade and Market in the Early Empires*, p. 197.
102 Cerulli, *Etiopia occidentale*, vol. II, pp. 83–4, translation by H. S. Lewis; *ibid.*, p. 55.
103 d'Abbadie, Nouv. Acq. Fran. no. 21303, folios 287, 360.
104 Abir, *Ethiopia*, p. 44.
105 Beke, *Letters on the Commerce*, p. 27.
106 d'Abbadie, Nouv. Acq. Fran. no. 21300, folio 218.
107 R. Pankhurst, *Economic History of Ethiopia*, p. 363.
108 d'Abbadie, Nouv. Acq. Fran. no. 21300, folios 218 and 236.
109 Beke, *Letters on the Commerce*, p. 23.
110 *Ibid.*, p. 21. See also d'Abbadie, Nouv. Acq. Fran. no. 21300, folio 388.
111 Abir, *Ethiopia*, pp. 86–7. See also Cecchi, *Da Zeila*, vol. II, p. 516; J. Borelli, *Ethiopie meridionale* (Paris: 1890), pp. 344–6, 361.
112 Cecchi, *Da Zeila*, vol. II, p. 31. See also the Jimma Interview Programme, folio 27.
113 d'Abbadie, Nouv. Acq. Fran. no. 21300, folio 569.
114 Abir, *Ethiopia*, p. 88. See also Beke, *Letters on the Commerce*, p. 33.
115 See, for instance, Shaykh Ahmad Abdullahi Rirash, *Kashf as Sudul as Sumal wa Hamalikahum as-sabca* ("The Uncovering of Somali History and Their Seven Kingdoms") (Mogadishu: 1974), pp. 36–67.
116 Hassen, "The Oromo of Ethiopia," pp. 113–16.
117 Braukamper, "Islamic principalities in southeast Ethiopia," pp. 27–8.
118 The Jimma Interview Programme, folio 33. See also Cerulli, *Etiopia occidentale*, vol. II, p. 130.
119 The Jimma Interview Programme, folio 35.
120 *Ibid.*, folio 55. See also Massaja, *In Abissinia*, pp. 279, 282–8; *idem, I miei trentacinque anni*, vol. IV, p. 79.
121 Cerulli, *Etiopia occidentale*, vols. I and II, p. 93.
122 Trimingham, *Islam in Ethiopia*, p. 272.
123 Beckingham and Huntingford, in *Some Records of Ethiopia*, pp. lxxxi, lxxxvi.
124 Massaja, *In Abissinia*, p. 279. See also d'Abbadie, *Athenaeum*, no. 1042, p. 1077.
125 e.g. Crummey, "European religious mission in Ethiopia," p. 361.
126 Massaja, *I miei trentacinque anni*, vol. IV, p. 10.
127 Trimingham, *Islam in Ethiopia*, p. 258.
128 Lange, *History of Southern Gonga*, pp. 20, 23, 25.
129 Trimingham, *Islam in Ethiopia*, p. 269.
130 *Ibid.*, p. 271.
131 Massaja, *In Abissinia*, p. 284.
132 d'Abbadie, *Athenaeum*, no. 1042, p. 1078.
133 The Manuscript of Abba Jobir, pp. 8–9.
134 On the *butta* ceremony and *gerarsa* poems recited at this time, see the Introduction, pp. 12–13.
135 The Manuscript of Abba Jobir, pp. 8–9.
136 *Ibid.*
137 Trimingham, *Islam in Ethiopia*, p. 272.
138 *Ibid.*, pp. 262, 272, 274.
139 *Ibid.*, p. 263.
140 See below, pp. 158–9.
141 d'Abbadie, *Athenaeum*, no. 1042, p. 1077.

142 d'Abbadie, Nouv. Acq. Fran. no. 21300, folios 788–90.
143 *Ibid.*
144 The Jimma Interview Programme, folios 26–7.
145 The Jimma Interview Programme, folios 5, 21.
146 Massaja, *In Abissinia*, p. 284.
147 Harris, *The Highlands of Aethiopia*, vol. III, pp. 53–5.
148 J. S. Trimingham, *The Influence of Islam upon Africa* (London: 1980), p. 43.
149 *Ibid.* See also his *Islam in West Africa* (Oxford: 1959), p. 36.
150 The Jimma Interview Programme, folios 26–7.
151 The Jimma Interview Programme, folios 6, 26–7.
152 *Ibid.*
153 Harris, *The Highlands of Aethiopia*, vol. III, p. 54.
154 Massaja, *In Abissinia*, p. 284.
155 Cecchi, *Da Zeila*, vol. II, p. 160.
156 Trimingham, *Islam in Ethiopia*, p. 201.
157 Cecchi, *Da Zeila*, vol. II, p. 239; see also J. S. Trimingham, *ibid.*, p. 200.
158 Cecchi, *Ibid.*
159 Cecchi, *Da Zeila*, vol. II, p. 239. Translation by Huntingford in *Some Records of Ethiopia*, Preface, p. lxxxix.
160 Anonymous, *Rabi-al-Qulub* (Cairo: 1927), pp. 13–23 *et passim*. This is an Arabic book which deals with the life history and miracles of Shaykh Hussein of Bale.
161 The Jimma Interview Programme, folios 34, 59.
162 Cerulli, *Studi Etiopici*, vol. I, p. 44; see also Trimingham, *Islam in Ethiopia*, p. 240.
163 The Qadiriya traces its origin to the Baghdad Sufi and jurist Abd al-Qadir al Jilani (470–561 A. H. – 1077/8–1166 A. D.). In Harar the Qadiriya claimed that Abd al-Qadir himself miraculously flew to Harar, where he died and was buried. There is a mosque in his name, and his tomb at Qorobe Limay, in the southwestern part of the city of Harar, is one of the holy places of the city. See E. Wagner, "Eine liste der Heiligen von Harar," *Zeitschrift der Deutschen Morgenländischen Gesellschaft:* 23, 2 (1973): 274. According to Trimingham, *ibid.*, 234, the order is said to have been brought to Harar by a Sharif Abu Bakr Ibn Abd Allah al-Idarus (or Aydarus) called al-Qutb or Rabbani (the divine axis) who died at Aden in A. H. 909 (A. D. 1503).
164 The Jimma Interview Programme, folio 3.
165 Cerulli, *Etiopia occidentale*, vol. II, p. 96.
166 Cecchi, *Da Zeila*, vol. II, p. 239.
167 Cerulli, *ibid.*
168 Harris, *The Highlands of Aethiopia*, vol. III, p. 60.
169 Trimingham, *Islam in Ethiopia*, p. 272.
170 Cecchi, *Da Zeila*, vol. II, p. 240.
171 *Ibid.*
172 A. d'Abbadie, Nouv. Acq. Fran. no. 21300, folio 206, states that the spirit of proselytization among the Muslims was strong and that Abba Bagibo encouraged and compensated those Christians who changed their religion.
173 *Ibid.*, folios 633–5.
174 The affirmation that there is only one God – Allah – and that Muhammad is his last and final messenger.
175 The five daily prayers, which are fundamental obligations for a believer.
176 Fasting once a year during the holy month of Ramadan.
177 The donation of alms to the poor.
178 The pilgrimage to Mecca and Medina, which is obligatory only for those who can afford it, once in a lifetime.

179 See below, p. 158.
180 d'Abbadie, Nouv. Acq. Fran. no. 21302, folios 126–7.
181 d'Abbadie, Nouv. Acq. Fran. no. 21300, folios 788–90.
182 Cecchi, *Da Zeila*, vol. II, p. 291.
183 The Jimma Interview Programme, folio 27.
184 Lewis, *A Galla Monarchy*, pp. 41–2.
185 Interview with Abba Jobir Abba Dula, Mecca (Saudi Arabia), June 13, 1982.
186 *Ibid.* See also the Jimma Interview Programme, folio 60.
187 Massaja, *I miei trentacinque anni*, vol. VI, p. 10.
188 *Ibid.*
189 The Manuscript of Abba Jobir Abba Dula, pp. 33–4.
190 The mosque of Abba Boka, which is still found in the city of Jimma, is said to have been the first to be built in that country. The writer had visited the said mosque several times during his stay in Jimma in 1974/5.
191 Lewis, *A Galla Monarchy*, p. 43.
192 The Manuscript of Abba Jobir Abba Dula, p. 11.
193 Cerulli, *Etiopia occidentale*, vol. II, pp. 95–6.
194 Cerulli, "Folk literature of the Galla," p. 20.
195 The Manuscript of Abba Jobir, p. 11.
196 Cerulli, *Etiopia occidentale*, vol. II, p. 95.
197 *Ibid.*, p. 24.
198 *Ibid.*
199 e.g., The Manuscript of Abba Jobir, p. 40.
200 Cerulli, *Etiopia occidentale*, vol. II, pp. 95–6.
201 Beke, "On the countries south of Abessinia," pp. 258–9.
202 According to the "Chronicle of the Kingdom of Gumma" the first Muslim king of the land "abolished the festival of butta." See Cerulli, "Folk literature of the Galla," p. 154.
203 Cecchi, *Da Zeila*, vol. II, pp. 268–9. See also Trimingham, *Islam in Ethiopia*, p. 202.
204 Cerulli, "Folk literature of the Galla," p. 46.
205 *Ibid.*, p. 52.
206 Abba Rago died before accepting Islam though many Muslim teachers, preachers, and traders were said to have been active at his court.
207 Massaja, *I miei trentacinque anni*, vol. III, p. 34.
208 Cecchi, *Da Zeila*, vol. II, p. 267.
209 *Ibid.*, pp. 268–9.
210 *Ibid.*, pp. 305–6.
211 Cerulli, *Etiopia occidentale*, vol. II, p. 94.
212 e.g., The Manuscript of Abba Jobir Abba Dula, pp. 34–41. See also the Jimma Interview Programme, folios 8, 61.

6 The era of Abba Bagibo, 1825–1861

1 A. Cecchi, *Da Zeila*, vol. II, pp. 157, 173. See also Massaja, *Lettere e scritti minori*, vol. II, pp. 371–2.
2 See above, p. 4.
3 Bahrey, "History of the Galla," p. 113.
4 Three other Gibe states namely, Gumma, Gomma, and Jimma invented legends which glorify their dynastic origin.
5 Huntingford in *Some Records of Ethiopia*, Preface, p. lxi; see also Bieber, *Kaffa*, vol. II, pp. 510–11.
6 Huntingford, *ibid.*; see also Cecchi, *Da Zeila*, vol. II, p. 157.

7 Cecchi, *Da Zeila*, vol. II, p. 173.
8 All sources agree that Abba Bagibo was very handsome, fair in color, tall and well-built.
9 Antoine d'Abbadie, Nouv. Acq. Fran. no. 21300, folio 572.
10 Massaja, *Lettere e scritti minori*, vol. II, p. 372.
11 Abba Bagibo married another wife, the daughter of Kamo, the reigning king of Kaffa in 1843. In other words, Abba Bagibo married two wives from the ruling house of Kaffa.
12 Antoine d'Abbadie, Nouv. Acq. Fran. no. 21300, folio 572.
13 *The Journal of C. W. Isenberg and J. L. Krapf*, p. 14.
14 Beke, *Letters on the Commerce*, p. 15.
15 *The Journal of C. W. Isenberg and J. L. Krapf*, p. 14. See also Pankhurst, *Economic History of Ethiopia*, p. 445.
16 See above, pp. 139–40.
17 Massaja, *Lettere e scritti minori*, vol. II, p. 372.
18 d'Abbadie, Nouv. Acq. Fran. no. 21300, folio 199. See Abir, "The emergence and consolidation of the monarchies," vol. 6, p. 210. *Idem, Ethiopia*, p. 79.
19 Massaja, *Lettere e scritti minori*, vol. II, p. 372.
20 *The Journal of C. W. Isenberg and J. L. Krapf*, p. 14.
21 A. d'Abbadie, Nouv. Acq. Fran. no. 21300, folio 199; see also Abir, *Ethiopia*, p. 79, note 2.
22 See below, pp. 173–4, 189–91.
23 Cecchi, *Da Zeila*, vol. II, pp. 159–60.
24 Massaja, *I miei trentacinque anni*, vol. VI, pp. 16–17.
25 Massaja, *Lettere e scritti minori*, vol. II, p. 372.
26 *Ibid.*
27 *Ibid.*
28 See below, pp. 175–7.
29 See above, pp. 136–8.
30 J. L. Krapf, *Travels, Researches and Missionary Labours*, p. 64. See Harris, *The Highlands of Aethiopia*, vol. II, p. 53.
31 Abir, *Ethiopia*, p. 80.
32 Beke, "On the countries south of Abessinia," pp. 258–9.
33 d'Abbadie, *Géographie de l'Ethiopie*, p. 21.
34 d'Abbadie, *Athenaeum*, no. 1042, p. 1078.
35 d'Abbadie, Nouv. Acq. Fran. no. 21303, folio 220.
36 Cecchi, *Da Zeila*, vol. II, p. 158. See also Massaja, *In Abissinia*, pp. 158–9. Another *massera* on which we have adequate information is that of Jiren in Jimma.
37 Lewis, *A Galla Monarchy*, pp. 68–70.
38 The Jimma Interview Programme, folio 24.
39 Cecchi, *Da Zeila*, vol. II, p. 154.
40 Lewis, *A Galla Monarchy*, pp. 68–70.
41 Cerulli, *Etiopia occidentale*, vols. I and II, p. 120.
42 Lewis, *A Galla Monarchy*, pp. 68–72.
43 Cecchi, *Da Zeila*, vol. II, p. 158.
44 *Ibid.*
45 Massaja, *In Abissinia*, p. 159.
46 *Ibid.*, p. 283.
47 *Ibid.*, p. 160.
48 Cecchi, *Da Zeila*, vol. II, p. 158; see also Cerulli, *Etiopia occidentale* vols. I and II, p. 121
49 Cecchi, *Da Zeila*, vol. II, p. 381.
50 *Ibid.*, p. 158.
51 *Ibid.*, pp. 163, 166, 205.
52 *Ibid.*
53 See below, p. 191.

54 e.g., Lewis, *A Galla Monarchy*, p. 70.
55 *Ibid.*
56 Cecchi, *Da Zeila*, vol. II, p. 289.
57 *Ibid.*, p. 289. See also the Jimma Interview Programme, folio 2.
58 Cecchi, *Da Zeila*, vol. II, p. 290.
59 Beke, "On the countries south of Abessinia," pp. 258–9.
60 *Ibid.*, p. 295.
61 A. d'Abbadie, Nouv. Acq. Fran. no. 21300, folio 572.
62 Massaja, *Lettere e scritti minori*, vol. II, p. 372.
63 See below, pp. 177–8.
64 d'Abbadie, Nouv. Acq. Fran. no. 21300, folios 789–91.
65 The Jimma Interview Programme, folio 5.
66 Harris, *The Highlands of Aethiopia*, vol. III, p. 56.
67 A. d'Abbadie, Nouv. Acq. Fran. no. 21300, folios 718–19.
68 See above, pp. 7–8.
69 The Jimma Interview Programme, folio 5.
70 d'Abbadie, Nouv. Acq. Fran. no. 23851, folios 351–6.
71 Massaja, *In Abissinia*, p. 283 *et passim. Idem, I miei trentacinque anni*, vol. VI, p. 17 *et passim.*
72 d'Abbadie, Nouv. Acq. Fran. no. 10223, folio 34.
73 Harris, *The Highlands of Aethiopia*, vol. III, p. 56.
74 d'Abbadie, Nouv. Acq. Fran. no. 23851, folios 351–6.
75 Among others, see Crummey, "European religious missions in Ethiopia," pp. 358–61.
76 Krapf, *Travels, Researches and Missionary Labours*, p. 64.
77 See below, p. 173.
78 d'Abbadie, Nouv. Acq. Fran. no. 21300, folios 199–200.
79 Lewis, *A Galla Monarchy*, p. 72.
80 Abir, *Ethiopia*, p. 84
81 The Jimma Interview Programme, folio 30.
82 A. Cecchi, *Da Zeila*, vol. II, p. 159. See also Massaja, *Lettere e scritti minori*, vol. II, p. 372.
83 d'Abbadie, Nouv. Acq. Fran. no. 21300, folio 199.
84 Cecchi, *Da Zeila*, vol. II, p. 159.
85 *Ibid.* See also Massaja, *Lettere e scritti minori*, vol. II, p. 372.
86 See below, p. 191.
87 d'Abbadie, Nouv. Acq. Fran. no. 21300, folios 199–200. "Since there was not enough water in the river to drown the men, they dug a hole into which they put the heads of the guilty until they suffocated. They then buried all three in a trench next to it."
88 d'Abbadie, Nouv. Acq. Fran. no. 21300, folios 189–91.
89 Cecchi, *Da Zeila*, vol. II, p. 153.
90 See below, p. 197.
91 Beke, "On the countries south of Abessinia," p. 258.
92 Harris, *The Highlands of Aethiopia*, vol. III, p. 54.
93 A. d'Abbadie, Nouv. Acq. Fran. no. 21303, folios 622–3. *Idem, Athenaeum*, no. 1041, p. 1057.
94 Harris, *The Highlands of Aethiopia*, vol. III, pp. 54–5.
95 See below, p. 192.
96 Abir, *Ethiopia*, p. 90. See also d'Abbadie, Nouv. Acq. Fran. no. 21303, folio 218; Massaja, *I miei trentacinque anni*, vol. IV, p. 144; Rochet d'Héricourt, *Voyage sur la côte orientale*, pp. 223–4.
97 See, for instance, Krapf, *Travels, Researches and Missionary Labours*, pp. 64–5.
98 Plowden, *Travels in Abyssinia and the Galla Country*, pp. 305–6.
99 According to Antoine d'Abbadie, Nouv. Acq. Fran. no. 21300, folio 784, the land of Gudru was densely populated and they had *c*. 15,000 cavalry, altogether 64,000 warriors.
100 See above, p. 96.

101 Plowden, *Travels in Abyssinia and the Galla Country*, pp. 306–7.
102 d'Abbadie, Nouv. Acq. Fran. no. 21300, folio 784.
103 See for instance Fantahun Birhane, "Gojjam 1800–1855," B. A. thesis, Haile Sellassie I University, Addis Ababa, 1973, p. 14.
104 Harris, *The Highlands of Aethiopia*, vol. III, p. 55.
105 Bibliothèque Nationale catalogue des manuscrits Ethiopiens de la collection Antoine d'Abbadie 249, Ethiopien Abbade 249. Traduction litteral faite sur la version Arabe, de la lettre Ilmorma d'Abba Bagibo roi d'Enarea au dejasmatch goschou prince de Gojam, Damot et Agoo. See the Preface to the translated version.
106 *Ibid.*, 249.
107 *Ibid.*
108 Manuscrits Ethiopiens de la collection Antoine d'Abbadie, 249, folios 1–2.
109 e.g., Harris, *The Highlands of Aethiopia*, vol. III, p. 55.
110 Manuscrits Ethiopiens de la collection Antoine d'Abbadie, 249, folio 2.
111 See above, p. 163.
112 Birhane, "Gojjam 1800–1855," p. 16.
113 Harris, *The Highlands of Aethiopia*, vol. III, p. 55.
114 Goshu himself was of Oromo origin and he won decisive battles in his rise to power with Oromo cavalry. He spoke the Oromo language and also indulged in secret correspondence with Arnauld d'Abbadie in the same language. See, for instance, Birhane, "Gojjam 1800–1855," pp. 6, 12 and also Appendix no. 1, Document no. 4.
115 d'Abbadie, Nouv. Acq. Fran. no. 21303, folio 231. See also Beke, "On the countries south of Abyssinia," pp. 259–60.
116 Sahle Sellassie's expansion in Shawa in the late 1830s and early 1840s limited the scope of Abba Bagibo's influence and political control in the region of Soddo.
117 See below, pp. 197–200.
118 The manuscript of Abba Jobir Abba Dula, p. 33. See also the Jimma Interview Programme, folio 51.
119 See above, p. 139–41.
120 See below, p. 186.
121 Antoine d'Abbadie, *Géographie de l'Ethiopia*, pp. 79–80.
122 *Idem*, Nouv Acq. Fran. no. 21300, folio 639. See also no. 21303, folio 639.
123 Harris, *The Highlands of Aethiopia*, vol. III, pp. 56–7.
124 d'Abbadie, Nouv. Acq. Fran. no. 21303, folio 289.
125 *Ibid.*
126 Antoine d'Abbadie, Nouv. Acq. Fran. no. 21300, folios 196–7.
127 Massaja, *I miei trentacinque anni*, vol. VI, p. 6.
128 d'Abbadie, Nouv, Acq. Fran. no. 21300, folios 196–7.
129 *Ibid.*
130 *Ibid.*
131 See below, p. 189.
132 Cecchi, *Da Zeila*, vol. II, p. 352.
133 d'Abbadie, Nouv. Acq. Fran. no. 21300, folio 797.
134 Cecchi, *Da Zeila*, vol. II, p. 352. See also Abir, *Ethiopia*, p. 92.
135 d'Abbadie, Nouv. Acq. Fran. no. 21300, folio, 797. See also Abir, *Ethiopia*, p. 92.
136 The Manuscript of Abba Jobir Abba Dula, p. 33.
137 *Ibid.*
138 Lewis, *A Galla Monarchy*, p. 41.
139 *Ibid.*, p. 42. See also Cecchi, *Da Zeila*, vol. II, p. 541.
140 The Manuscript of Abba Jobir, *ibid.*
141 Massaja, *Lettere e scritti minori*, vol. III, p. 24.

142 *Ibid.* See also *idem, I miei trentacinque anni,* vol. VI, p. 6.
143 The Jimma Interview Programme, folios 7, 9, 11.
144 Massaja, *Lettere e scritti minori,* vol. III, p. 24.
145 *Ibid.*
146 The Jimma Interview Programme, folio 11.
147 The Manuscript of Abba Jobir, p. 33.
148 See above, p. 160.
149 Massaja, *Lettere e scritti minori,* vol. II, p. 371.
150 Massaja, *In Abissinia,* p. 160.
151 Beke, "On the countries south of Abyssinia," p. 260.
152 Abir, *Ethiopia,* p. 91, citing d'Abbadie, *Athenaeum* no. 10427, p. 1847.
153 Abir, *ibid.,* p. 92; see also Beke, "On the countries south of Abyssinia."
154 See below, p. 194.
155 Abir, *Ethiopia,* p. 92.
156 According to one recently published piece of information, the king had as many as twenty
    wives. See Massaja, *Lettere e scritti minori,* vol. II, p. 372.
157 See, for instance, Grühl, *The Citadel,* p. 173.
158 d'Abbadie, Nouv. Acq. Fran. no. 21302, folio 420.
159 Harris, *The Highlands of Aethiopia,* vol. III, p. 315. See also Abir, *Ethiopia,* p. 164.
160 Massaja, *Lettere e scritti minori,* vol. II, p. 372.
161 d'Abbadie, Nouv. Acq. Fran. no. 21300, folio 740.
162 *Ibid.,* folios 654–5.
163 See above, pp. 139–40.
164 Antoine d'Abbadie, Nouv. Acq. Fran. no. 21300, folio 714. *Idem,* no. 23851, folios 588–9.
165 Abir, *Ethiopia,* p. 91.
166 d'Abbadie, *ibid.,* no. 21300, folio 639.
167 Beke, "On the countries south of Abyssinia," p. 260.
168 d'Abbadie, Nouv. Acq. Fran. no. 21300, folio 639.
169 *Ibid.,* folio 186.
170 *Idem,* no. 21303, folio 641.
171 *Ibid.,* folio 639.
172 By 1842, the king of Shawa had already gathered more than 1,000 muskets, half of which were
    in good working order. In addition he had several pieces of cannon which were carefully
    looked after by the king's armorers, gun makers, and smiths. See, for instance, *The Journal of
    C. W. Isenberg and J. L. Krapf,* p. 344; Abir, *Ethiopia,* p. 176.
173 Krapf, *Travels, Researches and Missionary Labours,* p. 31. See also Rochet d'Héricourt,
    Voyage sur la côte orientale, pp. 285–6.
174 Abir, *Ethiopia,* pp. 90–1. See also d'Abbadie, *Géographie d'Ethiopie,* p. 97.
175 See below, pp. 191–2.
176 Sahle Sellassie died in 1847, and his death triggered off a wave of rebellion in Shawa itself.
177 Antoine d'Abbadie, Nouv. Acq. Fran. no. 21300, folios 797–8.
178 *Ibid.*
179 Massaja, *I miei trentacinque anni,* vol. IV, p. 83.
180 Cecchi, *Da Zeila,* vol. II, p. 160.
181 Massaja, *I miei trentacinque anni,* vol. IV, pp. 82–3.
182 *Ibid.*
183 Massaja, *Lettere e scritti minori,* vol. II, p. 373.
184 Massaja, *I miei trentacinque anni,* vol. IV, p. 84.
185 Antoine d'Abbadie, Nouv. Acq. Fran. no. 21300, folios 797–8.
186 Massaja, *Lettere e scritti minori,* vol. II, p. 373.
187 *Ibid.*

188 Antoine d'Abbadie, Nouv. Acq. Fran. no. 21300, folios 797–8.
189 The sudden death of the wife of Abba Dula and his only son seems to have persuaded the crown prince to plan the elimination of his father.
190 d'Abaddie, Nouv. Acq. Fran. no. 21300, folios 797–8.
191 Cecchi, *Da Zeila*, vol. II, p. 160. The crown prince had a deep hole dug, in which sharp spears were kept, under the place where the king was supposed to sit alone in the evening of the wedding-day and the hole was covered with carpets. The spears were erected upright with sharp sides to kill the king. The hole was to be the king's grave. One of the slaves of the crown prince who dug the hole went and told the king.
192 Cecchi, *Da Zeila*, vol. II, p. 160. See also Massaja, *I miei trentacinque anni*, vol. IV, p. 84. *Idem, Lettere e scritti minori*, vol. II, pp. 372–3.
193 Massaja, *I miei trentacinque anni*, vol. IV, p. 84.
194 *Ibid.*
195 Antoine d'Abbadie, Nouv. Acq. Fran. no. 21300, folios 797–8.
196 *Ibid.*
197 Massaja, *I miei trentacinque anni*, vol. IV, p. 84.
198 Cecchi, *Da Zeila*, vol. II, p. 172.
199 *Ibid.*
200 *Ibid.*
201 Antoine d'Abbadie, Nouv. Acq. Fran. no. 21300, folios 797–8.
202 Cecchi, *Da Zeila*, vol. II, pp. 157, 160.
203 d'Abbadie, *ibid.*, p. 797.
204 *Ibid.*, p. 799.
205 Massaja, *Lettere e scritti minori*, vol. III, pp. 33–4.
206 Antoine d'Abbadie, Nouv. Acq. Fran. no. 21300, folio 799.
207 *Ibid.* See also his *Géographie d'Ethiopie*, p. 101.
208 Massaja, *In Abissinia*, p. 160.
209 See above, pp. 142–3.
210 Abir, *Ethiopia*, p. 80.
211 Massaja, *I miei trentacinque anni*, vol. VI, p. 15. See also his *In Abissinia*, pp. 283–4.
212 Massaja, *I miei trentacinque anni*, vol. IV, p. 17.
213 *Ibid.*
214 Massaja, *Lettere e scritti minori*, vol. II, p. 381.
215 See below, p. 194.
216 According to the Jimma Interview Programme, folio 35, Abba Bagibo ruled for thirty-five years. However, "The History of the Matcha Kings" in *Mitteilungen des Seminars*, p. 181, claims that Abba Bagibo ruled for forty-two years.
217 Massaja, *I miei trentacinque anni*, vol. IV, p. 14.
218 Massaja, *In Abissinia*, p. 283.
219 Massaja, *I miei trentacinque anni*, vol. IV, p. 17.

Epilogue

1 Massaja, *In Abissinia*, pp. 283–4.
2 Grühl, *The Citadel*, p. 146.
3 Ta'a, "The political economy of western central Ethiopia," p. 129.
4 Addis Hiwet, *Ethiopia: From Autocracy to Revolution* (London: 1975), p. 5.
5 H. G. Marcus, *The Life and Times of Menelik II of Ethiopia 1844–1913* (Oxford: 1975), p. 44.
6 E. J. Hobsbawn, *Industry and Empire* (Penguin Books, reprinted 1971), p. 310. See also Walter Rodney, *How Europe Underdeveloped Africa* (Howard University Press, Washington, D.C.: 1982), p. 186.

7 Hiwet, *Ethiopia: From Autocracy to Revolution*, p. 4.

8 This is summarized from Mohammed Hassen, "The Oromo nation under Amhara colonial administration: past and present and Oromo resistance to colonial oppression," 1981, unpublished MS., p. 3.

9 Menelik was imprisoned by Tewodros for ten years.

10 Bairu Tafla, "Three Portraits: Ato Asma Giyorgis, Ras Gobana Daci and Sahafi Tezaz Gebra Selassie," *Journal of Ethiopian Studies* 5 (2) (1967): 145. See also Cecchi, *Da Zeila*, vol. II, p. 161.

11 Hassen, "The Oromo nation under Amhara colonial administration," p. 17.

12 *Ibid.*, pp. 16–18.

13 I am deeply indebted to my friend Tamene Bitima for providing me with this information and other rich Oromo oral literature which he recorded, translated, and published recently.

14 Ta'a, "The political economy of western central Ethiopia," p. 159.

15 *Ibid.*

16 Getahun Delibo, "Emperor Menelik's Ethiopia 1865–1916: national unification or Amhara communal domination," Ph.D. dissertation, Howard University, 1974, p. 81.

17 Bairu Tafla, "Three Portraits," p. 148.

18 Delibo, "Emperor Menelik's Ethiopia," p. 82.

19 Hassen, "The Oromo nation under Amhara colonial administration," p. 20.

20 It is not far-fetched to assume that Gobana's personal ambition and energetic campaign to quicken the pace of the conquest was because he wanted to be king of the conquered Oromo territory under Menelik's suzerainty. However, Menelik was too clever to appoint Gobana king over the conquered Oromo territory.

21 Paul Baxter, "Ethiopia's unacknowledged problem: the Oromo," *African Affairs* (1978): 288.

Selected bibliography

Primary sources

Unpublished primary sources

1. The manuscript of Abba Jobir Abba Dula, the last king of Jimma Abba Jifar. This contains recent history, oral traditions, as well as fantastic legends of bygone ages. It is particularly strong on the history of four kings of Jimma Abba Jifar, who reigned between 1830 and 1932.
2. The manuscript of Shaykh Bakri Sapalo, entitled "Kitab Irsāl Al-sawarikh Ila Samā Al-tawarikh." This sketches an overall panorama of Oromo history from early times to the present. Although it is not free from major limitations on early Oromo history, it contains much useful data on the gada system.
3. Bakre's manuscript. Although this deals with the history of the Oromo briefly, its main thrust is the history of the Oromo in Wallaga. It depicts the struggle for power and traces the rise to power of, and the prominence of, the Bakre family in Wallaga.

Archival

Bibliothèque Nationale, Paris (Département des Manuscrits Orientaux, Nouvelles Acquisitions Françaises). Of the twenty-seven volumes which come under the heading of "The papers of Antoine and Arnauld d'Abbadie," the following contain notes, personal observations and oral information gathered by Antoine d'Abbadie during his travels in Ethiopia. It was these notes, personal observations, and oral information gathered in the Gibe region itself which were useful to me.

10,222	21,301	21,305	22,433	23,851
10,223	21,302	22,430	23,848	23,852
21,299	21,303	22,431	23,849	23,853
21,300	21,304	22,432	23,850	

Institut de France (TF)
MS 20 84, Correspondance, Observations 1839–42
Antoine d'Abbadie
Ordre des Frères Mineurs Capucins (MAE)
Manuscrit de la bibliothèque de la province de Paris 185: 28 Letter from Taurin de Cohogne, dated Harar, June 29, 1884.
  1970B Ethiopia
  Etats religieux, politiques, géographiques, etc.
  Antoine d'Abbadie

234

Bibliography

Published primary sources

Ethiopic, Amharic, Arabic, and others

Ameida, M. de. "The history of High Ethiopia or Abassia." *Some Records of Ethiopia 1593–1646*, trans. and eds. C. F. Beckingham and G. W. B. Huntingford. London, 1954 (The Hakluyt Society).

Al-'Umari, Ibn Fadl Allah. *Masalk Al-Absar fi Manalek el Amsar: L'Afrique Moins L'Egypte*, trans. M. Gaudefroy-Demonbynes. Paris, 1927.

Alvarez, F. *The Prester John of the Indies*, trans. Lord Stanley of Alderley, 1881, revised, eds. C. F. Beckingham and G. W. B. Huntingford, 2 vols. Cambridge, 1961 (The Hakluyt Society).

Arab, Faqih (Chihab Eddin B. Abdel Qadir). *Futuh Al-Habasha*, trans. and ed. R. Basset. Paris, 1897.

Bāhāyla, Mika'el. *Māshafā Mistirata – Sāmay Wāmidr*, trans. in part by J. Perruchon. *Patrologia Orientalis* 1 (1904):1–97. It was translated and edited in full by E. A. W. Budge, *The Book of the Mysteries of Heaven and Earth*. London, 1935.

Bahrey, "History of the Galla." In *Some Records of Ethiopia, 1593–1646*.

Basset, R. "Etudes sur l'histoire d'Ethiopie, Paris, 1882." *Journal Asiatique*, ser. 7, vol. 17 (1881).

Budge, E. A. W. *The Life and Miracles of Takla Haymanot*. London, 1906.

Cerulli, Enrico. "Documenti Arabi per la storia dell'Etiopia." *Memorie della Reale Accademia dei Lincei*, ser. 6, vol. 4 (1931):37–101.

"Il sultanato dello socio nel secolo XIII secondo un nuovo documento storico." *Rassegna di Studi Etiopici* 1 (1941):5–42.

"Gli emiri di Harar del secolo XVI alla conquista Egiziona" (1875). *Rassegna di Studi Etiopici* 2 (1942):1–20.

"L'Etiopia medievale in alcuni brandi de scrittori Arabi." *Rassegna di Studi Etiopici* 3 (1943):272–94.

Conti-Rossini, C. "La storia di Libna Dingil, re d'Etiopia." *Rendiconti della Reale Accademia de Lincei*, ser. 5, vol. 3 (1894):617–40.

"Historia regis Sarsa Dengel (Malak Sagad)," 2 vols. *Corpus Scriptorum Christianorum Orientalium Scriptores Aethiopici* 3 (1907):1–191.

"L'autobiograpfia di Pawlos Monaco Abissino del secolo XVI." *Rendiconti della Reale Accademia de Lincei*, ser. 5, vol. 27 (1918):279–96.

Conzelman, W. E. *La Chronique de Galawdewos, rai d'Ethiopie*. Paris, 1895.

Coquat, A. "Histoire Amharique de Gran et des Gallas." *Annales d'Ethiopie*. Addis Ababa, 1957 (Institut Ethiopien d'Archéologie).

Foster, William. *The Red Sea and the Adjacent Countries as Described by Joseph Pitts, William Daniel and Charles Poncet*. London, 1948 (The Hakluyt Society).

Fotti, C. "La cronoco abbreviato dei re d'Abissinia in un monoscritto di Dahra Berhan de Gondar." *Rassegna di Studi Etiopici* 1 (1941): 87–123.

Gabra, Sellassie. *Tarika Zemen Ze Dagmawe Menelik Nigusa Nagast Ze Ityopya*. Addis Ababa, 1965.

Guidi, Ignazio. "Historia gentis Galla," 2 vols. *Corpus Scriptorum Christianorum Orientalium* 3 (1907). Bound together with "Historia regis Sarsa Dengel (Malak Sagad)."

"Annales Johannis I, Iyasu I et Bakaffa," 4 vols. *Corpus Scriptorum Christianorum Orientalium* (1903–5).

"Annales regum Iyasu II et Iyo'as," 2 vols. *Corpus Scriptorum Christianorum Orientalium* 6 (1910–12).

"Storieri e brevi testi Amarici." *Mitteilungen des Seminars für Orientalische Sprachen* 10 (1907):167–84.

"Leggende storiche di Abissinia." *Rivista Degli Studi Orientali* 1 (1907):5–30.

"Due nuovi manoscritti della 'Cronoca Abbreviata' di Abissinia." *Rendiconta della Reale Accademia de Lincei*, ser. 6, vol. 2 (1926):357–421.

235

Bibliography

Haber, L. "The chronicle of Ba'eda Maryam (1468–78)." *Ethiopia Observer* 5 (1962):68–80.

Huntingford, G. W. B. *The Glorious Victories of Amda Siyon, King of Ethiopia.* Oxford, 1965.

"Arabic inscriptions in southern Ethiopia." *Antiquity* 29 (1955):230–3.

Ibn Haukal Muhammad. *Configuration de la terre,* trans. J. H. Kramer and G. Wiet, 2 vols. Paris, 1964.

Ibn Khaldun. *Histoire de Berbères et des dynasties Musulmanes de l'Afrique septentrionale,* trans, de Slane. Paris, 1927.

Leo Africanus. *The History and Description of Africa and of the Notable Things therein Contained,* written by Al-Hassan Ibn-Mohammed, Al-Wazeb Al-Forsi, better known as Leo Africanus, trans. John Pory, ed. R. Brown, 3 vols. London, 1896 (The Hakluyt Society, ser. 1, nos. 92, 93, and 94).

Maqrizi. *Historia Regum Islamitcorum in Abyssinia,* ed. and trans. F. T. Rinek. Leiden, 1790. (At the Library of the School of Oriental and African Studies there is an English translation from the Latin version of this work by G. W. B. Huntingford in typescript.)

Narazzini, C. *La Conquista Musulman dell'Etiopia nell Secolo XVI.* (Tradizione di un manuscritto Arabo, 1891.)

Pereira, F. M. E. *Historia de Minas, Rei de Ethiopia.* Lisbon, 1888.

Chronica de Susenyos, Rei de Ethiopia, 2 vols. Lisbon, 1892–1900.

Perruchon, J. "Histoire des guerres d'Amda-Seyon roi d'Ethiopie." *Journal Asiatique,* ser. 8, vol. 14 (1889):271–363, 381–493.

Les Chroniques de Zar'a Ya'eqob et de Ba'eda Maryam, rois d'Ethiopie de 1434 à 1478. Paris, 1893.

"Histoire d'Eskender d'Amda-Seyon II et de Na'od, rois d'Ethiopie." *Journal Asiatique,* ser. 9, vol. 3 (1894):319–66.

"Notes pour l'histoire d'Ethiopie le règne de Lebna-Dengel." *Revue Sémitique* 1 (1893):274–86.

"Légendes relatives à Dawit II." *Revue Sémitique* 1 (1893):157–71.

"Notes pour l'histoire d'Ethiopie, la règne de Galawdewos (Claudius) ou Ashaf-Sagad." *Revue Sémitique* 2 (1894):155–66, 263–70.

"Notes pour l'histoire d'Ethiopie, règne de Minas ou Adamas-Sagad (1559–1563)." *Revue Sémitique* 4 (1896):87–90.

"Notes pour l'histoire d'Ethiopie, règne de Sartsa-Dengel ou Malak-Sagad Ier (1563–1597)." *Revue Sémitique* 4 (1896):177–85, 273–78.

"Notes pour l'histoire d'Ethiopie, règnes de Ya'qob et Za-Dengel (1597–1607)." *Revue Sémitique* 4 (1896):355–63.

"Notes pour l'histoire d'Ethiopie, règne de Susenyos ou Seltan-Sagad (1607–1632)." *Revue Sémitique* 4 (1897):75–80, 173–89.

"Notes pour l'histoire d'Ethiopie, le règne de Fasiladas (Adam-Sagad), de 1632 à 1667." *Revue Sémitique* 6 (1897):360–72, and 6 (1898):84–92.

'Notes pour l'histoire d'Ethiopie, le règne de Yohannes Ier roi d'Ethiopie de 1667 à 1682." *Revue Sémitique* 7 (1899): 166–76.

"Notes pour l'histoire d'Ethiopie, le règne de Iyasu Ier roi d'Ethiopie de 1682 à 1706." *Revue Sémitique* 9 (1901):161–7, 258–62.

Sergeant, R. B. "The Portuguese off the south Arabian coast." *Hadrami Chronicles.* Oxford, 1963.

Tafla, Bairu. *Asma Giyorgis and His Work "History of the Galla and the Kingdom of Sawa."* Franz Steiner Verlag Wiesbaden GMBH, Stuttgart, 1987.

Umarah Ibn Ali, Al-Hakami. *Yaman: Its Early Mediaeval History,* trans. H. C. Kay. London, 1892.

Wendt, Kurt. "Amharische geschichte eines Emirs von Harar im XVI jahrhundert." *Orientalia* 4 (1935):484–501.

Whiteway, R. S., trans. and ed. *The Portuguese Expedition to Abyssinia in 1541–1543, as Narrated by Castanhaso with Some Contemporary Letters: The Short Account of Bermudes, and Certain Extracts from Correa.* London, 1902 (The Hakluyt Society).

236

Anonymous. *Kitāb Rabī Al-qulūb fī Dhikr Manāqib Wa Fadā'il Sayyidinā Al-Shaykh Nūr Husain*. Cairo, 1927.

Secondary sources

Unpublished sources

Gidada, Negasso. "People and tribal divisions of Oromo in Qellem." Mimeograph, 1979.

Giyorgis, Asma. "Ya Galla Tarik." MS, Ethiop, 302, Bibliothèque Nationale, Paris.

Hassen, Mohammed. "Menelik's conquest of Harar, 1887, and its effect on the political organization of the surrounding Oromos up to 1900." *Working Papers on Society and History in Imperial Ethiopia: The Southern Periphery from the 1880s to 1974*, eds. D. L. Danham and Wendy James. African Studies Centre, Cambridge, 1980, pp. 227–46.

"The Oromo nation under Amhara colonial administration: past and present and Oromo resistance to colonial oppression." 1981.

Hultin, J. "The historical development in Matcha." Mimeograph, 1977.

"The Galla expansion reconsidered." Undated mimeograph.

Huntingford, G. W. B. "Historical geography of Ethiopia from 1st century A. D. to 1701." Unpublished MS at SOAS, 1969.

Mekurya, Bulcha. "Land ownership and social class formation among the Matcha of southwestern Oromia-Ethiopia." Mimeograph, University of Stockholm, 1980.

Merga, Tasaw. "Senna Umatta Oromo: jalqaba Jarra Kudha Jahafti hama dhumiti Jarra Kudda Sagalafanti." MS, 1976.

Published sources

Abbadie, Antoine d'. *Géographie de l'Ethiopie*. Paris, 1890.

"Sur les Oromo, grande nation Africaine." *Annales de la Société Scientifique de Bruxelles* 4 (1880):167–92.

"Les causes actuelles de l'esclavage en Ethiopie." Extract from *Revue des Questions Scientifiques*. Loubsin, 1877, pp. 409–34.

The Athenaeum: Journal of Literature, Science and Fine Arts, no. 1041 (1847):1056–8; no. 1042 (1847):1077–8; no. 1044 (1847):1126–8; no. 1105 (1848):1329–31.

Abbadie, Arnauld d'. *Douze Ans de Séjour dans le Haute-Ethiopie (Abyssinia)*, vol. I. Paris, 1868.

Abdulahi Rirash, Ahmad. *Kashrif as Sudul Can Tarikh As-Sumal, Wa Hamalikahum As-Sabca*. Mogadishu, 1974.

Abir, M. "The emergence and consolidation of the monarchies of Enarea and Jimma in the first half of the nineteenth century." *Journal of African History* 6 (2) (1965):205–19.

"Brokerages and brokers in Ethiopia in the first half of the 19th century." *Journal of Ethiopian Studies* 3 (1) (1965):1–5.

"Salt, trade and politics in Ethiopia in the 'Zamana Masafent.'" *Journal of Ethiopian Studies* 4 (2) (1966):1–10.

Ethiopia: The Era of the Princes 1769–1855. London, 1968.

"Southern Ethiopia." In *Pre-colonial African Trade: Essays on Trade in Central and Eastern Africa before 1900*, eds. Richard Gray and David Birmingham. London, 1970, pp. 119–37.

"Ethiopia and the Horn of Africa." *Cambridge History of Africa (1600–1790)* vol. IV, ed. Richard Gray. London, 1975, pp. 537–77.

Ethiopia and the Red Sea. London, 1980.

Ahmad, Yusuf. "The household economy of the amirs of Harar 1825–1875." *Ethnological Society*, 10 (Addis Ababa, 1960):7–61.

Andrejeweski, B. S. "Some preliminary observations on the Borana dialects of Galla." *Bulletin of the School of Oriental and African Studies* 19 (1957):354–74.

Bibliography

"Ideas about warfare in Borana Galla stories and fables." *African Language Studies* 3 (1962):116–36.

"Shaikh Hussen of Bali in Galla oral traditions." *IV Congresso Internazionale di Studi Etiopici*. Rome, 1974, pp. 463–80.

Aregay, Merid Wolde. "Population movement as a possible factor in the Christian–Muslim conflict of medieval Ethiopia." In *Symposium Leo Frobenius*. W. Germany, 1973, pp. 261–81.

"Political geography of Ethiopia at the beginning of sixteenth century." In *IV Congresso Internazionale di Studi Etiopici* vol. I, Rome, 1974, pp. 613–31.

Arnold, Rosemary. "A port of trade: Whydah on the Guinea Coast." In *Trade and Market in the Early Empires: Economics in History and Theory*, eds. K. Polanyi, C. M. Arensberg, and H. W. Pearson. Illinois, 1957.

Aubury, L. "Une mission au Choa et dans les pays Gallas." *Bulletin de la Société de Géographie* 8 (1887).

Aylmer, L. "The country between the Juba river and Lake Rudolf." *Geographical Journal* 3 (1911):289–97.

Azais, R. P. and R. Chambard. *Cinq Années de Recherches Archéologiques en Ethiopie, Province du Harer et Ethiopie Meridionale*, 2 vols. Paris, 1931.

Bardey, Alfred. "Notes sur le Harar." *Bulletin de Géographie Historique et Descriptive*. Paris, 1896.

Barker, W. "Extract report on the probable geographical position of Harar." *Journal of the Royal Geographical Society* 12 (1842):238–44.

Bartels, Lambert. "Studies of the Galla in Wallaga: their own view of the past." *Journal of Ethiopian Studies* 8 (1) (1970):135–59.

Oromo Religion Myths and Rites of the Western Oromo of Ethiopia: An Attempt to Understand. Dietrich Reimer Verlag: Berlin, 1983.

Bartinicki, A. and J. Niecko. "The role and significance of the religious conflicts and people's movement in the political life of Ethiopia in the seventeenth and eighteenth centuries." *Rassegna di Studi Etiopici* 26 (1970):5–39.

Bates, Darrel. *The Abyssinian Difficulty: The Emperor Theodorus and the Magdala Campaign, 1867–68*. Oxford, 1979.

Beke, C. T. "Reports on slavery." *Friends of Africa* 1 (1841 a):28–9, 88–9, 120–1, 168–9, 203–4.

"Abyssinie, extrait d'une lettre du Dr. Beke, datée d'Ankobar capitale du royaume de Choa." *Bulletin de la Société de Géographie* 15 (1841 b):373–6.

"Reports on slavery." *Friends of Africa* 2 (1842 a):40, 155–6, 171–2.

"Communications respecting the geography of southern Abyssinia." *Journal of the Royal Geographical Society* 12 (1842 b):84–102.

"On the countries south of Abessinia." *Journal of the Royal Geographical Society* 13 (1843):254–69.

"Abyssinia, being a continuation of routes in that country." *Journal of the Royal Geographical Society* 14 (1844):1–76.

"On the languages and dialects of Abyssinia and the countries of the south." *Proceedings of the Philological Society* 2 (33) (1845):89–107.

"Christianity among the Gallas." Reprinted from the *British Magazine* (1848 a).

"On the origin of the Gallas." Reprinted from the *British Association for the Advancement of Science* (1848 b).

Letters on the Commerce of Abyssinia and Other Parts of Eastern Africa Addressed to the Foreign Office and the Board of Trade, 1852.

Bent, Francisco. "Explosive markets: the Berber highlands." *Trade and Market in the Early Empires: Economics in History and Theory*, eds. K. Polany, *et al*. Illinois, 1957, pp. 188–218.

Berhane Sellassie, Tsehai. "The question of Damot and Walamo." *Journal of Ethiopian Studies* 13 (1975):37–45.

Beshah, G. and M. Wolde Aregay. *The Question of the Union of the Churches in Luso-Ethiopian Relations (1500–1632)*. Lisbon, 1964.

Bianchi, Gustavo. *Alla Terri dei Galla*. Milan, 1884.

Bieber, F. J. *Kaffa: Ein Alt-Kuschitisches Volkstum Inner-Afrika* vol. II. Vienna, 1923.

Black, Paul. "Linguistic evidence on the origins of the Konsoid peoples." *Proceedings of the First United States Conferences on Ethiopian Studies*, ed. Harold G. Marcus. Michigan, 1975, pp. 291–302.

Bloch, Marc. *Slavery and Serfdom in the Middle Ages*, trans. William R. Beer. London, 1975.

Bloch, Maurice, ed. *Political Language and Oratory in Traditional Society*. London, 1975.

Borelli, J. *Divisions, subdivisions, langages et races des régions Amhara, Oromo et Sidama*. Paris, 1889.

Ethiopie meridionale. Paris, 1890.

Bottego, Vittorio. *Viaggi di Scaperta Nil Cuore dell'Africa: Il Gueba Esporato*. Rome, 1895.

Brielli, Domenico. "Recordi storici dei Wallo." *Studi Etiopici*, ed. C. Conti Rossini. Rome, 1945.

Braukamper, U. "Islamic principalities in southeast Ethiopia between the thirteenth and sixtenth centuries." *Ethiopianist Notes* 1 (1) (1977):17–55; 1 (2): 1–43.

"The ethnogenesis of the Sidama." *Abbay* (1978):123–30.

Geschichte der Hadiya Süd-Athiopiens. Wiesbaden, 1980.

"Oromo country of origin: a reconsideration of hypothesis." *Ethiopian Studies Proceedings of the Sixth International Conference*, ed. Gideon Goldenberg. Tel-Amir, 14–17 April 1980, offprint, pp. 25–40.

Bruce, James. *Travels to Discover the Source of the Nile in the Years 1768–73*, 7 vols. Edinburgh, 1805.

Budge, E. A. W. *A History of Ethiopia: Nubia and Abyssinia*, 2 vols. London, 1928.

Burton, R. F. *First Footsteps in East Africa*, 2 vols. London, 1856.

Caulk, R. "Territorial competition and the battle of Embabo, 1882." *Journal of Ethiopian Studies* 13 (1975):64–88.

Cecchi, A. "Da Zeila alle frontiere del Caffa." *Viaggi di Antonio Cecchi spedizione Italiana nell' Africa equatorialo*, 3 vols. Rome, 1886.

Cecchi A., and G. Chiarini. "Relazione sui mercati principali dello Scioa e dei paesi Galla." *Bollettino della Società Geografica Italiana* 16 (1879 a):445–55.

"Sugli usi e costumi dei Galla." *Bollettino della Società Geografica Italiana* 16 (1879 b):456–62.

Cerulli Enrico. "Folk literature of the Galla of southern Abyssinia." *Harvard African Studies* 3 (1922).

"Notes su alcuni popola zioni Sidama dell'Abissinia meridionale." *Rivista degli Studi Orientali* II (1923–5):597–692.

"Ancora dell' orinamento della tribi Galla." *Bollettino della Società Africana d'Italia* 5 (1926).

Etiopia occidentale, 2 vols. Rome, 1933.

Studi Etiopici vol. I. *La lingua e la storia di Harar*. Rome, 1936.

Studi Etiopici vol. II. *La lingua e la storia di Sidama*. Rome, 1938.

Studi Etiopici vol. III. *Il linguaggio dei Giangero ed alcune lingue Sidama dell'Omo*. Rome, 1938.

Studi Etiopici vol. IV. *La lingua Caffina*. Rome, 1951.

Storia della litteratura Etiopicia. Rome, 1956.

Somalia: Scritti vari editi ed inediti, 3 vols. Rome, 1957–64.

Chambard, R. "Sur l'organisation sociale des Oromo du Harar." *Revue d'Ethnographie et des Traditions Populaires* 25 (1926):68–79.

Chedeville, E. "Quelques faites de l'organisation sociale des Afar." *Africa* 36 (1966):173–96.

Chernetsov, S. B. "The history of the Gallas and the death of Za-Dangel King of Ethiopia (1603–4)." *IV Congresso Internazionale di Studi Etiopici*. Rome, 1974, pp. 803–8.

Clark, J. D. *Prehistory of the Horn of Africa*. Cambridge, 1954.

Cohen, D. W. "The river-lake Nilotes from the 15th to the 19th century." In *Zamani: A Survey of East African History*, ed. B. A. Ogot. Nairobi, 1974, pp. 135–49.

Cole, S. *Prehistory of East Africa*. London, 1954.

Bibliography

Combes, E., and M. Tamisier. *Voyage en Abyssinie dans le pays des Gallas de Choa et d'Ifat*. Paris, 1838.

Conti Rossini, C. "Due squarci mediti di cronica Etiopica." *Rendiconti della Reale Accademia dei Lincei* (1893).

——— "Cataloga dei nomi propri di luogo dell'Etiopia contenui nei testi Gi'iz," ed. Amharina Finora Publicoti. *Atti del Primo Congresso Geografico Italiano* 2. Genoa, 1894.

——— "Sulla dianastia Zague." *L'Oriente* 11 (1897):144–59.

——— "Lettera a J. Halevy sulla caduta degli Zague." *Revue Semitique* 10 (1902):373–7; II (1903): 325–30.

——— "Studi su popolazioni dell'Etiopia." *Rivista degli Studi Orientali* 3 (1910):849–900; 4 (1912):599–651; 6 (1913):365–425.

——— "Popoli dell'Etiopia occidentale." *Rendiconti della Reale Accademia dei Lincei*, ser. 5, vol. 30 (1919):251–85, 319–25.

——— "La guerra Turco-Abissinia del 1578." *Oriente Moderno* 1 (1921–22):634–6, 684–91; and (1922–23):48–57.

——— *Storia d'Etiopia*. Milan, 1928.

——— *Etiopia e genti d'Etiopia*. Florence, 1937.

——— "I Galla raia." *Revista degli Studi Orientali* 19 (1941):58–64.

Cooper, J. Omer. *The Zulu Aftermath: A Nineteenth Century Revolution in Bantu Africa*. London, 1966.

Coulbeaux, J. B. *Histoire politique et religieuse d'Abyssinie*, 3 vols. Paris, 1929.

Cox, P. Z. *Genealogies of the Somali Including Those of the Aysa and Gadebursi*. London, 1896.

Crawford, O. G. S. *Ethiopian Itineraries, ca. 1400–1524*. Cambridge, 1958 (Hakluyt Society, ser. 2, vol. 109).

——— *The Funj: Kingdom of Sennar*. Gloucester, 1951.

Crummey, Donald. *Priests and Politics: Protestant and Catholic Missions in Orthodox Ethiopia, 1830–1868*. Oxford, 1972.

Curle, A. T. "The ruined towns of Somaliland." *Antiquity* 10 (1937):315–27.

Darkwah, R. H. K. *Shewa, Menelik and the Ethiopian Empire, 1813–1889*. London, 1975.

Davidson, Basil. *Black Mother: A Study of the Pre-Colonial Connection between Africa and Europe*. London, 1970.

Davis, J. "The 16th century jihad in Ethiopia and the impact on its culture." *Journal of the Historical Society of Nigeria* 2 (1960–63):113–28; 3 (1964):567–92.

Deressa, Yelma. *Ya Ityopya Tarik, Ba'asra Sedestannaw Kefla Zaman*. Addis Ababa, 1957, Ethiopian Calendar.

Doresse, J. *L'Empire du Prêtre-Jean*, 2 vols. Paris, 1957.

——— *Ethiopia*, trans. Elsa Coult. London, 1959.

Drake-Brockman, R.E. *British Somaliland*. London, 1912.

Engels, Frederick. *The Origin of the Family, Private Property and the State*. Peking, 1974.

Ferret, P. V. A., and J. G. Galinier. *Voyage en Abyssinie*. Paris, 1847.

Ferry, R. "Quelques hypothèses sur les origines des conquêtes Musulmanes en Abyssinie au XVIᵉ siècle." *Cahiers d'Etudes Africaines* 11 (1961):24–36.

Fortes, M., and E. E. Evans-Pritchard, eds. *African Political Systems*. London, 1940.

Grottanelli, V. "The peopling of the Horn of Africa." *East Africa and the Orient: Cultural Synthesis in Pre-colonial Times*, eds. H. Neville Chittick and Robert I. Rotberg. New York, 1975.

Grühl, Max. *The Citadel of Ethiopia: The Empire of the Divine Emperor*, trans. I. F. D. Marron and L. M. Sieveking. London, 1932.

Gwynn, C. W. "A journey in southern Abyssinia." *The Geographical Journal* 85 (1911):133–39.

Haberland, Eike. *Galla Süd-Athiopiens*. Stuttgart, 1963.

——— "The influence of the Christian Ethiopian empire on southern Ethipia." *Journal of Semitic Studies* 9 (1964):235–38.

Hable-Sellassie, Sergew. *Ancient and Medieval Ethiopian History to 1270*. Addis Ababa, 1972.

Halevy, J. "Notes pour l'histoire d'Ethiopie le pays de Zague." *Revue Sémitique* 4 (1897):275–84.

Harris, W. C. *The Highlands of Aethiopia*, 3 vols. London, 1844.

Hayward, R. J., and M. Hassen. "The Oromo orthography of Shaykh Bakri Sapalo." *Bulletin of the School of Oriental and African Studies* 44 (1981):550–66.

Heichelheim, F. M. *An Ancient Economic History* vol. i, trans. Joyce Stevens and A. W. Sijthoff. Leiden, 1968.

Hiwet, Addis. *Ethiopia: From Autocracy to Revolution*. London, 1975.

Hobsbawn, E. J. *Industry and Empire*. Penguin, London, 1972.

Hodson, A. W. *Seven Years in Southern Abyssinia*. London, 1927.

Honea, K. "A contribution to the history of the Hamitic peoples of Africa." *Alta Ethnologica et Linguistica* 5 (1958).

Hultin, Jan. "Man and land in Wallaga, Ethiopia." *Working Papers of the Department of Anthropology*. University of Gothenburg, no. 10, 1977.

Huntingford, G. W. B. *The Galla of Ethiopia: The Kingdoms of Kaffa and Janjero*. London, 1955. *The Land Charters of Northern Ethiopia*. Addis Ababa, 1965.

Isenberg, C. W. "A few remarks concerning the nation of Gallas." In J. L. Krapf, *An Imperfect Outline of the Elements of the Galla Language*. London, 1840.

Isenberg, C. W., and J. L. Krapf. *The Journal of C. W. Isenberg and J. L. Krapf Detailing Their Proceedings in the Kingdom of Shoa and Journeys in Other Parts of Abyssinia in the Years 1839–1842*. London, 1968.

James, F. L. *The Unknown Horn of Africa*. London, 1888.

Jensen, A. E. *Im Lande des Gada*. Stuttgart, 1936.
   "Das Gada-System der Konso und die Alterklassen-system der Niloten." *Ethnos* 19 (1954): 1–23.

Jewsiewicki, B., and David Newbury, eds. *African Historiographies: What History for Which Africa?* Sage Publications, Beverly Hills, California, 1986.

Johnston, C. *Travels in Southern Abyssinia through the Country of Adal to the Kingdom of Shoa*. London, 1844.

Jones, A. M., and E. Monroe. *A History of Ethiopia*. Oxford, 1955.

Kammerer, A. *La Mer Rouge, l'Abyssinie et l'Arabie depuis l'Antiquité*, 3 vols. Cairo, 1929–52.

Knutsson, K. E. "Social structure of the Mecca Galla." *Ethnology* 2 (1963):506–11.
   Authority and Change: A Study of the Kallu Institution among the Matcha Galla of Ethiopia. Gothenburg, 1967.

Koehn, P., and S. R. Waldron. *Afocha: A Link between Community and Administration in Harar, Ethiopia*. New York, 1979.

Krader, Lawrence. *Formation of the State*. New Jersey, 1968.

Krapf, J. L. *Travels, Researches and Missionary Labours during an Eighteen Years Residence in Eastern Africa*. London, 1860.

Landor, A. H. S. *Across Widest Africa: An Account of the Country and the People of Eastern, Central and Western Africa, as Seen during a Twelve-months Journey from Djibouti to Cape Verde*. London, 1907.

Lange, W. *Domination and Resistance: Narrative Songs of the Kaffa Highlands*. Michigan, 1978. *History of the Southern Gonga (Southwestern Ethiopia)*. Franz Steiner Verlag GMBH, Wiesbaden, 1982.

Lebel, P. "Oral traditions and chronicles on Gurage immigration." *Journal of Ethiopian Studies* 12 (1974):95–106.

Lefebvre, C. T. *Voyage en Abyssinie executé pendant les années 1839–1843*. Paris, 1845.

Legesse, Asmarom. "Class system based on time." *Journal of Ethiopian Studies* 1 (1963):1–19. *Gada: Three Approaches to the Study of African Society*. London, 1973.

LeGrand, J. *Voyages historiques d'Abyssinie du R. P. Jerome Lobo*. Paris, 1728.

Leslau, W. *Ethiopians Speak I: Studies in Cultural Background Harari*. Los Angeles, 1965.

Bibliography

Levine, Donald A. *Wax and Gold: Tradition and Innovation in Ethiopian Culture*. Chicago, 1972.
   Greater Ethiopia: The Evolution of Multi-ethnic Society. Chicago, 1974.
Lewis, H. S. "Historical problems in Ethiopia and the Horn of Africa." *Annals of the New York Academy of Sciences* 96 (1962):504–11.
   "Reconsideration of the socio-political systems of the western Galla." *Journal of Semitic Studies* 9 (1964):139–43.
   A Galla Monarchy: Jimma Abba Jifar, Ethiopia 1830–1932. Madison, 1965.
   "The origin of the Galla and the Somali." *Journal of African History* 7 (1966):27–46.
Lewis, I. M. *Peoples of the Horn of Africa: Somali, Afar and Saho*. London, 1955.
   "The Galla in northern Somaliland." *Rassegna di Studi Etiopici* 15 (1954):21–38.
   "The Somali conquest of the Horn of Africa." *Journal of African History* 1 (1960):213–30.
   A Pastoral Democracy: A Study of Pastoralism and Politics among the Northern Somali of the Horn of Africa. Oxford, 1960.
   Ed. *Islam in Tropical Africa*. London, 1966.
Lobo, Jerome. *Voyage to Abyssinia*, trans. from French by Samuel Johnson. Reprinted from 1789 edition. London, 1978.
Ludolf, H. *A New History of Ethiopia: Being a Full and Accurate Description of the Kingdom of Abyssinia, Vulgarly though Erroneously Called the Empire of Prester John*. London, 1682.
Marcus, H. *The Life and Times of Menelik II of Ethiopia (1844–1913)*. Oxford University Press, 1975.
Massaja, G. *I miei trentacinque anni di missione nell'Alta Etiopia*, 12 vols. Milan, 1885–95.
   Lettere e scritti minori 1836–66. A Cura di Antonio Rosso, 6 vols. Rome, 1978.
Melbaa, Gadaa. *Oromia: A Brief Introduction*. Finfine, 1980.
Metaferia, Seifu. "The eastern Oromo (Kottus) of Ethiopia and their time reckoning system." *Africa Rivista Trinnestrale di Studi e Documentazione dell'Istituto Italo-Africano*, 33 (4) (1978):475–507.
Mizzi, Angelo. *Semplici constatazioni felologico-etnologike Galla*. Malta, 1935.
   Cenni etnografici Galla ossia organizzazione civile use e costumi Oromonici. Malta, 1935.
Mokter, Mohammed. "Notes sur le pays de Harar." *Bulletin de la Société Khediviale de Géographie* (1877):357–97.
Oliver, Roland. "The problem of Bantu expansion." *Journal of African History* 7 (3) (1966): 361–76.
   "The East African interior." In *The Cambridge History of Africa, III c. 1050 to 1600*, ed. Roland Oliver, Cambridge, 1977, pp. 621–69.
Pankhurst, R. *An Introduction to the Economic History of Ethiopia from Early Times to 1800*. London, 1961.
   "The Maria Theresa thaler in pre-war Ethiopia." *Journal of Ethiopian Studies* 1 (1) (1963):8–26.
   "Primitive money in Ethiopia." *Journal de la Société des Africanistes* 33 (1963):213–47.
   "The great Ethiopian famine of 1889–1892: a new assessment." *Journal of the History of Medicine and Allied Sciences* 21 (1966):95–124.
   "Some factors depressing the standard of living of peasants in traditional Ethiopia." *Journal of Ethiopian Studies* 4 (2) (1966):45–98.
   State and Land in Ethiopian History. Addis Ababa, 1966.
   "Tribute, taxation and government revenues in nineteenth and early twentieth century Ethiopia." *Journal of Ethiopian Studies* 5 (2) (1967):37–87.
   Economic History of Ethiopia 1800–1935. Addis Ababa, 1968.
   History of Ethiopian Towns. Wiesbaden, 1982.
Pankhurst, S. *Ethiopia: A Cultural History*. London, 1955.
Paulitschke, P. *Die Geographische Erforschung der Adallander und Harar's in Ost Afrika*. Leipzig, 1884.
   "Notes per la storia dell'Harar." *Bollettino della Sezione Fiorentina della Società Africana d'Italia* 2 (1886).

"Gli Oromo O Galla dell'Harar." *Bollettino della Sezione Fiorentina della Società Africana d'Italia* 3 (1887).

Beiträge zur Ethnologie und Anthropologie der Somal, Gala, und Harari. Leipzig, 1888a.

Harar – Forschungsreise nach den Somal und Galla – Ländern Ost-Afrikas. Leipzig, 1888b.

"Die Wanderungen der Oromo Galla Ost-Afrikas." *Mittheilungen der Antropologischen Gesellschaft in Wien* 19 (1889).

Ethnographie Nordost-Afrikas I. Die Meterielle Kultur der Danakil, Galla und Somal. Berlin, 1893.

Pearce, N. *Life and Adventures in Abyssinia*, 2 vols., 2nd edition. London, 1980.

Plowden, W. C. *Travels in Abyssinia and the Galla Countries.* London, 1868.

Rey, C. F. *The Romance of the Portuguese in Abyssinia.* London, 1929.

Robecchi-Bricchetti, L. *Nell' Harar.* Milan, 1896.

Rochet d'Héricourt, E. C. *Voyage sur la côte orientale de la mer Rouge dans le pays d'Adel et le Royaume de Choa.* Paris, 1841.

Seconde Voyage sur les deux rives de la mer Rouge dans les pays des Adels et le royaume de Choa. Paris, 1846.

Rodney, Walter. *How Europe Underdeveloped Africa.* Howard University Press, Washington, D.C., 1982.

Rubenson, S. *The Survival of Ethiopia's Independence.* London, 1976.

Sahlins, Marshall. *Stone Age Economics.* Chicago, 1972.

Saincano, M. "L'Abyssinie dans la seconde moitié du XVIᵉ siècle ou le règne de Sartse-Dengel (Malak-Sagad) (1563–1594)." *D'après des annales éthiopiennes médites.* Leipzig, 1892.

Salt, Henry. *A Voyage to Abyssinia, etc., in the Years 1809 and 1810.* London, 1814.

Salviac, Martial de. *Un Peuple antique au pays de Menelik: les Galla, grande nation africaine.* Paris, 1905.

Sanderson, G. N. "Contribution from African sources to the history of European competition in the upper valley of the Nile." *Journal of African History* 3 (1962):69–85.

Scorin, Emilio. *Hararino ricerce e studi geografici.* Florence, 1942.

Simon, Gabriel. *Voyage en Abyssinie et chez les Gallas, Raias, L'Ethiopie, ses moeurs, ses traditions, le Negouss Iohannis.* Paris, 1885.

Smith, A. Donaldson. *Through Unknown African Countries: The First Expedition from Somaliland to Lake Lamu.* London, 1897.

Soleillet, Paul. *Voyages en Ethiopie, Janvier 1882–Octobre 1884: notes, lettres et documents divers.* Rouen, 1886.

Swayne, H. G. C. *Seventeen Trips through Somaliland and a Visit to Abyssinia.* London, 1903.

Takla Sadiq Makurya. *Ya Gran Ahmad Warara.* Addis Ababa, 1974–5.

Tamrat, Taddesse. *Church and State in Ethiopia, 1270–1527.* Oxford, 1972.

"Ethiopia, the Red Sea and the Horn." In *The Cambridge History of Africa, III, c. 1050–1600*, ed. Roland Oliver. Cambridge University Press, New York, 1977, pp. 98–182.

"The Horn of Africa: the Solomonids in Ethiopia and the states of the Horn," in *UNESCO General History of Africa IV – Africa from the Twelfth to the Sixteenth Century*, ed. P. T. Niane. Heinemann, California, 1984, pp. 423–58.

Taye, Alaka. *Ya Ityopya Hizeb Tarik.* Addis Ababa. 1956.

Tedeschi, Salvatore. "L'emirato di Harar secondo un documento inedito." *IV Congresso Internazionale di Studi Etiopici.* Rome, 1974, pp. 481–500.

Tellez, B. *The Travels of the Jesuits in Ethiopia*, trans. John Stevens. London, 1710.

Thesiger, W. "The Awash river and the Aussa sultanate." *The Geographical Journal* 85 (1935):1–23.

Traversi, L. "Estratto di lettera sul viaggi negli Arussi, Guraghi, etc." *Bollettino della Società Geografica Italiana* 24 (1887).

Trimingham, J. S. *Islam in Ethiopia.* London, 1952.

The Influence of Islam upon Africa. London, 1980.

Bibliography

"Escursione nel Gimma." *Bollettino della Società Geografica Italiana* 25 (1888):901–23.

Turton, E. R. "Bantu, Galla and Somali migrations in the Horn of Africa: a reassessment of the Juba/Tana area." *Journal of African History* 16 (4) (1975):519–37.

Tutschek, K. *A Galla Dictionary*. Munich, 1844.

Ullendorf, E. *The Ethiopians*. London, 1960.

Vansina, Jan. *Oral Tradition: A Study in Historical Methodology*, trans. H. M. Wright. London, 1961.

Wagner, E. "Eine Liste der Heiligen von Harar." *Zeitschrift der Deutschen Morgenländischen Gesellschaft* 123 (2) (1973):269–92.

    Trans. and ed. *Legende und Geschichte der Fatah Madinat Harar von Yaha Nasrallah*. Wiesbaden, 1978.

    "Neues Material zur Ausa-Chronik." *Die Islamische Welt zwischen Mittelalter und Neuzeit*. Festschrift für Hans Robert Roemer zum 65 Geburtstag, 1979, pp. 657–73.

Werner, A. "Some Galla notes." *Man* 15 (1915):10–11.

    "The Galla of east African protectorate." *Journal of African Society* 13 (1913):121–42, 262–87.

Woldemariam, Mesfin. *An Introductory Geography of Ethiopia*. Addis Ababa, 1972.

Wrigley, E. A. *Population and History*. London, 1969.

Zurla, Placido. *Il mappamondo di Fra Mauro*. Camaldolese, Venice, 1806.

Theses

Abir, M. "Trade and politics in the Ethiopian region 1830–1855." Ph.D. thesis. London University, 1964.

Aregay, Merid Wolde. "Southern Ethiopia and the Christian kingdom, 1508–1708, with special reference to the Galla migrations and their consequences." Ph.D. thesis. London University, 1971.

Asfera, Zergaw. "Some aspects of historical development in Amhara (Wallo) *c*. 1700–1815." B.A. thesis. Addis Ababa University, 1973.

Baxter, P. T. W. "Social organization of the Galla of northern Kenya." D. Phil. thesis. Oxford University, 1954.

Birhane, Fantahun. "Gojjam 1800–1855." B.A. thesis. Addis Ababa University, 1973.

Crummey, D. E. "European religious missions in Ethiopia, 1830–1868." Ph.D. thesis. London University, 1967.

Delibo, Getahun. "Emperor Menelik's Ethiopia 1865–1916: national unification or Amhara communal domination." Ph.D. thesis. Howard University, 1974.

Ege, Svein. "Chiefs and peasants: the socio-political structure of the kingdom of Shawa about 1840." M.Phil. thesis. Havedoppgave i Historie ved Universitetet e Bergen Hasten, 1978.

Gidada, Negaso. "History of the Sayyoo Oromoo of southwestern Wallaga, Ethiopia, from about 1730 to 1886." Inaugural dissertation. Zur Erlangung des Grades Eines Doktors der Philosophie in Kechbereich Geschichtruissenschoften der Johann Wolfgang Goethe-Universitat Zu Frankfurt am Main, 1984.

Goto, Paul S. G. "The Boran of northern Kenya: origin, migrations and settlements in the 19th century." B. A. thesis. University of Nairobi, 1972.

Hassen, Mohammed. "The relation between Harar and the surrounding Oromo 1800–1887." B.A. thesis. Addis Ababa University, 1973.

    "The Oromo of Ethiopia, 1500–1850: with special emphasis on the Gibe region." Ph.D. thesis. University of London, 1983.

Hunde, Daba. "A portrait of social organization and institutions of the Oromo of Jibat and Matcha in the nineteenth century till the conquest of Menelik II." B.A. thesis. Addis Ababa University, 1972.

244

Luling, Virginia. "Government and social control among some peoples of the Horn of Africa." M.A. dissertation. London University, 1966.

Orent, Amnon. "Lineage structure and the supernatural: the Kaffa of southwestern Ethiopia." Ph.D. thesis. University of Boston, 1969.

Ta'a, Tesema, "The political economy of western central Ethiopia: from the mid-16th to early 20th centuries." Ph.D. dissertation. Michigan State University, 1986.

Interview materials used in this work

Borrowed materials

I used much oral interview material which was collected by others from the Gibe region and Wallaga. This was of three kinds:

1 The Jimma Interview Programme, which consists of several hundred pages, and was the product of extensive field work conducted in the Gibe region in 1974 by a team of history students of Addis Ababa University. I owe a debt of gratitude to my former teacher, the late Dr. Richard Caulk, for providing me with photocopies of the Jimma Interview Programme;

2 Interviews with *Blatta* Dressa Amante, recorded between April 3, 1962 and December 15, 1962, in Bishofitu (Debre Zeit), which cover Oromo history, the Gada system, and Bakre's rise to power in Wallaga;

3 Oral interviews conducted by A. Triulzi as follows:

 A Interview with *Qannazmach* Abdisa Musa in Nāqāmte on August 3, 1972;

 B Interview with *Ato* Na'a Bassa, in Nāqāmte on January 27, 1972;

 C Interview with *Ato* Tāmasgan Gāmada and others in Nāqāmte on February 5, 1972; and

 D Interview with *Fitwarari* Yāmānā G. Eggiabhir in Nāqāmte on February 4, 1972.

I am greatly indebted to Alexander Triulzi for his kindness in allowing me to use all this material.

Personal interviews

When I went to Mogadishu to participate in the First International Somali Congress in July 1980, I was lucky enough to interview many Oromo nationals who lived in the Somali capital. In June 1982, when I went to Saudi Arabia, I was able to interview many Oromo nationals there. Of the many people I saw, only the information which I received from the following has been really helpful: (1) Shaykh Mohammed Rashad, aged 50, in Mogadishu on July 17, 1980, who has a thorough knowledge of the history of the Harar Oromo; (2) Abba Jobir Abba Dula, aged 80, in Mecca, June 10–13, 1982, who is well-versed in Oromo history in general, and the history of the Gibe region in particular; and (3) Mohammed Abdukarim, aged 50, in Jeddah on June 17, 1982, who is well informed on Harar Oromo history and lived in northern Somalia, where he gained much knowledge of the previous presence of the Oromo in that region.

OTHER BOOKS IN THE SERIES

246

247

Index

Index

Index